T0369737

Failure by Design

∴

Failure by Design

∵

THE CALIFORNIA ENERGY CRISIS AND
THE LIMITS OF MARKET PLANNING

Georg Rilinger

THE UNIVERSITY OF CHICAGO PRESS

CHICAGO AND LONDON

The University of Chicago Press, Chicago 60637
The University of Chicago Press, Ltd., London
© 2024 by The University of Chicago
Subject to the exception mentioned above, no part of this book may be used or reproduced in any manner whatsoever without written permission, except in the case of brief quotations in critical articles and reviews. For more information, contact the University of Chicago Press, 1427 E. 60th St., Chicago, IL 60637.
Published 2024
Printed and bound by CPI Group (UK) Ltd, Croydon, CR0 4YY

33 32 31 30 29 28 27 26 25 24   1 2 3 4 5

ISBN-13: 978-0-226-83440-5 (cloth)
ISBN-13: 978-0-226-83320-0 (paper)
ISBN-13: 978-0-226-83439-9 (e-book)
DOI: https://doi.org/10.7208/chicago/9780226834399.001.0001

Library of Congress Cataloging-in-Publication Data

Names: Rilinger, Georg, 1985– author.
Title: Failure by design : the California energy crisis and the limits of market planning / Georg Rilinger.
Other titles: California energy crisis and the limits of market planning
Description: Chicago : The University of Chicago Press, 2024. | Includes bibliographical references and index.
Identifiers: LCCN 2023057787 | ISBN 9780226834405 (cloth) | ISBN 9780226833200 (paperback) | ISBN 9780226834399 (ebook)
Subjects: LCSH: Electric utilities—Social aspects—California. | Electric utilities—California—Finance. | Electric utilities—California—Planning. | Electric power distribution—California—Planning. | Finance—Social aspects—California.
Classification: LCC HD9685.U6 C365 2024 | DDC 333.793/2—dc23/eng/20240130
LC record available at https://lccn.loc.gov/2023057787

♾ This paper meets the requirements of ANSI/NISO Z39.48-1992 (Permanence of Paper).

To Arthur and Katrin,
who make this life
so very wild and beautiful

Contents

INTRODUCTION 1

Part One
A CASE OF MARKET DESIGN FAILURE · 21

CHAPTER ONE
Two Tales of a Crisis · 23

CHAPTER TWO
A Framework to Study Market Design · 55

CHAPTER THREE
Breaking Bad in California's Energy Markets · 83

CHAPTER FOUR
A Structural Explanation of the Energy Crisis · 110

Part Two
WHY THE DESIGN PROCESS FAILED · 137

CHAPTER FIVE
Politics, Politics! · 143

CHAPTER SIX
The Perils of Modularization · 165

CHAPTER SEVEN
The Chameleonic Market · 193

CONCLUSION 219

Acknowledgments 239
Appendix A: Data and Methods 243
Appendix B: Key to Archival Sources 253
Notes 255   References 285   Index 301

Introduction

Markets are the ambivalent gods of our societies. Powerful and fickle, they become subject to our collective hopes and fears. Some believe that they will deliver us from evil by reconciling us with our rivals and fostering innovation. To others, they will forever corrupt nature, spread inequality, and alienate us from our communities. True to this ambiguity, markets variously appear as omnipotent information processors, evolving ecologies, or physical places in our collective imagination.[1] Social scientists describe them as emerging from networks of social relations, fields of power positions, ecosystems of competition, or diffuse configurations of material objects, ideas, and human beings.[2]

Diverse as these conceptions and theories of market creation may be, they share one assumption. Regardless of the mechanism that may create and organize the market, its global order is *emergent*.[3] The distinctive feature of the invisible hand, that secularized deity, is its invisibility. Whatever coordination it provides results from a myriad of decentral decisions that follow stochastic principles. For all our efforts to steer, regulate, and construct markets, for all the ways in which markets are embedded in other institutions of modern societies, market order is emergent.

This assumption is so central that it shows up in practically all theories of market creation.[4] As much as economics and sociology may disagree, they are aligned in the fundamental assumption that there is no global plan to the order of markets. Whether we search for the origin of markets in political struggles over institutions, the decisions of rational individuals, or the configurations of social networks, emergence is always assumed. It organizes the very nexus of contrasting concepts that give meaning to the term market. For example, we frequently distinguish between markets and firms along the lines of this assumption: the market begins where the planning capacities of the firm end.[5] Similarly, we think of regulation as deliberate intervention into open-ended processes of exchange. Even the foundational opposition between capitalism and socialism is often understood along these lines. To the defenders of capitalism, socialism appears to be a misguided attempt to replace the market with a centralized planning board.[6] Just as we can only ever hope to sway, but never control, the gods with sacrificial offerings, so too does the order of markets remain beyond the pale of intentional planning.

A new form of social engineering—market design—challenges this basic assumption.[7] Market designers build infrastructures that shape the interactions between market participants in such a way that they enact the calculative logic of a theoretical market mechanism. They rely on the power of virtual platforms to implement such mechanisms, but they also build administrative structures, organize enforcement, and set legal rules. In other words, they use a panoply of techniques to plan the minutia of economic interactions and enforce the logic of their theoretical mechanisms. They are social engineers who wield the tools of bureaucratic control and digitalization in the service of abstract ideals. And if they succeed, their economic machines produce the allocative benefits promised by the theory. In a strange twist on the socialist calculation debate of the early twentieth century, we no longer live in times when socialist technocrats are trying to replace markets with planning. Rather, we live in times when their heirs set out to plan markets.[8]

Originally a rather academic pursuit, market design is quickly becoming a guiding principle behind the organization of commerce in the digital age. As more and more of our economic life migrates into the platform economy, the opportunities for economic engineering multiply. Software engineers can manipulate the form and content of economic interactions and thus shape the resulting process.[9] Indeed, in this day and age, we can find designer markets practically anywhere: in the matching algorithms of dating platforms and online labor markets, the delivery services of the gig economy, and the clearing rules of financial exchanges.[10] They help to allocate donations to food banks, medical students to residences, and spectrum licenses to broadcasting companies.[11] In the words of a practitioner, market design is "a form of applied economics that promises to improve outcomes in almost every domain one can imagine."[12]

Though it may perhaps surprise the sociologist, many designer markets work very well and produce the outcomes their designers promise. The most prominent examples are matching markets for medical residencies, public school enrollments, and food donations. These applications do not only resolve a variety of market frictions that impede efficiency.[13] They often produce results that are fairer and more transparent than those of the byzantine bureaucracies they replace.[14] The ambition to realize substantial, ethical objectives resonates in the catchphrase "Mechanism Design for

Social Good," which currently circulates in the market design community.[15] But successful examples are not limited to the public sector. Market design stands behind Uber's matching software, Amazon's famous "Buy Now" button, and online labor markets that match freelance workers with employers. It drives the world of online transactions.[16]

Politicians and regulators are attracted to the idea that perfect market mechanisms can remove market failures and replace administrative solutions. Willing, as ever, to abdicate responsibility for hard distributional choices, they follow the lure of market design as they once followed the promises of deregulation and entertain its use for increasingly complex collective goods.[17] Who would deny that global warming requires markets for emission certificates, that overfishing must be addressed by dividing the oceans into markets for fishing quotas, and that health-care plans are best allocated via exchanges?

But while market design works well for a variety of self-contained and well-defined matching problems, it is not clear whether it applies equally to complex problems regarding the allocation of collective goods.[18] Providing and distributing essentials like water, electricity, or clean air often requires the management, maintenance, and expansion of vast technological infrastructures. The managers of these infrastructures have to deal with conflicting goals along various temporal horizons, a complex array of stakeholders with competing interests, a variety of contingencies, uncertainties, and complicated technical challenges.

Though market designers are not deterred by these complexities, their record is somewhat more mixed here. While many markets for public goods work well most of the time, they also experience breakdowns and even the occasional disaster. When the market for US Treasuries began to sway wildly in March 2020, commentators called for "design changes."[19] When the lights went out in California in August, an internal report blamed in part supply shortages that could be traced to bad incentives.[20] When Europe's carbon certificate market crashed between 2008 and 2013, experts pointed to design flaws.[21] Texas's blackouts in February 2021 can be traced, in part, to missing incentives for maintenance work.[22] More recently, a governmental report determined that the world's largest water markets—for Australia's Murray-Darling Basin—are seriously flawed and subject to destructive behavior.[23]

Market designers often pin such problems on market actors' cognitive limitations or the influence of politics, while politicians blame political exigencies or bad advice. But market design always takes place in political processes with conflicting interests, and it always faces imperfect knowledge and cognitive limitations. Yet it both succeeds and fails under these conditions. To explain this variation, self-serving arguments of science versus politics will not lead us very far.

What we need is a theory that can explain both the success and the failure of market design on its own terms. This is the purpose of this book. It seeks to understand what designers' goals are, how they go about meeting them, and how these goals can become reality. With these scope conditions for success in place, the book then asks why designers may fail to meet them in practice. To this end, the book studies a case where market design was difficult and failed catastrophically. This is a strategic choice. Because the details of software algorithms and organizational routines are commercially sensitive, it is often hard to study market design in action.[24] But disasters produce a public record—litigation, congressional hearings, newspaper reports, and, most importantly, internal documents of the organizations that host the market. Such records allow us to pierce the veil of secrecy that normally obscures the prospects and perils of market design. But even more importantly, cases of breakdown can help us understand how something works. Cases of extreme failure maximize the number of obstacles we can observe and the reasons designers might fail to meet them. From this, we can infer the practical requirements of success.

That being said, the book does not just choose any convenient example. It focuses on a famous and iconic case that may even, at first sight, appear to be an unlikely choice: the creation and collapse of California's electricity markets between 1993 and 2001. When the markets derailed during the Western energy crisis of 2000–2001, they triggered what is still one of the worst financial disasters in US history. The events are wrapped up with the fall of Enron, the start-up culture of the 1990s, widespread corporate crime, regulatory failure, and political paralysis. And even after twenty years of litigation, the roots of the crisis continue to elude us. While this case has usually been seen as a classic instance of deregulation gone wrong, this book suggests that some of these most vexing puzzles may be resolved if we recognize that this was not a case of flawed deregulation but a failure by design.

The Creation and Collapse of California's Electricity Markets

In the early 1990s, California struggled with high electricity rates that stifled the growth of the fledgling tech industry. The regulatory structures seemed overly complex and unable to solve the problem. Deregulation, or restructuring, promised a solution. Within the span of just a few years, California transformed its electricity industry from a set of vertically integrated monopolies into "the most complicated electricity market ever created."[25] In

1998, these markets opened their doors to newly created classes of buyers and sellers. Initially, everything went according to plan: rates declined, new entrants crowded in, and everyone was happy. But after two years of relatively smooth operation, price spikes started to rattle the markets. April 2000 marked the beginning of the Western energy crisis, which lasted almost a year and drove the state's three biggest utilities to the brink of bankruptcy. Amid rolling blackouts and an electricity system at the verge of collapse, the government finally stepped in to take over the provision of energy.[26] The scandal was perfect: it turned out that the sellers of energy had manipulated the market to drive up the prices and profit from the resulting disaster.[27]

Decades of litigation and economic and journalistic work have probed into the causes of the Western energy crisis. Dominated by stakeholders, this voluminous body of research has pursued one question above all else: Who is to blame? In collective memory, this question is inextricably linked to the collapse of Enron. For many years, Enron was America's darling and the symbol for the new economy. In 2001, its fall from grace captivated the nation as the company collapsed amid revelations about corporate abuse and financial fraud.[28] Soon, memos surfaced that described in colorful language how Enron's traders had manipulated California's electricity markets. Their language was as lurid as it was cynical and revealed a merciless culture of greed at the heart of the company.

A public relations disaster, the Enron collapse quickly became a central anchor for litigation and research on the crisis. It neatly partitioned the debate into two camps. One side stresses the role of economic fundamentals and places the blame on politicians' attempts to meddle with market forces, and the other tells a story of Texan companies that conspired to raid California.[29] Even after twenty years of sustained inquiry, no unified version has crystallized, and the two narratives continue to coexist in uneasy tension. To this day, researchers puzzle through evidence to identify the precise combination of causal factors that produced the price spikes. The crisis continues to be shrouded in ambiguity.

The opening chapter of the book explores these interpretative difficulties in detail. It reconstructs the events of the California energy crisis and the genesis of the two dominant narratives. But rather than taking a side, it suggests that we approach the case from a different perspective altogether. Less interested in identifying the exact combination of factors that drove up prices, the book focuses on their structural antecedents. It does not ask how much problematic behavior occurred or what specific operational configurations triggered it. Instead, it looks for the reasons it was possible in the first place.

California's market system was not just another case of deregulation gone wrong but a sophisticated attempt to solve a difficult problem. The physical characteristics of electricity and the technical complexity of the grid turned electricity market design into a tremendous intellectual challenge that drew some of the country's brightest minds to the state. Among the designers were Nobel laureates from the most prestigious institutions in the country, as well as accomplished utility executives, engineers, and lawyers. Their blueprints articulated an ambitious vision for designer markets that would perform a closely circumscribed function in the management of the electricity system. Yet, when all was said and done, the designers had helped to create a system that was riddled with incentives and opportunities for destructive behavior that could undermine the reliability of the electricity system. Why, then, did some of the world's foremost authorities on market design create such a flawed system? And what can this case teach us about the more general conditions of market design failure? To answer these questions, the book develops a theoretical framework for studying designer markets as planned structures. Before outlining this theory and the empirical analysis it informs, this chapter will briefly consider why a new theory is necessary in the first place. Why not simply rely on frameworks that are already available?

The Creation of Markets and the Literature on Market Design

Despite considerable research on market creation in general and market design in particular, the practical conditions for the success and failure of market design remain inadequately explored. Within the academic community of market designers, most research on design failure concerns the internal flaws of design blueprints. This focus can be explained by the methodological training of economists and computer scientists that emphasizes the evaluation of theoretical models.[30] Most research therefore considers the feasibility of designers' blueprints on the basis of formal criteria. For example, designers might explore whether a proposed mechanism is algorithmically feasible. They analyze whether there are realistic trading processes that would converge on equilibria whose existence is theoretically possible. Designers might also use laboratory experiments and simulations to explore whether a market mechanism leaves room for strategies that would substantially undermine designers' objectives.[31] To evaluate the mechanisms' robustness, they might study whether the mechanism would produce the same outcomes under a variety of starting parameters. If a model is sensitive to deviations from base assumptions, it would not be considered robust to implementation.[32] While this work is important, it does not consider the obstacles to implementation directly. Instead, the designers think about robustness and feasibility in terms of the internal consistency of the models or their formal characteristics. But even a perfectly consistent and formally robust model may be impossible to implement in practice.

Applied market designers go into the field and help to build customized markets. They have frequently drawn lessons from these practical experiences. Their insights are invaluable, but they take the form of advice to other practitioners rather than systematic reflections about the conditions of design work. For example, designers stress that blueprints must be amenable to political compromises because politicians will frequently disregard expert advice and insist on problematic design features.[33] This is a good piece of practical advice, but it does not provide much insight into the political dynamics that produce workable or unworkable compromises. Practitioners also highlight that a workable market mechanism must account for market actors' cognitive limitations and that real market participants may have "larger strategy sets" than those in the model.[34] They suggest keeping designs as simple and intuitive as possible. But they do not systematically evaluate how the vagaries of technical implementation processes affect their ability to deal with these problems. In other words, market designers have rarely studied how the conditions of design work bear on their ability to realize the internal logic of their models.[35]

Normally, this is where the sociologist would enter the picture. For decades, the discipline has studied the empirical details of market creation. It has shown that all marketplaces are constructed and that various types of experts contribute to their organization. But there have been no attempts to identify the general conditions for the success or failure of market design. Consequently, little empirical research indicates why these conditions may be met or violated in practice. There are three traditions that study how markets come about, how they stabilize, and how they change over time. Each approach has slightly different reasons for avoiding the question at the heart of this book.

The embeddedness perspective is associated with the names of Mark Granovetter and Harrison White.[36] Studies in this vein ask how social networks organize actors' mutual expectations and how these networks are structured by them in turn. Work that follows Granovetter's lead typically explores how actors' relations shape aggregate patterns of trading behavior, while Whiteian analyses are more interested in processes of perception and the network dynamics they engender.[37] Fluid interactions, mutual perceptions, and communication produce network structures that determine trade and become the basis for future processes of signaling and observation.[38] In each case, studies search for the relational dynamics of economic life and trace them to economic outcomes on the aggregate level.

This conceptual setup requires the assumption that market order arises from stochastic processes—rather than intentional planning.[39] The network structures that organize the market emerge endogenously from decentral interactions. Practically all contemporary methods for the analysis of social networks rely on this assumption. They evaluate whether an observed network could have resulted from a few interactional dynamics on the level of the group.[40] Because markets do not appear to be something that could be planned, the conceptual framework precludes questions about variation in market design success and failure.

That being said, the embeddedness perspective still reveals important obstacles to market design. To the extent that a market mechanism requires actors who make decisions independently of one another, the designers must first neutralize or mitigate the impact of social networks. Similarly, the emergent properties of trading networks may be relevant for the global allocation designers seek to create. In other words, the embeddedness perspective offers useful tools for identifying the problems that designers must overcome. But it has little to say about the designers' ability to do so.

The second tradition constitutes neo-institutional work. Most research on market creation falls under the banner of field theory.[41] Field theory emerged from Pierre Bourdieu's work and is most famously associated with Neil Fligstein's "markets as politics."[42] Field theory focuses on the political struggles that establish market institutions. These institutions are both formal and informal rules that structure what actions are possible. Studies of market creation from the nineteenth to the twenty-first century indicate that institutions evolve in a gradual and endogenous process of political contestation that takes place inside and around the market. Politicians, stakeholders, and regulators struggle to impose their ideas of legitimate action on the field. Cultural frames, the status quo, and power structures influence how these struggles play out.[43] The literature has produced important insights about how state actors make markets by creating regulatory and legal infrastructures in a dialectic back-and-forth with market actors.[44]

Similar to the embeddedness perspective, the neo-institutional framework makes it hard to study market design on its own terms. Designers try to impose a particular institutional structure on the market. But field theory assumes that no individual actor, and particularly no economic expert, can have that much power.[45] Market institutions are not the product of intentional planning but endogenous political dynamics. It would therefore make little sense to ask under what conditions designers could build the market they envision—they could not. Instead, designers appear to be just one group among many that compete for influence over the institutions of the market. Their expertise is seen as either a rhetorical tool for establishing political influence or an epistemic framework that structures the logic of political contestation.[46] This view is problematic for online marketplaces where the tools of software design place unprecedented power over the market process in the hands of small groups of market design experts.

Of course, any work on market design failure must consider how exactly formal and informal political dynamics enable or constrain designers' ability to realize their blueprints on different levels of the design process.[47] Once we turn to the empirical case to understand why these conditions may be broached, neo-institutional resources will help to explain the difficulties of design work. But to get a sense for what designers are trying to do and what they need to do to succeed, we require a different approach.

The last tradition is attuned to the designers' intellectual project. The "social studies of finance" focus on the materiality of markets as well as the technical experts who work to build them.[48] Michael Callon once launched this line of inquiry with the provocative claim that economic knowledge is complicit in creating the economic processes it purports to merely describe.[49] Since then, the literature has tried to understand how social processes make reality conform to theoretical propositions about it. These social processes are said to perform the theory.

At first sight, this seems like the perfect starting point for a sociology of market design. In some ways it is. Indeed, practically all sociological research about market design starts from this viewpoint.[50] Those who study successful cases show how laboratory experiments translate theoretical propositions into material arrangements.[51] Studies of failed experiments have traced what goes wrong as theoretical propositions travel from the laboratory to the field or how market designers' blueprints shape the political negotiations that set the rules of the market.[52] By now, we have a rich catalog of descriptive studies showing that it is possible to perform economic knowledge—though in highly limited and contingent ways. Of course, market designers will not be too surprised or provoked by this finding: performing theories is their explicit goal.[53]

This book frequently draws on insights from this literature. In particular, it often comes back to ideas about the distance between theory and practice in different organizational settings.[54] But for metatheoretical reasons, the literature is committed to description rather than general explanation.[55] Theoretical concepts are designed to shed light on a given phenomenon rather than pick out general features that explain variations between cases. To give an example, a recent study examines the "material political economy" of high-frequency trading in an attempt to explain how the automation of trading occurs in the US and the UK in a complex political and technical process.[56] The study is not trying to explain under what conditions a particular project of automation could succeed in one setting but not in another. Of course, description is not inherently problematic. Quite the contrary. But it remains inconclusive for the explanatory purposes of this book.

A couple of examples illustrate the point. In studies of failed market design projects, researchers noted an "epistemic gap" that exists between the conditions under which markets work in a laboratory and the real-world conditions to which they must be transplanted.[57] It is true that this epistemic gap can become a source of failure. If designers do not anticipate the problem, the rules may be indeterminate and allow market actors to violate the mechanism. But such gaps always exist. Every time a market is transplanted from one context to the other, questions emerge that were not predetermined by the blueprint describing the market mechanism. Yet designers can handle this challenge in some cases but not others. A purely descriptive approach has little to say about the factors that explain this variation.

Conversely, studies of successful market design have occasionally identified "felicity conditions" that helped a market work as intended.[58] But these conditions tend to be inherently local and concrete. For example, honor has been described as a felicity condition for the operation of New York's financial markets in the eighteenth century.[59] This doubtlessly facilitated trust between market participants, but an honor system is not required for the success of stock exchanges or of market design; designers do not manipulate the honor system in society.[60] As these examples show, a descriptive approach makes it difficult to study the conditions for success or failure.

In sum, none of the three traditions is well suited to help us understand the conditions under which designers can build the markets they envision and those under which they would fail to do so. While the embeddedness paradigm and institutional work assume the order of markets to be emergent and place designers at the periphery of market creation, the social studies of finance adopt a descriptive approach that does not move beyond the individual case to explain success and failure. What we need is a theoretical framework that reconstructs the internal logic of market design projects—what designers are trying to do—and then identifies the requirements that designers have to meet to realize these projects as well as the factors that may make this easier or harder.[61] Against this backdrop, we can then draw on the existing analytical tool kit to determine empirically why designers may fail to live up to these requirements.

Designer Markets as Organizational Forms

To study markets as things that can, in principle, be planned, I propose that we think about them as organizational forms.[62] This perspective highlights two characteristics of these markets. First, they are built inside organizations. Designers work in a formal division of labor to build, manage, and alter the infrastructures of the market. Second, designer markets perform a function similar to that of formal organizations: they are systems to coordinate people's activities in line with higher-order goals As the second chapter shows in depth, designers view market mechanisms as custom-tailored search algorithms that solve specific optimization problems.[63] This is not just a metaphor. The idea of the market as computer and the market mechanism as algorithm unify market design as a profession. Designers come from a variety of different disciplines and subfields in academia. Economics, engineering, computer science, and system operations research all contribute to their expertise. They work in the university environment, but we can also find them in specialized companies, governmental agencies, and think tanks. What makes them distinct is their commitment to the vision of markets as computers and market mechanisms as *search algorithms*.

Designers need market actors to engage in calculative activities that realize subroutines of the larger algorithm. In combination with software, the market process then produces aggregate distributions that solve the optimization problem at hand. Designers build the infrastructures of the market to cause actors to follow the correct logic of action. They write the rules, procedures, and interfaces that constitute the actors' choice environment and create organizational structures to monitor and adjust the resulting market process.

This yields a definition for the analytical object at the heart of this book: the designer market. A designer market is the organizational arrangement of transaction platforms and technical systems that work together to execute a search algorithm for producing allocative results that resolve an optimization problem. Understanding designer markets along these lines has two advantages. First, it directs analytical attention to the economists, engineers, technical experts, and administrators who build and manage these systems of interrelated components. To explain the success or failure of design projects, we might look at the political, organizational, and cognitive conditions under which they work.

Second, and more importantly, differences between formal organizations and designer markets reveal the core challenge of market design. In formal organizations, employees are nominally committed to the organization's objectives, and their employment contracts give managers a broad set of tools to coordinate them in line with these goals. For example, they can assign tasks directly, run performance reviews, or host team-building events to align employees' interpretations of tasks and inculcate them into the organizational culture.

In contrast, market designers are dealing with independent actors who are beholden only to their own interests. This substantially limits designers' tool kit. It forces them to coordinate market actors indirectly. They have to align market actors' interests with their own by structuring the actors' choice environment. The rules, procedures, and interfaces must make it beneficial and easy to follow the intended logic. Most market designers worry about getting this right—or figuring out what to do when they do not. In other words, "market design is the art to structure institutions in such a way that incentives and behavior harmonize with higher-order goals."[64] This is very difficult.

To use an analogy, designers are like developers of a peculiar board game where every session is supposed to end with a predefined distribution of resources between players. The game's structure and rules would have to ensure that all possible moves propel players toward this goal. This is hard because designers need to write rules in anticipation of countless different situations.[65] In addition, market actors always have a reason to assume a reflexive stance vis-à-vis the system and search for loopholes that allow them to extract bandit profits—riskless profits that derive from flaws in the administrative system of the market rather than from superior information about market fundamentals. Even when the market can withstand some deviant behavior because designers have specified the objectives for the market with a sufficient margin of error, they must keep a close check on the permutations of possible behavior in the market. Otherwise, they run the risk that actors will systematically exploit a loophole that can derail the market mechanism.

To contain the complexity of the market and keep destructive behavior at bay, designers rely on three general strategies: simplifying, bounding, and controlling. Simplifying means reducing the behavioral options inside the market as well as the information participants need to consider. It is an effort to limit options to a level that both designers and participants can manage. Bounding refers to an effective insulation of the market from other spheres of action. Control refers to ongoing efforts to identify novel behavior and either constrain it or adjust the market mechanism to accommodate it. In each case, the point is to limit the ways in which market actors can interpret and act in the situation to the calculations required by the design.

Control structures are *always* necessary to enforce designers' mechanisms. Markets generate the benefits they do because they rely on decentral decisions. Self-interested actors best know the problems and possibilities of their local contexts. They know how much to produce, what methods to use, and how they might solve their local problems more efficiently than they did in the past. They have, in the language of designers, private information that is not accessible in the center. Designers are therefore trying to *coordinate* rather than overdetermine these local decision-making processes. They aim to shape the form but not the substance of economic transactions. Users provide the inputs; designers set up the formal structure that elicits these inputs in such a way that they aggregate toward the global objective.

Even if the designers make the market rules extremely restrictive, there is always room for creative reinterpretation in practice and thus deviation from the expectations of designers—what it means to follow a rule is necessarily and contingently established by practice, as the old philosophical insight goes. Designers can therefore never get away by just simplifying and bounding the market. They also need to put an oversight structure into place. Due to the possibility of variation on the local level, synthetic markets are organizations that work with cybernetic *feedback-control* mechanisms. Though particularly theoretical market designers do not always recognize this, no synthetic market can exist without some form of control structure.

Successful market design, then, requires that designers strike a workable balance between all three techniques. Depending on the level of simplification and bounding, designers may need to put more or less active control into place. But the success of the design depends on finding a workable balance between these strategies. Generally, this means simplifying the market as much as the allocation problem admits and never allowing the permutations of behavior to increase beyond what a centralized control regime can monitor and manage. Where exactly the limits of control are located will vary from case to case—it depends on the hazards associated with deviant behavior. But there is a hard limit, nonetheless. The control structure must be able to evaluate transactions by applying some set of formal criteria. It needs to be able to apply some formal rule that will indicate whether or not a transaction conforms to the blueprint. Otherwise, the control structure would need to know the right, local decision or the correct solution to the optimization problem. Either the market would then be obsolete as a coordination device because the center would know the correct local decisions or centralized oversight would fail because it would not have that information. At that point, the market would collapse into centralized planning.

The center must evaluate each local decision substantively. As research on centralized planning has shown, this is not generally feasible.[66]

In sum, market design failure occurs when the balance among simplifying, bounding, and controlling is off. Actors can then profit by acting in ways that undermine the designers' objectives without being visible to the center. Designer markets can be complicated but not complex; while there must be room for actors to introduce novel information into the system, the permutations of possible behavior cannot exceed what the centralized observer can sort through and manage.[67] Containing the market's complexity—the various ways in which actors can relate to the rules of the system as a whole—is the only way to handle the meta-incentive to search for profit beyond the letter of the rules for a given context.

Though general, this analytical framework does not yet explain market design failure or success in any particular case. It translates questions about market failures into questions about human design decisions and the limits of social control and thereby provides a guideline for empirical research that can help us understand market design on its own terms. An empirical investigation of market design failure can establish how and why the balance between simplifying, bounding, and controlling may be broached in practice. From this, we may then derive insight into social dynamics that can push market design projects off course. This is where the book turns back to the mystery of the Western energy crisis.

An Explanation of California's Energy Crisis

After developing the conceptual framework for the book in the second chapter, the third and fourth chapters turn to California's electricity markets and show how the system violated the balance among simplifying, bounding, and controlling. Chapter 3 begins by reconstructing how the market architecture worked under ideal circumstances. It discusses in detail how a system of more than fifteen interrelated forward markets helped to coordinate and prepare the management of the electric grid—the vast network of transmission and distribution lines that connected California with eleven western states and parts of Canada and Mexico. The chapter then shows how three broad types of destructive behavior violated the precarious and sophisticated interrelations between the different submarkets. In each case, the actors no longer followed designers' plans, and the market mechanism no longer served to coordinate the management of the electricity system. Indeed, to execute these profitable strategies, market participants had to actively damage the system's physical infrastructure.

The fourth chapter traces the incentives and opportunities for the destructive behavior in the underlying market design. It develops a structural explanation of the energy crisis: each class of deviant behavior responded to a design flaw that I call *differential simplification*. The design teams simplified rules, products, and even the representation of physical reality itself in an effort to constrain the space of possible actions in each market. But they simplified different submarkets to different degrees, creating inconsistencies between the market rules and temporal horizons of decision-making. These inconsistencies multiplied market actors' behavioral options relative to the desired course of action. Almost paradoxically, the designers achieved the opposite of their intentions. By simplifying different parts of the system unevenly, they increased the global complexity of the market system far beyond the range of desirable behavior.

In principle, the system may still have worked if the designers had controlled the interdependencies of the different subsystems effectively. But several design features made the boundaries between the system extremely porous. Though the designers had created strong boundaries around core features, they left a variety of gaps and weak spots in other parts of the system. Because market actors always acted with respect to the system as a whole, the boundaries were only as effective as their weakest part. Sneaking through a few porous boundaries made it easy for actors to circumvent the others as well.

With each failure of simplification and bounding, the control requirements grew. Indeed, by the time the markets opened, the requirements eclipsed what any centralized control system could have accomplished—the market had grown too complex to allow oversight on the basis of formal criteria for desirable behavior. Nonetheless, designers might have avoided some of the worst consequences of the crisis if they had put a stronger system into place. Yet, despite the need for a nearly omniscient control structure, they opted for a weak and fragmented solution. As we tally these various design failures, a deeper question emerges: Why did the designers implement the features that derailed California's market design so completely? And what can we learn about the limits of market design more generally? This is the topic of the book's second part.

Why the Designers Built a Flawed System

To explain the problematic features of California's system, the book turns to the design work that put the markets into place. Unfolding between 1993 and 1998, the process was highly fragmented and generated various path dependencies. Political negotiations among stakeholders, politicians, regulators, and designers produced a broad architectural baseline. Vastly complex, technical implementation processes then began to hash out increasingly concrete plans. Finally, the designers created new organizations and assembled the infrastructures that would operate the markets. Throughout, their work was split between several different venues: political negotiations in Sacramento and San Francisco, technical working groups that met at changing locations, and regulatory conferences in Washington. Chapters 5–7 construct the design process and trace problematic decisions to different levels of this institutional field.

The fifth chapter looks at the decisions made during political negotiations at the California Public Utility Commission. Between 1993 and 1996, stakeholders increasingly rallied around a compromise proposal that violated core principles of market design. Designers recognized these problems early on and bitterly opposed the political compromise. They tried to demonstrate that the provisions violated core technical constraints of market design and that they, the designers, should sort out the relation between markets and the system operator. But the stakeholders and politicians did not recognize designers' expertise as authoritative. The chapter explores why designers' rhetorical strategies were destined to fail in an environment where everyone thought they knew how markets worked.

The empirical argument in the fifth chapter expands, but is broadly consistent with, research that traces the crisis to the flawed legal foundations of the system. It identifies political reasons for certain design flaws. But the book does not stop here. If the design process were an iceberg, the political process would be merely its tip. Submerged below the surface of public attention lay technical work that turned the broad political compromise into the vastly complex reality of the market system. In the sixth and seventh chapters, the book turns to this technical work. Here, market designers changed from peripheral expert witnesses into decision-makers. They concretized the vague political compromises into a workable blueprint and then implemented the corresponding market infrastructures in software, hardware, and institutional rules. While they could not ignore the political compromise proposal, they had ample room to work around key issues and were optimistic that they could do so. However, despite careful planning, they ended up making things worse.

The political process imposed on the designers a system architecture that was more complex than necessary. It also created several roadblocks for strategies to resolve the resulting inconsistencies and complications. Unable to simplify the basic architecture of the system, they adopted a division of labor that promised to keep the complex interdependencies between different parts of the system in check while allowing the designers to iterate quickly through solutions. This technique, called modularization, is used to break down complex problems into manageable chunks. Because modules are exchangeable, it allows decentral innovation, robust design, and concomitant work processes.[68] It was the only choice for a complex system that had to be built very quickly.

But as the sixth chapter shows, the organizational technique ran up against the logic of designer markets. Working within the confines of their respective modules, designers made decisions about rules and interfaces that worked well for the specific problems they were trying to solve. In particular, they made reasonable decisions about the minimal level of physical complexity they needed to represent in their markets. But because of the modular division of labor, the teams could not systematically consider corresponding decisions in other modules. After all, these were supposed to be independent. But from the perspective of market actors, differences between the modules encouraged violations of the structure of the system. Inconsistencies created incentives to link the modules in ways that contradicted the intended logic of action. Intermediaries and managers looking for such problems had to consider design issues on a level of abstraction that obscured the relevant inconsistencies and made it difficult to fix problems iteratively. The problems of differential simplification and porous boundaries thus go back to the division of labor in the design process.

The seventh chapter asks why the designers did not compensate for this escalating complexity by erecting a rigid control structure or shoring up boundaries. To explain this last puzzle, the book considers the cultural and cognitive dimension of design work inside the modularized organization. The designers were fragmented into several intellectual camps, working on different subparts of the larger system. They used similar formalizations and concepts for their mechanisms. But underlying the shared, formal language were different imaginations of the market as algorithm. Engineers and economists of various stripes thought about the market in different ways. The models for the new system thus had a *chameleonic* character.

Depending on the context of the work, designers thought differently about how the markets would operate and how they related to the management of the grid. As a consequence, the designers had different conceptions of deviant behavior and therefore protected some elements of the larger architecture better than others. This left open several loopholes that sellers of energy could use to circumvent the stronger boundaries. These inconsistencies proved fatal for designers' efforts to separate different parts of the market. Relatedly, the teams also arrived at different understandings of the control requirements for the new system. Their different perspectives led each group to overlook crucial problems that the others were aware of, and they each concluded that a limited oversight structure would suffice.

After politics had dealt the designers bad cards, the organizational and cognitive dynamics of design work overwhelmed their ability to build a globally consistent system of market rules with limited behavioral complexity and deceived them about the need for an extensive oversight regime. In this way, then, the California energy crisis was a catastrophe waiting to happen—the permutations of possible behavior constantly grew larger than the oversight structure could handle. Several of these behaviors undermined the reliable operation of the system, and as soon as market actors discovered them, the system began to unravel.

The Limits of Market Design for Complex Allocation Problems

In sum, the book shows that three practical problems explain why the designers ended up with a flawed market design in California. First, designers did not have the *political standing* to control central design decisions. Second, designers' *organizational tools* were insufficient to meet the consistency requirements of designer markets and contain the behavioral complexity of the system. Modularization tended to produce only locally optimal sets of rules and practices, while the markets required globally consistent rules and practices. Third, different groups of designers did not agree about the requirements to implement their blueprints. Their *practical meaning* was not sufficiently stable across the different parts of the design process. Unlike in architectural or engineering projects, the practices for the interpretation of blueprints' formal language could not draw on stable institutional standards. Together, these three problems overwhelmed even the most sophisticated designers. They prompted decisions that were locally prudent but led to differential simplification, porous boundaries, and weak control structures.

To conclude, the book considers what general lessons can be drawn from the highly idiosyncratic situation in California at the turn of the millennium. It starts with the observation that designers faced practical problems that are fairly common. All market design involves political negotiations with nonexperts, some degree of organization, and practical problems related to translating formal models into working institutions. The conditions of market design work are therefore always in latent tension with the requirements for successful market design—the need to simplify, bound, and control markets as closely as possible.

The nature of the allocation problems is directly related to the seriousness of this tension. Some problems involve clearly defined objectives, are largely static, and are separable from other contexts. Such problems can be solved in market environments that are exceedingly simple and bounded. Control is therefore relatively easy. For such allocation problems, the issue of political standing should be more minimal because designers have to control fewer decisions and their technical work faces fewer material and institutional constraints from adjacent systems. The organizational structure of the design process can likely be more centralized, and it should be harder for distinct cultures to form with respect to the practical interpretation of the blueprints.

Conversely, the tension exacerbates allocation problems where designers have to contend with multiple objectives over different temporal horizons, technological and organizational changes, and dependencies with the markets' environment. In these cases, the required market architectures are rather large and have to work in close alignment with complex technological requirements. Varying temporal horizons are particularly tricky: the more scenarios designers must consider for the system to be reliable, the more markets there need to be that enforce the relevant perspective on the future and coordinate their interrelations. Because of the inherent tension between short-term and long-term logics of action, failure to control these temporal horizons tends to generate incentives to deviate from the required long-term logic of action. This makes design more difficult. Political negotiations become harder because designers have to control more decisions in situations where stakeholders with disparate intellectual backgrounds vie for dominance. Organizational structures have to be larger and more differentiated, prompting difficulties in meeting the consistency requirements behind the imperatives for simplification and bounding. This escalates control requirements until the project either becomes prohibitively costly or falls prey to the pitfalls of centralized planning.

All this has a clear implication. For simple problems, market design brings together the best of two worlds—markets and organizations. It uses the tools of bureaucracy to centrally enforce a logic of decision-making that aligns decentral decisions. While the center ensures that the collective objectives are maintained, decentral decisions are driven by self-interest and rich contextual information. The discipline of markets beautifully combines with intentional planning. But for complex allocation problems, market design conjures the worst of both worlds. Self-interested market actors exacerbate the problems that complex organizations face in coordinating decision-making and undermine the tools that could fix these problems. This turns designer markets into fragile and error-prone social systems. In the end, even successful electricity markets are operating in a precarious balance that requires vast and constant control far beyond the oversight required for administrative bureaucracies. Failures of control can have devastating consequences because the market turns against the reliable operation of the underlying system. For complex allocation problems concerning essential goods, market design is therefore *not* going to be the most sensible or even feasible solution. The organizational, political, and cognitive conditions of design work run up against the steep consistency requirements of working markets, constantly pitting actors against the reliable solution of the underlying problem. Indeed, I show that a complex division of labor in both the design process and the control structure makes it impossible, *on principle*, to rule out behavior that can subvert the market mechanism.

Perhaps, then, the solution is to use the tools of market design not for markets but for other types of organizations that do not involve the structural antagonism of market actors. But before this implication can become accessible and plausible, we still have a long way to go. The book will therefore now come back down from the lofty heights of abstraction and approach its empirical case: the California energy crisis.

PART ONE

A CASE OF MARKET DESIGN FAILURE

CHAPTER ONE

Two Tales of a Crisis

The unthinkable happened at 11:40 a.m. on January 17, 2001. The control room of California's Independent System Operator, or CAISO, had grown silent over the last few hours. People no longer moved to and fro, bantered, or cracked jokes. They sat at their control stations and worked. Occasionally, a telephone punctuated the silence. Hunched over their desks, operators picked up and stated terse requests, all the while observing signals from screens that covered every surface of the room.[1]

The operators sat at semicircular stations of the "fishbowl," so named for the large windows that allowed the rest of the organization to peer in. The stations were arranged around a large map board that covered the entire front wall. It provided a schematic overview of California's high-voltage electricity grid. Hundreds of small red and green lights represented every major generation facility and electric switchyard in California as well as the energy flows between them. Each workstation provided the operators with specialized information on technical parameters such as voltage support levels and path protection. Glancing up, operators could check the real-time status of the grid on the board.[2] What they saw was not good.

The complex setup of screens, dials, and control panels served a singular purpose. CAISO managed the network of high-transmission lines that delivered energy from generators to local distribution networks and from there to end users. At first sight, the technical sophistication of the control room may seem surprising. The blinking LEDs, the large map board, and the control stations seem to better fit the world of interstellar travel than the mundane task of moving electricity from a generator to someone's toaster. But the veneer of the mundane often belies great and fragile complexity. The production and delivery of electricity is such a case: it depends on a complex process of adjustments, unparalleled by other infrastructures.

As soon as a generator releases energy into the grid, it travels at nearly the speed of light through a vast network of transmission lines. Following Kirchhoff's laws, it takes all available paths through this network. This means that the inputs from different generators combine and interact with one another. In 2000, the California network had about 3,500 buses and 25,526 miles of circuit power lines. This network was tied into the larger framework of the Western Interconnection, which had over twenty thousand nodes and connected parts of Mexico, Canada, and eleven states in the western United States.

For energy to traverse this system reliably, frequency and voltage must be kept within a tight band of error. Even minor differences can lead to equipment failure and cascading blackouts with potentially devastating effects on people's lives. The characteristics of energy production further complicate this precarious balance. Since it is not yet feasible to store large quantities of electricity, production and consumption need to be adjusted to each other nearly instantaneously. If someone switches a light on in San Francisco, a generator somewhere in the service territory of Pacific Gas & Electric (PG&E) needs to have produced that energy just a fraction of a second earlier.

These characteristics require that the central system operator—CAISO, in this case—constantly adjust the production of energy to balance the changes in consumption, all the while maintaining the security standards required for reliability. Because each fluctuation in input can influence the available transmission capacity, voltage, and frequency anywhere in the system, even just one change in one part can require wide-ranging adjustments in all other parts. To get a feeling for this complexity, you can imagine electricity as a concert of light pulses in which each generator influences the pattern and rhythm of the whole—an infinitely complex performance that may collapse with little more than a single node falling out of rhythm. The technical sophistication of this constant coordination explains the futuristic look of the control room.

Since about 5:00 a.m. on January 17, 2001, the operators at CAISO had been fighting to keep the system going. Many of the crucial indicators on the board had been worrisome. Now they suggested an impending disaster. Information from a dozen different feeds added up to one simple message: there was not enough capacity. Californians were using a lot more electricity than usual to heat their buildings. Meanwhile, the supply to satisfy the growing demand had virtually disappeared. During the summer, many generators inside California had produced in excess of their ideal operating conditions, and they were now shut down for maintenance. Generators in adjacent states that normally sold to California did not offer their energy. Even pumped-storage facilities, whose water could usually be relied on to deal with bottleneck situations, were depleted. "We could see that we were at the ragged edge," CEO Terry Winter said to the reporters who had gathered in the blue-box area, a special zone for press who visited the system operator during the crisis.[3]

Increasingly desperate, the operators relied on informal channels to cope with the situation. They had long stopped relying on CAISO's official imbalance markets, which could be used to adjust supply to sudden fluctuations in demand. Rather than trusting the numbers on their screens, they called friends at other utilities, begging them to send whatever they had at whatever price. "Everybody around here was doing everything they possibly could," said Jim McIntosh, the director of grid operations. But at 11:00 a.m., the balance of forces shifted against the team. A large generating plant in the Central Coast area declared an engine failure and went offline. In the little time that remained before the impact would materialize, it was impossible to find sufficient energy. "We begged. We borrowed. We tried to steal, but there wasn't anything to steal," remembered Ed Riley.[4] At 11:40 a.m., the operators gave up.

The system operator had to institute rolling blackouts in California. As a despondent McIntosh recalled: "That one day, there wasn't anything left."[5] Then, about 320,000 customers in the San Francisco area lost electricity. After two hours, the blackouts moved up north into Central and Northern California. Traffic lights, refrigerators, and ATMs stopped working.[6] Images of mechanics opening elevator doors with crowbars were shared around the world. It seemed absurd that widespread blackouts would affect the state that was home to the computer revolution and the world's fifth-largest economy. And yet it had happened—the system operator had failed in its mission to provide reliability at all costs. "We all just stood there, kind of shocked," said Riley.[7]

But the operators did not have much time to catch their breath. On January 18, the drama repeated itself, and they had to cut twice as much electricity as the day before. After that, the system teetered on the brink of collapse for another thirty days. Pulling together everything they could and working sleepless nights, the operators managed to improve the situation slightly. But despite their combined efforts, blackouts rolled across the state for three more days, affecting millions of Californians. As of May 2001, the system operator had declared thirty-eight Stage 3 emergencies. Rolling blackouts swept across the state.[8] Nonetheless, the operators almost pulled off a miracle: they largely prevented blackouts in residential areas, pulling the system back from collapse by the sheer force of their will. For several months, the nation watched aghast as California's electrical infrastructure teetered on the brink of system failure.[9]

The dramatic fight to keep the lights on formed the climax of a crisis that had begun about a year earlier, in April 2000. The events followed a pattern that is familiar from many industrial disasters: a problematic development was left unrecognized for long enough to turn into a self-sustaining process. This process escalated as its effects spilled over into adjacent domains. Everything began with problems in the energy markets, which quickly spiraled out of control and led to a financial crisis among the most important utilities. Political paralysis allowed the financial crisis to spill over into the operation of the grid, which led to reliability problems that dragged the electricity system as a whole to the brink of collapse. Desperate attempts to bring things back under control eventually required state intervention. The government took over the procurement of electricity and ultimately socialized the problem. This, finally, turned the reliability problems into a (temporary) budget crisis for the state of California.[10]

To appreciate the different steps in the crisis's rapid escalation, it is necessary to zoom in from the ten-thousand-meter view just presented. Everything began in California's brand-new energy markets. In 1996, the California legislature passed a law with the colorful title "AB 1890" to restructure the industry. Only two years later, the new markets opened their doors for business and replaced a century-old system of regulated monopolies. Figure 1.1 provides a simplified sketch that contrasts the old system with the new and gives a sense of the profound transformation.

Before the restructuring, three investor-owned utilities had dominated California's electricity industry. They operated as vertically integrated monopolies that produced, sold, and transmitted energy in distinct service territories. Pacific Gas & Electric (PG&E) controlled the northern part of California; Southern California Edison (SCE), the southern. San Diego Gas & Electric (SDG&E) operated in the area around San Diego, while four cooperatives and thirty-four small utilities ran the systems of municipalities and rural irrigation districts. These companies sold energy at regulated rates to end users, retail customers and such industrial users as cement factories, chemical plants, and large companies in Silicon Valley. The California Public Utility Commission (CPUC) set the prices that utilities could charge their customers in rate cases.[11]

Restructuring radically transformed this system and introduced several new players. I will provide a more detailed picture later, but a simple sketch suffices for now. The new system unbundled utilities' monopoly and introduced markets in the production and sale of electricity. CAISO took over the management of the grid, effectively merging the service territories of the three investor-owned utilities. Meanwhile, the sale and production of energy moved into two sets of markets. In the retail markets, end users could sign contracts with the old utilities or with a new group of "alternative retail suppliers." Despite substantial publicity efforts, these alternative

California Electricity Industry

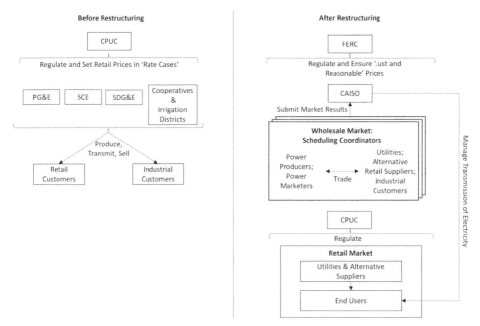

FIGURE 1.1. Illustration of California Electricity
Industry, Before and After Restructuring

suppliers never gained a meaningful market share. The retail market therefore remained in the hands of the three utilities. More significant changes
occurred on the level of production. Utilities had to divest most of their
generation assets. Together with industrial users, they now had to buy
their power in wholesale markets. So-called scheduling coordinators operated these markets, which traded electricity contracts for delivery at
future points—a year, a month, or a day in advance. The most important
scheduling coordinator was the Power Exchange, a public auction house
for same- and next-day contracts. About 80 percent of all transactions took
place here.[12] The buyers could choose between two classes of sellers: power
producers, which owned generation assets and sold power outright, and
power marketers, which engaged in arbitrage trading, profiting from price
differences between locations and time points. After the wholesale markets concluded trading, the scheduling coordinators turned the resulting
obligations into schedules of anticipated generation and consumption.
They submitted these schedules to CAISO, which then executed them as
closely as possible. This way, the market prepared for the work of the system operator, approximating the best way to dispatch generators to meet

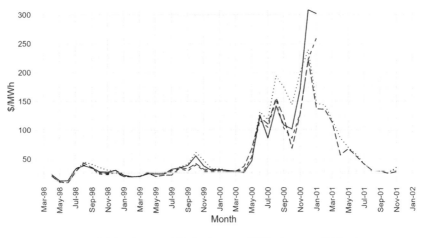

FIGURE 1.2. Average Prices in the PX Day-Ahead
Market and CAISO Imbalance Market

demand. Because the wholesale markets included sellers from the Western Interconnection, most regulatory responsibility shifted from the California Public Utility Commission to the Federal Energy Regulatory Commission (FERC), which had to ensure that the markets were competitive.

For about two years, this structure worked well and produced low prices. But in April 2000, the prices for wholesale electricity began to fluctuate dangerously: they first spiked to unprecedented heights, then fell drastically, only to jump back up and remain high for several months. Initially, the utilities, regulators, and politicians thought the price spikes were just a minor hiccup. Nothing but the growing pains of competitive markets, driven by minor supply shortages during unusual weather. Not only were such events expected in a new and untested market environment but insignificant spikes had also occurred at the end of 1999.

But the new markets defied these hopeful expectations. The spikes kept disrupting the markets and rapidly pushed the average price above actors' keenest expectations. Figure 1.2 displays the monthly average prices in the Power Exchange's day-ahead market and CAISO's imbalance market for the time between 1998 and 2001.[13] Between the second half of 1999 and the second half of 2000, the average price increased by 500 percent.[14] Since the figure reports averages, it hides significant fluctuations: for certain hours, the prices would spike as high as $1,400 dollars, while at other times they would be as low as before the crisis.

The high prices were bad news for all buyers, but they posed an existential threat to the three utilities.[15] As part of restructuring, they had divested about 60 percent of their generation assets. In addition, they had very few long-term contracts from the time before restructuring. Such long-term contracts would have protected them from price spikes, by allowing them to cover their energy needs at fixed prices. During the creation of the new markets, the California Public Utility Commission had implemented a rule that blocked the utilities from entering such contracts. They had worried that there would be little competition in the new short-term markets if the biggest buyers had already procured their energy elsewhere. At the time, the policy had seemed like a good idea to increase the liquidity of the new markets. But without long-term contracts or independent generation assets, the utilities could not protect themselves from the volatility in the new spot markets. It was a perfect trap, and the price spikes hit the utilities with full force.

Normally, the utilities would have recovered these high costs of wholesale energy by increasing the rates they charged to retail customers. Basic economic theory suggested that this would have led to a decline in demand that exerted downward pressure on wholesale prices. But the utilities did not have recourse to such rate hikes. A state law had imposed a retail-price freeze for the first few years after restructuring.

The retail freeze had been a product of political negotiations between the utilities and the California Public Utility Commission. During the negotiations about restructuring, the utilities fought for the right to recover "stranded costs." This was a euphemism for investments that regulators had approved but that would become uneconomical in the context of a competitive market.[16] The utilities demanded compensation for these investments. Their point was straightforward: they had made these investments under a regulated system. The California Public Utility Commission and the California Energy Commission had granted the right to recover these costs from rate payers, and the utilities therefore felt that it would be only fair if the regulators now provided a way to recover these "stranded costs" under the new system. After all, these investments had been made in good faith, in the belief that the established system would cover them.

The utility commission—having long-standing and comfortable relations with the utilities—found this argument convincing and decided to honor the commitments from the old regulatory consensus. To do so without imposing excessive costs on consumers, they came up with a complicated and nontransparent legal construct called the "competitive transition charge." Though the details were complex, the gist was simple. Since everyone assumed that wholesale prices would be lower than retail rates, the regulators froze the retail rate at the level established on January 1,

1996.[17] At low wholesale prices, the utilities would then quickly recover their stranded costs from the difference between wholesale and retail price. After that period, the freeze would be lifted, and consumers would be exposed to the price risk of the wholesale markets.

Of course, the entire mechanism would only work if the wholesale costs remained low. When the crisis began in May 2000, the logic quickly turned on its head. Because wholesale prices were suddenly far above the retail price, the utilities no longer made profits from the difference. Instead, the price freeze prevented utilities from charging their customers the wholesale price. Not only were they barred from charging their customers the true costs of energy but they were also unable to cut demand because they had a legal obligation to serve all customers.[18] In this situation, they had no choice but to buy the required energy at any cost and without a way to recoup their losses. What used to be an almost riskless fountain of profit now turned into a formidable trap that drained the utilities' cash reserves with breathtaking speed.

The utilities' vulnerability to high wholesale prices created the foundation for the next phase of the crisis. With no means to defend themselves, the utilities would quickly bleed out unless something changed. Since they were the crucial intermediary between most of California's end users and the wholesale markets for energy, their demise would undermine not only the markets but also the reliability of the electricity system. Recognizing the danger as early as March 2000, the utility executives began to plead with politicians and regulators for help. But during the early months, it was not clear how long the price spikes would last or what exactly was driving them. Trying to navigate a murky and increasingly dangerous situation, utilities, regulators, and politicians commenced a complicated dance that paralyzed the regulatory system and left the crisis unresolved.

First, the utilities tried to appeal the restrictions on long-term contracts. If they could buy more of their energy over longer periods of time, they would become less vulnerable to price swings in the short-term markets. Initially, the California Public Utility Commission worried that the higher average price of long-term contracts would lock utilities into bad deals. These would then lead to retail-price increases and an unhappy public. When they recognized the danger of the volatility in the short-term markets and relented, the legislature quickly overrode the decision and reinstated the restrictions.

In August 2000, it finally became clear to everyone that the state was in a full-fledged crisis, and the California Public Utility Commission was able to lift restrictions on forward contracts purchased through the Power Exchange markets. But while the agency now encouraged utilities to enter these contracts, it still withheld the guarantee that the prices would be considered "reasonable." The utilities could not be sure that they would be allowed to recoup the costs from their customers when the crisis was over. The California government desperately wanted to avoid giving the utilities carte blanche—if they had declared the price of these contracts to be reasonable, the utilities could have justified high retail rates for years to come. It was therefore unclear whether the utilities would be able to recover the costs of the long-term contracts. For whatever reason, the utilities decided *not* to take the risk and avoided the long-term contracts despite the escalating spot prices.[19] And when it finally became obvious that forward contracts were the only way to avoid a financial disaster, the cheap options had long disappeared from the long-term markets.

Without the ability to hedge their position, the utility executives now hoped that the regulators might release them from the rate freeze in the retail markets. If they had to pay astronomical prices for wholesale energy, they at least wanted a chance to pass the prices on to customers. But the political establishment in California tried to avoid such increases with all its might. The firm stance formed as a reaction to the first time the crisis burst from the obscure world of utility experts who traded in wholesale markets onto the stage of everyday life, in San Diego in August 2000.

San Diego Gas & Electric had sold most of their generation assets before restructuring. Since they now had low stranded costs, they had managed to recover their money through the spot markets by 1999. No longer beholden to the rate freeze, the utility started to charge customers in San Diego the price of the wholesale markets. The results were spectacular.

Consumer electricity bills suddenly doubled. "The prices in San Diego went crazy, and the small businesses were affected," remembered one interviewee, whose parents had a restaurant in the city. "San Diego is a very small part of our big state, but it was sort of a canary in a coal mine."[20] The prices were so high that some restaurants could not stay open in the evening. Some people could not pay the bills at all. The public was outraged. "There were demonstrations in the streets," one of the CAISO board members recalls. "FERC came out to meetings in San Diego [and the buildings] were surrounded by protestors."[21] For the most part, people did not want to think about electricity markets or the best way to induce long-term efficiencies in energy production. They only cared about restructuring to the extent that it reduced the high rates for electricity. People did not care about markets; they wanted cheap, reliable energy.[22] When the prices suddenly skyrocketed, the outrage was commensurate with the desire not to be bothered with a simple and taken-for-granted thing like electricity.

The situation in San Diego first put the crisis at the center of public attention and created significant political pressure to rein in the markets. As the CEO of the PX remembered, "The howling, and the crying, and the screams, the hearings, the everything. This just blew up, this whole political fiasco, and created a situation in which there was panic, and at which price caps were put on that we didn't have before. The state legislative branch had several hearings on this problem caused by San Diego in May and June."[23]

San Diego Gas & Electric filed a complaint at FERC, which was responsible for "just and reasonable" prices in the wholesale markets. Steve Peace, the senator who had spearheaded the efforts to pass the legislation for restructuring, started a crusade against the system operator. The California legislature reimposed the retail-price controls and closed off the utilities' route to cost recovery.[24] From then on, it was clear to politicians that it would be political suicide to allow the rate increases that would be necessary to reflect the cost of wholesale energy. Accordingly, they rejected the utilities' requests as the crisis got worse. They also continued to resist pleas to sanction the escalating costs for long-term contracts as reasonable, thus effectively leaving the utilities defenseless.

Apart from political reasons for leaving utilities to fend for themselves and protect customers, the government also had a substantive reason. The California Public Utility Commission and the governor's office had become increasingly convinced that the wholesale markets were not working properly. Until about August 2000, the dominant narrative had been that California suffered from a shortage of supply and that the high prices would eventually attract new generation assets that would drive down prices. Because of an investigation by the California Public Utility Commission and another regulatory organization, the Electricity Oversight Board, the governor became convinced that the crisis was primarily attributable not to supply shortages but to the exercise of market power.[25] Market power is a company's ability to influence the prices unilaterally, either by physically withholding generation capacity or by influencing the clearing prices in auctions, also called economic withholding. In a written statement to the press from July 2000, Governor Gray Davis declared that the current situation was "unjust and totally unacceptable" and said there was not yet sufficient competition among electricity suppliers to strip away regulations without hurting consumers.[26]

Despite their determination to end price gouging, the California Public Utility Commission and the governor's office were unable to curb what they perceived to be problematic behavior—they did not have the requisite jurisdiction. Because the markets had a regional structure that transcended state lines, it was the federal regulator, FERC, that had this authority. However, FERC's leadership was committed to restructuring and had close ties with companies like Enron, Dynegy, and Williams that heavily lobbied in Washington. Accordingly, FERC did not agree with California's allegations. Not only did they react comparatively slowly to events that were unfolding at a rapid pace but a staff investigation in August 2000 responding to the problems in San Diego concluded that the crisis was mainly a problem of supply-and-demand imbalances.[27] They acknowledged that there were some design problems and that market power might play a role, but they decided that these were subsidiary issues. The commissioners were therefore hesitant to curb the prices in the wholesale markets or remove sellers that might be driving up prices. They thought the best way to resolve the crisis would be to incentivize new generation and change the market protocols. The staff report therefore led to various suggestions for a gradual reform of the market protocols and the creation of incentives for new generation.[28] Ideologically, politically, and historically at odds with each other, the agencies at the federal and state level had increasing difficulties agreeing on a joint course of action, and the atmosphere between California and Washington turned sour.

The tug-of-war between the state and the federal level played out not just before FERC but also at CAISO. The organization had a governing stakeholder board that decided on the best strategy to deal with the crisis. The twenty-six representatives came from all branches of the energy industry. Before the crisis, this board was usually able to agree on the development of the energy markets, but when the crisis began, most of those who made money began to disagree with most of those who were losing it. Technical issues rendered unclear whether price caps would help with the crisis and, if they would help, how high they should be. Soon, the California government leaned on the board to apply lower price caps. FERC insisted that any price caps could only be remedial. Torn between the different political pressures and divided among its members, the board could no longer reach majority decisions. The conflicting demands from the political apparatus, combined with the internal interest conflicts, turned the atmosphere toxic, and the board became dysfunctional.

When the situation continued to worsen, FERC eventually sanctioned price caps in the system operator's imbalance markets. But it mandated that the prices had to be high enough to attract new entrants. Even after they finally became convinced that the markets were not workably competitive, in November 2000, they did not implement strong behavioral constraints for sellers of energy. But because the California system was tied to regional markets that were also facing supply shortages, the moderate price caps did not lead to improvements. Instead, they reduced the available supply in the wholesale markets further, pushed the prices to the allowed limit, and did nothing to relieve the utilities, even though the resulting market prices were still far above the retail price. In December 2000, Southern California Edison sued FERC for failing to ensure reasonable wholesale prices, and on January 2, 2001, Governor Davis joined the lawsuit. Paul Joskow, a Massachusetts Institute of Technology (MIT) economics professor who helped to create the markets and analyzed them during the crisis, summarized the situation like this: "When it became clear it was not just a supply problem, the state and feds stared at it for months, pointing fingers at each other."[29]

A minor episode in December 2000 captures how helplessly the government stood by as the crisis raged on. Davis attended a traditional ceremony to celebrate the beginning of the Christmas season and presided over the lighting of the state's Christmas tree in Sacramento. After the four thousand bulbs lit up in festive colors to the delight of a cheering crowd, he waited a few minutes and then switched the tree off. The utilities had begged Californians to forgo Christmas decorations to save energy, and the governor was trying to set a precedent with a symbolic gesture. Davis closed his speech with bitter words that stood in contrast to the season's spirit: "We're going to send FERC a picture of the tree going dark."[30]

With no authority to regulate wholesale prices, a limited ability to reduce demand, no affordable forward contracts, and infeasible rate increases, there were seemingly no good options. Boxed into an impossible situation, the governor and the utility commissioners put their heads down, accused generators of market manipulation, and denied requests for rate increases. Various attempts to implement demand response programs and expedite the approval of new generation facilities did not do much to improve the situation.[31]

Since the crisis had paralyzed the political and regulatory apparatus, the utilities approached insolvency after a few months. The retail price remained fixed, the wholesale price remained high, and the supply remained scarce. In December 2000, the utilities' credit became so poor that the sellers of energy were not sure that they would get paid.[32] Accordingly, generators became increasingly unwilling to sell energy into California and chose other western states that offered better conditions. Some of the independent energy producers had not been paid in such a long time that they could not afford to buy fuel anymore or risked bankruptcy themselves.[33] Even if operators promised to pay arbitrary prices, it became almost impossible to find enough energy to keep the system going. This, of course, drove prices up further, made the crisis worse, and increased the risk of selling energy in California, as no one knew how long the system would last before it broke or what the regulatory response might be. Would the generators be paid for their energy? No one knew with certainty. Around the turn of the year, the utility companies' financial crisis therefore turned into the reliability crisis we encountered in the control room on January 17, 2001.

Because the Power Exchange markets increasingly came up short of needed supplies, the system operators were desperately trying to make up the shortfall of scheduled supply in the imbalance markets—sometimes within a few hours, sometimes within minutes before dispatch. Under immense pressure, the California Public Utility Commission finally approved a 10 percent rate increase in January 2001. But this was too little, too late. Shortly after the events of January 17, the utilities became unable to pay their bills, and central pieces of the market collapsed. Without utilities or willing sellers, the Power Exchange markets became illiquid, and the organization declared bankruptcy in February 2001. Shortly after, it ceased operations. In April, PG&E declared bankruptcy.[34] Edison had been on the verge of bankruptcy since November 2000.[35] Amid rolling blackouts and system emergencies, it was increasingly unclear how the majority of end users could be served, and a system collapse seemed possible.

To prevent a disaster and guarantee that the demand for energy would be served, the state finally took over and vouched for the utilities. On February 1, the governor signed a law that authorized the Department of Water Resources to purchase power under long-term contracts for sale to Pacific Gas & Electric and Southern California Edison. The employees moved into the CAISO headquarters and largely replaced the auction markets with a centralized purchasing program. This move finally turned the financial crisis of the utilities into a budgetary crisis of the state. Because these contracts were signed at the climax of the crisis, their terms were unforgiving, at three to four times the national average. Through August 31, 2001, the state paid $10 billion for electricity, which was then sold back to the utilities at the regulated price of about $3 billion.

When all was said and done, the state lost about $7 billion from the state budget. But the implied costs of the crisis were much higher. The long-term contracts committed the state to purchase $42 billion worth of electricity over the next ten years. This represented about 3.5 percent of California's yearly total economic output at the time. In comparison, the savings and loan debacle of the 1980s amounted to a total cost of $100 billion, but that represented just 0.5 percent of the total US economy.[36]

During the subsequent litigation, California managed to renegotiate many of the long-term contracts and recovered $7.5 billion of the money they had paid to sellers of energy in 2001. So, from today's perspective, the total cost of the crisis remains somewhere below $5 billion. These costs were ultimately shifted onto rate payers. But before two decades of litigation commenced, it looked as if the crisis would cost the state somewhere between $40 billion and $47 billion. The market crisis had morphed from a financial crisis to a technical disaster and finally to a state budgetary crisis.[37] It prematurely ended Gray Davis's career as governor, in 2003, and paved the way for Arnold Schwarzenegger. It also led to a second restructuring of California's energy industry in the years to follow. Seven states that had prepared to follow in California's footsteps canceled their plans for restructuring. On September 20, 2001, the five members of the California Public Utility Commission voted to end power competition in California in the present form. The grand experiment to create competitive markets to bring reliable electricity at low prices to California's customers had failed.

Two Narratives of the Crisis

Long before the crisis was over and years after the dust had settled, the stakeholders fought to take control of the narrative that would explain what had happened. Amid blackouts and a mounting state deficit, the search for the culprits had begun. Politicians, regulators, utilities, and power marketers released economic analyses, ran advertisement campaigns, and published legal statements that explained what had happened and why they were blameless. In the two decades that have elapsed since the crisis ended, a complex tableau of court cases, congressional hearings, and regulatory investigations has unfolded.[38] The legal and economic scholarship that has tried to explain the crisis cannot be understood in isolation from these processes.

Perhaps because of the vast complexity of the electricity system, most of those who have written about the events were insiders in one way or another. They were closely related to the court proceedings or wrote about matters whose relevance only emerged in these proceedings. The academic literature therefore mirrors the development of the central positions in the court cases. Indeed, the literature is also animated by the same overriding question as the litigation: Who is to blame for the high prices?[39]

Despite enormous efforts, a single answer has never materialized. There continue to be at least two explanations that coexist in uneasy tension. One is the narrative of those who made money during the crisis, and the other belongs to those who lost it. Each party blames the other, and the existing scholarship divides relatively neatly into the two camps.[40]

The first narrative has its origin in newspaper articles about looming supply shortages in 1999. It explains the crisis as the result of basic market forces — there simply was not enough generation capacity in the summer of 2000. But clueless politicians and regulators blocked the incentives to provide the missing capacity and thus caused the high prices. Energy marketers and independent power producers quickly adopted this narrative when the crisis broke out. The details are complicated because on the surface, the narrative's central empirical claim seems implausible. California had added substantial generation capacity throughout the 1980s and 1990s.[41] Meanwhile, the growth of real demand was moderate and did not exceed the California Energy Commission's projections by much.[42] Supply had been added in line with these projections. Politicians and stakeholders in California were therefore quick to declare any claim about supply shortages laughable. To make their case, the proponents of the first narrative had to substitute a more complex analysis that focused on California's interdependencies with other states.

California was one of the few net importers of energy in the Western Interconnection. In the summer, it imported roughly 25 percent of its total energy from (primarily) hydro sources in the Pacific Northwest and coal plants in the Southwest. In the winter, it also exported to the Pacific Northwest, where temperatures were lower. But the average energy sales to consumers exceeded the average net generation. Reductions in supply outside of California could therefore have a direct effect on the composition of its energy production.

In contrast to California, other western states had not added much generation capacity in the 1980s, even though demand had grown rapidly.[43] Not only were fewer exports available for sale to California but the states' generators also operated with tighter and tighter reserve margins—they could keep less capacity on reserve for contingencies.[44] Like California, the entire Pacific Northwest relied heavily on hydro resources. This type of power depends on the annual level of rainfall. A drought can therefore severely reduce the available capacity. If the reserves are low, even minor increases in demand beyond those anticipated can threaten the reliability of the system. Recognizing the danger, utilities committed more of their energy in long-term contracts. This helped to lower the risk of capacity shortfalls because it made supply from other sources more predictable. But it also reduced the amount of energy that was available for short-term exports to California. Together, these developments led to a precipitous decline in net imports.

Between 1992 and 1996, strong rainfall kept the hydro reserves in the Northwest full and counterbalanced declining imports from the Southwest. But in 2000, a drought reduced the hydro reserves and led to decreased imports from both regions. As figure 1.3 shows, these declines were substantial.

In response, the power plants in California had to increase their output to meet the moderately grown demand in the state. Citing data from

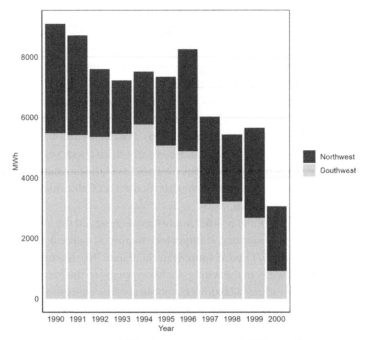

FIGURE 1.3. California Imports, Average MW/h per Year

the California Energy Commission, proponents of the first narrative claim that the increase in domestic production was significant—around 12 percent per year between 1997 and 2000.[45] This pushed almost all existing generators to their capacity limits and required older and much more expensive natural gas plants to increase their output as well. To keep the costs of production low, new generation would have had to be built rapidly, but while restructuring led to a lot of applications, these were not processed fast enough to bring sufficient power plants online in 2000.[46] With generation in other states increasingly tied up in long-term contracts, supply could be simply insufficient. Massive price spikes could occur without any untoward behavior—it would simply be a consequence of market forces indicating real scarcity. To the extent that there was any market manipulation, the first narrative contends, it was minor. Instead, the high prices simply reflected scarcity. The real culprits were regulators and politicians who tried to repress market forces with retail-price freezes, price caps, and restrictions on forward contracts—instruments that could have dampened the effect of scarcity on prices. The account changed several times between 1999 and today, but its core claim about supply shortages always remained the same.

Starting in August 2000, the utilities and the California government argued against this narrative. They suggested that price spikes could not be explained with supply shortages—regardless of whether they were viewed in terms of California or in terms of the Western Interconnection as a whole. Instead, they argued that only manipulative behavior could have caused the high prices.[47]

Initially, these analyses did not point fingers at anyone. They merely contested the dominant narrative of economic fundamentals to cause FERC to act against severe market imperfections. The analysts' approach was seemingly straightforward. They looked at episodes of high prices during the summer of 2000 and asked, Can these prices be explained by the kind of marginal cost pricing that perfectly competitive markets would create?[48]

To answer this question, they conducted markup studies, simulations of sellers' behavior, and analyses of confidential data about bidding behavior. The authors of these studies calculated the factors that influenced the cost of electricity production. More specifically, they calculated the cost for the plants that would serve peak demand at different times because those plants would set the market price in a competitive environment. Because all peak energy was provided by natural gas plants whose operating characteristics were well known, it was possible to determine their marginal cost. Considering the impact of various external factors, the market clearing price could be developed from these marginal costs.[49] By comparing the hypothetical, ideal prices with the actual prices during the summer, the authors developed a sense of the markup that had to be explained by "market imperfections"—over and beyond the supply shortages that the first narrative asserted.

The principal difficulties with such studies derive from the construction of the counterfactual: In a competitive market with given marginal costs, what composition of resources would clear the market? An example makes clearer why this can be a tricky question. Consider imports: How many imports would have been available at a different price level? In the real world, the extremely high prices during the summer presumably drew more imports than they would have if the prices had been lower. Therefore, the imports in the counterfactual would need to be adjusted. This changes the level of demand that in-state generators would have needed to serve. Such adjustments can have follow-on effects on other variables—for example, the level of forced outages on generators that now had to produce higher outputs or the impact of emission certificates on the availability of supply at different prices.

As soon as anyone began to think carefully about the counterfactual that informed the computation of ideal prices, all manner of variables could start to change. To fend off objections, the defenders of the second

narrative chose conservative assumptions and ran sets of sensitivity analyses to account for the different effects assumptions could have on the market clearing price. Even with conservative models, the economists found
that 21 percent of the increased prices were due to increased production
costs, 20 percent was due to increased competitive rent (scarcity prices),
and the remaining 59 percent was attributable to market power.[50] These
studies effectively argued that the claims of the first narrative left unex-
plained a gap between the real prices and the prices that would exist under
the associated logic.

Despite massive pushback by defenders of the first narrative, FERC
eventually came around to the second narrative.[51] By the end of April 2001,
the commission began to systematically cut off a variety of different avenues for the exercise of market power. When this combined with California's efforts to sign long-term contracts for the delivery of energy, the crisis
began to abate. This seemed to support the second narrative. In December
2001, FERC determined that refunds would be issued for the period when
the prices had exceeded what a competitive market would have charged.

Despite this apparent victory for the second narrative, the commission
hesitated to assess the behavior of individual sellers.[52] The economists' arguments pertained to market power in general and the level of the market
as a whole. They did not point fingers at individual players, and neither did
FERC. Between 2000 and 2001, *market power* was a term without a clear
referent—a demon that hovered above the markets and pulled the strings
rather than a specific culprit. Indeed, it seemed that FERC was trying to
move on as quickly as possible. Initial cases that dealt with accusations of
"physical withholding" ended in settlements that did not even cover the
profits the culprits had made. For a while, it seemed as if things were going
to just disappear in the murky depths of refund proceedings.

But then everything changed with the spectacular, unexpected, and
complete collapse of Enron in December 2001. More specifically, everything changed when the infamous Enron memos appeared in the press. In
colorful detail and with the trademark cynicism, these memos described
several strategies that a group of traders had designed to manipulate the
California energy markets.[53] The memos quickly made it onto national and
international television, getting even late-night talk show hosts like Jon
Stewart to discuss electricity markets—a topic that normally does not rank
high in terms of hilarity. Even *The Simpsons* had a skit about a roller coaster
called "Enron's Ride of Broken Dreams."

The scandal reverberated around the globe because the company held
a symbolic significance for the neoliberal ideology of the 1990s. Before the
bankruptcy in December 2001, Enron was one of America's most prestigious

companies. It had been voted the country's most innovative company for years. It stood for the promise of unlimited growth and the superiority of markets over socialism. The largest natural gas merchant in North America and the United Kingdom, Enron had turned itself into a poster child for the new economy. Besides investing in large infrastructure projects, it actively participated in financial markets for energy. It invented a variety of new products, pioneered online trading, pushed for deregulation in several different industries, and developed a vast trading operation.[54]

After it fell into bankruptcy, it suddenly turned out that Enron's continued success had been a mirage of fraudulent accounting practices. Wielding a suite of financial tricks, Enron had generated fictional profits and used them to inflate its share price. The world stood by in morbid curiosity as details emerged of a corrupt corporate culture that put a premium on greed and cynicism while producing no real value. The memos surfaced during these investigations. They put the litigation of the California crisis on a new trajectory and provided new vigor to the elaboration of the second narrative.[55]

During the energy crisis, no one made more money than the large trading firms. In 2000, Enron's trading operations reported an operating profit of $1.6 billion. This represented an increase of 160 percent from 1999. Another large trading company, Williams, tripled their profits with reported earnings of $1.56 billion.[56] Sellers of energy like Mirant, Duke, and Calpine made similarly spectacular profits.[57] Enron, just like the other trading firms, had been one of the main beneficiaries of the crisis. When it fell, and when it became apparent with how much delight the traders had watched the system crumble, the second narrative's perfect culprit had emerged: big energy companies from Texas had manipulated the markets at the expense of ordinary rate payers.

Of course, this narrative ignored the fact that *all* net sellers of wholesale energy made the profits of a lifetime: independent energy producers, municipalities, and even government energy projects collected millions of dollars in revenues. Several of these episodes have the same shady character as the Enron revelations, but they were quickly swept aside by the larger story. For example, S. David Freeman, who managed the design process for the new energy markets, later became the head of the Los Angeles Department of Water and Power. During the crisis, this department used some of the same tactics as Enron, presumably fueled by insider knowledge.[58]

Another nugget is the fact that Pacific Gas & Electric, which moved into bankruptcy in 2001, had an unregulated affiliate—as did all three utilities. The affiliate had the nondescript name National Energy Group and was financed with money that Pacific Gas & Electric received during its stranded cost recovery. In 2000, the National Energy Group made $162 million in reported revenue. These remarkable profits came from various investments in unregulated power companies in the Northwest and also from the California energy markets. Of course, none of these profits ever made it to the ailing utility that would soon find itself in bankruptcy court, begging the state to lend a helping hand. Instead, the profits of the National Energy Group quickly disappeared into Pacific's parent company, PG&E Corporation.[59]

The annals of the energy crisis are full of such stories. But the constant and ever-escalating revelations about Enron and the other "Texan energy companies" easily eclipsed shady deals by beloved state icons. Either way, FERC had no choice now but to consider the behavior of individual sellers explicitly. In response to cases brought by the California government and buyers of electricity, the commission determined that several of the strategies outlined in the Enron memos fulfilled the definition of behavior proscribed by the tariffs that governed market operations. They accused twenty-two firms of engaging in illegal strategies that involved false exports, sixty-five of gaming the CAISO congestion management system, and twenty-six of misrepresenting their capacity to sell ancillary services. Ten entities, finally, stood accused of having cooperated with Enron to implement its manipulation strategies. Another proceeding revoked Enron's market-based rates. Though virtually all sellers contested these allegations, most eventually settled.

Since the accusations were based on the strategies in Enron's memos, they were relatively limited in scope—FERC did not have an independent standard to define manipulative behavior. But in 2009, a Ninth Circuit remand opened the door to additional litigation under a broader definition of manipulative behavior. In 2012, a judge decided, on a transaction-by-transaction basis, that sellers had violated the market tariff in over *thirty thousand* transactions. The decision was affirmed on November 14, 2014, and refunds were ordered.[60] This decision finally established that the California markets had indeed been manipulated. But it did not, in the last analysis, allow a definitive conclusion about the root cause of the crisis. The fraudulent transactions represented only a small subset of all trades that had taken place, and there was no definitive proof that they were the true cause of the high prices. In short, though the commission adopted the second narrative and diagnosed both market power and manipulative behavior, it never settled the question about the relationship between these problems and the high prices that drove the utilities to the brink of bankruptcy. Even though the evidence of outrageous trader behavior is crushing, the second narrative therefore never triumphed in the courts.

The Strange Persistence of Both Narratives

It does not matter how sophisticated the second narrative has grown over time. Regardless of how many different versions of the story exist in legal, academic, and journalistic treatments, an equal number will appear to tell the other story. The battle of the two narratives also continues to be the decisive concern of most stakeholders. To give just one example from my own fieldwork, I met George Sladoje, the former CEO of California's Power Exchange, for the first time at the Union League Club in downtown Chicago. We sat across from each other at a table in the vast, empty dining hall, and I had just started to record the conversation.

Before I could ask a question, he started by saying, "I have a first comment, even before we start talking about the exact situation that we're researching here. The purpose of the study is to determine why the California markets were designed in a way that made them unable to counteract destructive behavior by market participants. So, your professor has already concluded that the problems were due to destructive behavior by market participants? I wonder what his conclusion is based on."

I responded that we meant "behavior that contradicts the reliability requirements of the grid" and that I did not assume that the behavior caused the crisis or arose as the intended consequence of particular design decisions. But he pressed on: "My point is that the political situation and primarily the California government had a lot to do with creating the conditions, which enabled things to go on, which were not all unethical or, which were not all unreasonable."[61]

The statement illustrates that he felt the need to defend the behavior of market actors as rational and reasonable, even after I tried to explain that I did not intend to presume which of the two narratives was right. His most urgent interest was to straighten out my misconception that the crisis had been caused by sellers of energy. Practically all my interviewees fell on one side or the other of the debate and tried to convince me to believe the same. Their urgency illustrates well how unsettled the divide continues to be. For each revelation that the proponents of the conspiracy story raise on their flagpole, the defenders of the first narrative have a riposte.

It is easy to disregard the arguments of the first narrative and suggest that they are blatant attempts to deny what is obvious. But that would be too easy. It is certainly true that the California markets saw manipulative behavior that drove up the prices and sustained them at high levels. But this behavior could have been a surface phenomenon, distracting from more fundamental factors driving the crisis and enabling this behavior. As one traverses the vast record of studies, analyses, and legal and journalistic accounts, one gets the impression of a fundamental ambiguity at the heart of the crisis.

To gain a sense of the problem, consider the following episode from January 16, 2001, the day before the fateful blackouts in California. It involves Bill Williams, one of the traders who worked at Enron's West Desk in Portland, Oregon. The West Desk was a tight-knit operation that traded electricity in the western states: all traders worked in a single large room equipped with telephones and computers. Throughout the day, the different desks cooperated to identify and execute speculative trades in energy markets.[62] Bill Williams was one of twelve employees who specialized in short-term trades. This involved buying and selling electricity at different locations to realize arbitrage profits. Most trades were executed via phone. In the following conversation, Williams talks to an operator at a small plant in Las Vegas that usually exported energy to California. After the operator picks up, Williams says, "This is going to be a word-of-mouth kind of thing. We want you guys to get a little creative and come up with a reason to go down." The operator responds that he could certainly switch off the plant. Somewhat uncertain, he asks, "OK, so we're just coming down for some maintenance, like a forced outage type of thing? And that's cool?" Bill responds, "Hopefully." At this, both men begin to laugh.[63] On January 17, the plant declared technical outages and did not come online. It was one less resource that McIntosh, Riley, and the other operators at CAISO could draw on.

An administrative law judge at FERC released the tapes of this and similar conversations in 2005. Some members of the press heralded them as the smoking gun that finally proved power marketers had created artificial shortages of energy to drive up the prices in California, deliberately risking the system's breakdown.[64] Yet, while there can be no doubt that the conversation documents how Enron's traders orchestrated the physical withholding of electricity at a crucial moment, it is not at all clear whether this attempt was successful: the power plant could not possibly have provided the energy necessary to prevent the blackouts on January 17. So, even if it had sent all its energy to California, the prices would not have changed, and the blackouts could not have been avoided.

But if the energy from the power plant could not have made a difference, how can we say that this action really did have anything to do with the crisis? Conversely, while it was obvious that *other* outages did in fact affect prices and system reliability, it could rarely be established with certainty that the generators were shut down to influence prices. Researchers found that such shutdowns for maintenance became much more frequent during the crisis and lasted longer than they had in previous years. Between 1995 and 2000, plants shut down between 5 to 10 percent per year on average. In 2000, the average went up to *50* percent.[65] Similar increases pertain to the duration of these shutdowns. In June 2000, power plant engineers working for Duke accused their company of virtually sabotaging one of their own plants by "running it up and down like a yo-yo," shutting the plant on and off.[66] Observers noted that the patterns of shutdowns and bids represented an image of the existing generation capacity that was highly unlikely to correspond to the facts.[67] Indeed, they suggested that the Texas-based company Industrial Information Resources had sold a daily generation-outage-notification service to power industry subscribers. The information was plant and unit specific, disclosing the expected start date for an outage and the expected return-to-service date. This would have allowed Duke, Dynegy, and Williams (among others) to coordinate the shutdown of generators.

Yet it could never be proved conclusively that they had done so. When the regulators showed up at the power plants that were under maintenance, the operators always provided some plausible explanation: algae were stuck in the turbines, a rotor had malfunctioned, or a generator had overheated because of overuse during the summer. These explanations often pointed to the first narrative's insistence that generators had operated above efficient levels for too long to make up for the shortages. For every piece of evidence that seems to provide incontrovertible proof that manipulation explains the price spikes during the Western energy crisis, other information or arguments that undermine these certainties creep up, demonstrating the workings of economic forces while revealing political interference that distorted them.[68]

Underneath the ambiguities created by inconclusive evidence and political maneuvers, there is a deeper reason that both narratives persist: the criteria guiding the evaluation of evidence are not clear or set in stone. This begins with the law. At the time of the crisis, FERC did not have a clear standard of market manipulation. To detect the market power in California, they first had to change their metrics. This change redefined the understanding of the nature of market power and arguably changed the substance of their regulatory approach.[69] Only after the Enron memos appeared did the commission declare their provisions to be in violation of the CAISO/PX tariffs. For almost a decade, illegal behavior was almost exclusively defined in terms of these memos. This arguably imposed a new legal standard into the past. More importantly, it represented an extremely limited view of market manipulation as the Enron memos were highly specific and covered only a subset of behaviors that had the same effects on the system.

On top of these problems, FERC did not appear as a neutral arbiter of the law. Several writers have suggested that the agency was subject to regulatory capture.[70] Many power marketers, but particularly Enron, had actively lobbied for deregulation during the 1990s. On the federal level, they had spent vast sums of money on campaign contributions for politicians on both sides of the aisle. In a *New York Times* editorial, Senator Ernest Hollings put it bluntly: "In my 35 years in the Senate, I have never witnessed a corporation so extraordinarily committed to buying government. In the last decade, Enron gave campaign contributions to 186 House members and 71 senators, including $3,500 to me."[71] Enron's influence with the George W. Bush administration was even more pronounced and problematic. Famously, Ken Lay, Enron's CEO, was close friends with Bush himself. The resulting connections between the company and the government were tight and have been examined extensively.[72] In a comprehensive article on the California energy crisis, a legal commentator writes: "Enron's relationships with policymakers illustrates how corporate interests are interwoven with legislative and administrative decision-makers to the point that they are often unable to consider the broader public interest when formulating and implementing policy."[73]

Where the legal foundation and standing of the regulators was shaky, the political and econometric standards were even more so: What looked like a clear form of manipulation to some appeared to others as contributions to an evolutionary market logic that was the cornerstone of American success. What was to one set of economists a good econometric model to understand market power was to another group a terribly flawed abstraction from the reality of business decisions. When studying the two narratives and the back-and-forth of argument and analysis across a variety of different venues, we therefore do not simply see attempts to determine "what really happened." We see a negotiation over the criteria of evaluation and the weight that should be given to any particular factor. On top of this negotiation, we face the problem of missing or ambivalent evidence.

Both narratives fundamentally agree that the California markets enabled manipulative behavior, at least to some degree. Both also agree that political, regulatory, and criminal activities worked together under conditions of scarcity to drive up the prices. But they disagree about what weight should be placed on the different factors, what has been proved, and what has not. And because the legal system could never find its way to a general conclusion, which would have settled the score by virtue of its position in the institutional hierarchy of truth making, the debate continues. While one side continues to argue that the crisis would never have occurred if the politicians had not tried to frustrate the logic of the market, the other side insists that the politicians only protected the population from a corporate conspiracy. In the final analysis, it is impossible to declare which factor was most influential. Perhaps, then, it is time to shift the conversation into a different register.

A Case of Market Design Failure

So far, the crisis has been analyzed in terms of cause-effect sequences. Most of the effort has gone into stabilizing counterfactuals for different combinations of factors that could have influenced the wholesale prices at specific moments in time. The assumptions behind these arguments are not stable enough to ever point a way out of the labyrinth. Instead, I will therefore switch to a *structural* point of view. I start by observing that there *was* destructive behavior that violated the way these markets were supposed to operate. Rather than ask how much problematic behavior occurred or why it happened in specific instances, I ask what the different types of problematic behavior were and why any of this behavior was possible in the first place.

Not only does this shift enable us to leave behind the fruitless attempt to establish "what really happened"; it turns the very ambiguity at the heart of the crisis into part of the phenomenon to be explained. The markets did not produce the information that would have enabled an external observer to establish how much of this behavior actually occurred or how bad it was. Doubtlessly, this lack of information itself helped to make problematic behavior possible. So, in pursuing my line of inquiry, we also ask why it was so difficult for regulators, monitoring teams, and the legal system to know what was going on in these markets and thereby trace the origin of the deep ambiguity that sustains the battle of the two narratives.

All of this points to an overarching question this book pursues: What structural features of the system created opportunities and incentives for behavior that was incompatible with the reliable operation of the electricity system? With this question, we are now looking for the discrepancies between an ideal image of the market system and its implementation. This vantage point highlights an aspect of the crisis whose significance has rarely been appreciated: California's markets were not simply deregulated or restructured; they were *designed*.

To turn electricity into a tradable commodity, a vast amount of social engineering had to take place: new organizations had to be created, ownership structures had to be changed, new institutions needed to be invented, new ways of doing business had to take hold. Practically everything the utilities had done in the past had to change. And this project was guided by a plan, albeit roughly and not always as the architects had intended. The markets were the creation of experts, stakeholders, and politicians who tried to engineer markets according to a new vision of how the system should work. The question about the structural preconditions for the crisis require us to investigate what these people were doing, what they created, and why it did not work the way they wanted it to. It requires us to look at the crisis as a failure by design.

Most existing studies view the design period as yet another instance of the 1990s' obsession with deregulation and focus on the political process that led to the creation of AB 1890, the law that provided the foundation for restructuring.[74] The political history is full of interesting characters, such as Steve Peace, a charismatic senator who forced compromise by debating people to exhaustion, berating them, or ridiculing them during the night-long sessions of the "Steve Peace Death March" in the California Assembly in August 1996. The stories prominently feature Enron executives like Jeff Skilling, influential lobbyists, and Washington supporters. They tend to explain the architecture of the California system in terms of political compromise, naive utility officials, or cunning power marketers who tried to create a system they could game.[75]

But while politics, special interests, and utilities' inertia did play their roles, many technical design decisions originate in working groups, teams, and public forums where experts' voices held sway. Without considering the enormous technical challenge of electricity market design, we may easily forget how much intellectual firepower the task brought to the table. The stories of political naivete and seduction by the empty promises of Texan companies capture some of the situation in California during the 1990s. But they ignore that it was also a moment of tremendous hope and ambition.

Joan Didion once observed, "California is a place in which a boom mentality and a sense of Chekhovian loss meet in uneasy suspension; in which the mind is troubled by some buried but ineradicable suspicion that things had better work here, because here, beneath that immense bleached sky, is where we run out of continent."[76] This sentiment captures the spirit of the moment well. At the time, California was facing the early trembling of the internet industry's spectacular growth, but it had the highest rates of electricity in the nation. There was a sense that the utilities were wasting rate-payer money, that the regulatory structure was deficient, and that the industry might choke the economy. But there was also the firm belief that California was a special, visionary place with untold potential. This led politicians in California to pursue restructuring more aggressively than anywhere else. Not only did they want California to be the first state to move to a market regime but they also wanted to execute the transformation in the shortest period of time and in the most complete way. While other states explored opportunities for a gradual transformation, California quickly decided on a comprehensive design project.

The urgency and ambition of the project made being in the industry *cool*, as one of my interviewees put it.[77] What had, for decades, been a backwater for engineers with low grades from public schools suddenly turned into a promised land for young go-getters who had picked up their self-assured mannerisms in the classrooms of the Ivy League.[78] To the market designers, the California industry was a welcome laboratory to try out the limits of market design.

As Paul Joskow and Richard Schmalensee wrote in their landmark study of potential avenues toward deregulation, "Currently electric power is supplied by complex and highly developed systems with unusual technical characteristics. These make it likely that reliance on an economist's instinct, developed through countless examples drawn from agriculture and manufacturing, will produce incorrect conclusions."[79]

Because of its unusual characteristics, the industry served as an exciting terra incognita. From all over the country, intellectual talent began to head to California. Market designers came from Harvard, MIT, Caltech, Berkeley, and Stanford to collaborate with utility officials, engineers, and lawyers.[80] United under the banners of game theory, mechanism design, operations research, information economics, and industrial organizations, the designers followed an intellectual vision that had first been imagined during the late 1970s. It is now time to take a closer look at these people and what they came to California to do; to truly understand what the California system was, we have to take a closer look at the intellectual ambitions of those who dreamed it up.

The Vision of Electricity Market Design

As we trace the path of electricity market design through history, we are in for a surprise. The path does not lead to an economics department. Instead, we end up in MIT's engineering workshop on "Homeostatic Control" in the academic years of 1977–78, almost fifteen years before the creation of California's markets.[81] These workshops served as playground for a diverse group of scientists who speculated about the future of electricity systems. Until the 1960s, the utility industry had improved power plants by optimizing economies of scale. But by 1977–78, the opportunities to improve the thermal efficiency for large power plants had all but vanished. The workshop posed the question of how one might gain efficiency in other ways.

Initially, the debates on "Homeostatic Control" had little to do with the creation of markets. Few people doubted that the electricity industry was anything but the most obvious case of a natural monopoly. Instead, the experts wondered whether control theory might help to identify new solutions. Among the engineers and operations researchers who discussed the topic, four scientists were central: Fred Schweppe, Richard Tabors, Mike Caramanis, and Roger E. Bohn. Tabors had an undergraduate degree in biology and studied geography as well as economics for his PhD. As he remembers, their research interests and backgrounds could not have been more diverse.

> We had Schweppe, who was originally a control theory guy. He started out his career sort of worrying about rockets. He was an electrical engineer, but, professionally, he ended up worrying about rockets going up and where they were going to come down. Mike Caramanis was an operation research guy by training. He and I have been together working on, of all unlikely things, population. . . . The third person is Roger Bohn. In between [working in operations research at] Harvard and coming to MIT to grad school, he'd worked with an engineering economics and consulting firm that focused entirely on energy down in Washington, DC.[82]

Given their research on rockets, population dynamics, energy systems, and the geographic structure of economic activities, they made for an unlikely team. But even though they worked in four different disciplines, they shared an interest and a common language: "We had an overlap on the energy side. All of us could talk optimization and control theory. . . . On the economics side, Michael, Roger, and I were capable of doing economics. . . . Fred understood the math, and he certainly understood supply and demand at fifty thousand feet. But when it got down to how you combine them, that wasn't Fred originally—we basically all had to teach each other what we needed to know."[83]

The language of control theory and energy systems provided them with a bridge between their different areas of expertise. As it would turn out, it provided a powerful set of metaphors and techniques that would fuse the worlds of markets and of electricity systems.

Control theory is a set of mathematical techniques that are common in both economics and engineering. It can be used to describe the properties of continuously operating dynamic systems. The current condition of the system is represented as a state space—a set of vectors with state variables. Stochastic differential equations then describe transformations of this state space.[84] Control theory helps designers to develop models of control actions that keep the system within acceptable parameters. It effectively measures an error, or a discrepancy between desired outputs and current outputs, and then applies a corrective action described as a control function on the basis of the equations that describe the system's transformation.[85]

In the 1980s, several participants of the workshop, including Schweppe and Tabors, published the first, programmatic statement for a philosophy of "homeostatic utility control." Homeostasis is a concept that was first developed in biology and that describes the existence of a state of equilibrium between the interdependent parts of an organism. For example, it may describe how a body can retain a steady temperature despite changing environmental temperatures.[86] A balance of internal adjustments between parts of the system maintain a stable system state. Schweppe and Tabors applied this concept to electricity systems.

So far, the utility industry adhered to the philosophy of "load following."[87] Since consumers simply consumed energy without any way to consider the conditions of energy production, the supply side always needed to react to whatever was happening on the demand side. But it was costly and inefficient to deal with completely unresponsive demand. Utilities had to build large spinning reserves—plants that are running without load and can quickly link into the system. The gap between the lowest and highest possible demand also required excess capacity that was not used most hours of the year.

Like many scientists today, the workshop participants wanted to tackle the inefficiencies of load following. Indeed, their programmatic paper anticipated the guiding ideas behind the Internet of Things and the smart grid in its vision for "an electric power system in which the supply systems and demand systems work together to provide a natural state of continuous equilibrium to the benefit of both the utilities and their customers."[88] The authors imagined a process of mutual adjustment that would retain an efficient balance between both production and consumption—a global equilibrium with desirable efficiency characteristics. If demand adjusted to supply and supply to demand, variation would decline, and excess capacity could be reduced in terms of both spinning reserves and installed capacity.

This was supposed to happen *automatically*. The paper proposed that a "Frequency Adaptive Power Energy Rescheduler" (FAPER) would measure changes in the standard frequency of the electric power system and use this information as an indicator for the availability of supply. If too little energy was in the system, the frequency of the alternating current would decrease for brief intervals. If the FAPER noticed a frequency loss, the device could switch off a machine to reduce load on the system. This would provide the basis for automatic adjustments to the demand in the system, depending on the supply situation. In short, the envisioned system was meant to balance itself in a complex interplay of signal processing—hence, it was called homeostatic. Instead of operators in the control room of a utility, a fleet of distributed FAPER devices would now exercise generation control. The operators would merely guide these adjustment processes on the basis of the calculations for optimal power flows.

The theory introduced a couple of new ideas about the management of energy systems. First, production and consumption were now seen as parts of a large machine whose mutual relation needed to be optimized. Second, this was supposed to happen in a process of mutual adjustment, driven by the exchange of information among a variety of devices that represent consumers and generators.

The punch line is perhaps becoming obvious already. Though Schweppe and Tabors did not think about markets when they proposed the homeostatic framework, their conceptual innovations made the electricity system look much like the perfect market of microeconomics. Such markets are nothing but homeostatic systems—supply and demand constantly react to each other, constantly balance the overall market process toward equilibrium. Indeed, with the conceptual equivalence in place, these ideas began to present themselves when participants in the workshop wondered what kind of information might best guide the adjustment between the generators and FAPER devices. The answer was simple: a spot price would carry all relevant information. It would reflect the true marginal cost of providing energy at a given location at a given time. The fluctuating prices would signal whether generation was in short supply. This signal could be used to adjust consumption and guide the system to a position where consumption would converge at the level of the most efficient production. Since the costs of production were known, it was not necessary to have a separate, real market. If you could just calculate the costs and then automatically adjust all consumption with FAPER devices, no one needed to make any decisions. The price signals would be an administrative tool, implemented by the centralized controller—a pure signal in a Hayekian sense, but without a decentralized market process.

In short, they envisioned a perfectly planned, centralized assignment process devoid of human participants that was conceptually identical to a perfect market.[89] While Schweppe and his collaborators initially thought about the market as a heuristic, the formal similarity quickly justified a political argument. If perfectly competitive markets now performed the same task as a utility, why not replace the utility and its potentially inefficient and complacent bureaucracy with a *real* market?

In 1988, Schweppe, Caramanis, Tabors, and Bohn published *Spot Pricing of Electricity*, which brought the different strands of research in the workshop together and fully bore out this connection. The idea of spot pricing replaced the concept of homeostatic control and equated central-ized optimization via control theory with the optimization processes of perfectly competitive markets. Clothed in this politically more appealing garb, the book then sketched a set of institutional arrangements that would split the coordination tasks between these two types of control regimes—between markets and centralized control. Though the authors' precise ideas about the optimal division of labor would never be realized, their core idea persisted.[90] Even today, electricity market design begins with this premise. It just divides up responsibilities between the markets and the centralized system control differently.

When California's government began to ponder restructuring in 1992, the MIT-Harvard vision quickly made inroads into the design process. The academic world of market designers was relatively small in the 1990s, and the group of experts who considered electricity market design was even smaller. It included a variety of academics but also engineers and econo-mists who worked in the utility industry and maintained connections with the academic centers. Apart from organizing and attending conferences with the designers from the East Coast and meeting them at the Harvard Electricity Policy Group, the scholars and practitioners engaged with one another's work and frequently acknowledged the associated feedback.[91]

Several members of Schweppe's original design team entered Califor-nia's process as expert witnesses or consultants.[92] Many of them had long-standing institutional ties to the California Energy Commission or the three utilities.[93] Another important institutional touch point was the Electric Power Research Institute, an independent nonprofit with federal funding and several branch offices. The laboratory in Palo Alto had close connec-tions to Stanford and different schools at the University of California. Most of the technical solutions to California's design problems were developed, discussed, and advocated within the larger context of this institute. Its di-rectors Hong-po Chao and Stephen Peck collaborated with Robert Wilson, a professor at Stanford and one of the founding fathers of game theoretical market design.[94] In turn, Wilson brought Vernon Smith, Charles Plott, and Stephen Rassenti from the University of Arizona into the Western Power Exchange (WEPEX) process to test market designs in an experimental electric power market simulation model.[95] In this way, electricity market designers from the East Coast collaborated with some of the most prom-inent mechanism designers and experimentalists in the US. In California, these designers took a shot at realizing some of the conceptual ideas that had emerged in MIT's workshops almost fifteen years earlier.

This book asks how the markets deviated from their vision of coordinating the electricity system. It asks why those who followed this vision could not build the markets that would have realized it. In following this path to the structural antecedents of California's energy crisis, the book tells a story different from the familiar narratives. The story is not about the follies of neoliberalism, the incompetency of politicians, or corporate corruption. It is a story about the limits of social engineering. The first step is to develop a theoretical framework that enables us to study the conditions for the success and failure of market design as a form of social engineering. In search of general scope conditions, we must therefore step back from the intricacies of electricity market design and ask, more generally, how we might think about the challenge to plan markets.

CHAPTER TWO

A Framework to Study Market Design

The last chapter peeled away the layers of rhetoric and guilt from the history of California's energy crisis, uncovering a case of social engineering. A group of market designers came to remodel the electricity industry from the ground up, in an effort to plan and build new markets that would solve a difficult allocation problem. They followed in the footsteps of an intellectual vision that had first been articulated in the intellectual nexus of Harvard and MIT during the 1970s and 1980s. It is easy to gloss over the words *planning* and *building* and simply treat the crisis as a case of deregulation gone wrong. Many studies have done so, and this would certainly fit the rhetoric of the 1990s, the age of "market triumphalism."[1]

But while the ideology of free markets has an important role to play in this book, it does not serve well as an analytical tool kit. To take the premises of market design seriously, we need a theoretical framework that conceptualizes markets from the perspective of designers' intellectual ambition—as something that can be planned and that has to operate in a specific way. From this framework, we can then derive general scope conditions for the success of market design. Once we understand what designers are trying to do, we can see what conditions they require to succeed.

This is what this chapter does. It develops a theoretical framework that describes market design as a form of *organizational planning* that has to strike a balance between imperatives to simplify, bound, and control the market. Because the book seeks to understand market design on its own terms, the chapter begins by recovering the intellectual project designers pursue. At its core, market design views markets as search algorithms that solve constrained optimization problems. This is not just a matter of the formalizations designers use to conceptualize markets. It reflects how designer markets are supposed to operate. A combination of human activity and software should realize the search algorithm and produce custom-tailored results. If market actors follow the desired calculative logic, they realize the subroutines of the larger search algorithm. In that way, market design is similar to organizational planning.

Just as the founders of new organizations create structures that coordinate employees to meet group objectives, market designers impose structure on the interactions between actors to meet higher-order goals. Designer markets are therefore best understood as organizational forms rather than emergent phenomena.[2] The designer market is a set of material, legal, and social infrastructures that coordinates actors to execute the desired search algorithm and converge on an allocation that solves the underlying optimization problem.

After putting these preliminary considerations into place, the chapter develops the core challenge for successful market design. In contrast to the founders of formal organizations, market designers have to coordinate actors that are not beholden to the goals of the organization. Participants do not work for the organization that hosts the market and therefore have no special reason to cooperate with the designers. Instead, they have a constant meta-incentive to identify flaws in the system and extract bandit profits. This creates the central and distinct challenge for market designers: to coordinate without cooperation. Specifically, they need to make it easy and beneficial for market actors to follow the calculative logic of their blueprints, and they need to do so while relying on little more than incentives and ongoing control.

To meet this challenge with the tools available to them, designers have to strike a balance between strategies to simplify, bound, and control the market. They must ensure that the market represents all aspects of the allocation problem adequately and remains sufficiently flexible to adjust to changes in the underlying reality. But at the same time, they must strive to simplify and bound the system as much as possible. This ensures that the spectrum of possible behavior remains closely tied to the range of actions that their blueprints envision. In that case, a control structure can apply formal criteria to evaluate whether transactions might violate designers' objectives. Conversely, if the market becomes more complex than the oversight structure can handle, the design will fail. As I will show, this marks a crucial and general scope condition for market design. The designers must contain the complexity of the market at a level where formal tools are still available to assess hazardous transactions.

The last part of the chapter suggests that the nature of the allocation problem determines how difficult it is to strike this balance. Complex problems involve multiple, potentially conflicting objectives over different temporal horizons, are changeable, and are not easily separated from other domains of social life. They make the use of simplification, bounding, and control precarious. Indeed, if simplification and bounding do not succeed, market design can collapse into a form of centralized planning that runs into the aporias that have always characterized bureaucratic overreach. This sets up the analytical agenda for the rest of the book: to understand in what ways the California system violated the required balance between simplifying, bounding, and controlling as well as to explore why this happened. I will begin by recovering the basic ambition behind market design.

Market Mechanisms as Search Algorithms

Market design has roots in economics, engineering, operations research, and computer science. Even within economics, market design is not contained by a single subfield. Mechanism design, information economics, behavioral economics, and industrial organization contribute ideas and concepts, overlap, and diverge.[3] Disciplinary labels therefore tend to obscure more than they reveal. Instead, market design is best conceived as a collection of tools that can be used to formulate, test, and analyze market mechanisms for a variety of allocation problems. These tools share the underlying idea that markets are information processors. Prices contain information, and trading regimes aggregate and process this information in optimal ways to solve allocation problems.

We can think about markets in this way because we live in an age when the computer has become the dominant metaphor for thinking in general—our brain is often viewed as a kind of biological computer. But we might just as well imagine the market as a physical place, an evolving ecology, or a virtual casino where speculative narratives of the future drive action.[4] These imaginaries of the market are not innocent. They produce different ideas about how markets can and should operate. Accordingly, they come with different intuitions about the way markets should be regulated or, in the case of market design, built.

Early versions of the idea of the market as an information processor can be traced back to the marginalist revolution in the late nineteenth century. But for the development of market design, the socialist calculation debate at the beginning of the twentieth century is the more decisive point of reference.[5] As the somewhat revisionist history has it, this debate began when the Austrian philosopher Ludwig von Mises published the article "Economic Calculation in the Socialist Commonwealth" in 1920.[6] This article developed a novel argument against socialism. Unlike previous authors, Mises did not depend on philosophical and intractable questions about the malleability of human nature. Instead, he offered an *epistemological* argument to demonstrate that socialism was *logically impossible*.[7]

He started with the assumption that economic action always responds to a universal calculation problem. *All* economic action involves choice under scarcity. Regardless of what social system we live in, we always need to choose between different production methods to make the best use of scarce resources. Since production processes generate inputs and outputs for one another, societies must coordinate the choice of methods relative to these variables. The number of possible combinations constantly changes, growing geometrically with the number of products, production methods, resources, and wants. Identifying the optimal combination requires not only a stable metric of comparison between different uses for a given resource but also a lightning-fast information processor that can sort through all possible permutations to identify the best combination of methods and resources.[8]

Mises argued that markets are the only social institution that can satisfy both requirements. Markets generate prices for resources. Because these prices are determined in a world of alternative uses, they contain information about the resource's value for these alternative uses. They can therefore guide the entrepreneur to the optimal production method for a specific purpose. The market works like a giant information processor that minimizes the cognitive burden of producers and consumers. The entrepreneur simply needs to follow the price to optimize the choice of production methods overall and over time.

In a society without money or private property, a socialist planning board would have to take over the role of the market. But they would not be able to draw on market prices to coordinate the use of resources. They would have to identify the best combination from a central location and without the benefit of a *tertium comparationis*. Naturally, the permutations of possible combinations for resources and production methods would be too complex and variable for humans to compute fast enough. As a result, the planning board would end up with poorly aligned processes, and the socialist economy would either disintegrate entirely or fall far below the threshold of efficiency that capitalist systems achieve.[9]

Mises's work prompted heated responses because it articulated an epistemological argument against the logical possibility of socialism. However, the central idea turned on the assumption that the market qua information processor is inherently unknowable to humans. It is a secularized deity that guides our fates with a genial but mysterious purpose.

Ironically, it was the socialist response that became the linchpin for market design. Socialist economists at the University of Chicago's Cowles Commission argued that mathematical models of the economy could decipher the mysterious information processor. Enrico Barone had already presented a mathematical model for a general economic equilibrium in 1908. Formalizing Leon Walras's theories, he envisioned the economy as a giant set of supply-and-demand functions for all commodities in the system. This model reached equilibrium when supply and demand matched, which could be represented as a solvable system of simultaneous equations. Not only did these models articulate mathematical proofs for the idea of an invisible hand—proofs that would become more complex and general as economics went through a process of formalization in the 1940s and 1950s. The models also suggested that economists might decipher the invisible hand and thus step into its place. And if economists could solve the equations of the formal models, they would not need private property and money to plan the economy.[10] A centralized planning office packed with socialist economists might do this just as easily as a market.[11] While Mises had articulated an argument against the very possibility of socialism, the socialist economists concluded that it was merely a *practical* question whether the planning board could collect, process, and disseminate the information to estimate the models in time.

To save their argument, the Austrians attacked the idea that it might be possible to model the economy mathematically. Friedrich Hayek, for example, argued that static models do not capture the dynamic transformations in a real economy, that they misrepresent the nature of information, and that equilibria are irrelevant fictions that never exist in reality.[12] Overall, they tried everything to shore up the fundamental assumption that mathematical models can never decipher the mystery of the market.

Initially, these arguments carried some plausibility because the debate took place before John von Neumann and Alan Turing invented the mathematical foundation for computers. But as the first computers began to spread, the Austrian position became increasingly implausible to economists. Indeed, they eventually turned that argument on its head. Operating with the idea of the market as an information processor, economists soon began to argue that computers are *better* information processors than markets. In the 1960s, one of the leading socialists looked back at the calculation debate and summarized this sentiment: "the market process with its cumbersome tâtonnements appears old fashioned. Indeed, it may be considered a computing device of a pre-electronic age."[13]

This idea began to spread as empirical research demonstrated the divergence between real markets and the mathematical models of markets in equilibrium. For example, game theory revealed that markets suffer from adverse selection. It can be rational for market actors to misrepresent information. Not just socialist bureaucracies encourage mendacity and opportunism; markets do too if they are not structured well. Other research has demonstrated that markets impose a variety of transaction costs that make it hard to find trades a rational actor would prefer. Economists also began to recognize that human actors have severe cognitive limitations that distort market results.[14] With the rise of information and behavioral economics in the 1960s and 1970s, it thus became increasingly clear that markets produced many problems that inhibited the wonderful information processor Hayek and Mises had envisioned.

This did not just open the door for persistent dreams about computational socialism; it also triggered the invention of market design.[15] If real markets do not work as promised, maybe economists can create the perfect information processors assumed by the mathematical models. In contrast to socialist pipe dreams, the designers' goal was not to replace markets with a board of socialist planners. This was no longer necessary. Instead, they envisioned boards of planners that could realize the information processors that markets were meant to be *by their very nature*. If markets operate like computers, we do not have to replace them. We just have to fix them.

The first efforts in this direction trace back to the work by William Vickrey during the 1960s. Vickrey explored how different kinds of auctions generate incentives for market actors to reveal private information.[16] He was fascinated by the problem that certain markets generate incentives to lie. To ensure truthful offers, he explored different institutional settings that might shift these problematic incentives. Something like a market designer might then create the correct institutional frameworks. Vickrey's work gave rise to the discipline of mechanism design, which systematically searches for systems of rules that structure the strategic interactions between market participants in a way that aligns with designers' objectives.[17] Mechanism design is central to market design, but it is also a highly mathematized and formal discipline. Accordingly, it is a largely academic and theoretical branch. Analysts are limited to a few stylized auction formats that can rarely be implemented as stated.[18] This lack of flexibility limits practical applications.

Economists like Vernon Smith, Charles Plott, and Stephen Rassenti moved market design one step further by using laboratory experiments. In the lab, they could create artificial markets by simulating different institutional frameworks for exchanges between individuals. No longer constrained by formal models, the designers could use trial-and-error learning to identify combinations of rules and constraints that optimized the market process along different dimensions.

Market design leaped forward once again when the experimentalists introduced computers to the laboratory in the 1980s.[19] Before that, the strategic interactions between individuals could be understood as analogous to a computer. Now, the market actually moved *into* the computer. Human actors no longer confronted one another directly but interacted with a software interface that structured their choices. The software could play an active part in constructing the market: it could perform various operations on the inputs from human traders.

Today, the computer is no longer just a metaphor for the market. The market consists of humans and software that jointly execute a search algorithm. Characteristically, market designers now talk of their laboratory constructs as "smart markets" — the market software contributes some thinking of its own.[20] An interesting consequence is that parts of designer markets do not have to work like markets at all. Classic markets are composed of bilateral trading processes. Mathematically, these may be deciphered as simple search algorithms that can be analyzed with the tools of calculus (e.g., Lagrange multipliers). But once part of the market is software, the designers can draw on a whole suite of search algorithms to identify globally optimal solutions. Examples of such algorithms are neural networks, genetic searches, or simulated annealing.[21] They proceed on the basis of principles that have no direct relation to the generation of efficient allocations by economic interactions. As computer-human hybrids, designer markets may operate unlike any trading system that has existed before. Human inputs form subroutines for a larger search algorithm that is completed by the market software. The rise of machine learning accelerates this trend in today's digital transaction platforms and algorithmic market design has become a new subfield of computer science.

In sum, designers conceptualize market mechanisms as algorithms that solve specific optimization problems. While economists used to think that there was a universal logic to markets, contemporary designers view their constructs as akin to custom-tailored software that runs on the market as a more universal information processor. The objectives can be specified in a variety of ways. By tweaking rules and constraints, the designers can optimize on complex trade-offs between competing goals. These do not have to be formal goals, such as a Pareto-efficient distribution, but can also be substantive goals, such as a minimum total revenue. The market mechanism can then unfold in different ways. It often works as a hybrid that divides the execution of the algorithm between person and software.

The paradigmatic examples of contemporary market design are digital transaction platforms like Uber or Upwork or platforms for the trade of public goods like school slots. The interactions in the market are organized according to the logic of strategic games, making it rational for agents to behave in ways that conform with the theory. Human actors receive a particular set of information, combine it with their private information, and then calculate the best course of action. The result is a trade, or a bid, that enacts the desired subroutine of the algorithm. Once all trades have been made, the software computes the rest of the algorithm and produces the allocative outcome the market requires. The desired outcome can be straightforward, or it can be a complex trade-off between competing goals like efficiency and equity. Note that we are now quite far away from the commonsense understanding of a market as a place where people exchange money for goods and services. The designer market is a matching mechanism that combines human and software processing. With this picture in mind, we can now develop an analytical definition of designer markets, explore how market designers try to create these systems, and ask what it takes to succeed.

Designer Markets as Organizational Forms

When we hear the term *market*, we usually think of open-ended, evolutionary processes that are loosely bounded by rules and regulations. While designers frequently draw on this imaginary, it is misleading. The last section has revealed the socialist tendencies behind market design—it is a genuine effort to plan market interactions in line with higher-level objectives. Market designers try to get participants to enact subroutines in a larger search algorithm. The actors need to make decisions that closely follow the calculative logic of designers' blueprints. The designers create rules, procedures, and interfaces that shape market activities and gently guide the actors to the right decisions. The core of a designer market is therefore usually a software platform where buyers and sellers interact according to the designers' rules and procedures.

But the software platforms do not exist in a vacuum. To work as intended, designer markets have to relate to other parts of larger sociotechnical systems in the right way.[22] A platform is hosted on computers that belong to specific organizations. But the platform is also connected to a larger environment. The electricity system is a good example. It consists of generators, wires, and a myriad of other technical components. Various organizational structures manage these technical structures. The market process is closely tied to the sociotechnical system and the organizational structures that manage it.

While this is particularly true for complex infrastructures like the electricity system, even simpler systems have such interdependencies. For

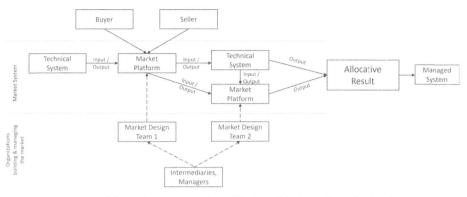

FIGURE 2.1. Schematic Representation of Designer Market as Organizational Form

example, a matching market for residencies is tied to the administrative system of different hospitals, databases that store the information, and multiple organizational layers that manage these interdependencies. Even as relatively self-contained software platforms, designer markets are therefore elements of larger systems, they play a role for coordinating them, and they are intertwined with their organizational structures.

Because a single market only deals with a single product, complex allocation problems usually require multiple markets. These are then linked more or less directly to one another and to the larger, sociotechnical system. (See fig. 2.1 for a schematic illustration of the setup.)

Submarkets are platforms that mediate the interaction between buyers and sellers for the exchange of a particular commodity. They use inputs from technical systems or other submarkets and produce outputs for other parts of the market system. The individual platform does not directly control the actions of buyers and sellers (top of fig. 2.1). Rather, actors follow the rules and procedures of the market, use the inputs from other systems as information, and trade on the basis of that information. In regular intervals, the software submits the results of the trading process to other parts of the system. Together, the different components produce the allocative outcomes that meet designers' goals. This allocative result is then used in the larger system the market system helps to coordinate and manage. This discussion yields the following analytical definition of a designer market: the organizational arrangement of submarkets and technical systems that work together to execute the algorithm and produce the allocative result that solves the optimization problem at hand.

Market designers work with lawyers, economists, managers, administrators, and other professionals in the organizational structures that build, manage, and alter these platforms. They also manage and regulate the interplay between the different components of the larger system. These organizations operate bureaucratically. Formal authority relations between divisions, departments, and teams split up the labor and establish oversight responsibilities. Designers follow rules and protocols that establish how they are to manage the market and its relation to other parts of the system. They, in turn, create and modify the rules and procedures to organize participant interactions. All this happens so that the actions of the market participants align with the higher-order goals of the organization—the allocative outcome the designers desire.

There are two fundamental differences between such designer markets and traditional markets. First, the market system is tightly engineered to produce a predefined allocative outcome. The different pieces of the architecture have to work together just right to solve the intended optimization problem. Second, the system does not primarily depend on the interactive dynamics between market participants but hinges on the organizational actors that construct and manage the market process. In that way, designer markets can be understood as organizational forms. They are built, maintained, and altered within organizations; they reflect designers' attempts to coordinate a social process in line with higher-order objectives; and they rely on various tools that formal organizations deploy. Yet a crucial difference between organizations and designer markets defines the core challenge for market designers.

The Core Challenge: Antagonistic Actors

Unlike the managers and founders of formal organizations, market designers cannot simply create a division of labor and assign tasks. Market actors are not members of the organization that hosts the market; they use the market for their own ends. Therefore, designers have to coordinate these actors indirectly—by creating a choice environment that makes it beneficial for them to follow the path of action decreed by the designers' abstract ideal. Designers are effectively trying to "govern by abstraction"—via formal systems of rules, procedures, and interfaces that shape actors' decision-making. As Arthur Stinchcombe has observed, any attempt to govern social life on the basis of such formalisms must fulfill three very basic requirements.[23]

First, the market logic must represent all relevant aspects of the domain the designers seek to regulate. The governing abstractions—commodities, transaction rules, and procedures—must effectively represent the issues that characterize the activities coordinated by the market. For example, a virtual market for bananas that does not allow actors to communicate the date of harvest would miss crucial information. The rules and procedures must enable trade processes that are useful for the actors who are trying to buy and sell the product.

Second, the system must have a trajectory of improvement. Since the underlying reality is always changing, designers need to create procedures to observe these changes and adjust the system accordingly. Designer markets must evolve in lockstep with the reality they seek to organize. If a new form of energy becomes available, the market rules must be adjusted to trade this new resource as easily as the old ones. This can be trickier than it might at first appear. For example, most electricity markets have uniform market clearing prices. The last seller necessary to meet demand sets the price for the market as a whole. Every seller receives that price if they are among the winning bidders. This system works when the marginal generators are relatively expensive. They push up the clearing price and cover the fixed costs for generators that provide the baseload—the steady output by nuclear and coal plants that is always needed. When solar energy enters the system, it takes over the role of marginal supplier, but it can sell its energy for close to zero dollars. This can depress the market price, making it harder for baseload plants (coal, nuclear, etc.) to cover their cost. However, these baseload plants cannot quite be substituted by renewable energy yet.[24] Since all resources are interdependent inputs to a single system, market rules for all other products must be adjusted once renewables enter. These kinds of interdependencies always exist in market design projects. Maintaining a trajectory of improvement is therefore crucial.

Third, actors need to relate to the rules and procedures as intended. They should have no practical reasons to circumvent the formal structure of the system. This third requirement presents the core challenge to market design. All market mechanisms assume, and indeed require, that participants further their own interests strategically. This assumption is so central that altruistic or prosocial behavior can become a problem. For example, eBay and Amazon use review systems to improve trust and resolve information asymmetries.[25] These systems can be understood as markets in which participants trade information in kind. Designers want users to exchange honest reviews. But social expectations loom large behind decisions to write a review. Often, buyers will give sellers a good review not because they liked the product but because they received some positive feedback themselves.[26] From the perspective of market designers, this behavior is deviant because the reviews no longer express the quality of the product. They therefore use a variety of tricks to disable norms of reciprocity and encourage self-interested behavior.

In short, the mechanisms behind designer markets always presuppose actors who are committed only to their own interests and act strategically to further them. This is another reason market actors have no commitment to designers' objectives. What is more, they are placed in a position of latent antagonism toward the designers. Designer markets usually—though not always—coordinate actors via price competition. The market constantly limits actors' pursuit of profits and places them at odds with the system. Regardless of how well the rules are structured, participants now have a constant incentive to look for ways to subvert the system and escape its discipline. The danger of actors circumventing the system is therefore omnipresent. It is a fundamental structural feature of designer markets. This makes market design difficult.

In most organizations, members share a baseline level of cooperation. Of course, this does not mean that everyone always selflessly furthers the organizations' goals. Decades of sociological research have debunked this myth. Employees primarily follow career imperatives, engage in struggles over political influence in the firm, and work on local projects whose goals may be at odds with those of the organization.[27] However, there is a distinct difference nonetheless: members of organizations do not have a generalized incentive to actively undermine the organization's goals.[28] Instead, there is a basic normative expectation that everyone furthers the goals of the organization—whatever this may mean in practice.

Given this generalized norm of cooperation, organizations can use a variety of formal and informal tools to reinforce members' commitment. Managers can foster a culture of cooperation and identification with the organization, rely on decision rights to reorient members' work toward different goals, structure vocal rights to identify problems, install recursive learning mechanisms to reveal and resolve pathological tensions in the workflow, run performance evaluations, impart bonuses, increase or reduce wages, and so on.[29]

These tools for improving actors' commitment are crucial because formal rules are practically indeterminate. A simple example illustrates this issue.[30] To build a house, an architect draws up several kinds of blueprints that serve as formal abstractions to govern the construction workflow. Workers, supervisors, owners, and public officials derive different instructions from the blueprints and then try to execute them. When they translate the abstractions into concrete activities, they always confront ambiguities and uncertainties. They will each use different standards of good artisanship to fill in what the blueprint leaves out. But at some points— usually where their knowledge touches on that of other experts—they will need to make decisions that are presaged by neither the blueprint nor their expertise. Whenever workers run into such problems, they can switch to an informal channel, go to the architect or owner, and ask how best to proceed. These informal negotiations clarify misunderstandings, realign interpretations, and focus the work on the same goal. In other words, a cooperative orientation toward a similar goal binds practical activities to abstractions governing the work process—even in exceedingly undifferentiated organizations.[31]

Much research on highly reliable organizations backs up this basic insight. Reliable systems require members' mindful and cooperative orientation to the safety of the technical system—precisely because there are always stopgaps and unintended consequences in the everyday routines of such organizations. These only show up when the operators on the ground are committed to noticing and revealing them to one another.[32]

But market designers need to coordinate participants without their explicit cooperation and without the standard tools to ensure such cooperation. If they define market rules that allow for two types of decisions—one in line with the goals of the system and one not in line—the actors have no prima facie reason to call the designers and alert them to the problem. Rather, they have an incentive to choose the option that maximizes their profits. Similarly, if software interfaces leave the actors room to violate the blueprint, market actors have an incentive to figure out whether such behavior would be profitable. Designers cannot simply tell them their goals and direct them to interpret the rules in line with those objectives.

Of course, actors in regular organizations will also act on incentives to undermine goals. But designers can structure the organization to make this difficult: they can get other employees to report on them, they can screen their activities in detail, they can assign them different tasks directly, and they can foster identification with the organization to preempt such behavior. Market designers cannot draw on any of these tools because they do not have employment contracts with the actors. The lack of a cooperative baseline and the informal tools to enforce it creates extra requirements for success.

Designers need to structure the market environment in such a way that the actors find it both beneficial and easy to follow the intended logic. Without special interference from the designers, the market participants need good reasons to do what the blueprint requires. To understand why this is hard, consider the problem of incentives for a moment. To create a market setting where actors always have an incentive to do the right thing, designers must meet two stringent requirements.

First, they must create an internally consistent system of rules and procedures. Market actors take a holistic approach when they enter a designer market. They do not just respond to individual rules and constraints. Like players who begin a board game, they observe the entire system of rules and constraints to figure out how they can act within the system. Each time there are unintended ambiguities or inconsistencies between rules, participants gain new ways of acting. These may be beneficial to the actors, but they may not align with the designers' objectives. Achieving this global consistency between rules can be very difficult.

Consider mechanisms that match students to schools.[33] They are meant to find stable matchings, in the sense that there are no pairs of schools and students who are *not* matched to one another but who would mutually prefer to be matched than to accept the matching produced by the designer.[34] To ensure such matchings, designers try to find strategy-proof rules for the software that guarantee that it is always in the best interest for participants to state their true preference. A mechanism is *not* strategy-proof if individuals can increase their chances for a desired matching by misrepresenting their preferences. Since misrepresentations can affect a variety of other matchings, they can quickly derail the market from its path to the desired equilibrium.

In the matching system, applicants will always be asked to rank their preferences for different schools — and schools will do the same for applicants. Some algorithm then identifies an optimal allocation of students to schools. This allocation usually has to accommodate multiple constraints. Individual schools may have preferences for different types of students. Complications like that mean that the designers have to develop relatively sophisticated algorithms that consider different rank positions separately. It considers all first-ranked options and develops a set of matches, then moves on to all second-ranked options, and so on. While it is pretty straightforward to specify rules for each stage of this process, the different stages can interact. It can then be beneficial to misrepresent one's true preference to gain advantages at a later stage.

In an early version of the Boston school algorithm, students might "waste" their highest-priority slot by ranking a highly sought-after school as first priority if that school assigned a low priority to them. To avoid wasting one's voice, it became rational to mispresent one's true preference and elevate a less desirable school to the highest slot. In the aggregate, this led to inefficient matching.[35] Now, participants suddenly had two ways to behave: for some parents, it made sense to simply offer their preferences — as the designers had intended. But for others, it became rational to strategically misrepresent their preferences. The inconsistencies increased the space of possible behavior and introduced room for actions that were not aligned with the algorithm. The example shows that setting incentives requires designers to create a system of internally consistent rules. Indeed, most formal work in mechanism design sorts through the possible permutations of strategic actions under different configurations of rules and preferences. This gets more difficult as the number of rules and the structure of preferences grow more complex.

But designers are not done when they have created a system of consistent rules and procedures. They also need to fix actors' perception of the context of decision-making in the market. That is, the interpretation of rules is tied to the context in which they are applied. For example, when you are playing a board game, you can decide on moves relative to the game or relative to the social relations between the players. And people can think about these relations in terms of a variety of parameters (e.g., contributing to a fun party versus respecting a long-standing friendship). As Alfred Schutz put it, the world within potential "reach" is extremely flexible and temporally variable.[36] If rules set the correct incentives under one description of the situation, the same rules may produce different incentives under another description. When I think about the board game in terms of the social dynamics at the party, my incentive to win may disappear.

Robert Wilson, a famous designer from Stanford and winner of the Nobel Prize for his work on market design, describes this problem in an interview: "The big lesson of market design is that marketplaces are small institutions in a big economic environment: participants have bigger strategy sets than you can see, and there are lots of players, not all of whom may even be active participants in the marketplace, but can influence it. So, we needed a way to design mechanisms that had both good equilibrium properties for the rules we knew about, and good stability properties for the strategies we didn't know about."[37]

What Wilson refers to as actors' "bigger strategy sets" is the designers' definition of the context. Depending on how actors define the context within which they act, what counts as optimizing on their preferences may shift. What is irrational with respect to one market can become rational if it is understood in relation to another market. Interlinked financial markets provide an intuitive example. If you place a bet on a negative price trend in a derivative market, you could benefit from accelerating that trend by selling a product in the primary market at a loss. For an observer who looks only at the primary market, this seems irrational—the seller is making a loss. But for those who understand that the actor is optimizing over two markets and therefore see the "full strategy set," this sale is rational. To control which incentives participants face, market designers must constrain actors' definition of the context. Specifically, they must *inoculate* the logic inside the market from contexts outside the market.

But designers' work is not done when they have fixed the context of choice and created a consistent system of rules that sets the right incentives within that context. Next, they have to make sure that it is also easy and intuitive for real humans to follow the existing incentives. This requires that designers account for cognitive limitations and stabilize the temporal horizon of decision-making.

Humans have a variety of limitations and biases. They use heuristic shortcuts to make decisions and are not good at executing complex computations. If designers want actors to realize subroutines of a search algorithm, these limitations need to be accounted for. For example, real people struggle to report what market designers refer to as the actors' "type"—a set of ordered preferences that defines the person as belonging to a particular class of actors. Designers found that real humans may not be able to express their preferences in this format.[38] While objective incentives exist for actors of a particular type, individuals may be unable to identify with a given type. Ultimately, this is a problem of stabilizing the interpretation of rules and procedures in line with actors' cognitive limitations.

Designers also need to fix actors' perspective on the future—the point where the consequences of an economic decision manifest. How participants imagine the future is a contingent construction of the present. Internal deliberation generates ideas about how competing choices would unfold along imaginary lines of cause and effect.[39] The resulting projections are open and subject to change as new experiences and reinterpretations shape the present moment.[40]

But designers' market mechanisms generally assume that the future is a set of possible states. The available information determines the probability distribution for the different possibilities. Actors use the information to their best ability and therefore predict the future with only random errors. Individual predictions may be off the mark, but in the aggregate the true future will be discerned. As an information processor, the market accounts for and optimizes on the true future. This model of the future clearly diverges from the contingent, socially mediated, and plural ways in which actors construct and reconstruct narratives of the future. Accordingly, market designers must influence actors' perceptions of the future—what they deem likely or unlikely and how many different scenarios they consider. To come back to the school example, designers need to explain to parents how exactly their choices will translate into future assignments. Only if the parents understand the causal chain from choice to outcome do they understand the incentives the designers have set. Actors' perceptions of the future need to be standardized.

In sum, designers' main problem is dealing with antagonistic market actors. They need to coordinate the actions of participants who share no specific allegiance to the designers' goals and who do not have employment contracts with the platform organization. To work around this problem, designers create rules and procedures that make it beneficial and easy to do what the blueprint requires. First, they make the systems of rules and procedures internally consistent with the intended incentives. Second, they fix market actors' perceptions of the context of choice. Once they have met these first two requirements, the designers also need to make it easy for actors to perceive these incentives. They must therefore accommodate the cognitive limitations of real humans and enforce a shared understanding of how the future derives from choices in the present.

If these requirements are all met, market actors will always find it worthwhile to follow the logic that designers lay out for them. However, designers will not usually be able to perfectly isolate a market or remove all inconsistencies in the rule structure. I later explore a variety of practical reasons that this is difficult. But for now, it suffices to point to a logical reason. Any system of incentives leaves discretion to market actors. In some ways, this is the very point of market design. It is not a form of centralized planning. Instead, designers want to facilitate decentralized decisions in cases where market actors have more private information than is available to those who plan the system. Market mechanisms that assign children to schools or organ donations to patients give a voice to those who are affected. Parents know best which would be the best school for their children, and using that information to determine the final allocation is usually more efficient than using a bureaucratic formalism like wait-listing. In a designer market, those who know the situation best get to provide the input. The core idea behind market design is to use systems of incentives to elicit this information in a way that conforms to an ideal market logic and thus benefits the global goals. But this means that the designers never have all the information—the actors know more than they do. To accommodate this fact, every designer market gives discretion to market participants. Even if the market rules are extremely restrictive, there is always room for creative reinterpretation and thus deviation from expectations; what it means to follow a rule is necessarily and contingently established by practice, as the old philosophical insight goes.[41] Accordingly, market actors can choose not to follow the designers' plan.

Therefore, market designers must ensure that nonideal behavior does not derail their global objectives—the "stability properties" that Wilson mentioned. This insight does not surprise market designers. Deviance is not a problem unless it creates hazards for the system as a whole. Now, because of the fundamental antagonism of market players, the only way to know that the market cannot realize such hazards is to understand the space of possible behavior. That is, it must be possible to identify and constrain behavior that would violate designers' objectives. The market cannot become more complicated than designers can cognitively process and control from within their administrative structure. This point may seem obvious, but the implications hold the key to understanding the practical limits of market design.

A comparison with Charles Perrow's theory of normal accidents draws out this point.[42] Perrow was interested in accidents that occur in complex technical systems like nuclear power plants, spaceships, chemical plants, or military infrastructures. He argued that such systems will *necessarily* experience accidents if they are characterized by high interactive complexity and tight coupling. High interactive complexity refers to a situation involving many different processes that can interact in unfamiliar, unexpected, or unplanned ways. Tight coupling means that these interactions can happen very quickly. Both concepts are relative to the observer—they describe a system in which the observer cannot understand all potential interactions between elements in the available time.[43] In such systems, seemingly trivial failures in different parts of the system can interact in ways that no one anticipated. Before anyone can react, they trigger failure cascades that spiral out of control. These accidents are "normal" because they occur beyond the edge of the possible knowledge of the system and can therefore not be avoided—they are a necessary part of complex systems with these properties. But, Perrow argues, such accidents will be rare because they depend on improbable interactions between failures in technical components.[44] In that sense, then, we might accept them as a kind of calculated risk that is minimal enough to keep using the systems.

This last step of the argument does not work for designer markets. In markets with high interactive complexity and tight coupling, something like a normal accident would occur not rarely but frequently because the designers would not be dealing with random interactions between technical components. They would be dealing with guile. Consider this more carefully. A market with high interactive complexity and tight coupling would allow actors to interpret rules and procedures in many different ways and thus define contexts of action and futures arbitrarily. In such a system, decisions informed by different perspectives on the rules and procedures can interact. If one agent assumes something about the situation and another agent assumes differently, then the combination of these actions can produce room for trades that no one anticipated. Just as in Perrow's analogous example, certain configurations of decisions—or events in the system—can create incentives for behavior that violates the objectives of the market. But this possibility will not be up to negligible probabilities. If the incentive exists, actors will identify the possibility and act on it as quickly and secretively as possible.

While the interactions between technical components in Perrow's examples follow physical laws, market actors are always searching for profitable moves. They always have reasons to leverage inconsistencies between the rules that emerge as the market proceeds—the more, the better.[45] If it is impossible for designers to understand and constrain such behavior, their markets will constantly experience the equivalent of "normal accidents." As a result, the epistemic problem Perrow points out is much more serious in designer markets than in technical systems.

To be clear, my point is not that complex markets necessarily produce opportunities to bring down the system. Hazards differ by the problem addressed by the market. Some markets may be compatible with extensive deviation from ideal behavior. But markets will definitely fail if there are opportunities for behaviors that derail designers' objectives. The designers cannot risk the dangers that are associated with high interactive complexity and tight coupling. They can only rule out the existence of such moves by controlling the space of possible behavior in some way. This does not mean that designers have to rule out all unintended consequences; for time immemorial, sociologists have shown that this is impossible.[46] But it means that market designers can never make their market more complicated than they can control given the hazards they need to avoid. They must be able to understand the space of possible behavior to a degree where they can identify unintended consequences and react to them. Because of market actors' antagonism, the market process can be complicated, but it cannot be more complex than the administrative structure can handle. While I am not yet able to give a substantive definition of this scope condition—the limits of oversight depend on the nature of the allocation problem the market is meant to solve—it is possible to specify the formal limit more closely.

Again, the organization that manages the market does not have the knowledge of the participants—that is the reason the designers put a market into place. The organization can therefore never know exactly the correct decision on the local level or the substantive solution to the allocation problem. The center may have historical benchmarks for acceptable solutions, or it may be able to specify limit conditions that will not be breached. But in the end, the center can only apply formal standards to screen transactions. Accordingly, there must be a standardized way to determine whether a given decision fits designers' expectations. If the allocation problem is complex enough to require many different decisions over multiple temporal horizons, this formal standard necessarily becomes vaguer.

Behavior that is acceptable along one dimension may not be acceptable along another, but which dimension actors choose depends on their local information. For example, a company may declare maintenance outages on a generator. This could be because they are legitimately trying to protect their hardware or because they are trying to exercise market power. What fits the designers' algorithm under one description does not fit it under another description. The center can only know whether the action follows a legitimate calculation if it assesses the situation on the ground—for instance, by sending a regulator to see whether the generator is actually broken. Not only is this not feasible in a system with thousands of transactions but it also violates the intent behind market design.

As soon as the center needs to know the right local decisions, the value of decentralized decisions evaporates. Market design then collapses into centralized planning—the center would need the local information to determine whether the transaction fits the design's logic. But this would defeat the whole point of market design. Moreover, it would also pose insurmountable bureaucratic obstacles, as we know from the literature on the failures of centralized planning.[47] For one, the centralized oversight structure would have to impose a substantial division of labor that would inevitably lead to blind spots and misaligned incentives between the different departments. This would inhibit its ability to control the market process effectively. Accordingly, the limits of control are located where the formal definition of acceptable behavior no longer suffices to discriminate between legitimate and illegitimate activities. Note that this applies even if designers use machine-learning techniques to identify problematic behavior from patterns of past behavior relative to some substantial threshold. Because markets are employed when the substance of correct decisions cannot be predicted in advance, such machine-learning techniques produce conclusive results only when there is a formal definition of acceptable behavior. The availability of such a formal definition is directly related to the complexity of the rules and procedures that define the market.

To sum up, designers need to make market systems that are useful to the actors; they need to provide procedures to ensure a trajectory of improvement; and they need to prevent actors from circumventing the rules of the system. As I have shown, the last requirement poses the highest barriers to success. Not only do designers have to create consistent sets of rules and stable contexts of action but they also have to adjust to the cognitive limitations of humans and stabilize the perception of the future. To the extent that they cannot meet these standards, they have to control the space of possible behavior. That space must be narrow enough for a control structure to apply formal criteria to evaluate the legitimacy of transactions in the system. How, then, do market designers go about meeting these challenges?

Simplifying, Bounding, and Controlling

Designers can pull several different levers in their design work. They can define the commodities, set the rules that determine what kind of transactions are possible in what order and at what time, organize information flows, define the mix and starting positions of players, and structure the interfaces that define the available options. To the extent that the market interactions are mediated by software, they can create structures to monitor the market process and intervene in real time. In short, they can comprehensively define the possible moves, the accounting structure behind the market, and the information that actors receive to make their choices. In pulling these levers, they generally follow three strategies.

First, they do everything to simplify the market process. If designers give actors few behavioral options, limit the information they need to consider, and make the rules as simple as possible, they decrease the chance of any ambiguities and inconsistencies between rules and procedures. Further, they limit the permutations of possible behavior to a level that a control structure can easily assess. Simple rules and procedures also make it easier for actors to understand the incentives and what it means to follow these incentives.

Strategies of simplification are somewhat analogous to the operation of a Taylorist factory. The physical organization of an assembly line reduces actors' freedom to behave in ways that do not cohere with the optimal production process.[48] The design of software interfaces offers a good example. In one of the early auctions for the spectrum licenses of the Federal Communications Commission, market actors could use smaller numbers in bid amounts to send signals to other bidders, thus colluding to hold down the price for specific items.[49] The players had redefined the context of choice: the bid was no longer just a representation of their commitment to pay but a tool to send signals to other players. The solution to this problem was relatively straightforward: the designers forced the actors to submit lump-sum bids, thus removing the signaling potential from the market. By reducing the complexity of the information that traders could communicate through the interface, they reduced behavioral options and fixed actors' definition of the context of choice.

In simplified systems of rules, actors have few options that do not align with the calculative logic of the blueprint. Sometimes, designers refer to market mechanisms with highly constrained choices as zero-intelligence mechanisms. These structures always work as intended because the space of possible behavior—as modeled by agents who behave randomly and without strategy—is equivalent to the space of desirable behavior.[50] Still, even zero-intelligence mechanisms require that actors follow the rules and define the context of action and the horizon of future consequences as designers want them to. Simplification makes this more likely.

Second, designers bound their systems. They engage in a variety of strategies to close the market system off from its environment—by making the environment irrelevant, by erecting legal or technical boundaries, or by regulating the interaction with other markets. Bounding is a timeworn strategy to organize social processes: by building a wall around a bullfight, we can ensure that the fight plays out among the torero, the riders, the bull, and no one else. Designers may prohibit some actors from entering the market; they may limit the time of operation, the types of transactions, and the products. If actors can move in multiple markets, the designers can set rules to limit the factors in one market that can become relevant in another. In each case, they try to fix the context of choice to stabilize how actors interpret rules and procedures.

Third, the designers create structures of control. As outlined before, it is always possible that the rules and procedures of the market will generate ambiguities and inconsistencies in the flow of events. Designers therefore need to create administrative structures that monitor the process and check its match with designers' blueprints. If the process does not deliver on designers' objectives or does not unfold as intended, the administrative structure either intervenes or changes the rules of the market to accommodate changes in the underlying reality, thus producing a trajectory of gradual improvement. The general need for such control structures cause designer markets to follow a feedback-control logic.[51] Market designers sometimes speak of their markets as systems of rules that continuously create a perfect social process once the markets get going. But this is misleading. The market system must be closely observed and adjusted by the organizational structures surrounding it. Digital platforms have multiplied designers' powers of control far beyond what was possible in traditional markets. Designers can record and analyze activities in the market on a granular level. They can use machine-learning techniques to identify suspicious patterns of activity autonomously, they can intervene in individual transactions, and they can adjust the structure of the market with relatively little effort. They can also design the market to unwittingly enlist participants in one another's control. Review systems discipline market participants in a fully decentralized manner.[52]

Together, the three strategies of simplifying, bounding, and controlling help designers to keep the systems of rules consistent, the context of choice stable, and the actors' understanding of the situation in line with the blueprint. This reduces the overall complexity of the system and makes it easy for the control structure to identify deviant behavior. Accordingly, designers generally aim to simplify, bound, and control the systems as much as possible to ensure that actors follow the logic they envision. This is crucial because the system may never become more complex than they can manage from within the control structure. It is therefore important to appreciate what increases market complexity. I will now show how the nature of the allocation problem affects designers' ability to rely on the three strategies.

The Complex Problem of Electricity Market Design

Designer markets solve allocation problems. When a problem is well defined, static, and separable from other contexts, a single algorithm can solve it. For example, the task may be to find the combination of matches between schools and students that optimizes the satisfaction of first preferences and the diversity of the groups' composition. This is a discrete problem that does not change over time, can be solved in the same way repeatedly, and requires information with a clear and unchanging structure (preferences from both sides and information on personal characteristics). A single market can solve this problem with highly simplified interfaces that ask users to volunteer little more than their preferences. While it is still difficult to make sure that users find it rational to submit their true preferences, the problem's properties make it easy to simplify the market and thus control how users can interpret the rules and the horizons against which they operate. Similarly, because the information is highly circumscribed, it is easy to bound this market from other contexts of action. Complex allocation problems do not allow designers to simplify and bound the market quite as easily, and thus the control requirements increase. Complex problems involve multiple, potentially conflicting objectives over different temporal horizons; they are changeable and not easily separated from other domains of social life. I will now turn to electricity systems to illustrate how these features affect designers' ability to rely on techniques of simplification and bounding.

At the core, an electricity system consists of generators that produce electricity and then send it via a shared transmission system to end users. But this simple statement can be unpacked into bewildering complexity, beginning with the fleet of generation assets. Different generators have vastly different operational characteristics.[53] While some may have to run for hours or days to come online and achieve efficient output levels, others can produce efficiently within a few minutes. Their "ramp rate" varies. Some produce a steady output over long periods of time, and others produce vastly different levels of energy from one hour to the next. The degree to which generators can produce steadily is also called their intermittency.[54]

Each electricity system contains a mix of different generators. Consumers use different amounts of electricity throughout the day and the year. While there is always a certain amount of baseload, usage will fluctuate around peak times. Generators in the system have to react to these fluctuations at all times because it is still relatively expensive and inefficient to store electricity in reservoirs or batteries. Consumers also do not perceive the overall status of the system and therefore do not adjust their consumption to its needs. Despite the dreams about homeostatic systems, electricity systems have largely remained load following. This means that some plants (peak and cycling plants) need to be able to come online and produce energy very quickly, while others (baseload plants) need to produce a steady output over long periods of time.

The optimal mix of generation assets does not just meet the existing demand at all times; it also minimizes the cost of energy production at each moment and over time. The cost structure for power plants is complicated. There are fluctuating input costs, maintenance costs and personnel costs, as well as a variety of fixed costs of investment. In the short run, the system must use the available generation capacity to meet all demand in the system at the least cost. This is also referred to as the "unit commitment problem." Since generators must run for different periods of time to come online and produce energy efficiently, operators constantly need to consider when to start a generator and commit its resources to the grid. This decision depends not just on the ramp rates of different generators but also on their operating costs, which themselves depend on a complex mix of considerations (e.g., input costs, salaries, wear and tear at different levels of output, etc.).

The problem is complicated further by the physical characteristics of energy flows. Power moves at close to the speed of light across the transmission grid. All power flows interact with one another according to Kirchhoff's laws on all available paths. Flows in opposite directions can cancel each other, and flows in the same direction add to each other, depending on the structure of the network. In a network with circularities, complex interdependencies between the inputs from different generators are the norm. These dynamic interdependencies must be managed carefully and at all times when considering the optimal level of generation output.

Transmission lines have thermal limits that determine how much energy they can transport. If too much energy were to flow in a line, the current would first increase and then collapse, or the line would sag and rip. The sudden voltage drop would suddenly leave the system without enough energy to meet consumption. If there is too little energy in the system, the frequency, the alternation of current that moves energy, drops. If it falls too far from the US standard of sixty cycles per second, generators will switch off because they are unable to produce output at lower frequencies. This further reduces the frequency in the system, leading to more generators disconnecting. Soon, the chain reaction can cause cascading blackouts that can bring down the system. This is dangerous because many crucial services of our civilization depend on electricity and because the system cannot be brought back online easily after a system-wide blackout. Many plants need electricity to come online. To prevent such a catastrophic event, the power flows in the grid must always remain in balance. And since the energy moves at the speed of light, the generators' outputs must be controlled relative to one another. To ensure that all of this works reliably, the engineers require that backup generators run in the background to provide emergency reserves if necessary.

Electricity systems thus confront a difficult allocation problem in the short run. They must find the cheapest combination of generator outputs to meet demand at all locations at each moment while obeying the transmission and related security constraints. This requires not only finding an optimal solution to the unit commitment problem for different intervals but also ensuring that a cost-effective combination of backup services is standing by. Solutions to this problem are sensitive to error. The associated hazards are substantial: incorrect solutions can trigger cascading system failures.

In the long run, things become even more complicated. Equipment must be updated and maintained. The electricity system consists of thousands of components—not just generators and transmission poles. There are transistors, circuit breakers, relays, transmission towers, substations, and many other pieces of equipment that must be maintained and integrated. Since demand changes over time, this system must gradually but steadily expand. New generators must be built and connected to the system. Depending on the location and the type of generator, this process can take years. The transmission system must be expanded and updated. This depends on plans for additions of generation capacity and their effects on power flows. Finally, as new technologies emerge, the whole system needs to be adjusted. For example, to introduce renewable energy into the system, the grid needs to be updated to account for the fact that the output of renewable energy sources cannot be adjusted at will (e.g., battery storage needs to be updated and integrated). Because the system is vulnerable to even small imbalances, the safety standards are unforgiving. They require that the system be able to deal with a variety of scenarios, ranging from interlocking component failures to cyberattacks and extreme weather. These possibilities need to be anticipated and accounted for.

As these details show, electricity systems solve an exceedingly complex allocation problem at each moment and over time. This problem is not well defined. Identifying the best combination of generators requires the solution of multiple problems over different temporal horizons. Their solutions might be conflict with one another. For example, as in many other engineered systems, there is a trade-off between cheap and reliable production. Reliability requires redundancies and generous safety margins, but the cheap provision of energy requires that the system be as lean as possible. Solving one problem well means solving the other poorly. The allocation problem is also not static — new technologies can change the calculus behind efficient dispatch. For example, solar energy has low fixed costs and practically zero operating costs. But the high intermittency requires backup facilities that may be expensive. This changes the search for the optimal dispatch. Finally, it is not easy to isolate the components of the allocation problem. Electricity systems are tied into a variety of other upstream and downstream markets, technical systems, and administrative structures. These systems cannot easily be isolated: whatever role markets play, their results are directly relevant to the technical management of the grid, and the markets for input resources will affect how the electricity markets operate.

These properties make market design difficult. Whatever role markets are going to play in the larger system, designers are severely limited in their ability to simplify. To accommodate the different trade-offs and functional requirements, there must be multiple interrelated products and relatively complex rules that determine how they relate to one another. Market actors need to be able to act with respect to multiple time horizons. Further, there are uncertainties: some generators may confront technical difficulties, the weather may change, and demand patterns may fluctuate randomly. Finally, innovation is key in electricity systems. It requires not only a complex system of rules but also much discretion from market actors. To build structures that successfully coordinate the electricity system, designers must therefore tolerate a substantial level of complexity in the rules and procedures for the market.

Similarly, bounding will be more difficult because electricity markets depend on other market contexts, like natural gas or derivative markets. Within each of these markets, actors must be able to make different and relatively sophisticated decisions in the short and long run. Designers need to allow substantial amounts of outside information into the market, and that requirement makes it harder to restrict both the context of choice and the degree to which outside influences can matter in the market.

With a proliferation of rules, markets, and procedures, there will be an increase in the possibilities for actors to interpret rules and relate to them to one another at different points while making decisions. Substantial ambiguities and inconsistencies become a real possibility. The more possible permutations of behavior, the more ways actors might find it rational to deviate from the requirements of the blueprint. Since the designers cannot rely on participant cooperation to identify these avenues of problematic behavior, oversight requirements grow. Designers need to put more and more emphasis on a workable control structure.

However, the capacity for centralized oversight is not infinite. While the precise limits of control differ from case to case, the comparison with Perot's theory of normal accidents yields one basic and formal insight. The permutations of possible behavior cannot become larger than the administrative structures can handle. This happens if the system can no longer rely on standardized ways to assess the legitimacy of transactions.

In sum, then, certain properties of complex allocation problems push up against the core strategies that designers use to ensure success. As simplifying and bounding become more difficult, the control requirements grow until they might exceed what market designers can guarantee. Importantly, this argument does not imply that market design is impossible for complex problems in general or for electricity in particular. While doing so is difficult, there are avenues for designers to simplify and bound these markets, some of which will be the topic of the next chapter. But the argument also does not imply that market design can always be used to solve complex allocation problems. Even after twenty years of refinement, contemporary electricity markets are far from perfect. Both Texas and the PJM Interconnection, generally considered role models for good electricity market design, experience manipulative behavior and can, as the recent blackouts in Texas remind us, stumble into disaster.[55] From what has been said, these cases of failure may be inherently preventable — market designers simply run into practical obstacles that prevent them from striking the correct balance. But is also possible that these failures are symptoms of a deeper problem. Maybe market design fails on principle here; maybe electricity markets make it impossible to strike a workable balance among simplifying, bounding, and controlling in the long run. We cannot tell at this point.

This chapter has only established two basic insights. First, a simple imperative operates behind all successful systems: simplify and bound the market system enough that the control structure can still identify hazardous transactions on the basis of formal standards. Second, complex allocation problems make it harder to rely on simplification and bounding. The question for a sociology of market design failure is now twofold. First, in what ways can market design projects violate the balance among simplification, bounding, and control—how do they produce incentives and opportunities for behavior that derail the search algorithm and cannot be detected? Second—and this is the crucial question—what exactly leads market designers to adopt features that violate these scope conditions? What drives decisions to adopt rules, procedures, and administrative structures that create inconsistencies and ambiguities whose implications can no longer be controlled? The first question will be the topic of the next two chapters. The second will be the topic of chapters 5–7. In the conclusion, we will return to the question of what this tells us about the limits of market design more generally.

[CHAPTER THREE]

Breaking Bad in California's Energy Markets

There is an infamous phone call between Enron's headquarters and the West Power Trading Desk in Portland. The employee at the trading desk, Tim Belden, suggests with substantial glee that his boss "steals money from California to the tune of about a million." Somewhat indignant, the operator responds, "Will you rephrase that?" and without losing a beat, Belden says: "Ok, he . . . arbitrages the California market to the tune of a million bucks or two a day."[1] The recording of the call became a smoking gun in the court cases against Enron because it captures nicely both the cynicism and the intent to defraud at the heart of Enron's operations. But the call is also interesting for another reason.

It drives home how *easily* the true intention (stealing money) could be translated into the language of legitimate business (arbitrage). Enron and its peers knew they were doing things that violated the intended logic of the market design, and in that sense, they were stealing. But it was also not entirely clear whether they were breaking any rules. In another sense, they were simply being creative arbitrageurs and could easily code-switch to justify what they were doing. Precisely such ambiguities are at the heart of the market design failure and the reason the battle of the narratives cannot be resolved. There were few formal standards by which traders' behavior could be unambiguously classified as legitimate or illegitimate. And where such standards existed, there was not enough evidence to assess what was happening. Accordingly, little could be done about this behavior.

And there was a lot of variation. Though the literature still debates the pervasiveness of market manipulations and the extent to which they caused price spikes, no one denies that such manipulations occurred frequently. The casual reference to "a million bucks or two" suggests as much. An overly restrictive focus on Enron would be misleading as well. Although Enron has always been the face of the California crisis, practically all sellers of energy either developed their own games or collaborated with Enron. For example, Enron helpfully listed in its recruitment material trading desks that were amenable to risk-free profits in exchange for a bit of ethical flexibility. Some of the games were even named after counterparties. A strategy with the catchy title "Red Congo" involved the city of Redding. Other, perhaps surprising players were public entities like the Bonneville Power Administration or the Los Angeles Department of Water Resources. These counterparties surely were in on the joke and made a healthy profit during the operation of the markets.

These strategies often operated in legal gray areas—a fact that poses problems for attempts to resolve the battle between the two narratives. But this ambiguity becomes the very object of inquiry once we study the crisis as a case of market design failure. The market rules and procedures were inconsistent enough to sustain a variety of behavior that conformed to the rules but still undermined the system. "Stealing money" and "arbitraging" were in some ways equivalent activities within the purview of the rules the designers had set up. Regardless of their legality, the games reflect a reaction to the problematic incentives created by the designers. They represent possible behaviors in the system that deviate from the intended actions— they represent a failure to simplify, bound, and control the system at a level where only legitimate behavior is possible. *This* is what a structural explanation has to make sense of. It has to identify which rules and procedures created the games, what made it difficult to identify and enforce them, and why the designers built the system in this way.

During the design and initial operation of the markets, most market designers, politicians, and regulators had no idea what the future had in store for them. Champagne corks popped as the first set of orders ran over the screens in CAISO's control room in April 1998. Sure, there were some bugs that had to be dealt with, some wrinkles to be ironed out, but in a general way, the system seemed to be working as advertised. Low prices kicked in almost immediately, electricity flowed reliably, and commentators began to hail the California model as the pinnacle of market design. Some of the system's architects toured the country and advertised the model to dazzled politicians and regulators everywhere.

The positive image of the system persisted for quite some time. Even after cracks started to become obvious to insiders, some designers remained confident. A researcher at the University of Cambridge and codesigner of the Power Exchange concluded as late as July 2000 that "California's market structure with respect to forward trading is more robust than PJM's."[2] The article was published mere days before the retail spikes would hit San Diego and the crisis would move into the public eye. While price spikes were already tearing at the utilities' credit, operators were nervously looking for reserve capacity, and companies like Duke and AES ran their plants up and down like yo-yos, watching scarcity translate into dollars.[3]

On the one hand, we have dozens of sellers who pitted the markets against the reliable operation of the electricity system with almost perverse ease. On the other, we have economists, market designers, and regulators who celebrated the system as a triumph of social engineering. It is tempting to discard the view of the designers and call them naive. But that would not do the case justice. Many of the problems were simply not as obvious as they might seem in hindsight. This chapter will therefore try to make both perspectives plausible. First, I explain why the system could, from the right point of view, seem like a success. I highlight the ways in which it was a genuine accomplishment, an elegant and sophisticated solution to a difficult problem. I show how exactly the designers deployed the strategies of simplifying, bounding, and controlling to create the behavior their blueprints required. The immense complexity of the system will help us understand both the excitement and the difficulty of identifying many of the problems. But as "the mind is its own place, and in itself / can make a heav'n of hell, a hell of heav'n,"[4] we then switch perspectives and turn to the other side of the story.

Descending into the offices of the traders and producers, I catalog three types of behavior that brought problems into California's markets. These strategies violated the design and turned the market logic against the reliable operation of the technical system. Practically, all problematic behavior can be classified under three headings: market power, arbitrage games, congestion games. I reconstruct how each of the strategies worked, why they were profitable, and how they undermined the system. The next chapter then traces these behaviors to specific design features, thus developing a structural explanation of the crisis.

California: A Cathedral to the Ambitions of Market Designers

Those who manage the electricity system have to solve two basic problems. In the short run, the operators need to find the security-constrained economic dispatch. They need to identify and deploy the combination of generators that can meet the current demand at the least cost while obeying transmission constraints and a variety of other reliability criteria. The size of the system and the complexity and sensitivity of power flows makes this no easy task. In the long run, the system's managers must ensure that someone updates, maintains, and expands the equipment to accommodate the

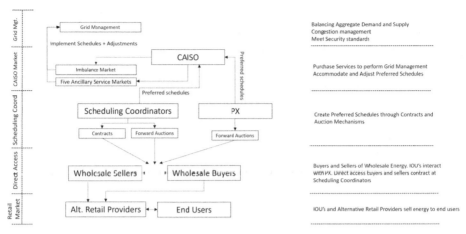

FIGURE 3.1. Illustration of California's Market Structure

evolution of demand, political mandates, and new technologies. The technical infrastructure has to evolve in lockstep with the society it serves.

Electricity markets are supposed to help with both short-term and long-term tasks. But they can never solve these completely. Shortly before electrons begin to dance, the system operator must take over and assume control over the grid. In every electricity system, there is a division of labor between the system operator and the market system. The crucial question is how much the markets can accomplish before the operator needs to take over. In California, the designers gave as much control to the markets as was possible at the time. They took the most radical approach available, and the system architecture turned out to be a cathedral to the ambitions of market design. Not only did the designers create a complex array of markets to identify an approximate solution to the dispatch problem but they also built markets to help the system operator with management tasks. They even delegated to the markets the long-term maintenance and expansion of the system. Figure 3.1 offers an illustration of the resulting architecture.

The actual system was even more complex than this figure suggests. But even just developing a working understanding of the basic architecture can be complicated. The most important thing to keep in mind is this: the financial markets were divided among a variety of organizations—the scheduling coordinators. All of them traded financial obligations for the delivery of energy at future times. CAISO collected this information and used it to run the system. In this way, the markets prepared the work of the system operator.

I will now discuss the basic architecture in quite some detail, for two reasons. First, I want to give the reader a chance to appreciate the elegance of the designers' solution. This was a sophisticated response to a difficult problem. Second, a working knowledge of the system is necessary to appreciate how the games that derailed the markets actually worked. We begin with the center of the system. The system operator, CAISO, formed the functional core of the larger system. It is marked in the top two brackets of figure 3.1. The engineers in CAISO's control room had wide-ranging authority not just over the grid but over all parts of the technological system, including the generators. In real time, during the actual operation of the system, they managed the flows of electricity on the basis of command-and-control principles. They adjusted inputs to meet the aggregate load while resolving transmission constraints, compensating for losses, and implementing various reliability services for emergencies.[5] This was very demanding technically—recall the description of the control room in the first chapter. In some ways, it looked like the bridge of a spaceship. To accomplish their tasks, the operators used resources from so-called imbalance and ancillary service markets (top of figure 3.1).

The wholesale markets in the brackets below prepared and supported the work of the operators. Three classes of participants interacted in these markets. Sellers owned generation assets in California or in the Western Interconnection. These were independent power producers, utilities in other states, public power administrations, and municipalities. Buyers either sold the energy to retail customers or consumed it themselves. The most important buyers were California's three big utilities because they satisfied the most demand in the state. Discounting old long-term contracts and generation from their own sources, they covered 90 percent of their daily power needs with purchases in the wholesale markets.[6] Other buyers included industrial direct-access customers who bought bulk energy for their production facilities in the wholesale markets. In addition, there were power marketers, who did not own generation assets and did not consume electricity. Instead, they profited by buying and selling energy between locations or time points—that is, they were speculators who benefited from the arbitrage opportunities that existed between the different markets. The group included financial trading firms like Enron and Calpine but also unregulated affiliates of the three big utilities.

These actors traded not "real" energy but financial obligations to deliver power at specific locations and at future times. The earliest products would be delivered a year later, while the latest markets traded energy that would flow on the same day. Together, these markets formed an interrelated cascade of forward markets. Each subsequent market could be used to adjust obligations from the previous ones. For example, those with obligations from yesterday's day-ahead market could buy or sell energy to adjust their

| Year & Month-Ahead Market | Day-Ahead Market | Day-of Market | Real-time: Balancing Markets | Dispatch of Generators |

Forward Markets   Spot Market

FIGURE 3.2. Illustration of Electricity Markets' Temporal Structure

commitments in the day-of market.[7] Figure 3.2 displays the temporal structure of the market system.

The reason for such interlocking forward markets is straightforward. In an ideal market with perfect information, trading would automatically converge on the optimal dispatch. Buyers would search for the cheapest resource to serve their demand, while suppliers would lower their prices to marginal cost to compete for their business. In such a market, buyers would select the cheapest offers. When those were depleted, buyers would go to the second cheapest, and so on until all demand was met. In equilibrium, the market would find the ideal mix of generators to supply all demand at the least price—disregarding transmission constraints and other technical issues for a moment. As we saw in the first chapter, this is not a coincidence: the ideal and frictionless market of microeconomic theory is based on the same mathematical techniques as the optimization algorithms for identifying the optimal dispatch.[8]

However, financial markets always come with one drawback: the assumption of perfect information is never met. The future is open, and the actors are uncertain about the quantities of energy they might want to consume or produce. Designers solve this problem by employing market cascades like those in California. By adjusting their positions from previous markets, the actors can gradually reflect new information in the market, and as the system approaches the time of dispatch, the market solutions become more accurate. The cascade works as an iterative optimization algorithm.[9]

Scheduling coordinators operated the different marketplaces in this system (middle of fig. 3.1). Between 1998 and 2000, there were around thirty such entities, managing different types of markets. Most worked as brokers and facilitated bilateral contracts between buyers and sellers.[10] Others operated centralized auctions. The closer the markets operated to dispatch, the more constrained the environment. While the bilateral markets mainly dealt with long-term obligations and imposed few restrictions on buyers and sellers, auction markets operated closer to dispatch and regulated every aspect of participants' behavior.

This was true for geographic reach as well. California's grid was embedded in the larger Western Interconnection, which linked eleven western states and parts of Canada and Mexico. Bilateral contracts were the method of choice for importing energy from adjacent states into California. But to enter the auction markets, one had to schedule the energy at one of twenty-six scheduling points or three zones inside California. In other words, the closer you got to dispatch, the more firmly the market insisted on a particular representation of the grid, a particular trading process, and a structure for contractual agreements. In this way, the market process remained flexible and regionally open as long as grid management was not affected. Once the time for the actual dispatch came around, the market contracted and was more tightly controlled, ensuring that the match between market results and grid management would be perfect.

By far the most important auction house was the Power Exchange, which operated a day-ahead and a day-of market for energy. Since California's three utilities had to purchase their energy at the Power Exchange, the day-ahead auctions accounted for roughly 80 percent of all energy trades in the California system. Buyers and sellers had to submit bids that specified how much energy they were willing to buy or sell at different prices. The software then added all bids to form aggregate supply and demand curves, set the market clearing price at the intersection of these curves, and assigned the resulting obligations to buyers and sellers. By increasingly constraining choice and relocating components of rational action into computer software—that is, by simplifying the market—the designers ensured that accuracy increased over time. It became easier to act rationally, and there was less room for maneuvers that did not reflect the required logic.

To give an example: the auctions required a standardized input—a step function that established how much the buyer or seller was willing to buy or sell at a given price for a given hour. This information had to be submitted at a particular time. After the auction closed, the software calculated the optimal combination of trades and informed buyers and sellers about sales and purchases. The algorithm incentivized all generators to bid their true marginal cost and buyers to bid their true preferences. The setup made it easy and intuitive to do what the market design required.

Power marketers played a special role in the larger system of interlocking markets. They were supposed to mediate the trading process. On the one hand, their arbitrage trades increased the liquidity of different products. On the other, they facilitated price convergence across the marketplaces because their arbitrage business eradicated price differences between locations and time points. Given the fragmentation into multiple scheduling coordinators, the power marketers were an important source of information distribution and convergence between different marketplaces.[11]

The architecture also included a retail level (bottom of fig. 3.1) to ensure that the wholesale markets would be competitive. Market competition requires that buyers respond to increases or decreases in prices. But California's end users usually did not have the necessary equipment to learn about wholesale prices in real time. They simply used energy and paid at the end of the month. To create wholesale markets with elastic—or price-responsive—demand, it was therefore necessary to split the production and the consumption segments of the industry. In the retail markets, the utilities and other providers sold delivery contracts to households, districts, neighborhoods, and small businesses. These retailers made money by selling more expensively to the end users than they bought in the wholesale markets. Retail sellers thus became price-responsive buyers in the wholesale markets. In theory, the retail segment could have turned into a competitive market for delivery contracts, but end users never took much advantage of these markets and generally stayed with the incumbent utilities.

Overall, the system of interlocking forward markets created incentives to develop and upgrade the system over time. Price increases in the wholesale markets identified supply shortages. On CAISO's open-access system information system (OASIS), WEnet, all market participants could access load forecasts, transmission outages, capacity status, market prices, and even anonymized bidding behavior with a three-month lag. In addition, CAISO and the California Energy Commission released annual demand growth forecasts. These indicated where and how much demand would develop over time. This information system was supposed to make transparent what kinds of new capacity would be needed and where. The existence of long-term forward markets reduced the risks of investment because companies could secure future sales in advance. In that way, the system was supposed to meet both the short-term and long-term goals for the operation of the electricity system.

The picture is almost complete, but we are still missing a few more pieces.[12] In particular, I have not yet explained how the system operator procured the various services it needed for reliability purposes and how it dealt with transmission constraints (top of fig. 3.1). The scheduling coordinators generated financial obligations between buyers and sellers and aggregated them into balanced schedules. A balanced schedule is a table that shows how all buyers will be served by all sellers. Imports, exports, production, and consumption need to cancel each other completely. After the forward markets closed, the scheduling coordinators submitted these schedules to the system operator, who tried to implement the resulting schedules as accurately as possible.[13] To that end, the organization used a so-called imbalance or real-time market for energy, where they purchased increments or decrements of energy. Since the imbalance market set the prices and quantities for the real flows of energy and thus reconciled the financial with the physical side of the system, it was the de facto spot market—the market against which all financial obligations were settled.[14]

Yet the operators used the resources in these markets to adjust the balance in the physical system. The markets thus played two roles: settling the scores of the financial markets and procuring energy for the real-time grid management. For CAISO's central responsibility of maintaining the reliable operation of the grid, the imbalance markets were not enough. Strictly speaking, the cascade of forward markets only dealt with the unit commitment problem—when and for how long to switch on generators. But the unit commitment problem had to be evaluated in light of the transmission constraints and various reliability requirements that were central to the security-constrained economic dispatch. The system operator ran several markets of its own to reflect these constraints in the market and procure the additional reliability services.

Apart from the imbalance market for schedule adjustments, CAISO used four ancillary service markets to buy different types of standby capacity for use in various contingencies, like line failures, generator outages, and so on.[15] The four types were spinning reserves, nonspinning reserves, regulation, and replacement reserves. The services differed mainly by the speed with which they could come online. For each, the system operator bought the right to call on generators in a specific time frame, during which these generators had to remain ready. CAISO ran separate auctions for each of these services. Their interfaces were integrated with the auctions at the Power Exchange. After scheduling coordinators ended their day-ahead and day-of markets, the participants could enter a separate market where they could sell any or all of the four ancillary services. The system operator set the level of demand on the basis of reliability considerations, and auction software processed the bids. If their capacity was selected, companies had to remain on standby. If they were called to produce, they would be paid the ancillary service price plus the current imbalance price. Market actors therefore had to consider carefully whether they might make more money by selling their energy directly or by selling less of it but potentially at a higher price. Under ideal conditions, generators would offer ancillary services if their generators were not needed in the energy markets; in other words, the most cost-efficient generators would still show up in the imbalance markets. To incentivize this bidding behavior, the designers ensured that ancillary services were more likely to receive only the capacity price than both the capacity and imbalance prices.

The system operator also managed an implicit market for transmission rights that interacted with both forward markets.[16] Recall the problem of transmission congestion. If it turned out that the market's dispatch schedules violated transmission constraints, the schedules had to be adjusted to put the system back into balance. Generators that would ordinarily sell their output had to be backed off, and other generators whose transmission to the customers was not blocked had to step up their production. Congestion is thus a conceptual fiction that indicates a discrepancy between the market schedules and the physical flows of energy: there is not enough transmission capacity to implement the schedules the markets have produced. In principle, such congestion can occur anywhere in the physical grid—the real network that consists of thousands of buses and lines connecting them. Since congestion depends on the global patterns of all inputs and outputs, it can change at any moment. Given the complexity and temporal instability of congestion patterns, the system operator needed to resolve congestion with software that monitored all power flows and could adjust the system in real time.

However, some sources of congestion occurred frequently enough to be predictable. The resulting congestion could therefore be represented in a simplified network model and resolved through a market for transmission capacity. California's three zones roughly corresponded to the old service territories of the three utilities and marked transmission lines that were frequently congested. If the forward markets generated schedules that violated transmission constraints between the zones of the simplified model, participants entered the system operator's implicit market for transmission rights. On the basis of the schedule adjustment bids, the system operator calculated the opportunity cost of redispatch and informed the scheduling coordinators of the best adjustments.

Once the market had taken care of such interzonal congestion, CAISO would merely have to deal with the remaining intrazonal congestion on paths not represented in the market model. In this way, the market represented as much of the transmission system as possible and helped to price the cost of redispatches. This made the market more efficient because it now accounted for constrained transmission capacity—at least approximately.

To recapitulate: The system consisted of intricately linked markets that fed into the task of system management. Scheduling coordinators created balanced schedules and submitted them to the system operator. In the longer term, bilateral agreements prevailed. The closer you moved to dispatch, the more important the markets at the Power Exchange and the system operator became. The highly structured, centralized day-ahead markets generated schedules for the next day, which went through compatibility checks by the operators. If the schedules were not feasible in terms of the simplified network model, the system operator performed congestion management. On the basis of the day-ahead schedules, it acquired ancillary services. The day-of markets refined the resulting commitments.

Once the final revisions were locked in, the system operator implemented the schedules as closely as possible, adjusting them relative to the full network model and the contingencies of real-time operation. Operators in the control room used the imbalance market to buy these adjustments. The setup ensured that each market improved on the other and created increasingly accurate schedules for the moment of dispatch. The wholesale markets were competitive because buyers only profited in the retail markets if they found cheaper wholesale rates than they were charging on the retail level. This made them price responsive. Suppliers were competing because there a variety of sellers could serve any particular market. The resulting schedules therefore reflected an approximate solution to the least-cost-dispatch problem: the cheapest generators sold the most output, then the second cheapest, and so on until all demand was served.

The arbitrage business of the power marketers made sure that the solution transcended any individual scheduling coordinator market and converged on a global solution because they found price differences between marketplaces, locations, and time points. By arbitrage, the price differences disappeared and pushed the market to a global solution. This way, the interactions of the three groups of market participants generated schedules that the system operator could use and that tended to solve the unit commitment problem. High prices indicated places that required new generation; congestion indicated places that needed new transmission investments. As real time approached, the other markets made sure that the system operator received the resources to fine-tune the resulting schedules at the least cost. The integrated system of submarkets thus fed perfectly into the task of managing the system in real time.

To sum it all up, considering the complexity of the challenge and the many different parts that had to work together, the California electricity system was a gleaming, perfect machine. But, of course, demons were lurking in the wings. After two years, price spikes ushered in the Western energy crisis, and the designers' dreams lay shattered amid the smoldering ruins of the market system.

Paradise Lost

The Archimedean point of electricity market design is the mathematical equivalence between the logic of a perfectly competitive market and the computational techniques used to identify the security-constrained economic dispatch.[17] California's system of interlocking markets and technical systems was organized to approximate the logic of these technical tools in a complex division of labor between markets and the system operator. But the entire division of labor required that buyers, sellers, and power marketers play their preassigned roles. They had to follow particular logics of action in each of the different submarkets. In the financial wholesale markets for energy, buyers needed to search for the cheapest supplier given their anticipated needs. Suppliers needed to offer at marginal costs based on their anticipated production capacity. Depending on how likely their resources were to be needed, this meant either offering the energy outright or, if they were unlikely to be part of the optimal dispatch, offering the capacity to the ancillary markets. Both buyers and sellers needed to determine the opportunity costs for their transactions, relying on calculations of alternative trades that they might substitute for the missed business in the forward markets. Power marketers had to look for price differences between scheduling coordinators and geographic locations in the simplified grid. Suppliers needed to determine whether they might profit from investing into new generation capacity and how to allocate funds for the maintenance of their existing generation fleet.

Each of these calculations had to take particular information as input and follow a preordained rationale. Most importantly, the market actors needed to frame their decisions in terms of the simplified representation of the physical electricity system. When they traded in the financial markets, the buyers and sellers were supposed to consider power flows only to the extent that they showed up in the simplified representation of the grid. Similarly, the forward market traded generic products. Accordingly, sellers had to ignore operational differences between generators when they bid in the financial markets. The actors needed to think about the electricity system in the simplified ways the designers had decided to represent it in the software.

The designers' central task was to create the incentives for this behavior and then to ensure that it was easy to follow the intended path—and exceedingly difficult not to. This is where things became problematic. Though the actors followed the right course of action for a while, small glitches started to occur practically as soon as the markets opened. Seemingly irrational behavior proliferated, prices began to jump randomly, and lower-quality products garnered higher prices than higher-quality products. Initially, these problems seemed to be minor—just random bugs in the software, uninformed traders, mistakes, and nothing more.

A set of fascinating files from the early days of California's markets captures the work of the Power Exchange's compliance division.[18] They contain a transcript of a conversation between Enron traders and the CAISO's compliance division in May 1999. Karen, the compliance officer, has noticed that Enron has submitted an impossible schedule for power flows over a small line called Silver Peak. She calls to figure out why they would do something like that. As soon as the trader realizes who Karen is, he redirects her to his superiors, Tim Belden and Jeff Miller. Confused, Karen asks who she is talking to. After they tell her, the conversation proceeds like this:

> KAREN: Oh OK. Um, yeah. I had a question regarding one of your schedules over Silver Peak that's through the PX.
> TIM: Um-hm.
> JEFF: Yes.
> KAREN: Are you familiar with which one I'm—is the one for 2900 megawatts?
> JEFF: Yes, ma'am.
> KAREN: The—the path is only 15 megawatts.
> JEFF: Say 15?
> KAREN: Yeah.
> JEFF: Uh-hm.
> KAREN: And I was wondering if that was a—an error—for—to schedule 2900 megawatt over a 15-megawatt path. . . . Is that what you wanted to do?
> TIM: Yeah, that's what we did. And, so, we'll put it through the adjustment bidding process and—and see what happens.
> KAREN: Can I ask why?
> TIM: Um, there is a—there—we just, um—we did it because we wanted to do it. And I do not mean to be coy.

The conversation continues on like this, and Karen soon stops to inquire what prompted the traders to submit an obviously impossible schedule to CAISO. In fact, she eventually apologizes for checking in—she just wanted to make sure that there was no error. Today, we know that the Silver Peak incident was an early prototype for a strategy that Enron's traders developed so they would be paid to relieve artificial congestion.

The conversation reveals two important facts about how California's markets worked in practice. First, the compliance division was not at all prepared for traders who tried to play games. Perplexed, Karen says, "I mean it's like putting 29—2900 megawatts on a zero-rated path. I mean, it's kind of pointless. I am not sure. . . . What your intention is here." And Belden replies cheekily, "Well—if you are sitting at our chair, there was actually, um, some things happened this morning that caused us to—to do that." Despite these rather dissatisfying explanations, she gives up on probing the incident and simply logs the trade in. It was only weeks later that the compliance division began to investigate the incident, recovered the transcript, and tried to close the loophole.

The conversation also reveals how traders proceeded. They relied on trial and error to search for loopholes and then just experimented until profits occurred. While the Silver Peak incident derailed the dispatch schedule substantially, it did not generate revenue for Enron. Yet it became one of the foundations for the games they played all throughout the crisis. This is how we have to imagine the sellers: sitting in offices, pouring over the tariffs that determined how the market system operated, trying to gain an edge in any way possible.

Of course, the designers had expected problems with trader behavior because the market system was new and they had built it under considerable time pressure. Not even three years had elapsed between the technical work in 1995 and the market opening in 1998. The designers simply hoped that they would be able to iteratively push the markets toward perfection. Some even declared that attempts to game the market were part of an evolutionary process that helped to improve markets over time. During a congressional hearing about the prevalence of gaming in California, the economist and consultant Charles Cicchetti defended the power marketers along these lines. With substantial rhetorical heft, he drew the following parallel between gaming and training: "General MacArthur recognized that the nation is better off because kids compete when he said, 'On the fields of friendly strife are sown the seeds that on other days and other fields will bear the fruits of victory.' Modern game theory brings this verve and reality into economics and finance."[19] In other words, he viewed companies' efforts to game the system as a kind of training exercise for market designers—though one might be hard pressed to explain what kind of war these exercises would be preparation for.

As 1998 progressed into 1999, the issues with California's markets began to accumulate. The operators were spending more and more time correcting misalignments between markets and the system management. High prices distorted the markets and led to inefficient dispatch schedules. Shortly before the crisis started, toward the end of 1999, the CAISO management finally recognized that a fundamental redesign would be necessary. For every rule change proposed by the market monitoring units, new problems popped up somewhere else—one step forward, two steps back. But before the team could do anything, their efforts were overtaken by events, and they moved from reform to crisis management.

Before we can understand why the design was so susceptible to gaming, why Belden could get away with cagey answers, and why these games could proliferate to practically all sellers in the system, we have to understand what the players were doing exactly. We have to take stock of their bag of tricks. I will outline how the manipulative behavior worked, why it was profitable, and how it affected the relationship between markets and system management. Once we understand how the sellers derailed the system, we can begin to search for the design features that gave rise to these problems.

Market Power

The simplest and most serious way to derail the market mechanism was the exercise of *market power*—the designers' nemesis. Not only was it relatively easy to exercise when you had it but it had extremely complex and unfortunate effects on the identification of the economic dispatch. Even small amounts of market power could introduce deviations from the intended market logic, and these rippled across the system as a whole, moving the markets into misalignment with the rest of the system.

According to the economic definition of the term, a company gains market power if it can profitably alter the market price away from the competitive level.[20] This happens when the company does not face competition and consumers are willing to pay inflated prices.[21] In electricity systems, market power emerges from the interplay between the existing generation and load. Since electricity cannot be stored efficiently (yet), production must meet all demand the moment it arises. As the aggregate demand in the system increases, more and more of the available generators will be in operation. As soon as there are very few or no substitutes to meet the residual demand in the system, generators no longer face competition. Since the system as a whole can collapse if these "pivotal" suppliers do not contribute their generation assets, the resulting market power is substantial. The markets become less and less competitive, the closer the demand approaches to the industry's capacity limit.[22]

For two reasons, this market power is also extremely fluid. First, it does not depend on the size of the generator. On a hot summer afternoon when the system operator needs 97 percent of all generators running to meet demand, even a firm that owns less than 6 percent of capacity can exercise almost unlimited market power.[23] This means that the ability to exercise market power can be widely diffused through the industry—it does not fall on just a few large corporations. Second, the ability to exercise market power depends on conditions that can change quickly; the ratio of supply to demand is in constant flux.

The presence of limited transmission capacity complicates things further. In a system where certain geographic areas are connected via limited transmission lines, congestion can fragment the market and cut these areas off from competitors. Once a load pocket emerges, the number of possible competitors can shrink and endow the remaining companies with market power. Congestion patterns can change within minutes. Accordingly, a company can quickly move from having absolute market power to having none.

Companies employed two strategies to exercise market power. If they were uncertain whether some of their assets would be necessary to meet aggregate demand, they could simply shut down some of their plants to increase the likelihood that other plants would become pivotal. Since the in-state fossil fuel plants were old, there was always some reason to shut them down.[24] As one interviewee summarized the logic: "There were companies who said, 'I have three generators; if I take two down and I just let one on, I will make it ten times more money than if I keep them all three.'"[25]

The alternative strategy was economic withholding. If the sellers were sure that their capacity was necessary to meet load, they simply submitted an inflated bid curve to the Power Exchange and CAISO markets. If their plant was selected to provide output, it drove up the market clearing price because the California markets paid all sellers that price. This created windfall profits for anyone else in the queue. Even if the generator with the inflated curve was not selected, the substitution of a different generator increased the market clearing price. As a member of the market monitoring unit put it in an interview, "A part of your portfolio drives up prices, and the rest of your portfolio enjoys these wonderful high prices."[26]

The presence of market power was bad news for market designers because it came with a variety of problematic incentives. Generator shutdowns exaggerated an already-existing shortage and increased the risk of system failure. But the resulting price inflation in the markets had additional consequences. At high price levels, it became rational for all companies in the system to run the engines of generators far above their efficient output levels. Of course, this would lead to engine breakdowns later on. But such breakdowns were more than repaid by inflated prices. In addition, diminished supply could become the source of *more* market power for companies. Once a generator was truly necessary to keep the system running, it had the system operator over a barrel. Accordingly, destroying assets became rational because it increased the power asymmetry. At the very least, it created a perverse incentive for the timing of legitimate maintenance shutdowns. Periods of low demand now constituted the only time it was reasonable to schedule such shutdowns. Even before the restructuring, utilities had chosen these low-demand times, usually during the spring and winter months. But before the restructuring, they used to coordinate these shutdowns so that the maintenance work was spread over many days and weeks. This way, they ensured that there would be sufficient backup generation in case of unexpected events. Now, it is not clear to what extent power producers coordinated shutdowns to hold the market hostage. However, even if they did not directly coordinate shutdowns, the market signals were the same for everyone; accordingly, multiple shutdowns occurred at the same time even without explicit coordination. This led, once again, to incentives for the exercise of market power at the expense of system reliability.[27] Market power thus derailed the traditional coordination of maintenance shutdowns and created incentives to destroy the system's material infrastructure by operating it above safety margins.[28]

But this was not all. The exercise of market power could have substantial ripple effects. If an inefficient generator replaced a more efficient one, the power flows in the entire system could change. This would require additional adjustments that moved the system further away from the optimal allocation. Because all elements of the electricity system hang together, even small shifts away from the optimal dispatch order can feed on one another and move the system further and further away from equilibrium outcomes.[29]

Market power also undermined the sequential logic of California's forward markets. As outlined before, these markets were designed to improve on one another. In each market, buyers and sellers had to act on their best guesses about future production and consumption. Subsequent markets would then refine the schedules according to new information. The specter of market power disrupted this logic of sequential improvements because it drove all trading activities into the real-time markets. These markets were not designed to handle a lot of traffic—they were meant to procure less than 5 percent adjustment capacity. In addition, they operated close to dispatch, which left little room to correct errors.[30] This concatenation of market activities occurred because the presence of market power reconfigured the incentives in the forward markets.

As soon as market power started to affect the prices in the forward markets, buyers would try to relocate their demand into later markets. For example, by underreporting the anticipated demand in the day-ahead market, utilities would lower the aggregate demand in that market. This would depress the market clearing price at the intersection of supply and demand. But the utilities and retail service providers could not actually lower their demand. It depended on their customers' consumption. Accordingly, they had to buy the remaining energy in the system operator's imbalance markets. The desperate attempt to avoid being the victim of market power effectively pushed the buyers into the real-time markets.[31]

Yet this turned out to be a dead end. In the real-time markets, the exercise of market power was practically unlimited. The system operator acted as the only buyer in the imbalance markets and bought whatever was necessary to keep the system running; the markets were characterized by near-complete demand inelasticity. The operators had therefore practically no way to defend themselves against high prices; if a generator was necessary to meet demand, they would sell their energy regardless of what they charged CAISO.[32] As soon as the imbalance markets were affected by market power, the incentives in the system operator's markets for ancillary services shifted too. Offering ancillary services was an alternative to offering energy outright. Price increases in one market translated into price increases in the other.[33] Since not all generators in a system qualify to offer ancillary services, the number of potential suppliers was smaller to begin with, and they were even more vulnerable to market power than the imbalance markets.[34]

In that way, the exercise of market power derailed the market mechanism as well as the interrelation between the different markets, pitched the market system against the reliable operation of that system, and metastasized through the system wherever it entered. The first question for a structural explanation of California's energy crisis will therefore be why the design produced conditions under which sellers gained market power. But this is not all: two other types of manipulative behavior contributed to the crisis. Both of these enabled and reinforced the exercise of market power, but they also had their own problematic effects on the operation of the electricity system.

Arbitrage Games

The first set of games was designed to exploit illegal arbitrage opportunities.[35] Whenever the price differed between market locations or time points, power marketers had an incentive to trade on it. They bought cheap energy at one location or time and then sold it for a profit at another. As outlined before, these kinds of trades were allowed because of price discovery and market liquidity. If traders competed to execute arbitrage trades, those trades would tend to equalize price differences. By giving markets "thickness," the power marketers ensured that all conceivable obligations could be traded at a competitive price—even when such trades were "speculative," or based on uncertainty about future prices.[36] In a setting with many different marketplaces, the activities of arbitrage traders enabled the convergence of prices and thus the convergence of the dispatch solutions produced by the different marketplaces.

One potential arbitrage opportunity existed between the markets at CAISO and the forward markets of the Power Exchange. When prices differed between these markets, it would have been profitable to trade on them. However, these kinds of arbitrage trades were usually prohibited. The system operator used its markets to balance the grid in real time. For technical reasons, the operators could only buy energy from sellers who controlled their generators directly and could provide a variety of technical information if prompted. Power marketers typically did not control the resources they traded and did not have the necessary technical information. Accordingly, they were usually barred from entry into these markets. If prices differed between the financial and the physical markets, they had strong incentives to circumvent these rules.

The first strategy involved fraudulent export schedules.[37] CAISO allowed importers of energy to participate in the real-time markets as long as they could specify where the resources were sourced and what transmission interface they would use to deliver the output. Because energy from outside California was managed by other balancing authorities, the system operator did not require the immediate sellers to have physical control over the resources. The other balancing authorities, which were mostly composed of vertically integrated monopolies, would ensure that the schedules were met exactly as specified.

Power marketers used this rule to circumvent the limitations on their access to the imbalance markets. They found ways to launder energy from California to make it look as if it came from outside California. The trick was simple: they would first buy energy in California (either bilateral or in the Power Exchange) and then schedule this energy for export to another party outside California. This party sold the power right back to the power marketer for a small "parking fee." Since it now seemed as if the energy were coming from outside California, the power marketer could sell the energy as an "import" to the system operator and circumvent the control requirements of the tariff.

To obfuscate the movement of energy further, additional transaction partners could be added to the chain before the marketer would "import" the energy into California. One of Enron's presentation slides, titled "Real Time's Best Month EVER," summarized the strategy concisely: "Prices are sky high in Mid C, power is tight; we are buying from all over California through the PX market. Snohomish acts as Mid C sink and resells us energy for $10 more. We wheel it back to CAISO and collect our big fat check."[38] In the Enron memos, this strategy was referred to as "Ricochet" because the energy would bump around the (fictional) network model before "returning" to California.

Of course, the strategy moved no real energy. It was purely a financial fiction created to sell energy in the system operator markets without controlling the actual generation assets. During the "100 days of evidence," the California parties produced internal communications from the power marketers that aptly described the scheme like this: "They are stealing CAISO's lunch and selling it back to them."[39] (See fig. 3.3 for an illustration. The green lines indicate the import/export trades.)

A variation of this game allowed power marketers to sell ancillary services they did not possess—effectively a form of short sale. The trader would simply bid to sell fictional ancillary service capacity from resources outside the system operator's control area. Again, they would declare them as imports from other balancing areas, which resolved the need to specify the technical characteristics of the asset. If the power marketer was called on to provide these resources, the company would quickly procure them in a bilateral transaction.

Since ancillary services were usually requested to run in emergency situations with little time to spare, and since the power marketers did not actually have the necessary capacity, these sales could create real problems for grid management. If the seller could not find the missing capacity, it might simply disappear from the markets. The power marketers risked only a fine, but the system as a whole could collapse.

Another strategy along the same lines was referred to as "Fat Boy."[40] This scheme allowed power marketers to enter the real-time markets via fraudulent load schedules—false statements about anticipated demand. The sellers would pose as buyers in a scheduling coordinator's market and create some fictional load. They would use their generation to meet that load. In the real-time market, CAISO would recognize that some of the load was fictional and that the schedule was no longer balanced. The extra generation would count as "positive uninstructed imbalance." In other words, there would be unused extra generation on the scheduling coordinator's balance sheet. If there was insufficient generation to meet load in the imbalance

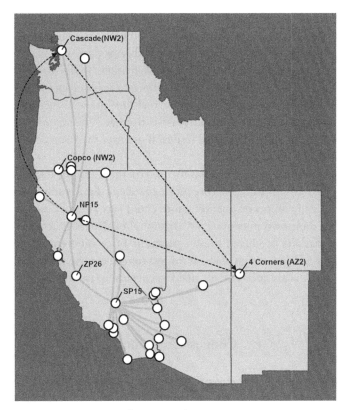

FIGURE 3.3. Illustration of Import-Export Game

markets, the system operator would use the extra energy to meet it, thus allowing the power marketer to passively sell in the imbalance market. The unused generation would be sold at the level of the real-time energy. In other words, by creating fictional demand in the forward markets, the power marketer could smuggle their production resources into the imbalance market.[41] Of course, this exacerbated the coordination requirements that CAISO had to perform. Rebalancing the schedules shortly before dispatch drained the slack out of the system and increased the risk of errors.

In sum, the first set of games constituted a form of illegal arbitrage trading. In each case, the power marketers found ways to circumvent restrictions on access to system operators' real-time markets. These strategies usually involved steps that obscured the origin of the resources they sold and that falsified bidding portfolios. Each strategy fed on incentives to arbitrage price differences between parts of the market that were supposed to be separate. Apart from the problems they created for operators in the control room, these strategies also interacted with the exercise of market power. As outlined in the previous section, this exercise of power concentrated all trading activities into the real-time market. To the extent that demand drained from the forward markets, the market clearing price of those markets could lie substantially below the real-time price. This created price differences that heightened incentives for arbitrage.[42] By entering the real-time markets via illegal arbitrage trades, the power marketers could exercise market power.

While research on the crisis has focused on the Enron strategies, which became the basis for FERC's prosecution of sellers, there is ample evidence that practically all power marketers invented variations of the arbitrage games for their own purposes.[43] A structural explanation needs to show why the markets produced these systematic price differences and what parts of the market design enabled traders to obscure their schedules. Before turning to this question, we need to cover one last form of manipulative behavior.

Congestion Games

The last set of games aimed to profit from incentives to relieve congestion in the transmission system. The California system also had a set of implicit markets for transmission capacity. They were designed to include the presence of scarce capacity in the pricing mechanism. Recall that "congestion" is a fiction that is used to point out problems in a planned dispatch schedule. All real flows of energy are instantaneous. If a given dispatch schedule is flawed because it would lead to overheated lines, it needs to be changed. Some generators need to reduce their planned production, and other generators have to step theirs up. The market for transmission capacity was supposed to find the most important adjustments ahead of time by pricing transmission on paths that were often congested.

The Power Exchange used a simplified network model with three zones and twenty-six scheduling points to represent the transmission network. If schedules produced in the forward markets created congestion in the network model, the system operator would use adjustment bids to determine who would get the greatest benefit from using the congested interfaces. This would help find the most cost-effective way to organize the necessary redispatch. The system thus generated incentives to back off generators that would make less money selling outputs to one location than another.

The situation changed when there was congestion that was not represented in the market's network model. In real time, the system operator used a full network model to see if the schedules could be implemented. If residual intrazonal congestion had not been resolved by the market process, CAISO would use the adjustment bids to pay for necessary last-minute changes. The costs of these adjustments were socialized. If generators were unable to fulfill their obligations because of "unpredictable" congestion, they might then be paid to back off.

Now, whenever it was possible to predict intrazonal congestion ahead of time, sellers had an incentive to make trades that profited from it. This encouraged them to either create intrazonal congestion or exacerbate it by selling energy on lines that were already congested. These incentives were detrimental to the market mechanism because they led sellers to make trades that compromised the efficiency of the aggregate dispatch, increasing the work for the system operator and generating payments to relieve congestion that would have been avoidable. Since such trades constituted violations of the market mechanism, the tariff generally prohibited them.

One strategy to profit from artificial congestion was the infamous "DEC game."[44] In the forward market, traders in two separate companies would schedule a trade between two locations in the same zone. This trade would far exceed the capacity limits of the line that connected the locations. But since the transaction took place within the same zone, the market for transmission capacity would not reflect this congestion. From the perspective of the simplified network model, it looked as if the trade had taken place at the same location. Accordingly, the trade was accepted, scheduled, and submitted to the system operator. In real time, the system operator would try to implement the schedules. Since it used the full network model, it recognized that the trade could not be executed. To deal with such real-time fluctuations, the system operator would buy "decrements" from the trader, paying the generator to decrease its output and relieve the congestion.

The price for the decrement was established via adjustment bids that specified how much the lost opportunity was worth to the trader. Conveniently, the DEC player had submitted very high adjustment bids and now reaped a massive windfall for *not* delivering energy—energy they could not have delivered in the first place. Since the system operator only had a couple of minutes to resolve the problem before dispatch, this game put strain on the reliability of the grid. The profits depended on the fact that the forward markets were supposed to be the best approximation of the real-time market. As soon as traders figured out how to get paid for their ability to predict or create congestion, they derailed the market mechanism (and system reliability), broke the precarious connection of mutual improvement between the two markets, and made a massive profit.[45]

The second game type, called Death Star, revolved around a similar flaw. Death Star comprised a variety of games with names such as Forney's Perpetual Loop, Red Congo, and NCPA Cong Catcher. Each relied on specific agreements with other market participants. The names indicated, with thinly veiled code names, which company served as counterparty.[46] The Enron memos described the point of these games succinctly: "The net effect of these transactions is that Enron gets paid for moving energy to relieve congestion without actually moving energy or relieving any congestion."[47] The game took advantage of the fact that power flows moving in opposite directions cancel each other out. Accordingly, certain decisions to produce energy can free up transmission capacity and render the overall usage of the grid more efficient. The transmission markets were designed to encourage such trades and reward traders who offered counterflows on congested pathways. The game took advantage of this incentive without actually moving energy.

CAISO only controlled parts of California's grid and was tied into the Western Interconnection. It therefore saw only those power flows on its network and optimized the use of the grid (as much as it was allowed to) within the boundaries of its jurisdiction. Of course, real-power flows move on all available paths. How exactly power flows interact therefore depends on the system as a whole, not just the part that CAISO managed. This made it possible to create schedules for energy flows that appeared to provide counterflows but in fact canceled the others out entirely. No energy would flow, but it would look as if the company were providing a counterflow.

The game would begin when traders could confidently predict congestion somewhere in the California network. For example, they could often tell when Path 15, the main line that connected Northern and Southern California, was congested. They would then schedule a counterflow in the opposite direction, which would generate capacity payments for relieving congestion. From the system operator's perspective, they had provided an important service and increased the available transmission capacity. At the northern delivery point, the company would then move the power outside of California, perhaps to Oregon or Washington. From there, they would send the power back south and then to the initial scheduling point in California. The complete schedule was therefore circular.[48]

Such circular schedules do not actually lead to power flows; they simply cancel each other out. But the incomplete market for transmission rights did not reflect this fact. It only reflected half of the complete schedule, so the company could reap payments for providing transmission capacity when they produced no energy at all. (See fig. 3.4 for an illustration. The solid black arrow indicates the congestion on Path 15, while the dotted black

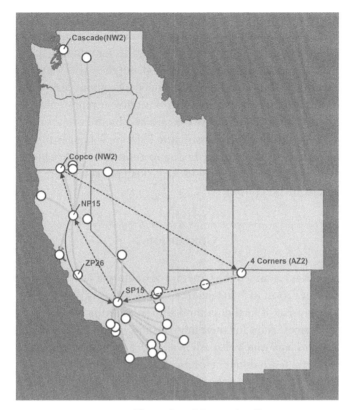

FIGURE 3.4. Illustration of Congestion Game

arrows indicate the direction of the circular energy flows; the light gray lines refer to connections between zones and scheduling points.) From the perspective of California's grid, these movements look like south–north counterflow trades. From the perspective of the system as a whole, they are circular trades that cancel each other out.

The game used the physical reality of power flows in the whole network to provide fictional counterflows to CAISO. It turned the physical reality against its representation in the software. There were other versions of these games, such as load shift, which was a corresponding strategy to create fake congestion in the day-ahead and hour-ahead markets. A trader needed two trades: one to serve load in the northern zone and one to serve load in the southern zone. These loads would be overscheduled—the amount of energy served at each location would be far in excess of the real demand. The trader could then increase the fictional load at one location to increase congestion and also increase the load at the other location to provide a fictional counterflow. Or it could reduce the fictional load, shifting it from north to south or vice versa to reduce congestion. Since the load at both locations was fictitious, they could move it around arbitrarily, depending on the best way to increase congestion and then reap rewards for relieving it.[49]

Further variations on this strategy existed, but the basic point should be clear: power marketers could use their knowledge about real power flows in the overall system to profit from their insufficient representation in the market model. These games were exacerbated by the exercise of market power. Changes in the dispatch structure led to new congestion patterns, and these new patterns led to further opportunities for congestion games. Conversely, congestion games could create load pockets where generators could exercise market power.

Conclusion

This chapter has examined the structure of California's energy markets between 1998 and 2001. Rich in technical details as it may be, the chapter has ignored a universe of further complications: additional markets for contingency services, rules for their interactions, subtle differences in operating protocols, and much else. All in all, more than fifteen different products could be traded at different locations and for different times. The tariffs that guided the operation of the markets were several hundred pages long, and the internal rules for selecting one resource over another resulted from complex negotiations. A surfeit of administrative procedures allowed stakeholders, designers, and managers to alter the rules of the market and determine the future direction of the system. While the view of the system has therefore remained fragmentary, I have reconstructed the core pieces of the architecture to explain how the system met the short-term and long-term goals. Each of the many different markets contributed to the larger search algorithm and set incentives for actors to do their part.

In a second step, I reconstructed three types of behavior that violated the market mechanism. The discussion revealed how thoroughly and quickly these behaviors could pit the market system against the reliable operation of the grid. When market power emerged, the incentives shifted almost completely, and actors were richly rewarded for decisions that exacerbated existing supply shortages, destroyed the material foundation of the system, and derailed the search algorithm from its path toward a good solution to the dispatch problem. Similarly, congestion and arbitrage games undermined the routines the operators used to manage the power flows on the grid. Now that we have a good sense of the ways in which the system broke down, it is time to explore the parts of the underlying market design that produced these problems. This will reveal how the California energy system violated the balance of strategies to simplify, bound, and control the market. It will also reveal the ways in which we can understand the crisis as a failure by design.

CHAPTER FOUR

A Structural Explanation
of the Energy Crisis

The archives are full of little instances that do not conform to the two narratives about the crisis. But as time polishes these stories down to their essential core, inconvenient details tend to disappear. Take the work of California's monitoring units as an example. Soon after the markets opened in 1998, they chanced upon an early version of the Ricochet game. They promptly interviewed traders at Enron's West Desk about their findings. Contrary to what one might expect, the traders were quite forthcoming and confessed the calculation behind these "experiments" freely. The design teams at the Power Exchange took note and quietly changed the rules to close the loophole.[1] But there were no special sanctions, no criminal proceedings, no disgorgements of profits.

This was no isolated event either. Between 1998 and 2000, the monitoring units identified and fixed dozens of problems like this. Terry Winter, the CEO of CAISO, made a statement to Congress: "With regard to the gaming of the type described in the Enron memos, the ISO consistently has monitored for such activities and, when appropriate, we have taken action."[2] As is well documented by dozens of FERC filings, there can be no doubt that he was right: the monitoring units kept finding and closing loopholes throughout the system's existence.

Neither of the two narratives can really deal with this fact. It does not square with the story about economic fundamentals because it proves that sellers were constantly engaged in a determined search for loopholes. But it also does not sit well with the idea of corporate raiders who descend on unsuspecting Californians. Not only do we encounter institutions that are far less blindsided by savvy traders than the story presumes but we also see Enron's traders cooperating with the market monitoring team when prompted to explain themselves.[3] Of course, the episode does not outright contradict the narratives either. It just does not fit well into their rhetorical setup. Over time, it has therefore all but dropped out of sight. But once we view the crisis as a case of market design failure, the work of the monitoring units gains new significance.

At the heart of the of market was an ongoing struggle to adjust the system to ever new forms of destructive behavior. Whatever the design flaws were, they transcended any individual game or manipulative strategy. Each time the designers patched a hole, another opened up. Each time monitors identified one source of market power, another opportunity arose elsewhere. For a structural explanation of the energy crisis, it is therefore not enough to identify the origins of specific games and manipulations. We must also understand why the architecture kept giving rise to new forms of destructive behavior and why the monitors could not get them under control.

This is the goal of the present chapter.[4] I begin by quickly clearing the deck of alternative explanations. Next, I identify those elements of the market design that created incentives for market power, arbitrage, and congestion games. That is, I identify the parts of the system that made it attractive for sellers to deviate from the intended logic of action in destructive ways. Though the resulting list will doubtlessly appear somewhat eclectic, the different items express problems of differential simplification: efforts to simplify the market along one dimension increased behavioral complexity along another dimension. Within the resulting space of action, market players gained incentives to deviate from the intended behavior.

If the actors had not also encountered opportunities to act on these incentives, things might have worked out after all. In particular, designers could have isolated the different markets to prevent considerations from one market context affecting others. But as I show in a third step, the designers had adopted porous boundaries between key parts of the system. This created room for traders to circumvent even the solid boundaries that designers erected elsewhere.

In a fourth step, I show that the existing control structure could not compensate for this problem. It was highly fragmented, blind, and toothless. I then deal with a counterfactual that is central to my theoretical framework. It is an important question whether *any* control structure could have dealt with the system that the designers put into place. If a capable control structure could have compensated for the problems of simplification and porous boundaries, California's ultimate issue might simply have been a lack of oversight. I argue that this was not the case. Even a highly capable control structure would have been unable to apply standardized tools to assess the legitimacy of problematic trades. The work at the market monitoring units was always going to be futile: with the setup the designers had created, manipulative strategies would have kept emerging, undermining the reliable operation of the grid. Incomplete simplification and porous boundaries pushed the system beyond the point where mere control could have saved the day. The system in California thus violated the formal scope condition for successful market design identified in the second chapter. Designers have to limit the systems' complexity to a level where an oversight structure can still apply formal criteria to evaluate potentially hazardous transactions. In California, they failed to do so.

At this point, we are left with a new question: Why would designers adopt features that violated the guiding principles behind market design so deeply? Why did they put into place structures that directly contradicted the imperative to simplify and bound the market to minimize control requirements? These questions direct our attention to the design process and its protagonists. But before we can go there, we first have to understand why the California markets failed. As always, the first step is to show why existing explanations do not get us there already.

Puzzles and Complications: Evaluating Existing Explanations

To the extent that the literature has focused on the design of California's markets, it usually identifies three design flaws: the lack of forward contracts, the must-buy requirement, and the retail-price freeze.[5] Regulators designed the first two policies to increase the liquidity in the new markets. By forcing the utilities to procure most of their energy in the spot markets of the Power Exchange, they wanted to encourage many sellers to congregate in these markets and thus promote a competitive landscape. But, so the argument, for three reasons it would have been better to allow utilities to procure most of their energy via long-term forward contracts outside the Power Exchange.

First, the utilities would then have been less vulnerable to price swings in the Power Exchange's spot markets. Most of their energy would have been delivered at fixed rates, and only peak demand would be covered through the spot markets. The supply shortages during the crisis would therefore not have affected their bottom line as much. Second, with more demand safely covered by long-term contracts, it would have been less likely that any one generator would become a supplier of last resort in the Power Exchange. That is, the literature suggests that the Power Exchange auctions would have been competitive even at a lower level of demand and that market power had more to do with the system's capacity constraints. Third, if suppliers had sold their energy via forward contracts, they would have lost incentives to raise market prices in the short term. Forward contracts are hedges for buyers. Any increase in spot prices relative to the established forward price will therefore cause losses to sellers. To the extent that the majority of a generator's supply portfolio is committed in advance, incentives to exercise market power disappear in the short term.[6] In that way, forward contracts reduce both the opportunities and the incentives for the exercise of market power in spot markets. Without the must-buy requirement and the corresponding restrictions on forward contracts, according to the argument, utilities would have covered most of their demand via forward contracts. This would have made them less vulnerable to high prices in the spot markets, and the spot markets themselves would have seen lower prices as well.[7]

A similar argument isolates the retail-price freeze as an important design flaw. The freeze made it impossible for utilities to pass the true costs of energy on to their retail customers. They had to carry the burden of the high prices without being able to adjust their demand because they had an obligation to serve—they were not allowed to curtail the delivery of energy to end users. At the same time, retail customers had no reason to change their consumption because they received their energy from the utilities at fixed-rate contracts. This demand inelasticity meant that sellers could raise the prices almost arbitrarily when they had market power.[8]

The law that established the retail freeze also introduced a mandatory 10 percent rate reduction. This meant that most consumers had no reason to switch from California's three utilities to an alternative supplier. The utilities therefore continued to serve most of the demand in California, concentrating the financial risk of market power on three entities. Their vulnerability to market power could quickly have systemic effects.

I do not want to dispute that the three design features are important in relation to the proximate causes of the crisis. They essentially explain why California's utilities were vulnerable to the exercise of market power and could do little in response to this problem. But the arguments do not take a structural point of view and do suffer from hindsight bias.

First, even if utilities had been allowed to buy long-term forward contracts, they also would have needed to know that energy prices would go through the roof beforehand. Just because forward contracts are available does not mean that companies will buy them. As hedges, these contracts are effectively bets on the future, and during the time of restructuring, there was strong evidence that wholesale prices would go down rather than up. In fact, this was one of the initial reasons California embarked on restructuring. Utilities had signed long-term contracts under unfavorable conditions throughout the 1970s.[9] These contracts drove up the rates in the 1990s, triggered calls for restructuring, and taught California's utilities to avoid long-term contracts at all costs. Accordingly, the utilities had good reasons to stay away from forward contracts. From a structural perspective, the mere availability of forward contracts does not solve the market power problem.

A rarely recognized fact highlights the importance of this insight. The literature often cites the California Public Utility Commission's restriction on forward contracting to explain why the utilities were exposed to the price risks. This restriction applied to bilateral contracts outside the main auction markets. But in July 1999, the Power Exchange introduced so-called block forward contracts. These gave utilities an opportunity to hedge some of their price risks inside the Power Exchange. Despite the must-buy requirement, they could now buy contracts for the delivery of energy up to twelve months in advance.[10] The commission also restricted the number of contracts the utilities could buy here. Each utility was limited to one-third of its historical minimum hourly load by month or to a combined capacity of 1,600 MW per month. After protests by Pacific Gas and Edison, these limits were scaled up to 5,600 MW. Even though 5,600 MW constituted a minor share of the utilities' combined average demand on any given day, they did not use the forward contracts to this level. In 1999, the highest trading volume occurred in September and amounted to a total of 3,175 MW. In 2000, July was the month with the highest trading activity: only 4,850 MW were sold. In other words, at no point did the utilities utilize even the limited amount of forward contracting they had access to.[11] Before the crisis, when cheap contracts were available, the utilities did not use them. And why should they have? When the markets started, wholesale energy prices were low, and the expectation of excess capacity suggested that they would stay that way. The sense that a more robust forward market could have prevented the crisis is therefore an anachronism.

The argument about the retail-price freeze suffers from a similar flaw. It is easy to see that the law stifled the development of California's retail markets. But while sound, this argument overstates the demand response that could have been expected from a more competitive retail market. The economic argument is that market power diminishes in the face of elastic demand. But the argument is generic. It does not consider that decision-making itself has a cost. For truly elastic retail demand, individual consumers would have to monitor the prices in the wholesale markets and redirect their consumption toward periods of lower prices. Not only is this a time-consuming bother—as the lukewarm customer reaction to the introduction of retail markets for electricity shows—but the consumption of electricity is also tied to the rhythm of the workday. Most people do not have the choice to wait to do their laundry until the early afternoon because they are at work at that time. Even today, as machines are increasingly taking over the adjustment of consumption, the demand in retail markets is not particularly elastic. Experiences in other regions support this conclusion. When Texas restructured its electricity markets in 1999, it made demand response a prime policy objective and introduced competitive retail markets to that end. Despite the absence of a retail-price freeze and incentives for distributers to improve metering, consumers did not take the opportunity to respond to wholesale prices.[12]

The retail-price freeze, the must-buy requirements, and the lack of forward contracts explain well why the utilities became highly vulnerable to market power in the spot markets in 2000–2001. But these arguments do not point to structural reasons why sellers could exercise market power in the first place. Moreover, none of the three factors explain why new games could constantly pop up throughout the existence of these markets. But if not these three factors, what are the decisive design flaws from the perspective of the system's architecture? In what follows, I go through each of the three problems—market power, illegal arbitrage, and congestion games— and identify structural features that created the incentives and opportunities for such behaviors.

Differential Simplification and Market Power

During the period from 1998 to 2001, companies gained market power whenever the system was pushed close to the capacity limit. At that point, their capacity became crucial to keep the system running. They no longer faced competition and could drive up the market clearing price easily.[13] With the problem stated in this way, the solution is obvious: the only sure way to prevent the emergence of market power is to provide ample reserve capacity. Consumers can still not be expected to react to price changes in wholesale markets quickly. Accordingly, it is necessary to generate competition for each part of the demand curve. At all locations in California, at all times, there had to be multiple sellers competing to serve the last bit of outstanding demand. The presence of highly inelastic demand required excess generation.

Consider these excess generators in analogy to Marx's Lumpenproletariat—unemployed workers who allow capitalists to hold down the wages. Similarly, electricity markets require unemployed generators to reduce the bargaining power of those who end up selling. Such excess generators pose a threat that forces sellers to keep their price low. But just as the Lumpenproletariat needs to be fed by the state, California needed to find a way to pay for these excess generators. More specifically, the designers needed to create incentives for sellers to build and maintain these generators. Because of the long lag times between the decision to invest and the moment a new generator comes online, these incentives had to exist perceptibly several years before the new generators were needed.

Even though the creation of California's markets led to an uptick in applications for new capacity, the system did not create these incentives.[14] To the contrary: the market mechanism kept the prices below the average operating costs of existing generators and thus undermined the maintenance and provision of excess capacity over time.

The designers had not created special markets for long-term investments, and the California Energy Commission (CEC) had gotten rid of the old regulatory instrument that it used to plan the system's evolution: the biennial resource plan update.[15] Instead, the designers wanted to fold the provision of long-term investments into the short-term markets for energy. In such energy-only markets, the short-term market thus has to perform two functions at once: identify an approximate solution to the economic dispatch in the short run and send price signals to encourage the creation of new generation capacity in the long run. Because the Power Exchange represented more than 80 percent of the market in California, the designers would have needed to set the relevant incentives here. Unfortunately, they only optimized the market structure to encourage the correct short-run decisions. That turned out to be the central design flaw.

To understand this argument, we have to look a bit more closely at how these auctions operated. If companies wanted to sell energy in the Power Exchange, they had to submit supply curves for each hour of the next day or the same day. For example, a generator might bid to sell 10 MW/h for forty dollars, 20 MW/h for fifty dollars, and 30 MW/h for sixty dollars at 11:00 a.m. the next day. There was a clear design reason for forcing everyone to submit their bids in this way: it simplified a complicated calculation. Competition fundamentally requires that goods be comparable. But electricity generators differ substantially from one another, and forward markets can operate against a variety of temporal horizons. Market designers wanted the markets to find the approximate solution for dispatch at specific intervals. Since everyone had to figure out how to express their bid in the same format and for the same hour of delivery, bids from generators with different operating characteristics became commensurable. But while simplification thus helped to align and enable the desired calculative behavior in the short run, it depressed incentives for long-term investments.

To understand the problem, assume for a second that California's system had *not* been at the capacity limit yet. We are imagining a system with multiple generators that might serve the last piece of the demand curve. The Power Exchange auctions incentivized generators to bid as low as they possibly could to sell as much of their output as possible. The least expensive generator required to meet the last MW/h of demand set the price for the market as a whole. What would such a generator bid? To make a profit, sellers had to express both their fixed and their operating costs in the different quantity-price pairings of their supply curve. That is, they had to figure out how to formulate their bid for a single hour in such a way that it would actually cover their expenses in the short *and* long run. In an ideal market, they would bid their cost of production, including a part of the fixed costs to represent the initial investment. However, reality fell short of the ideal when there was excess capacity in the system. Any generator would usually prefer to sell something rather than nothing. At the edge of the demand curve, such a generator would be worried that they might not be selected. They would then bid only their marginal operating costs—just enough to survive in the short term. Accordingly, generators' fixed costs would no longer be reflected in the bid.[16] At the edge of the supply curve, they would effectively operate at a loss relative to the initial investment costs to set up the plant.

This was the heart of the problem. The short-run market depressed the price below the level where sellers could sustain the existing excess capacity. With the fear of selling nothing, the market price falls to a level well below the average cost of producing electricity. This had two consequences: while excess capacity existed, the market did not produce prices that compensated the sellers for maintaining this excess. During this time, the prices therefore did not create incentives for investments in new capacity either.

What did this problem have to do with the temporal logic of the market? Constraining the market to an individual hour of operation meant that only the generation necessary in that hour of operation would be priced. The temporal horizon of the market regulated what counted as useful and what did not. From the perspective of a given hour of real-time operation, generation capacity represented waste if it was not needed to operate the system. Accordingly, an efficient market would not pay the owners of this superfluous generation. Though the excess capacity was a crucial precondition for the market mechanism to work as required, it was not reflected in the highly constrained time slice that the market represented. As long as the horizon of the market was an individual hour of operation and excess capacity already existed, the market also did nothing to encourage the construction of new generators.[17]

However, as we have seen, the presence of excess capacity was the crucial requirement to keep market power at bay. As soon as companies gained market power, they had no reason to follow the calculative logic that would produce the economic dispatch. The absence of incentives for the provision of excess capacity thus meant that the market would undermine the conditions required to keep it functional. The emergence of market power was then just a matter of time—regardless of forward contracts, must-buy requirements, and frozen retail rates. Without additional markets for long-term investments or an administrative mechanism like the biennial resource plan update, the fixed temporal horizons of the forward markets were a crucial design flaw. As of today, this problem has reasserted itself over and over again, leading to a return of the state in electricity system planning because markets consistently cannot produce the right incentives for the long-term expansion of the system.[18]

This is only the first part of the problem, though. Even in an energy-only market, there are incentives to invest in future generation at various points. The argument in defense of such markets goes like this: as long as there are incentives to build new generation at some point, there will usually be an excess because new generators almost always produce capacity beyond the anticipated level of demand. As demand grows, this excess will gradually be fed into the market, allowing the investors to recoup their costs. Even without an explicit pricing mechanism for excess capacity, a pure-energy market can therefore inspire new generation and stay ahead of growing demand. But the argument has several practical flaws.

First of all, it requires that a seller perceive the incentives to construct new generation in the short-term markets. But if a single seller can see that new generation will be necessary in the future, all sellers perceive these incentives at the same time. If they all act on these incentives, a boom in investments would occur. Because any real excess resulting from these investments would not be priced, most of these new generators would go bankrupt. Indeed, electricity markets often follow such boom-and-bust cycles. Not only is this wasteful but the bust phases also threaten the reliability of the grid.

Second, the argument requires a precarious dynamic that hinges on the temporal structure of the market. Companies would have to receive very high prices during a few hours of operation to provide generators that operated at the margin of the supply curve. If an expensive generator operated only a few hours a year, it would have to reap astronomical sums during those hours to make up the complete cost.[19] Of course, such price spikes can and do occur because demand is inelastic. Such spikes also immediately pull investors into the markets. If this dynamic unfolded, no special provision for excess capacity would be necessary. Formally correct, the argument ignores that regulators do not accept price spikes for very long.

The risk of regulatory intervention thus eviscerates incentives to build generators that rely on such spikes. Further, the required price spikes are almost completely indistinguishable from market power. They only occur when the system is close to the capacity limits. At that point, the competitive fringe has disappeared, and pivotal generators are beginning to exercise market power.[20] Absent a system to differentiate between legitimately high prices and market power, the market mechanism turns against the logic of system operation.

But even if designers allowed price spikes to occur and accepted boom-and-bust cycles as well as occasional blackouts, the investments would lag behind because it would be difficult for market actors to predict price spikes far enough in advance to start building new generation in time. To invest, companies would need to be sure that prices would go up when the plants came online a year or more in the future. For several reasons, this is difficult. If other companies make the same prediction, the investor might well end up with capacity that will not be recompensed by the market.[21] To avoid this risk, the investors would need to predict their precise location in the system operator's supply stack years ahead for specific hours of operation. This is practically impossible. The highly constrained temporal horizon of the market makes it exceedingly risky to venture such predictions. Not knowing what others would do, how exactly demand would develop, and when the capacity would come online turns such investments into a risky bet.

Of course, as soon as price spikes begin, it is obvious that new generators are necessary. But at that time, it is too late to act on the incentives. Market power has already turned the market against the reliable operation of the system, and attempts to build new generators would come too late to rescue the incentive structure. Thus, the slow expansion of the system could not be sustained by markets that only price the resources needed in specific hours of real-time operation.

In sum, two basic design flaws produced incentives for the exercise of market power. The first flaw was an absence. There was no market mechanism or regulatory requirement to protect excess generation capacity or ensure its construction. In a dynamic that is reminiscent of Polanyi's argument in the *Great Transformation*, the markets could not sustain their own foundations.[22] They did not generate payments to sustain the generation necessary to keep the system competitive. The second flaw was the simplified temporal structure of the financial markets. That structure made it both risky and difficult to express the long-term considerations about new investments in these markets.[23] There were therefore no clear signals for needed long-term investments even when incentives did exist. By the time it became obvious to human actors that new generation would become profitable, it was too late to construct it. The system necessarily led to shortages, which prompted actors to exercise market power. At this point, all incentives shifted against designers' plans, and the market activities moved into tension with the reliable management of the grid. Without provisions for long-term planning, California's system progressively undermined the stock of excess generation to a point where the markets no longer worked as intended. In that way, the system actively undermined the preconditions for its own operation.

This points to a more general problem. Designers made the interfaces of the auction markets as simple as possible because they wanted to minimize actors' ability to deviate from the intended logic. Rules and procedures restricted the range of possible actions considerably, fixed the context of choice, and standardized the perception of the future to a specific hour of system operation. But by doing this, the designers effectively excluded considerations that were crucial to the health of the system. Because long-term planning could not be reflected easily in the short-term markets, it became more difficult and riskier. The limited representation of the system's physical reality made things easier along one dimension but more complicated along another. As I go through the other games, this will become a recurring pattern. Simplification on one level causes escalating complexity on another, thus undermining the incentives for desirable behavior. I will now turn to the design flaws that produced the incentives for illegal arbitrage trades.

Illegal Arbitrage and the Simplification of Commodities

Illegal arbitrage trades took advantage of price differences between the financial markets and the different physical markets of the system operator. These were games with colorful names like Ricochet that drew considerable attention during the litigation of the crisis because they show Enron's traders at their most ingenious and corrupt. All of them enabled sellers to circumvent access rules that separated the financial and physical markets. To understand the structural reasons for the incentives that prompted these games, we first have to understand why the designers imposed access restrictions at all. Economic theory would not expect such restrictions between forward markets for the same products. The imbalance markets effectively settled the trades in the financial markets. That is, they determined the ultimate price of energy against which all other contracts were settled. All market action in prior markets therefore oriented itself toward this final horizon. Economic theory would therefore expect these forward and spot markets to be linked and consistent. Indeed, arbitrage trades should not be problematic but highly desirable because they would close price gaps between the different time points and thus improve the convergence of the markets. So why did designers impose access restrictions?

Again, we encounter a problem of simplification, albeit a somewhat more complex one. Financial markets must be liquid and competitive to function as intended. Many sellers must compete for many buyers relative to a standardized product that can change hands easily. When the market is illiquid because relatively few companies sell a given product, market designers can improve the situation by broadening the product definition. Sellers of similar commodities can then trade in the same market because their products have become nominally identical. For precisely this reason, California's financial markets abstracted from the vast, technical differences between generators and traded highly simplified products called firm and nonfirm energy. To make trading even easier, the Power Exchange auctions did not require sellers to make their bids resource specific. As long as traders stuck with the distinction between firm and nonfirm energy, they could offer energy from portfolios that contained a variety of different resources or even sell energy that they did not possess yet.[24] Once again, designers used simplification to bring the market process in line with their theoretical model and to simultaneously make the market process more manageable. They could define the products in this simplified way because the financial markets dealt only with obligations for future production and consumption. After CAISO received the resulting schedules, there was still enough time to align the commitments with technical reality. Operators could usually swap one resource for another or correct dispatch instructions if there was a problem. In other words, the forward markets could abstract from the technical details of the grid because CAISO would eventually intervene and align the financial with the physical reality.

However, for this reason CAISO could very much *not* abstract from the physical details of the generators that provided energy to its internal markets. The operators in the control room had to know where a given resource was located and what its technical characteristics were to ensure that it would harmonize with the other generators in the system. Most importantly, the operators needed to be able to give binding instructions to different generators in short periods of time. Accordingly, the sellers in these markets needed direct control over the generation assets. Short sales or portfolio bids were incompatible with the need to adjust the real outputs from generators quickly. Resources that provided ancillary services had to meet even higher control requirements.[25]

Yet, because the imbalance markets settled the financial markets, the markets had to harmonize with each other on the level of software. Obligations from the forward markets were supposed to progressively move into the next-closest market until they were matched against the real-time dispatch of energy. To allow this successive movement, the products had to appear to be equivalent from a financial point of view. The definition of the commodity needed to be the same in both places, even though the commodities were different from a technical point of view. The products in the Power Exchange were financial obligations that participants traded according to principles of financial markets. At CAISO, the same products stood for resources that could be used to solve technical adjustment tasks. Nonetheless, the designers could not reflect these differences in the definition of the commodity. To feed the results from the financial into the imbalance and ancillary markets, the products had to be identical.

Because they could not reflect the difference on the level of the product definition, the designers decided to restrict access around the CAISO markets. If only sellers with direct control over generation assets could act in these markets, it did not matter what the product was called—it would automatically fulfill the more sophisticated requirements. Isolating the two markets thus enabled designers to simplify the financial markets, feed the results into the spot markets, and still allow CAISO to operate with a more restrictive definition of the relevant products. The access rules effectively protected an effort to simplify different market settings to different degrees. They ensured that each sphere could operate on the basis of its own social and technical logic—a prime example of bounding.

The next question, then, is why the traders had a reason to circumvent these access restrictions. The imbalance markets settled the contracts from the financial markets against the real-time deviations of energy flows. They represented the horizon against which all other markets operated. In an efficient commodity market, all contracts—forward and spot—for the delivery of goods at the same time and location will, on average, transact at the same price even in the absence of arbitrage. In theory, price changes will simply reflect random changes in the information that becomes available between forward and spot markets. The deviation will have a distribution with a mean of zero.[26] If the two sides of the system had converged on the same price in this way, there would have been no incentives to circumvent the access restrictions because there would not have been systematic price differences.

But the markets displayed large and consistent price differences over time. As economic research has shown, these differences occurred regularly and predictably enough to be captured by traders who adopted simple

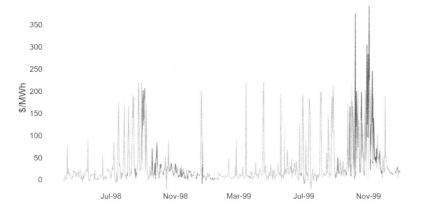

FIGURE 4.1. Max. Daily Price Differences Day-Ahead / Imbalance Market in 1998

trading rules.[27] Potential profits were enormous. (See fig. 4.1, which plots the maximal price differences between the two day-ahead and the imbalance markets in 1998—the first year of operation.) Differences occurred frequently and were substantial. On many days during the summer, they could exceed $200. With enough traded energy, they could turn into a gold mine for sellers.

These differences started to widen substantially in the summer of 2000 when companies began to exercise market power in the Power Exchange. In response, utilities tried to flee into the imbalance market, where price caps protected them. As outlined in the last chapter, the difference in the price ceilings distorted the differences between forward and real-time markets substantially, breaking their intended interrelation. But while the divergent price caps and market power are important reasons for these price differences during the crisis, they do not explain all of them. In fact, the price differences between the two markets were substantial even before the crisis. They were a constant companion practically from the moment the system began operation in April 1998.

The early price differences had mechanical sources. The scheduling coordinators and the system operator used different protocols to determine winning bids, set the prices, and clear the market. These divergences created artificial price differences that had nothing to do with the value of electricity or the balance of supply and demand. They simply went back to the way that the markets determined prices. Because these problems are subtle, I am going to choose a few illustrative examples to drive home the general point. In each case, price differences go back to divergences in how CAISO and the Power Exchange determined the order of dispatch—which generators would provide energy in what order.

At the Power Exchange, market participants' offers and bids were aggregated into separate supply and demand curves for a given hour. Cheap offers went to the bottom, and more expensive ones rose. The auction software then computed the market clearing price at the intersection of the supply and the demand functions. In a word, the Power Exchange used a simple rule to relate supply to demand and optimized on price-quantity pairings.

The CAISO imbalance markets worked differently. After receiving offers from generators, the market software constructed a so-called balancing energy and ex post energy (BEEP) bid stack—an ordered list of resources. The stack combined ancillary services and imbalance energy into a single list that operators could draw on. As in the day-ahead market, the stack represented the supply curve and stacked offers from cheap to expensive. But the clearing price for resources from this list was computed every ten minutes, relative to the demand the system operator had to meet. In other words, operators did not simply accept the proposed order in the BEEP stack but drew on the resources selectively. For example, they often skipped over low-cost energy bids if they wanted to retain them as ancillary services.[28] They also accepted more expensive bids when transmission capacity from the cheaper generator was scarce. In other words, while the Power Exchange simply intersected two curves that software had dynamically generated, CAISO used much more complex criteria to relate supply to demand. This meant that the imbalance energy price might suddenly rise in relation to the price in the Power Exchange as operators skipped lower-cost bids.

Partly, these differences resulted from operating protocols. The Power Exchange had a simpler procedure than the CAISO operators to determine the order in which supply was selected. Some of the differences also related to informal practices. For example, one source of price differences had to do with the way the interfaces in the control room displayed the resources from the BEEP stack. Generators could submit decremental and incremental bids for the real-time markets. The incremental bid was to supply an additional MW/h output should the clearing price be equal to or above the bid. The decremental bid was to reduce the output should the price be equal to or above the clearing price. Now, depending on the situation of supply, the use of generators may have been more cost effective if some generators increased their outputs while others decreased theirs. A price difference between the clearing price for increments and decrements would indicate as much. But the operators did not perform such delicate balancing operations systematically. Instead, they used the incremental bids when there was an undersupply and the decremental bids when there was an oversupply. Operators introduced a certain level of inefficiency into the combination of resources—at least from the perspective of the financial markets—and this pushed up the price in comparison to the Power Exchange, where the software simply calculated the ideal combination.[29]

So far, I have shown how differences in the protocols at the Power Exchange and the system operator created price differences. But other differences resulted from the relationships among the Power Exchange, the other scheduling coordinators, and the system operator. Because the electricity system is one integrated network, CAISO needed to optimize the global balance of inputs. However, not all generators sold their energy at the Power Exchange. The system operator therefore received trading results from different scheduling coordinators. If these different schedules did not add up to a globally consistent result, CAISO might have wanted to optimize *across* these schedules. Yet it was barred from doing so. A so-called equality requirement forced CAISO to make all adjustments within the portfolios of scheduling coordinators rather than the system as a whole. It might have been impossible to implement a more efficient solution at a lower cost. If the arbitrage traders did not resolve inconsistencies between the two sides of the system, the system operator could not impose the solution centrally. Naturally, inconsistencies between the different schedules could therefore produce price differences with respect to the imbalance markets.[30]

While I could describe even more reasons for mechanical price differences, the underlying problem was always the same. Because the markets played different roles for the management of the electricity system, the commodities and trading rules represented aspects of the electricity system differently in the different markets. In each submarket, designers simplified the definition of the market as much as possible to streamline trading and align actors' calculative behavior. Each market was optimized to create incentives for a specific type of calculation and make it easy to execute this calculation. Each therefore employed slightly different rules, definitions, and interfaces excluding or including different aspects of the underlying physical system.

However, these operational differences translated into *price differences* and thus encouraged traders to link the different contexts and stop following the logic of action that each individual market required. Paradoxically, the differential simplification therefore had the opposite effect from the one intended. While efforts to simplify submarkets made it easier to follow the desired logic of action in each individual market, the set of possible behavior steadily grew with respect to the system as a whole. The resulting inconsistencies generated price differences, which in turn created incentives to link formally independent parts of the system. It became reasonable for companies to consider their local actions in relation to all other markets.

Though the analysis has admittedly been rather complicated, the general takeaway is relatively straightforward. Designers aim to create a globally consistent set of rules and procedures. A core technique to achieve this consistency is simplification—it limits the ways in which actors can interpret the context of choice and the moves they can make within that context. But when differential or incomplete simplification produces markets that operate differently for seemingly identical products, problems start to emerge. Systematic price differences derail the assumption of independence between parts of the system. Suddenly, the different sets of rules begin to interact in ways that no one anticipated. The complex permutations of additional behavioral options also create incentives for behavior that violates the blueprint.

Congestion Games: Simplifying Power Flows

Congestion games are the last type of behavior that derailed the markets. Sellers of energy used a variety of strategies to create fictional congestion. Traders could profit from these strategies by taking payments to resolve the congestion with further, purely financial transactions or by partitioning the market and exercising market power in the resulting load pockets. Though the execution of these games required the most sophisticated tricks and chained transactions, they go back to the same basic design flaw we discovered behind the arbitrage games: differential simplification.

Since energy flows on all available paths, it could create congestion anywhere on the grid. A schedule that looked feasible in the simplified three-zone model of the financial markets could therefore turn out to be infeasible in terms of the real network. Whenever there was congestion that was not reflected in the simplified model of the three zones, the system operator paid generators to change their schedules and socialized the costs of these adjustments. The system worked well as long as the actors confined their calculations to the zonal model of the financial market. If they reacted only to the congestion that occurred between the three simplified zones and scheduling points, the software produced the best approximation to the ideal dispatch. The intrazonal congestion management then fixed all discrepancies and compensated everyone.

However, the discrepancy between the real system and its fictional representation created incentives to find or create congestion that was not represented in the financial market and then trade on it. Because the financial markets assumed that all predictable congestion was represented in the zonal model, actors could profit from predicting congestion that was not reflected in the financial markets. Of course, the best way to do this was to create such congestion oneself. Actors did so most easily by fabricating infeasible schedules and then taking payments to correct them. In other words, it was relatively easy to identify sources of congestion that were reflected in the intrazonal congestion management system but not in the interzonal system that the financial markets used. By exploiting this gap, the sellers figured out how to link the two markets and derail the internal logic of each.

Yet again, we encounter differential simplifications as the heart of the problem. Rather than choosing an integrated structure in which physical complexity is represented homogenously, designers adopted market structures that dealt with the system at different levels of detail. Since the divergent simplifications created incentives to leverage one market mechanism against the other, the designers would have needed to place boundaries that could have isolated the markets. Just as the access rules for the imbalance markets were supposed to keep speculative trades out of the CAISO markets, the congestion management software limited traders' inputs for schedule adjustment bids to the three zones. And just as in the case of the access rules, the provision was insufficient to bound sellers to the local context. With a good understanding of the design flaws the prompted the incentives for deviant behavior, the next question is what provided the opportunities to act on these incentives.

Porous Boundaries Create Opportunities

When sellers played illegal arbitrage games, they circumvented rules that kept different parts of the architecture separate. To create fake congestion, sellers first needed to over- and then understate production before stringing together fictional transactions. Doing so violated tariff rules to represent energy schedules truthfully. The sellers could violate these rules because the boundaries between the markets and their environment were porous and poorly enforced. There were two particularly weak spots.

First, traders could move energy in the larger Western Interconnection, but the system operator only controlled the parts of the grid inside California. Once they reimported the energy, its origin was no longer clear in the financial schedules. This was the foundation for arbitrage games like Ricochet or Death Star. By moving the energy out of California and back inside, the sellers could obscure its origin and create fictional power flows that were not visible to the system operator. When energy came from outside California, the system operator assumed that it belonged to one of the regulated utilities in the Western Interconnection. It neither could nor did verify the origin of these resources. Accordingly, sellers could use the Western Interconnection to circumvent the access restrictions in the imbalance markets.

The boundaries between California's markets and the Western Interconnection were so weak as to be imperceptible. In Enron's recruitment materials, for instance, the two are frequently represented as coextensive.[31]

The second problem was that participants could play multiple roles in the market. In particular, any company could become a scheduling coordinator. To apply, they merely had to prove that they could fulfill hardware and software requirements to interface with the CAISO databases, that they had a legal right to represent their clients, and that they had the necessary credit rating to act as an intermediary.[32] Power marketers could therefore easily become scheduling coordinators and effectively evade any direct control over their transactions.[33] For example, they could submit "balanced schedules" that overstated or understated the true demand or supply because no one verified scheduling coordinators' submissions. As scheduling coordinators, market players could effectively fake any formal requirement that CAISO imposed on the results of the financial markets. The rules for scheduling coordinators effectively put the foxes in charge of the keys to the hen house.

Another version of the same problem was companies' ability to play on multiple sides of the market via corporate restructuring. Holding companies organized multiple branches of business under the same corporate entity. For example, the three utilities had so-called unregulated affiliates that could play the markets as wholesale sellers. A legal firewall separated these companies from the utilities—they were not allowed to share information, offices, or employees. But they were still tied to the larger corporation via a holding company that acted as a parent to both. The utility could therefore easily funnel profits into the affiliate via the parent and vice versa. Because market designers assumed unified actors, these structures distorted incentives on both sides of the market. For example, the affiliate could enjoy the benefits from the exercise of market power, while the utility could enjoy the profits from the fixed rates in the retail markets when the wholesale prices were low. As long as there was no real crisis, the utilities' position was always hedged—they profited from low prices just as much as from high prices.[34] This is another reason that a market for forward contracts would not have helped much. The ability to play both sides acted as a more profitable hedge for the utilities than the genuine article would have as long as no crisis seriously undermined their ability to recover the cost from their consumers.

In sum, market participants could broach the boundary between California's markets and the Western Interconnection because of CAISO's limited jurisdiction, and they could violate boundaries between different roles in the market because it was easy to become a scheduling coordinator. These two flaws rendered all other boundaries ineffective. In the previous chapter I described how restrictive the system became close to dispatch. Bids had to meet tight input restrictions and underwent multiple feasibility tests. But if the technical information could be falsified, these tests were largely meaningless. Here, the chain was just as strong as its weakest link: with a few gaps in the boundaries, the rest could be circumvented easily.

A Weak Control Structure

Today, electricity markets are among the most closely observed and controlled markets in existence. With California's complex set of inconsistencies and porous boundaries, one might expect that the designers would have put into place an extremely capable oversight structure. But there was no effort to compensate for these weaknesses. California's control structure was woefully inadequate for even moderate oversight.

FERC was responsible for California's wholesale markets.[35] When the markets opened, FERC had no clear goals for market oversight, no means to oversee the markets in real time, and no effective means to intervene. The agency derived its jurisdiction from the 1935 Federal Power Act, which imposed on FERC the responsibility to ensure "just and reasonable" electricity rates.[36] FERC assumed that market prices were just and reasonable if they reflected what would be charged by a competitive market, defined as a market that does not suffer from market power. As we know, energy systems can produce substantial levels of market power in a matter of seconds. In principle, FERC could therefore have justified extensive oversight and control.

But the agency did not employ a definition of market power that took the dynamics of energy markets into account. Instead, it relied on static concentration measures to determine whether a company might have market power. If a company could prove that it would not hold too much of a market share in a predefined geographic market, FERC gave it the right to charge market-based rates. Apart from checking quarterly self-reports, the agency assumed that the firm was structurally unable to exercise market power and made no effort to monitor the markets on an ongoing basis.[37]

The Power Exchange and CAISO each had two market monitoring units. An internal unit conducted day-to-day monitoring, and an external unit staffed with academics provided independent analyses and advice. They were the beating heart of California's oversight regime, but they derived their jurisdiction from FERC. Because FERC considered the market power issue resolved, it neither provided them with strong enforcement powers nor specified monitoring objectives. This was true not just for the exercise of market power but for anomalous market behavior in general. None of the tariffs that governed the markets even contained the term *manipulation*.[38] The monitoring units therefore acted primarily as information-gathering entities that were tied into the slow, ponderous, and weak enforcement processes at FERC.

For example, at the Power Exchange the market monitoring unit was a subdepartment of the compliance unit.[39] Initially, there were only two market monitors. In August 1999, the CEO added four additional positions. If either of the two monitors discovered anomalous behavior, they would first alert the vice president of the compliance unit. The vice president then decided whether the problem required further investigation. If so, it would be conducted by an economist and a mathematician in the economic analysis unit, which would analyze the bid data to establish whether a violation might have occurred (an inquiry).[40] If something was amiss, they asked the accused party to react to the charge and potentially interviewed them. This, finally, opened a formal investigation. After analyzing the results of the interview as well as any other evidence, the compliance unit recommended to the CEO whether the matter should be pursued further. After holding a hearing on the allegations, the CEO determined whether a violation had been proved. If one had, the CEO still needed to go to FERC, open a proceeding there, and ask the agency to impose sanctions. This would, again, lead to comments and reactions to comments, with FERC eventually approving a settlement, revoking market-based authority, or disgorging profits. The process could take upward of a year. This encouraged early settlements, which tended to be at a fraction of the profits generated by the illegal activities.

At CAISO, the situation was not much different. There was an internal market monitoring unit and an external market surveillance committee. Their primary task was to watch out for market inefficiency, gaming, and the exercise of market power. In contrast to the Power Exchange, CAISO's committee closely cooperated with the internal unit and conducted original analyses on the basis of primary data. CAISO's external board consisted of economists from California's universities who were closer to the markets than were the members of the Power Exchange's external board. However, just like the Power Exchange, they had no authority to sanction or penalize rule violations directly. All sanctions had to be approved by FERC.[41]

Another weakness was institutional fragmentation. Though the four monitoring units cooperated, they did so slowly, their negotiations fraught with tension and information restrictions. The Power Exchange and other scheduling coordinators had information only about their own market transactions. When the system operator collected and integrated this information, the operators had no means to verify its integrity. There were also very few reporting requirements for companies. Only FERC had the authority to oversee the entire market, and it did not have an independent monitoring unit until 2001.[42] There was not even a specific employee in charge of systematically evaluating the quarterly trading data they collected from market participants.[43] In sum, then, the control structure was weak, fragmented, and underprepared to react to any manipulative behavior.

The Limits of Control

In light of the toothless control structure, we might wonder if the crisis was not simply a regulatory failure. Could the designers have compensated for the problems of differential simplification and porous boundaries with a strong control structure? The answer is no, and that brings us back to the beginning of this chapter.

Designers need to create a system of rules and procedures in which market participants find it intuitive and beneficial to follow the calculations laid out for them. As we have seen, participants act on incentives they encounter anywhere in the system—if it is beneficial and possible, they will have no compunctions about breaking the boundary between elements of the market architecture and linking different contexts of action. The designers must therefore create a set of rules and procedures that are globally consistent with the required incentives and actors' understanding. As chapter 2 has argued, perfect consistency is impossible, and ongoing oversight is necessary.

But there are limits to the number of inconsistencies that designers can compensate for. The range of possible behavior in the market may not exceed what a control structure can assess on the basis of formal criteria. The argument is straightforward but rather abstract. Recall that we use markets because private information is present in the system—buyers and sellers know best what price to buy and sell energy for. The center does not have this information. It does not know whether a generator really should offer its output for fifteen or twenty dollars per megawatt-hour at hour ten of day two. The center merely knows what kind of calculation will produce this substantive result, not what the result is in each case. To know whether a transaction conforms to the required logic, the center can therefore only apply formal criteria. These must be derived from the rules that govern the market and define desirable behavior. Consider the ideal case: if actors have only one way to follow the rules and this leads to the desired calculation, the control structure merely needs to check whether the transaction conforms to the rules.

However, inconsistencies between rules escalate the range of legitimate behavior in the market: actors can combine rules in ways that no one intended and thus act in unprecedented ways. As the space of possible behavior increases, the market becomes more complex. But the greater the space of possible behavior defined by the rules, the looser the connection between formal criteria and the substantively correct behavior. The behavior may conform to the bidding rules but manifest a different calculation. The control structure will therefore need to bring in more substantive criteria to evaluate the transaction.

For example, to identify whether a company is exercising market power, California's monitors would have needed to develop a sense for the bid that the generator should have submitted. Because excess capacity might only run for a few hours a year, a very high bid, in and of itself, did not convey any information about the legitimacy of the transaction. The greater the space of possible behavior, the vaguer the guidance provided by formal criteria. Of course, in some markets it may not be necessary to evaluate each transaction to meet designers' objectives. Oversight regimes might work with bright-line tests where it is enough for transactions to fall within a particular range of acceptable values. But even then, the control structure needs to establish substantive criteria for which range is acceptable relative to the designers' objectives and whether a violation is necessarily the result of illegitimate behavior.

I will give another example to show that this was not just a practical but also a logical problem. Recall the principle behind congestion games. Traders would use financial transactions to create artificial congestion and then get paid to relieve it. To execute this game, they had to schedule energy trades that overwhelmed transmission lines within one of California's zones. These trades did not conform to the designers' plans. Legitimate trades would have reflected an effort to provide the cheapest offer to meet some demand. In contrast, illegitimate trades were deliberate attempts to manipulate the intrazonal congestion management system.

Now, consider what a control structure would have needed to know to distinguish these two motivations. Formally, both kinds of trades looked the same—they were bids to sell a quantity of power at a particular location from a particular resource. To identify the intention to congest, the system operator would have needed to know whether the trade could be executed at all. Sometimes, this was just a matter of checking some formal requirement. As the Silver Peak incident shows, it was easy to see that a thousand megawatt-hours could not travel over a line with a carrying capacity of fifteen kilowatts. Here, monitors could employ a formal criterion to identify the problem.

However, most trades did not obviously violate any specific transmission limit. Power does not simply flow from A to B but interacts with all other putative power flows. Two seemingly innocuous transactions could easily interact to produce congestion in a different part of the system. The feasibility of the transaction therefore depended on how the trade fit into the optimal dispatch structure of all energy, relative to the available transmission capacity on the grid. The legitimacy of the transaction could only be decided by its relation to the ideal dispatch structure for the system as a whole. But the market was supposed to identify this ideal dispatch structure in the first place—and the market was potentially affected by the game. The control structure would have needed the information that the market was supposed to produce in the first place. The monitor only could have identified the problem trade if they knew the right trade. This poses two problems.

First, this information was constitutionally not available to the control structure. The very point of the market was that individual consumers and producers know best when and what to produce. These are the crucial inputs to the search for the optimal dispatch. Second, the control structure would effectively have to become a centralized planner. Even if the required information had been available, the required control mechanisms would have defeated the very point of using a market. If the control structure already knows what each generator and consumer needs to do, why not let the control structure run the system? It seems that the market becomes superfluous when the control structure can only ensure its functioning by knowing what results it should produce. Indeed, the market would appear much more cumbersome than centralized control because all decisions would have to be validated and checked for their intent to realize illegitimate profits. In that way, then, there is a distinct limit on the inconsistencies that a designer market can practically and logically compensate for with a control structure. In sum, incomplete simplification and porous boundaries thus escalated the complexity of possible behavior beyond a point where control would have been possible. Either way, California had nothing that came even close to a powerful control structure. The system violated the balance between the three imperatives completely.

Conclusion

Electricity markets must reflect the requirements of grid management. Inherently technical considerations must be translated into market mechanisms. But this is not always possible—there are breaks between the logic of electricity markets and the logic of grid management. While engineers seek to create systems that are safe, market designers seek to create systems that are efficient. Engineers try to plan for all possible ways in which a system can fail and put measures in place to deal with these problems. In contrast, markets only price what actors perceive as likely. They tend to optimize the system for the average hour of operation—by reducing excess capacity, minimizing maintenance, and using other techniques. To accommodate engineering concerns in markets, designers must therefore work against the logic of those markets. They must explicitly create mechanisms that incorporate reliability concerns into new markets. If they want redundant capacity, they need to create artificial market demand for it or create administrative structures that pay for this capacity out of market. If they want resilience in the face of unlikely scenarios, they need to create market mechanisms that price these scenarios. Each time they add a task to the market system, the permutations of possible behavior between the different submarkets become greater. The more tasks are trusted to the market, the more complex the resulting architecture and the more potential interactions between markets that designers will need to observe and control.

In California, the designers decided to relegate practically every important decision to the market. This quickly posed problems of escalating complexity as inconsistencies emerged between rules designed to simplify decision-making. If the market had required humans to identify profitable trades across the entire grid, the market would never have converged on the correct solution to the dispatch problem in the available time. Individuals would have had to consider millions of different possible trades at each moment and identify the best one for their position. Accordingly, the designers simplified the market mechanism as much as possible. This made it easier to control incentives and ensure that the cognitive limitations of humans did not overwhelm the search algorithm. Depending on what each market was supposed to do, the designers included different elements of the underlying system.

However, this turned out to be the system's Achilles' heel. Tracing the origin of manipulative behavior, we encountered the same problem over and over again. Efforts to simplify the submarkets created powerful incentives to connect parts of the architecture that were meant to be separate. Market power emerged because the highly streamlined structure of the forward markets made it difficult to reflect long-term decisions in the short-run markets. Arbitrage and congestion games responded to differential representations of the grid's physical complexity in the market. Since all markets and technical systems had to work together to achieve the security-constrained economic dispatch, they were inherently linked. Yet the market design required that actors limit their activities to the information and options represented in each of these subsystems.

The escalating complexity of problematic trades was in no way offset by strong boundaries. Since the actors could play multiple roles in the market and could easily move energy into and outside of California, they had no problems circumventing the rules that governed the auction markets in the center of the system. With strong incentives for problematic behavior and porous boundaries, the requirements for active control steadily escalated. But the oversight structure was toothless. The many flaws I have identified in this chapter pose a simple puzzle: Why did the designers adopt structures that violated the imperative to simplify, bound, and control the system? They were highly qualified experts who spent their days pondering market manipulation, the virtues of simplicity, and the need for control. Yet they somehow created a behemoth of a system with inconsistent protocols, weak boundaries, and a weak oversight structure—a system that could be gamed in dozens of different ways. Why? This question requires us to study the design process, which began in earnest in 1993.

WHY THE DESIGN
PROCESS FAILED

It is now time to shift the analysis to a different register. Even absent the proximate causes that the literature usually emphasizes as the trigger points for the price spikes in April 2000, we have seen that the energy crisis was a disaster waiting to happen. A variety of structural flaws produced social dynamics that not only failed to sustain but actively undermined the markets' foundations. Inconsistent rules and porous boundaries between different pieces of the architecture exacerbated this problem. They produced incentives and opportunities for destructive behavior and simultaneously escalated the complexity of the system beyond a point where even a powerful control structure could have kept problems in check. Yet the existing oversight regime was fragmented and weak. With this diagnosis of the problem, we arrive at the central question of this book: Why did the designers build the system in this way?

This question is much more difficult to answer than it might appear. If the literature has posed this question at all, it has provided three simple explanations. The most parsimonious argument asserts that the designers must simply have been ignorant. The system was so deeply and obviously flawed that only ignorance or incompetence could explain the relevant design decisions.[1] But we already know that this explanation does not get us far. The California system, devised by some of the brightest minds in the country, was an elegant solution to a difficult problem. A second explanation is more compelling but remains underdetermined. Some authors have suggested that the design process failed because the markets were created by committee. Decisions were not based on scientific truth but sprang from negotiations among special interests. The system was therefore always going to be a dysfunctional hodgepodge of political compromises.

Peter Cramton, a well-known market designer at the University of Maryland, summarized this perspective: "Just as one should be hesitant to fly on an airplane designed by a committee of stakeholders, one should be hesitant to trust electricity designs that are built from consensus among interested parties. Like airplanes, electricity designs should be largely the work of experts focused solely on the objectives of the market. The compromise inherent in the design should reflect the optimum balance among competing design objectives, rather than a distributional compromise among those with conflicting interests."[2]

In his comprehensive history of electricity restructuring in the US, Steve Isser echoes this sentiment, writing: "The market design was a 'camel,' a mishmash of concepts driven by compromise between competing interests, based on faulty assumptions and hastily enacted." A camel, he goes on to explain, is "a horse designed by committee."[3]

This explanation undeniably points to an important issue: the role of both formal and informal politics in market design. But the argument considers the problem as a simple matter of politics versus science. If the designers had been free to follow their technical expertise, as the argument indicates, the system would have worked. There are two problems with this way of thinking. First of all, the counterfactual is misleading. Regardless of whether we talk about markets, airplanes, or bridges, engineering decisions are always the expression of compromises among interested parties. No design process is purely technical or purely political. The two sides are always intertwined. In that sense, all complex market designs are "camels"—they are constructed by warring factions of politicians, regulators, experts, and stakeholders who work in organizational settings. Yet some structures deliver the promised results, and others do not. A complete explanation must therefore consider where the boundary between workable and unworkable compromises is located—and it must explore why some political processes heed this boundary and others do not. Politics is unavoidable, so when does it produce workable compromises?

Second, much of the design work in California cannot be classified as political in the formal sense of the term. It took place below the level of formal interest politics. Gary Ackerman, a close observer of the design process and a stakeholder representative, said in an interview, "I would say about 98 percent was the system operator and Power Exchange, and 2 percent was the top-level vision of AB 1890. Legislation never gets into detail."[4] If California's design process was an iceberg, the highly visible, political negotiations were its top, while technical work formed its mass, though it remained largely submerged below that surface of public attention.

This book argues that market design is an organizational activity and that designer markets are organizational forms. Accordingly, we find the market design experts who conducted the technical work in administrative structures that managed the markets. In their work, they dealt with issues that did not rise to the level of political debate—bidding rules, the structure of software interfaces, and details about organizational procedures. Some of the worst design flaws are located on this level. Of course, this kind of work was not devoid of politics. But it was not the brazen interest paddling by outsiders that the camel explanation posits. Rather, the technical work displayed the kind of informal politics that any organizational work would be subject to.[5]

Accordingly, the explanation that the crisis occurred because the markets were designed by committee is undetermined. It overemphasizes the role of political negotiations relative to technical design work and ignores that such design work is always political and always proceeds by committee. The goal has to be to better understand how politics crystallized into organizational arrangements that then developed problems of their own. The foregoing chapters have set the foundation for this kind of explanation: they have identified design decisions that directly violated the imperatives of market design and led to destructive behavior. Such decisions should have been made in line with technical considerations. In the next chapter, I explore why the political process did not heed these technical limits and what social mechanisms led politicians to ignore the technical constraints market designers pointed to and thus move beyond a simple view of science versus politics.

The literature has also offered a third, simple explanation for the design flaws—the elephant in the room. Journalists and energy scholars occasionally argue that Enron and some of the independent power producers conspired to create a system they could easily game. They used their political clout to rig the design process. By turning inherently technical questions into political ones, they could leverage their influential political position to engineer flaws into the market structure. In other words, California's market design was flawed because Enron wanted it to be flawed—not because anyone made a mistake.[6]

While the previous explanation was underdetermined, this one is overdetermined—it assigns too much influence to a single actor. On the one hand, it overestimates Enron's level of foresight. The transcripts of traders' conversations reveal a culture of cynicism and greed, but they also show us people who developed their manipulative games on the fly and by trial and error.[7] If they had known the problems beforehand, the conversations would have looked different, and their approach would have been less experimental.

The conspiracy theory also overestimates Enron's political power relative to other players. The games exploited inconsistencies between rules that constantly evolved between 1993 and 2001. To engineer these games in advance, the company would have needed to mastermind the tariffs of both the Power Exchange and the system operator at a granular level. It is true that the company wielded substantial influence on the legislative and federal level, where its campaign donations had created substantial goodwill.[8] Independent power producers with similar interests were also important players during the political negotiations.

But in regulatory proceedings at the state level and during technical implementation processes, the utilities and industrial users were far more important actors. They were established players, had long-standing connections to politicians, and were important employers in California. Most importantly, the utilities owned the transmission system and most generation assets. They were therefore in charge of implementing the new market system and were responsible for most of the granular design decisions. The utilities had no reason to cede ground to Enron, and they sidelined the power marketers wherever they could.[9] While Enron did have an important influence on the design process, it did not have the power to engineer the games the traders would later play. And power marketers did not create the conditions that would give rise to market power.

The existing explanations—ignorance, design by committee, and corruption—thus leave much to be desired. Indeed, they reinforce the central question of this book: Why did the designers build the California system in a way that so deeply violated the principles of market design?

The next three chapters answer this question. While they build on one another, the analysis will not converge on a single causal factor overriding all others. Monocausal explanations rarely do justice to the messy complexity of the real world. What follows systematically explores the three levels of the organizational field that created the markets: the interorganizational level of political negotiations where restructuring was first conceived; the organizational level where the markets were constructed; and the group level where teams decided specific design elements.[10] Each chapter points to the problems designers faced at different moments during the design process. But the list of problems nonetheless paints a comprehensive picture.

The organizational, political, and cognitive conditions of market design work gradually undermined designers' ability to follow the imperatives to simplify, bound, and control the market. That is, there was a systematic tension between the requirements of their craft and the conditions under which they had to work. These problems were interrelated in complicated ways, but each followed an independent logic. The next three chapters show that the designers' political standing was too weak to set an architectural baseline that they could have managed with the organizational and intellectual tools available to them under the political constraints they faced.

The conditions of design work quickly escalated the complexity of the market design project beyond the point where designers could have contained this complexity with a control structure. From this, I draw insights about the practical and conceptual limits of market design for complex allocation problems. I now turn to the first step of this argument and explore how politics created the flawed baseline for the new system. As so often, it all began with material discontent, interest politics, and backroom deals.

CHAPTER FIVE

Politics, Politics!

During the 1990s, the epistemic object *electricity market* did not yet refer to any tangible reality in the US. It was but a loose configuration of concepts, and the initial design process was little more than a sprawling conversation about these concepts. Because electricity is subject to substantial and highly concentrated material interests, these conversations were deeply imbued with interest politics. In envisioning what an electricity market might be or do, every stakeholder tried to further their own interests. Politicians and regulators searched for a compromise that would work for those whose cooperation was necessary to get the project off the ground.

In these strategic interactions, each party was simultaneously trying to gain a working understanding of the concepts and convince the others that their way of thinking was correct. While it is therefore impossible to understand these negotiations without attention to the power relations, it is just as important to ask why certain arguments and ideas appeared convincing while others did not. Some arguments were deemed technical, while others were related to "fairness" or purely material considerations. Some things were agreed to be unrealistic, while others seemed utterly possible. In other words, the early design process was a potent mixture of rhetoric, expertise, and material interests. In this chapter, I examine the relationship between these factors to explain how California's design process got off to a bad start.

First, I recount the early stage of the design process and outline how the battle between interests could give rise to the basic architecture of the new system.[1] Between 1992 and 1995, this process converged on a compromise that merged two basic visions for the new system into a hybrid. This hybrid proposal worked politically but contained two problematic ideas: the provision that separated the markets and grid management and the provision that the system operator had to treat the schedules from all markets equally. Both provisions violated the core principles of market design and saddled the system with an unnecessarily high level of complexity as well as a few irredeemable inefficiencies. As the next chapters show, this foundation made the subsequent work of implementation much more difficult and forced upon designers an organizational approach that effectively depleted their ability to follow the imperatives of simplification, bounding, and control.

After establishing why the stakeholders thought that the two provisions were a good idea, the chapter zooms in on the moment when the market designers began to contest the proposal. Despite occupying central positions in the design process and leveraging their substantial reputation as academic experts, they failed to convince stakeholders and regulators to give up on the compromise proposal.

To explain why they failed, I analyze the rhetorical moves designers made to convince their audience. Specifically, I trace how they tried to establish themselves as the authoritative experts who should be allowed to define the difference between a technical and a political issue. They did this in a two-step maneuver. First, they tried to frame the debate in terms of their expertise. Then, they used their superior skills of reasoning in terms of this expertise to reveal to audiences that they had a better understanding of the subject matter. But stakeholders and regulators had their own interpretations of central concepts like competition, market, and efficiency. Accordingly, they thought they understood the problems of electricity market design very well. From their perspective, what market designers said simply seemed counterintuitive and wrong—rather than indicative of superior understanding. Ironically, then, the popularity of economic language undermined designers' rhetorical strategies and thus their political authority. The audiences perceived the designers as just another interested party and sidelined them relative to more powerful actors. I now begin by reconstructing the play of interest politics that made the flawed baseline architecture plausible to the different stakeholders.

Political Negotiations and the Memorandum of Understanding

Early in 1992, the California Public Utility Commission asked its planning staff to evaluate the recent history of power company oversight. California's electricity rates were very high, and politicians worried that they might choke the fledgling development of the new computer industries. The commission published the report in 1993. It soon became known as the Yellow Book because it featured a remarkably ugly, bright yellow cover. The report laid bare a number of problems that beset the traditional, regulatory model of ratemaking in California.

Since the 1970s, the state's approach had evolved into a complicated and highly ineffective hybrid structure. While the rates for utilities were still set on the basis of cost-of-service principles, the payments to independent power producers, demand-side management efforts, and the operation of several newer plants followed the standards of performance-based ratemaking. The two paradigms created conflicting incentives because they were based on different ways of remunerating utilities for their investments. The contradictions prompted the creation of exceptions and complicated balancing rules. Over time, a maze of administrative processes developed in the gaps between these two systems.[2] Though no one really understood the rationale behind this byzantine structure anymore, utilities and other power producers managed to navigate it aptly to justify expenses for imprudent construction projects—thus pushing California's electricity rates far above the national average.

The authors of the Yellow Book considered several ways forward, including a proposal to radically restructure the industry. In the next few months of 1992, somewhat surprisingly, the radical option emerged as the most attractive one. There were several reasons. First, legislative efforts on the federal level produced a favorable environment for restructuring. During the 1980s, the commission had liberated the telecommunications and natural gas industries. Largely perceived as successful, these earlier precedents inclined most commissioners favorably toward restructuring.

More importantly, powerful stakeholders endorsed the radical proposal. Independent power producers accounted for about one-third of California's electricity production—more than in any other state. In a system dominated by utilities, these power producers could not easily sell to their customers. To gain unbridled access to the utilities' transmission networks, they formed a powerful coalition in favor of restructuring. To companies like Enron, electricity markets promised to be virgin territory for their role as arbitrageurs and market makers.[3] They lobbied heavily in favor of it, and once restructuring was on the agenda, additional power marketers like Dynegy, Reliant, and Williams joined the efforts.

Industrial users came on board as well. Throughout the 1980s, California had begun to aggressively implement conservation efforts, such as demand-side reduction and higher efficiency standards for new generation facilities. Instead of simply expanding the supply to keep up with demand, California preferred efficiency gains and demand reductions.[4] These measures cut into utilities' profits. Conservation threatened their sales, and they did their best to transfer the costs to industrial consumers, who already faced higher bills than in other states.[5] To the industrial users, restructuring promised an escape because it would enable them to contract with unregulated generators at much lower rates. They effectively wanted to get away from the socialized costs of demand-side management.

Despite these powerful supporters, the utilities would probably have derailed the project had they not been divided. While Edison and San Diego
were wary of structural changes and lobbied to protect their monopolies,
Pacific Gas & Electric quickly moved to support restructuring. In the preceding decade, Pacific had tried to push back on the deregulation of the
natural gas industry and had lost some of its political influence in the process. As one of my interviewees put it, "As [radical restructuring] gained
moment at the commission, we could see that the writing was on the wall."[6]
Accordingly, they tried to get ahead of developments, preferring to shape
rather than oppose restructuring.

With the utilities divided and business interests, power traders, and producers in favor of restructuring, the course was clear. The small group of environmental and consumer protection agencies that were against restructuring could easily be sidelined. Municipalities were granted the right to opt
in or out as they desired. After about a year of lobbying, meaningful pro-
test had been exhausted, and the utility commission decided that California
would become the first state to implement competitive markets for energy.
The outcome of these debates, *Order Instituting Rulemaking and Order Instituting Investigation*, published in 1994, came to be known as the Blue Book.

Apart from sketching a proposal for the new market structure, the Blue
Book opened a regulatory proceeding that would decide how to reform
California's energy system. With it, the market design process started in
earnest. Various stakeholders now had a chance to oppose the proposal,
suggest alternatives, or offer amendments. The commission also held formal hearings at its offices in San Francisco and Pasadena. During these proceedings, the most basic decisions about the California markets were debated and ultimately set in stone. They lasted from the publication of the
Blue Book in April 1994 to January 1996, when the commission published
the Preferred Policy Decision on the new market structure.[7]

Soon after the Blue Book proceedings started, the political establishment
in Sacramento recognized that the commission was infringing on their territory. The legislators asserted that restructuring required a legal foundation, and, in 1995, they began to work on AB 1890—the law that committed
California to restructuring. The design process thus bifurcated, with one
part playing out in San Francisco and another in Sacramento.

Much of the literature has focused on the process in Sacramento. Of-
ficially, Senator Jim Brulte sponsored the bill. But the Democratic Steve
Peace was the real force behind the legislative process. He was the chair
of the Senate Energy, Utilities, and Communication Committee and controlled the negotiation of the political compromise. Peace had a colorful
personality, and the negotiations in Sacramento had all the trappings of a

political thriller. There were nightlong negotiations that came to be known as the Steve Peace Death March, backroom dealings, and strong emotions. Furthermore, the bill implemented requirements that have often been associated with the crisis—including the 10 percent rate reduction and the retail freeze.

However, from the structural point of view that I have developed in the last two chapters, the legislative process mattered little for California's energy crisis. The bill practically implemented the architecture outlined in the California Public Utility Commission decision from January 1996. It added bells and whistles to gather political support, but it did not put into place any problematic structural features that had not already been agreed upon elsewhere.[8] Indeed, when the slender sixty-seven pages formally passed into law in September 1996, the technical efforts to implement their provisions had already been underway for more than a year. From the perspective of market design, AB 1890 and the dealings in Sacramento were an afterthought.

Instead, the defining moment occurred in August 1995 when a small group of special-interest representatives staged a minor coup against the California Public Utility Commission. It was a hot summer, and the Blue Book proceedings had been dragging on for several months. Two groups were fighting relentlessly against each other, unable to come to an agreement.

The first group had formed during the early months of 1994 when a conservative business foundation invited lobbyists, politicians, and utility executives on a trip to the UK—all expenses paid. Among the travelers were the president of the utility commission, Dan Fessler, and one of his commissioners, Greg Conlon. Their luxurious stay in a hotel in London's Mayfair district proved transformative when Fessler and Conlon met Stephen Littlechild, the primary architect of the UK's approach to electricity restructuring and a powerful man popularly known as the "Regulator." Mesmerized by his presentation, Conlon and Fessler fell in love with the UK's restructuring model. Upon their return to the States, the group advocated heavily for a PoolCo model inspired by Littlechild's approach.[9]

The PoolCo model was based on the British spot market, which was integrated with the grid operator. The pool would buy electricity from generators, sell it to distributors, and organize the transmission. While Fessler took over most features of this design, the Blue Book did not propose the complete separation of production, transmission, and distribution functions.[10] California's utilities had a vested interest in maintaining ownership in the transmission system. Fessler and Conlon were worried they would lose the utilities' support if they adopted these elements of the UK model.

The Blue Book thus envisioned a pool that would administer the transmission grid belonging to the utilities.

This difference from the UK model proved contentious, created a rift among the commissioners, and gave rise to the second group in the Blue Book proceedings. Commissioners Jesse Knight and Norm Shumway worried that utilities would take control of the pool and use their power over the transmission grid to distort access to the markets. This might turn the pool into an "überutility" displacing all competition. Accordingly, they proposed an alternative direct-access model that allowed retail and wholesale customers to choose their supplier on the basis of bilateral contracts. To weaken the utilities, they wanted a system operator that would manage the grid independently and merely provide equal access to the transmission system.[11]

Throughout 1994 and most of 1995, the stakeholders were deeply divided between the two models. The industrial users sided with the direct-access group because they thought that a system built around bilateral markets would enable them to contract with cheap qualifying facilities in the Northwest. They, too, were worried about the interference of utilities and wanted an independent market where they could easily contract with the cheapest offers. In their mind, the West had already had sufficient experiences with bilateral contracts, and they simply wanted access to more transaction partners.

The utilities were mainly concerned about cost recovery. A variety of investments had book values that far exceeded their potential profitability in the new markets. The principal concern was two nuclear power plants whose construction had been a disaster. The development of Pacific Gas & Electric's Diablo Canyon Nuclear Power Plant had started with a cost estimate of $400 million and ended up costing $5.8 billion. Similarly, Edison had initially estimated the costs for the San Onofre plant at $1.3 billion but ended up spending $4.3 billion. The cost overruns reflected various mishaps, and the utilities feared that a market would punish them mercilessly. Pacific decided to throw its weight behind the direct-access model and thus the interests of industrial customers. In exchange, it received a guarantee that it would be able to recover these stranded costs. For Edison, the situation looked different. Without an existing guarantee, they thought that only a power pool could promise cost recovery. They were worried that the industrial users would no longer buy their power in a bilateral contract market. Since this would prevent them from recovering their investments, they were firmly in favor of PoolCo.[12] For similar reasons, San Diego sided with Edison.

Because there were suddenly two powerful groups with disparate visions, the last months of 1994 and the first few months of 1995 went by with increasingly more hostile attempts to force a decision. The groups tried to pressure legislators in Sacramento as well as utility commissioners in San Francisco. But neither side could gain the upper hand, and it began to look as if the negotiations would fail.[13]

At this point, Governor Pete Wilson intervened. He was getting ready for a presidential bid in the Republican primary in 1996 and wanted the positive publicity of successful restructuring. Accordingly, he sent his chief of staff, George Dunn, and his chief economist, Philip Romero, to negotiate a deal between the major parties. The talks took place among a few top insiders from Edison, the California Large Energy Customer Association (CLECA), the independent power producers (IPPs), and the California Manufacturers Association (CMA). And so a small group of representatives began to negotiate the future of California's restructuring project outside the limelight of the public and without interference from consumer groups. Jan Smutny-Jones, the representative for independent power producers, remembered, "Throughout the summer of 1995, we met . . . once a week is probably overstating it, every other week is probably understating it. We met a lot."[14] The negotiations took place in the manufacturers association's meeting rooms in Sacramento and various hotel rooms.[15] "It was analogous to the Arab-Israeli peace talks," Romero remembered.[16]

At first, the more intimate setting only served to highlight the existing differences. Vikram Budhraja was Edison's representative in the negotiations. He had consulted extensively with William Hogan and the market designers at Harvard. To him, as well as most other market designers, there was no question that markets and grid management had to be integrated. Some form of PoolCo seemed inevitable.

Barbara Barkovich, the representative for CLECA, remembers their disagreements: "Vikram comes from that kind of technical background, likes the ideas [of the market designers in the East], thinks that they make sense. [He kept saying,] 'Why don't we do this? It's all going to work, right?' And our side is like, 'Well, we're not really sure. We haven't been convinced yet, and we want access to the grid. We want to be able to do retail choice. We don't necessarily feel that we need a centralized market.'"[17]

But despite pushback from the industry stakeholders, Budhraja did not relent. He was so insistent that Edison eventually added John Fielder, who was more sympathetic to the needs of the large customers, to the mix. He was willing to move Edison's position closer to the direct-access model Pacific Gas & Electric and the industrials favored. Barkovich remembers, "With Vikram, there was no moving him. So that's when Fielder came in, and he was more conciliatory and better able to understand the customer side. . . . So we finally said, 'OK, if you want a spot market, you can have one, but we want it separate from the grid operator.'"[18]

This offer of compromise marks the crucial moment in the negotiations. Just as the PoolCo group wanted, the industrial customers agreed to a power pool. There would be centralized auctions, and they would be used to help the utilities recover costs. But in exchange for this concession, the pool would be separated from the grid management. They wanted to chain the system operator to a minimal role as a "traffic cop," who would merely ensure that the markets obeyed technical constraints.[19] Otherwise, they feared, a more powerful system operator might discriminate against bilateral agreements. With the guarantee of cost recovery through the pool, both sides seemed happy, and a compromise was finally on the horizon.

Upon hearing the terms of the new agreement, Budhraja redoubled his efforts to object and reiterated that they would need to build markets that were integrated with the activities of the system operator. A senator who had dropped in on behalf of the manufacturers apparently listened to this demand, then slammed his hand on the table and cried, "It's going to be divided or there ain't no deal."[20] The sudden outburst marked the breaking point in the negotiations. As Barkovich recollected, everyone suddenly feared they might not arrive at a decision at all. A compromise seemed preferable:

> Through that long and hot summer, meeting after meeting after meeting, we finally realized that, well, that this is always the case. If an issue is really difficult and contentious, do you want to settle, or do you want to let the commission decide? I have settled many cases in my life because the bottom line is when the regulators get it, you have no idea what they're going to do. So, a lot of times, you will settle—that is, you will reach an agreement that is a compromise because you feel better about that than having five people have your fate in their hands.[21]

And so that was it: to prevent the regulators from making the decision for them, the group drafted a Memorandum of Understanding and resolved the fundamental conflict of interest that had blocked the Blue Book proceedings. The document was first signed in August 1995 and filed with the utility commission in September. As soon as the stakeholders agreed, the governor endorsed the memorandum and propagated the compromise in San Francisco and Sacramento. Already on the side of direct access, Pacific Gas & Electric endorsed the compromise without delay. The power marketers, represented mainly by Enron, supported the proposal as well. They could foresee that the memorandum would introduce significant inefficiencies into the communications between the markets and the system operators. Since their business model was premised on resolving such problems as intermediaries, they supported the proposal.[22] This is where we find the origins of the conspiracy theory that Enron designed a system they could game. They were in favor of provisions that expanded and multiplied the markets relative to grid management. This gave rise to the inconsistencies they would later exploit in their games. However, at the time, the provisions merely seemed to promise opportunities to sell services as an intermediary.

Either way, because the document brought consensus among the most powerful interests to some of the most divisive issues of the Blue Book proceedings, everyone saw it as a breakthrough accomplishment. The market design process could move forward. Not only did the document become the foundation for the utility commission's Preferred Policy Decision at the end of 1995 but the governor's influence in Sacramento ensured that it also informed the core of AB 1890. Even though it had been hashed out in the backroom dealings of a tiny group of special-interest representatives, the memorandum was the most transformative document of the political process.

Designers' Winter of Discontent

When it became clear that the California Public Utility Commission actually wanted to go through with the memorandum, market designers were uniformly aghast. Though they disagreed about a variety of other topics, they urgently, unanimously, and vigorously opposed the memorandum in personal interactions, published work, and expert testimony. Whenever asked, they repeated the objections throughout the technical processes to implement the markets as well as the legislative process in Sacramento.[23]

While market design is extremely flexible and can accommodate a variety of political compromises, the memorandum affected the very applicability of designers' tools. As we have seen, the markets were supposed to prepare the real-time dispatch of generation assets. By separating markets from grid management, the stakeholders effectively severed the connection between the optimization problem the markets were supposed to address and the markets themselves. Worse, the equality provision created inefficiencies by design. Without a mechanism to optimize across schedules, a gap would remain between economic dispatch and the markets' results. While it would have been possible to work around these problems to prevent a crisis, the resulting system would have been inefficient.

Some of the designers were rather marginal figures in the political process. But others occupied central positions. Take Dr. George Backus, a safety engineer who had worked for NASA and participated in the first Apollo mission. Starting in the 1980s and continuing on in the early 1990s, Backus conducted simulations to forecast the impact of deregulation on the electricity sector. As soon as the first design documents were released, he determined that players would quickly take advantage of the market structure, particularly through the exercise of market power. Later, he worked for Perot Systems, one of the vendors that integrated software packages for the new markets. In this role, he participated in the technical implementation of California's market design. Intimately familiar with the details of the design process, he presented his findings to the California Energy Commission and the Western Electricity Coordinating Council and offered his services to the California Public Utility Commission, the system operator, and the Power Exchange. As early as 1997, he argued for caution and suggested that the optimistic plans for restructuring were almost certain to fail. For some reason, regulators, politicians, and stakeholders ignored his warnings and sidelined his advice. It later turned out that he was more than happy to sell his insights to Enron and other power marketers—including the unregulated affiliates of the incumbent utilities. Under the cloak of secrecy, he revealed loopholes that proved instrumental to some of the strategies outlined in chapter 3.[24]

An even more powerful figure was the Harvard professor William Hogan, whom we have already met. He is known today as the premier architect of the nodal pricing system that is the standard for most electricity markets in the US. In the early 1990s, he was already one of the foremost authorities on electricity market design. A charismatic speaker with ties to the Pentagon and the most elite educational institutions in the country, he was a force to be reckoned with. In 1993, he founded the Harvard Energy Policy Group, which became the most important meeting place for industry stakeholders, academics, and regulators interested in electricity market design. In California, he testified as an independent expert and helped to draft an alternative market design proposal for San Diego Gas & Electric. He had amicable connections to the staff at FERC and frequently attended their technical conferences. While he received more time on political stages than the likes of Backus, he, too, was ultimately ignored. In an interview he suggested that he even became a persona non grata when he refused to cede opposition to California's design proposal.[25]

There were others like Backus and Hogan—highly visible experts like Charles Imbrecht, Paul Joskow, and Steven Stoft—who publicly and clearly derided the Memorandum of Understanding. They argued that the compromise made no sense, that it would create an inefficient system that would disproportionately serve the interests of speculators, and that it could potentially affect system reliability.

Take, for example, Charles Imbrecht's reaction to the memorandum in his official statement from the California Energy Commission: "In our view, the [memorandum's] signers have failed to demonstrate that this forced separation [between markets and system operator] makes any sense, that it solves some real problem, or that it makes the system operate better, more efficiently, or more fairly. . . . Moreover, our analysis suggests that the separation could be used as a pretext for denying the system operator the necessary tools and means to solve the congestion problem efficiently, while allowing arbitragers to exploit the resulting inefficiencies."[26]

While no one could anticipate quite how violently the memorandum's provisions would be exacerbated by the market rules and protocols, the designers' message was clear: do not implement them, or the system will not operate efficiently. Yet the politicians and stakeholders went ahead, ignored the warning cries of the experts, and set the compromise in stone.

Considering that market design is a highly technical activity and that designers considered the provisions of the memorandum grave mistakes, why were they unable to sway the politicians and stakeholders? After all, they had come up with the plans for market design in the first place, and they were prominent experts from some of the most prestigious universities in the world. Why could they not assert any control over these fundamental questions?

Politics and Rhetoric: The Battle over the Memorandum

In 1995, the political debates about electricity markets were really conversations about an imaginary object. Markets like the one California wanted to build did not exist yet. In their conversations, stakeholders tried to define a shared vision of these markets and possibilities for their creation. They reasoned by analogy to other industries, with reference to general concepts, and from personal experience. Of course, their positions mirrored their material interests. Utilities tried to recover stranded costs, independent power producers tried to gain access to the transmission grid, power marketers tried to improve business opportunities for intermediaries, and so on. Yet the debates also took place against a backdrop of hard, physical realities. Everyone knew that, when all was said and done, electricity still had to flow through wires to customers. Different forms of expertise — economics, law, market design, engineering — therefore inflected the political negotiations and shaped the terms of the debate. Engineers, economists, and utility officials helped to establish which arguments were acceptable and which were inappropriate, which issues could be negotiated and which could not. But experts did not simply point out the limits of political compromise. Rather, the boundary between technical and political matters was itself a matter of political contestation and negotiation.[27] Experts first had to convince audiences that their point of view was legitimate and that they should be in charge of the question at hand. This is where rhetoric enters the picture.

In the shifting terrain of the debate, the market designers tried to assert jurisdiction over decisions pertaining to the relationship between the system operator and the financial markets. They intended to establish themselves as the arbiters of truth regarding the separation and equality provisions. In lieu of political power, they relied on the power of rhetoric.[28]

To understand the logic behind these strategies, it helps to consider the figure of the expert more generally. An expert knows something the audience does not. If experts want to be *seen* as experts, they must therefore convince the audience that its members do not understand the matter at hand and that the experts know what should be done. They often do this by shifting the terms of the debate onto the terrain of their own professional knowledge. Since the experts can mobilize their disciplinary language with greater fluidity than outsiders, they can then demonstrate easily that members of the audience do not know what they are talking about.

For example, scientists can draw on the authority conferred by the "mechanical objectivity of numbers," and the "no-nonsense" rhetoric of instrumental rationality to showcase a superior understanding of, and training in, quantitative techniques that enjoy substantial respect among lay audiences.[29] They can use this superior skill to demonstrate flaws in the audience's reasoning. Or they can simply overwhelm the audience with considerations that seem relevant but arcane to outsiders. In each case, the audience's inferior ability to wield the language of the experts leads them to recognize that they do not know as much as the expert and to cede jurisdiction. This strategy works best when the experts have a monopoly on the abstract knowledge that defines the core of their profession.[30] The less the audience knows about the terms the experts dictate, the more willing they are to cede jurisdiction. Quantum physics enjoys an excellent reputation, partly because people do not generally have strong intuitions about answers in that field.[31]

Of course, the experts also need to get the audience to trust them. Rhetorical strategies are therefore highly tailored to appeal to specific audiences. Experts may praise the audience's understanding of the subject matter and draw them into the in-group of the knowledgeable, refer them to commonly agreed markers of competence (certification, education, etc.), or appeal to their sense of what counts as true knowledge.[32] But despite these moves to draw the audience in, the expert has to convince them that there is a substantial competence gap and that they should therefore defer their decision-making powers.

Market designers used such strategies to attack the separation and equality provisions. To give an example, I focus on regulatory hearings in 1994, when William Hogan debated several stakeholders. The memorandum did not exist yet, but proponents of the direct-access model for the new markets had already suggested these provisions. His argument was tailored to disqualify his audience and put the market designers in charge of the issue. Initially, he signaled his formal standing as an expert: "I, of course, have been involved in a lot of activities that have been looking at the competition in change through the Harvard Electricity Policy Group, research projects at Harvard."[33] After listing a variety of other qualifications, he asserts that "in this new era we're going to have the delight in working on a problem where . . . most things that everyone knows to be true, aren't. And because of that change in the world, we're going to have to rethink many of the elements of the operation of the market."[34] Among these elements, he argues, is the possibility of separating the transmission of energy from its generation and thus separating markets and grid management: "The distinction between short-run generation and transmission is false. They are actually parts of the same function. And separating the pricing is probably going to be as unnecessary as it would be difficult."[35]

The first part of the statement flatters the audience—he implies that they are all on the same page because they understand markets and electricity systems. But then he asserts that there is really a gradient: what everyone knew to be true is so no longer. Rather than just assert his superiority, he draws the audience in by suggesting that "as we work on this in the coming months, it's important to go back to basics."[36] Everyone needs to revise assumptions that they have reasonably held. After suggesting an imagined equality between himself and his audiences in this way, he confidently claims that a common distinction—that between generation and transmission—is false. An appeal to intellectual proximity to generate trust is followed by an indirect assertion of superior understanding. Then, he points to the source of this confusion: "You're getting a lot of submissions from people who are suggesting ways to think about these problems and what the criteria ought to be." This cacophony of different voices, he suggests, puts the burden on the utility commission to establish how the basic principles of restructured electricity markets should be understood. In the next statement, he argues that the commissioners might turn to the market designers for guidance: "A good next step, there's a group in California, the Power Group at the University of California that published a nice document that went through your proposal and tried to distill principles under the headings of economic efficiency, equity, technical efficiency of transmission and distribution."[37] To underline the importance of listening to the experts, he provides lengthy explanations of his technical filings that explain what can work and what cannot, where attention is misdirected and where it should be moved.

Take this passage: "The first step is to implement a competitive wholesale market with readily available spot price against which generators can sell power at a profit or loss. This is going to happen anyhow because of the FERC requirements under the EPAct. There are many ways to implement such a market; some are better than others. . . . An efficient pool-based wholesale market design will simplify many of the complex interactions, in the best case, lead to locational prices that reflect the congestion of the transmission grid."[38]

He confidently asserts what would happen under different arrangements, and which arrangements would be superior, given the actual workings of the interaction between markets and grid management. The references to "locational prices" and "transparent spot-prices" draw on the framework established by Schweppe and his colleagues. Accordingly, he uses them in a highly technical sense with which the audiences were likely not familiar.

Other examples of such rhetorical maneuvers can be found in all parts of the political discussions before the California Public Utility Commission and also at FERC. They show up in formal filings and the transcripts of official hearings. Initial moves to establish trust are followed by gentle demonstrations of the audience's ignorance and dense arguments in a highly technical language. But again and again, stakeholders listened politely to such rhetorical appeals, furrowed their brows, and then merrily continued to negotiate about issues the designers had declared off-limits.[39]

Indeed, the designers' rhetorical challenges failed almost completely. For example, after Hogan finished arguing that the separation between production and transmission was fictional, the next speakers simply continued to invoke this distinction, reiterating arguments that he had declared misinformed just a moment earlier. The speakers did not reject or refute Hogan's arguments. They simply ignored that they had ever been made. Clearly, Hogan's impassioned appeal had appeared to be little more than another opinion.

When Dan Fessler, the president of the California Public Utility Commission, ended the discussion, he closed with an ironic statement: "We have a problem in that it should be anticipated that in dealing with any group of distinguished citizens who are also called experts that it would be possible for them to take anything less than the 21 [minutes] of the allotted time for the entire period, and perhaps by precluding questions in this manner, one maintains one's posture as an expert."[40] He makes a joke here, but the statement is nonetheless revealing. He sees the market designers as citizens who *pose* as experts rather than actual experts who get to define the difference between political and technical.

The designers tried to make up for these losses with extensive behind-the-scenes negotiations. We have already seen that Vikram Budhraja tried his best to dominate the negotiations that led to the memorandum and tried to find allies among utility executives who would support his objections. But political pressure from the governor's office led Southern California Edison to add a more pliable executive to the negotiations. Members of the Electric Power Research Institute in Palo Alto organized behind-the-scenes conversations with staff from the governor's office and important stakeholders. In 1996, Hogan made a last-ditch effort to outmaneuver the coalition behind the memorandum. Before FERC, California's decision to separate and fragment the market structure became the center of attention at multiple technical conferences. After convincing San Diego of his approach, Hogan and his collaborators produced a set of "proposed amendments" to the proposal the utilities filed in 1996—shortly before AB 1890 became law.[41] The "minor adjustments" were a Trojan horse for a completely different market design that would have abolished the separation and equality provisions. The FERC commissioners were apparently sympathetic to the alternative because it had some backing from technical staff. Again, political pressure from the governor's office prompted San Diego to withdraw the proposal at the last moment—an unprecedented maneuver that left FERC commissioners stumped and required that legal staff hurry back to the general counsel to determine whether it was legitimate. Again and again, designers' rhetorical or strategic gambits led nowhere.

This is surprising because engineers could easily assert jurisdiction in these negotiations. When they testified that the system would need a separate mechanism to plan for updates to the transmission system, arguments about the introduction of market mechanisms more or less immediately ended. Why were market designers unable to define technical questions as technical when engineers managed to do so with questions about the system's physical infrastructure?

Everyone Is an Expert When It Comes to Economics

In the previous section, I have argued that claims to jurisdiction require that the expert convinces the audience that the expert knows more than they do. In political negotiations, the key rhetorical move is to pull the debate onto the experts' turf and then display superior skill in wielding the concepts. This is precisely what the designers tried to do—but they failed. As I will now show, the reason for this failure is rather straightforward. For the audience to accept the experts' superior understanding, they first have to accept how the expert wields the conceptual tools. Because most of us do not have strong intuitions about how to reason about quantum mechanics, we allow the experts to talk as they please and assume that they are probably correct.

The problem with market design is that it uses the conceptual language of economics. But economists have long lost the monopoly on this language. Over the second half of the twentieth century, the conceptual tool kit of economics has diffused far beyond the hallowed halls of academia. Carried by countless bachelor's degrees, the Econ 101 view of the world permeates business, government, and common sense.[42] MBA programs translate more sophisticated economic concepts into applicable lessons for managers and propagate a "scientific" method of making business decisions, based heavily on Chicago-style economics.[43] Concepts that are central to market design—such as equilibrium, Pareto efficiency, competitive advantage, marginal cost, cost-benefit analysis, adverse selection, and moral hazard—therefore show up in common sense as well as in the repertoire of other professions.[44] Because California's design process took place in the 1990s, when the enthusiasm for free markets had reached a peak, the political debate made ample use of these concepts.

This created a distinct problem for designers: the various stakeholders and regulators had strong intuitions about how to understand central concepts that featured in the designers' statements. With their highly technical form of expertise, market designers had their own definition of most of these concepts.[45] But the resulting discrepancies were not immediately apparent to outsiders. The political debate therefore became multivocal. Different members of the debate had divergent interpretations of central concepts but were not aware of these differences.[46]

This multivocality fundamentally derailed designers' rhetorical gambits. Whenever they made arguments to display their skill, their audiences simply found them to be counterintuitive and wrong. Because everyone has a different understanding, there was no effective agreement about what constitutes a performance of correct knowledge—the epistemic form that settles how valid claims are made became unsettled.[47] Yet, instead of clarifying these underlying differences, the parties acted as if they disagreed on matters of fact alone. In this situation, the deck was stacked against the market designers. Attempts to convince audiences by masterfully wielding concepts, status symbols, and techniques invited doubt rather than awe.

Because this is a subtle problem, I will illustrate the issue with one extended example from the debates in California. This example stands in for a more general problem that was evident in most filings and discussions. Stakeholders used different conceptual frameworks to think about markets but did not recognize the resulting inconsistencies. Instead, they treated the debate as if they agreed on the framework and merely disagreed about matters of fact. This was the reason market designers' claims seemed implausible; under the assumption that all participants used the same conceptual framework, designers' statements simply appeared wrong. If the underlying disagreements had become visible, they might have begun to interrogate each other's assumptions about how electricity markets work and given the designers a foothold to establish their superior understanding. But, as it was, the disagreements about the nature of markets remained hidden from sight, pasted over by disagreements of fact.

I am going to focus on an episode during which the parties discussed the separation provision—whether or not to keep the market separate from grid management. Recall that the debates initially focused on the question of whether PoolCo or direct access was the preferable restructuring model. PoolCo, which was based on the British model, proposed a centralized market that would be integrated with the work of the system operator. Direct access proposed a system of decentralized, bilateral markets. In its comments, Enron made the following argument against PoolCo:

> Whether or not the Commission centralized the scheduling and operation processes for the sake of reliability, it should *not* centralize the market clearing mechanism. . . . Centralized control over the physical market would substantially reduce the economic advantages associated with the proposed industry restructuring. A market-based approach to the electric market benefits consumers through the combined effect of two forces: 1. Choice of service and 2. Choice of supplier. . . . A centrally controlled market offers the hope of multiple suppliers but not the choice among services which enables consumers to get the full benefit of an efficient market. In a centrally controlled market, the government, the grid owner(s) or some other organization will decide what types of physical delivery services the market needs. . . . A simple analogy will reveal the fundamental problem: if the housing market were centrally controlled,

a central board or regulatory agency would decide what choices were available.[48]

Enron argues that central control distorts the market because it blocks innovative services. Therefore, the market should be separated from grid management. This argument presupposes a generic understanding of markets. Largely disembodied, rational buyers with perfect information examine different offers from competing sellers and choose the cheapest one. This process creates constant pressure to innovate and reduce costs, which weeds out inefficiencies and leads to the best possible industry organization. This conceptualization makes plausible the comparison with the housing market at the end of the quote. Only if you think that there is no substantial difference between housing and electricity can you suggest that services in the two markets should be understood in analogy to each other. Further, the rhetorical thrust of the comparison depends very much on a contrast between "real" markets that are decentralized negotiations between buyers and sellers and pseudo-markets where centralized regulators make decisions about offers. The phrase "whether or not" in the first sentence also suggests that Enron views the question of whether the "market clearing mechanism" can be separated from grid management "operation processes" as a matter of political preference — and not a question of market efficiency. This can only be true if you assume that markets will automatically converge on workable equilibria.

Enron's argument thus depends on an evolutionary view of markets that contrasts strongly with the designers' views. However, the competing assumptions are not justified and discussed. Instead, the thrust of the argument is about an empirical matter: whether a centralized market would give customers the choice between different services. One of California's three big utilities, Southern California Edison, responded thus:

> This concern [about the choice of services] has no applicability with regard to Poolco. Poolco, like the English Pool, would provide market participants with complete freedom either to (1) purchase from the pool at spot market prices or (2) enter into bilateral trades with any party that provides for any prices, quality, or characteristics of service that the parties so choose. . . . If marketers can add real value by developing contracts that offer consumers guaranteed prices for interrupted service or virtually any other tailored service . . . they are free to do so. Once a pool is in place that allows buyers and sellers to have an assured source of efficiently produced power, the market can decide which financial instruments are valuable. . . . The first priority should be to establish an efficient

market for the actual purchase and sale of power, not to facilitate the creation of hedging instruments.[49]

Rather than contesting Enron's premises, Edison responds on empirical
grounds and suggests that the pool is compatible with a variety of services
that consumers are free to choose: "Poolco . . . would provide market participants with complete freedom." Implicitly, however, the argument presupposes designers' algorithmic idea of markets and is incompatible with
Enron's evolutionary view. Edison simply states that "a pool . . . allows buyers and sellers to have an assured source of efficiently produced power."
This presupposes that centralized organization is an asset rather than a
problem—because it best executes the search for the optimal dispatch of
production and consumption.

The argument only works if you assume that the market is an algorithm
and not a distributed, evolutionary process. From the evolutionary point
of view, centralization is a problem because it blocks innovation and free
competition, which are, by definition, decentral. The two arguments are ultimately incongruent. They hinge on different conceptual ideas about what
an "efficient market" actually is. But rather than recognizing and discussing
this ambiguity, the parties act as if their argument resides on the level of empirical facts, presuming that their respective framings integrate the debate.

This multivocality became even more pronounced when large industrial customers entered the debate and tried to negotiate a compromise.
They stated that it might not be necessary to decide the issue in the first
place. Rather than mandating the creation of a centralized market, the politicians might simply leave it to the market to decide the issue. If it became
necessary, the market would give rise to and sustain a centralized entity.
They argued that "the experience to date in the restructuring of the natural gas industry, in particular the development of regional market hubs performing pool-like functions, supports the conclusion that the marketplace
can be counted upon to look after its own clearinghouse needs."[50] Again,
the argument makes an empirical point: the natural gas markets produced
hubs, so electricity markets would too. But this argument presupposes that
electricity markets are like the markets in other network industries. This,
in turn, requires the assumption that power flows follow contract paths—
prespecified paths on the transmission grid between point A and point B—
closely enough to resemble natural gas flows and that the production and
transmission can therefore be separated on the level of contractual negotiations.

From the market designers' perspective, the natural gas industry is not
comparable to electricity systems. Energy never flows on a contract path

but on all available paths at the same time. From the evolutionary point of view, there is no reason to allow the creation of centralized hubs. Accordingly, the argument is inconsistent with both positions it reacts to. Yet the representative ignores the conceptual incompatibility and seems to be simply making an empirical point (hubs will emerge here as they have elsewhere)

In sum, the three arguments about the desirability of an integrated market rely on three different ways to imagine electricity markets. What the ideal electricity market should be and how it should work were objectively ambiguous. But all three parties simply presupposed their view and argued as if they simply disagreed about matters of fact.

This proved fatal to the market designers' efforts to take control of the debate. Each time they attempted to weaken the audience's confidence in themselves, the participants simply perceived these efforts as factually wrong. Several of my interviewees remember disregarding the economists' advice. Experiences with "bilateral contracting in the West" or "how business is done" had been considered better means for deciding the question than academic analysis. They said that the "economists did not know [what would be best] either." Despite substantial rhetorical esprit, the attempts to undermine the "folk theorems" fell flat. In a world where everybody seemed to know how to use economic reasoning, the market designers appeared to be just one group with strange opinions. Without stable conventions for the use of economic language, the designers could do little to demonstrate their superior understanding of the material. Accordingly, they and their concerns were sidelined. As the designers could not claim jurisdiction over the equality and separation provisions of the memorandum, the political debates reverted to a basic calculus of competing interests.

Conclusion

The success of market design requires that experts assert control over certain technical questions. While market design is a flexible suite of tools, the experts have to at least control the questions that affect the basic ability to apply these tools. Since grid management has to be performed by the system operator, market designers should be able to control how market activities relate to the activities of the system operator. This is not all that is necessary for market design to succeed, of course. It is a limiting condition that allows market designers to set a baseline with which they can work.

As I have shown, the designers failed to establish jurisdiction over the memorandum because the structure of the debate invalidated their rhetorical strategies. The language of economics pervaded the discussion as a multivocal "style of thought." Ideological common sense and other forms of expert advice collided with the designers' claims. The wide and inconsistent use of economists' conceptual vocabulary made it difficult to depict market design as a distinct and decisive form of expertise. Things may have been different if the designers had dealt with a more homogeneous audience. If their task had been to convince other engineers or economists, they might have been able to stabilize the debate sufficiently to establish their superior understanding of the market design issues. This happened in other parts of the country, where utilities operated power pools that transcended state lines. For example, at the PJM Interconnection, market designers had an easier time being heard because they talked to a more homogeneous audience of engineers. With a shared baseline understanding of power engineering, they could more easily convince their audience that they did not fully grasp the implications of different market design decisions. But with the highly eclectic mix of lawyers, politicians, managers, interest representatives, regulators, and engineers in California, there was no common ground from which the designers could have built a convincing rhetorical strategy.[51]

The first set of design flaws therefore relates to market designers' standing in political discourses. While market design does not require that every decision be made in line with their expertise, issues that touch on the applicability of their tools should conform to the principles of market design, if the system is not to violate these principles. But once their ideas entered the domain of interest politics, the designers did not have the political standing to control even these most foundational issues.

Part of the problem was that the debates took place on a high level of abstraction. Foundational questions about market structure and architecture resonated more easily with the commonsense view of free markets than narrower questions would have. For example, while anyone would agree that a free market requires a lot of competitors, the commonsense view would offer less intuitive answers about the choice between single-price and multiprice clearing rules. With such specialized questions, market designers would have found it easier to demonstrate their superior skills of reasoning.

In the end, the memorandum passed as a great political success but established a highly problematic baseline for the subsequent design efforts. Interestingly, the Blue Book negotiations also created another flaw that I have not discussed specifically: they got rid of the biennial resource plan update, the administrative structure that guaranteed sufficient excess generation capacity. The decision to remove the regulatory means of long-term planning was unanimous and was made almost without serious debate after the most radical option of the Yellow Book had been selected. Similarly, the participants quickly rejected the adoption of capacity markets. Politically, this made sense: the whole point of restructuring was to impose market discipline on investment decisions. The memory of Diablo Canyon was fresh, and utilities' imprudent long-term contracts loomed large in the political debate. If the very reason for restructuring was to replace imprudent planning guided by byzantine regulations, any argument that markets would have trouble making these decisions would be orthogonal to the project. It is therefore not particularly surprising that the political negotiations quickly moved in this direction.

But why did the designers not raise objections at this point of the design process? The lack of explicit mechanisms for long-term investments forced them to optimize the short-term markets for two temporal horizons — a task that they failed to accomplish, as we saw. However, to explore the designers' silence with respect to this issue, we have to wait until the seventh chapter. For now, we note that the political process saddled the designers with a problematic baseline. As the process moved toward implementation, the designers had to figure out how they could harmonize the activities in fragmented markets with the work of the system operator. They needed to work around the provisions of the memorandum. But though they were aware of this challenge, they not only failed to solve the problems but exacerbated them. The next question is why the implementation process adopted procedures and rules that led to the problems of incomplete simplification and porous boundaries. Here, we leave the trenches of political battle and travel into the highly technical work of WEPEX.

CHAPTER SIX

The Perils of Modularization

We are now approaching one of the central mysteries of the failed design project. Its cipher is WEPEX, the organizational process that translated the political compromises of the Preferred Policy Decision into tangible reality. WEPEX's beginnings were humble. Early in 1995, a small group of engineers, system planners, dispatchers, and lawyers began to meet in the conference rooms of California's three large utilities. Now that the writing was on the wall, the utilities had asked the group to sort through the technical implications of restructuring.[1]

The experts tried to figure out how the utilities might integrate their three service territories into a single system under the management of a system operator. This was no easy task because the utilities had developed their infrastructures independently.[2] The systems were living, complex configurations of machines that had grown in a largely decentralized process over the course of a century. They embodied different design philosophies, consisted of different components, and called for different operational practices. Integrating these three systems was not unlike merging three cars of different builds and ages into a single machine—if the cars were the size of a country.[3] This work was not glamorous but technically demanding and intellectually obscure, a proven combination to keep politicians at bay.

As 1995 progressed, the working groups became more and more influential. Practically every market design issue touched on the putative role of the system operator and therefore on questions of system integration. Once the experts started to put out statements and recommendations, stakeholders in the political negotiations realized that the center of gravity was shifting. They quickly petitioned to be included in the WEPEX process. Municipalities wanted to know how their systems would coordinate with the larger grid, power marketers wanted details about how they could trade in the Power Exchange, and direct-access customers were confused about how they would interact with the system operator.[4] Over the course of a few months, more than sixty interested parties joined WEPEX.

Formal groups like the Scheduling Coordinator User Group, the Electric Utility Restructuring Forum, and the Research and Development Planning Forum sprang up around WEPEX to facilitate communication. They tied experts and stakeholders together, bridging backroom negotiations, official proceedings, and technical work. Gradually, the proceedings became the center of the design process, the place "where the arguments took place."[5]

By August 1995, the utilities had established WEPEX as the official implementation process for the Blue Book proceedings. They imposed a bureaucratic structure on the division of labor and a clear hierarchy of decision rights. Early in 1996, the utilities hired the industry legend S. David Freeman to take over leadership. He had run the Tennessee Valley Authority and advised President Jimmy Carter on energy matters. Under Freeman, WEPEX became a tightly run, formal organization. It first transformed into two Trust Advisory Committees for the creation of the Power Exchange and the system operator. After these organizations assumed legal existence, most WEPEX veterans took up roles in the management or stakeholder boards.

In 1997, Freeman summarized the work that had been done since the earliest meetings: "We have moved the idea, the concept, the vision from the dreamers to the vendors. And that's a fairly serious move. All of the hardware and software to build, all of the equipment that's needed to dispatch the power plants, to do the scheduling, to do the billing, the whole shooting match has now been thought through and is in the hand of free enterprise vendors that have the incentives to get the job done on time, financial incentives, and penalties if they do not."[6]

In other words, WEPEX was the organizational machinery that turned the broad political vision into tangible reality. While the previous chapter explained the flawed foundation of California's system, we now turn to the processes that actually put together the nuts and bolts of new market system—as well as its many design flaws. WEPEX stands behind a system that suffered from differential simplification and porous boundaries, a system that constantly undermined its own foundations and gave rise to multiple incentives and opportunities for destructive games. Yet the reasons for these flaws are not as obvious as they might appear.

The literature has typically argued that WEPEX was as corrupted by interest politics as the Blue Book proceedings.[7] And it is true that the steering committee approved several rules that drew heated opposition from market designers:[8] the lax application standards for scheduling coordinators; rules that forced the system operator to balance schedules internally; rules that prohibited scheduling coordinators from bidding outside their preferred schedules; and rules that limited the Power Exchange's ability to redraw congestion zones. All four serious design flaws (which showed up in chap. 3) contributed to problems of differential simplification and porous boundaries.

However, closer inspection reveals that these rules represented the unavoidable implications of the equality provision in the Preferred Policy Decision. The steering committee did not have much of a choice in implementing these decisions. The lax application standards reduced the barriers to entry for new scheduling coordinators. The other rules kept the Power Exchange and the system operator from dominating the other scheduling coordinators because they complicated their attempts to offer the lowest transaction costs.[9] This protected the arbitrage business of the traders as well as the markets of the other scheduling coordinators. Without these rules, the Power Exchange would always have been the most efficient marketplace, jettisoning the equality provision. While the rules thus go back to interest politics, they reflect such politics at the level of the California Public Utility Commission. They do not allow us to infer that WEPEX was a mere extension of the political process.

Indeed, the archival record suggests that WEPEX was firmly in the hands of the three utilities. They owned the transmission system, executed all aspects of system integration, and filed with FERC the tariffs that contained the details of the evolving market design. They held the most powerful votes on the steering committee, negotiated most issues among themselves, and hired the experts who implemented the new system.[10] The legislators in Sacramento had no interest in getting involved in technical details, and because regulatory authority shifted from the California Public Utility Commission to FERC, there was little influence from state politics. Meanwhile, FERC was happy to let "a thousand flowers bloom." Indeed, power marketers and independent power producers complained frequently and impotently that their interests had not been taken into consideration.[11] With a disengaged legislature, a toothless public utility commission, and a lenient federal regulator, the WEPEX Steering Committee assumed almost unchallenged power over the implementation of the new markets. It delegated most design questions to small teams and then voted on their proposals. In principle, the designers were therefore free to shore up the system against the problematic provisions of the political process.

The final version of the memorandum was only twenty-four pages long, the Preferred Policy Decision's section on market structure amounted to forty-two pages, and AB 1890 totaled sixty-seven pages. That was not much text to spell out how to create an entirely new industry structure. With the exception of the rules that implemented the equality provision, the working groups thus had much room to impose their own interpretation on the system. Of course, they could not have fully resolved the problems they inherited from the memorandum. But they could have worked around them to produce a much more manageable market system. Their thorough knowledge of the problems, and their sense that they could be compensated for, explains why market designers joined the WEPEX proceedings so confidently.

Recall the basic problem: the memorandum mandated multiple markets but prevented the system operator from optimizing across the results because it had to treat each market equally. The four rules I just discussed concretized this problem: they blocked any design that would enable the system operator or the Power Exchange to optimize the results of the market from a central position. To stay with the metaphor of the algorithm, this was like distributing the computation over several processors without checking whether the different solutions converged. Only the arbitrage business of the power marketers could produce this convergence. This "solution" would always be limited because human traders could not possibly identify the security-constrained economic dispatch on the full representation of all power flows.

But the designers might have used the tools of simplification, bounding, and control to align the clearing protocols, set bidding rules for all markets, and make the work of the arbitrage traders easier. Today, most contemporary electricity markets reduce the transaction costs of arbitrage businesses in this way—they streamline the market platforms, enforce symmetries between different market interfaces, and automate much of the search process for profitable trades.[12] Much could have been done by creating a minimal, simple, consistent set of rules and procedures that would fix the context of decision-making and the actionable horizon of the future.

But this is not what designers did. Instead, they created inconsistent market clearing protocols for the different submarkets, divergent representations of the grid, and market interfaces for the spot markets that optimized on short-term decision-making at the expense of long-term decisions. These differential forms of simplification vastly expanded how actors could behave in the system and introduced ever-changing incentives and opportunities for destructive behavior. In other words, the memorandum may have saddled the system with a flawed baseline, but WEPEX created the rules, procedures, and administrative structures that prompted the destructive behavior and made it impossible to simply identify and fix these problems.

This is one of the central mysteries of the California energy crisis. WEPEX hired sophisticated market designers and gave them the power to follow their technical expertise. And yet these experts somehow made a variety of decisions that directly violated the imperative to simplify, bound, and control the market as much as possible. Why?

In what follows, I develop an organizational explanation for this mystery. Working with tight deadlines and a vastly complex architecture, designers adopted a radical division of labor to build the market—modularization. While modularization was a prudent organizational technique to address complex design challenges, it ran up against the internal logic of designer markets. As I will show, modularization split designers into teams that could not appreciate the consequences local design decisions would have on the global level. This effectively undermined their ability to simplify and bound the markets effectively. Behind the backs of the local teams, the complexity of the market constantly escalated, leading to problems of incomplete simplification and porous boundaries.

The Problem of Modularization

The designers faced an extremely difficult task when WEPEX put them in the driver's seat. They had to build a complex market architecture in a short period of time—less than three years remained until the projected opening date of January 1, 1998. They needed to create more than fifteen different markets for products with varying characteristics and to coordinate them with technical systems for grid management. The different pieces had to provide a variety of inputs and outputs for one another. Each market platform would receive information from a variety of technical systems. The platform would organize the interactions between buyers and sellers, collate results, and pass them on to other markets and technical infrastructures. Only if the resulting interrelations worked as intended would the system produce the aggregate results the designers hoped for.

To create this system, the designers had to manage the internal logic of each component as well as their interplay from within an organizational structure. Managing such interrelations is not an unusual requirement. A variety of advanced technologies like nuclear power plants, intercontinental missiles, or large damns and irrigation systems have similar interdependencies. It is usually impossible to build and manage such systems from a single central location.[13] There are simply too many local decisions that can influence other parts of the system for the center to manage the whole process. Yet airplanes, missiles, and nuclear power plants work with remarkable reliability, nonetheless. One key technique to achieve this feat is modularization.[14]

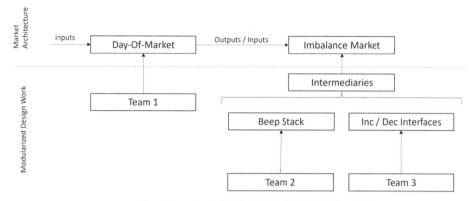

FIGURE 6.1. Illustration of Modularized Market Design Work

The idea is to divide a complex problem into self-contained chunks, or modules, that are related to one another via interfaces. An interface is an abstraction that selects only those elements of a module that are relevant to the operation of another. It effectively reduces the module's complexity by specifying in limited terms how the module interacts with the rest of the system. Once the interfaces are stable, the modules themselves become exchangeable. That is, one solution can be swapped out for another as long as the interface relations are preserved. The modules can therefore be designed by groups that work independently. As long as the teams working on module A know what inputs they receive and what outputs they have to produce for module B, they can ignore the question of how exactly module B works. This has advantages for the speed and reliability of design progress.[15] With a modularized approach, the design process mirrors the structure of the markets: modules with specific input-output relations correspond to teams with clearly defined, local tasks, creating results that other teams could work with.

Figure 6.1 illustrates modularized design work. There are two interrelated markets in the example. The day-of market receives clear inputs and has to produce certain outputs (preferred schedules, in this case). A team is responsible for designing this market. It only knows the imbalance market in terms of the outputs the team has to produce for it. The imbalance market is broken into two separate modules. Teams 2 and 3 are responsible for each module. Again, they only know the other systems in terms of simplified interfaces. Because the modules are closely related, intermediaries coordinate between teams 2 and 3, ensuring that their modules fit together in terms of the plan for the module imbalance market.

In California, there was really no alternative to modularization. With complex interdependencies between the different markets and very little time, the steering committee adopted this approach early on. "The ISO and PX will each consist of a number of subsystems," as a trustee summarized the architecture. Conceptually, "all of these systems were built so they could be procured separately or in an integrated package."[16] Modularization made it easy to develop the system in many concomitant work streams and hire different vendors who could work relatively independently to build the modules.

Each module was related to others via clear input-output relations. For example, the Dispatch Systems Integration Team was responsible for deciding how CAISO would tie the service territories of the three old utilities into one system. The team knew the format of the schedules that arrived from the markets and what to do with them. But the team did not know how the market filled the schedules with content. Each team knew the rest of the system only in terms of the interfaces relevant for the inputs and outputs of its own module.

Initially, the definition of the modules was extremely broad. Teams merely fleshed out how to realize the decisions stipulated by the political processes. As the project matured, the teams and modules were subdivided further.[17] By 1997, the designers had broken each module into submodules and tasks. With this intense differentiation, the number of teams multiplied. While the project started with only twelve teams, toward the end of 1997, there were seventy-seven working on implementation tasks at the system operator alone.[18]

Each team had members who were responsible for either definition or implementation. Those working on definition kept track of decisions and communicated them to other teams working on the same module. The other members implemented the decisions.[19] This ensured that work on related tasks fit together. Since many teams worked in parallel, large tables described deliverables and specified what functionality had to be implemented at what time. Project managers coordinated between teams and constantly checked the relationships between the different modules.

In the beginning, the designers working on staffing the teams recruited experts from the utilities and the larger industry. As tasks became more concrete and technical, the teams hired consultants and academics. This is how academic designers like Robert Wilson and the experimentalist Charles Plott entered the process. They not only helped with architectural questions but developed bidding rules for the auction markets and tested them in laboratory experiments. In the first half of 1997, the executive level finally hired specialized vendors that collaborated with the teams to write the software and set up the hardware.

This highly modularized setup enabled the rapid progress from concept to working system that Freeman praised in 1997. But it also had a price. It required the existence of design rules.[20] The steering committee had to specify ex ante how the different modules were related. Each designer market had to intersect with the rest of the system at clearly specified points, take clearly specified inputs, and turn them into clearly specified outputs. If the designers failed to enforce this structure, work on one module could influence the logic in other modules. The different modules would then no longer be exchangeable, input-output relations would no longer be aligned, and decentralized teamwork would produce incoherent results for the rest of the system. Without design rules, the logic of modularization collapses.

While markets seem to be good candidates for modularization because they are conceived as systems that process inputs to produce outputs, they are susceptible to violations of the design rules. To understand why, recall the central characteristic that distinguishes these markets from other kinds of organizations: the latent antagonism of market actors. Market actors do not cooperate voluntarily with the designers. They search for profits wherever they can. If they can benefit by leveraging information in one market against another, they will do so. If they can manipulate a technical system to change the input of the market in their favor, they will do so. On their quest for profitable trades, companies will thus break the interface relations between modules if doing so is possible and useful. They will violate the design rules.

As we saw in the third chapter, this latent antagonism is the key reason designers need to simplify, bound, and control the market as much as possible. To get actors to follow the blueprint, the designers have to make rules that are consistent with one another, fix the context of decision-making, account for biases, and fix the horizon of the future. This is true for all market contexts that actors can access simultaneously. Accordingly, the rules for interlinked markets have to be globally consistent; otherwise, the actors will identify inconsistencies between rules, exploit them, and thus violate the design rules of the system.

This is where modularization becomes a problem. The design rules do not necessarily specify modules and their interrelation relative to the perspective of market actors. Actors might be able to access different modules simultaneously, even if these are considered independent. They might also identify weak boundaries and link parts of the system that are meant to be independent. Decisions about nominally unrelated parts of the design process can therefore create consequences for one another. Specifically, designers face four distinct problems when they modularize design work.

First, teams that work on a given module do not perceive the consequences that their decisions have on the global level. Prudent design decisions in response to local problems can therefore create problematic incentives in other parts of the system. Conversely, designers working on other modules cannot perceive the impact that decisions elsewhere in the system have on the incentives in their own module.[21]

Second, standard techniques to discover precisely such problems tend to fail because any effort to coordinate the work between modules is incomplete. Most design projects have intermediary and executive levels on which managers examine the interface relations between subsystems, coordinate between teams, and redraw boundaries.[22] These managers are supposed to identify and resolve the problems that emerge when local decisions violate design rules—including incentives for manipulative games.[23] However, these intermediaries consider problems at a certain level of abstraction. They search for decisions that have an impact on other parts of the system. At the design stage, the negative effects of problematic decisions are not yet visible because market actors have not had a chance to act on the available incentives. To identify problematic decisions, intermediaries therefore search for decisions that are relevant to the problems they perceive on the global level—problems in the interface relations between modules. This leaves a variety of design decisions that occur in response to purely local challenges.[24] But these decisions might still interact with other contextual elements to produce gaming incentives. Because it is the interplay between local factors that creates these problems, intermediaries would have to understand the local context fully and then evaluate its relation to the larger system. This is not their job. Ironically, the insight that contextual information resists standardization and aggregation has often been an argument in favor of using markets rather than organizations.[25] But as soon as markets are built and controlled *as* organizations, they inherit this fundamental problem of centralized planning.[26]

A third problem derives from the timing of modularized design work. A frequent assumption in market design is that real market processes follow the logic of rules that have been established ex ante.[27] By this logic, it should be possible to iteratively discover and address global misalignments between rules in different modules. Once a module produces a problem, you go in and do some tweaking until the problem goes away. Once the rules have been realigned, the system is globally more efficient. In fact, this was a frequent defense of gaming during the congressional hearings on the Enron scandal.[28]

However, the logic of modularization makes such a process of iterative perfection unlikely. Local processes of creative problem-solving occur con-comitantly. Designers in different departments continuously and experi-mentally tweak rules in response to local problems. Each time they change a rule, they change the global baseline of incentives for market participants' behavior. The optimization of rules occurs against this shifting baseline. To the extent that this leads to new behavior, old fixes can interact with new ones to produce incentives for gaming.[29] For this reason, iterative problem-solving in different modules does not converge on a globally consistent set of rules. I refer to this as the problem of temporal instability. It was the true reason that California's market design kept generating new loopholes.

Finally, not all design challenges decompose neatly into modules. In-deed, to the extent that these challenges emerge during the design pro-cesses, new modules might become necessary long after the designers have drawn up the initial architecture. The need for new modules might necessi-tate changes to the entire configuration of the system. This is often difficult or even impossible to achieve. Even if this problem could be solved, the re-sponsibilities of identifying and planning for such modules may simply fall through the cracks between teams. Because the division of labor mirrors that of the system's architecture, tasks not adequately associated with spe-cific modules or their interrelation may simply fall by the wayside. This is the problem of incomplete decomposition.

The four problems have a simple takeaway. Designers can only enforce the correct logic of action inside any one market if it is consistent with the information and incentives actors confront anywhere in the system. Other-wise, actors will identify inconsistencies, break the required interface re-lationships, and derail the market design by deviating from the vision of the blueprint. Successful market design requires globally consistent sets of rules, contexts of action, and horizons of the future. Simplification and bounding have to provide these. However, modularized design work tends to produce only locally optimal sets of rules; the three techniques are bound to contexts that do not coincide with the perspective of market actors. If the allocation problem becomes complex enough to require modularized implementation processes, gaming incentives will emerge as a matter of course. Indeed, if they compound often enough, they will overwhelm any capable control structure—as in the case of California. I will now show how the problems of modularization explain why the designers adopted the rules and procedures that prompted market power, arbitrage, and conges-tion games. These problems also explain why efforts to simplify, bound, and control the market can have the opposite effect from the one intended— a more complex system whose behavior is less predictable.

Modularization Leads to Differential Simplification

The most basic flaws in California's system were incomplete and differential simplifications. These pervasive problems showed up in multiple forms. Financial and imbalance markets set prices for nominally identical products differently. The inter- and intrazonal market mechanisms represented the grid at different resolutions. The market software for the spot markets was designed to aid short-term decisions. This made it difficult for companies to understand when they should invest.

In each case, designers simplified an element of the market but did so in a way that was inconsistent with other elements of the system. Paradoxically, this exacerbated the complexity of the system by destabilizing the definition of the context of choice and the actors' ability to read rules together. The market actors turned from predictable processors of information into unpredictable wolves searching the system for weaknesses and finding them in the vastly increased permutations of possible behaviors. The three problems of modularization explain why designers adopted the rules and procedures that had this effect.

PROBLEM 1: FRAGMENTED ATTENTION

I begin with the decisions behind the market clearing protocols in the imbalance and financial markets. Operators in the control room used resources from the imbalance markets selectively. They received supply stacks for increments and decrements and chose separately from each of these two stacks. They also skipped bids, substituting more expensive resources for cheaper ones. In contrast, the Power Exchange simply computed an optimal supply curve and a corresponding demand curve. To determine the clearing price and the sales, it then intersected the two curves. Other differences pertained to the treatment of exceptions (e.g., how to represent so-called reliability-must-run contracts in the auctions) and reactions to problems like scarce transmission capacity. Generally, the operators satisfied their demand flexibly from the available supply stack, while the Power Exchange identified an ideal intersection of supply and demand automatically. This created a variety of mechanical price differences between the markets. These differences attracted illegal arbitrage trades. The question is why the designers did not ensure that the operators used the resources optimally.

The decisions about the market clearing protocols date from the second half of 1997. At that time, the design teams had already collaborated with external vendors to build the software and hardware for the new markets. The working groups had already migrated into the office buildings that would later become the system operator (in Folsom) and the Power Exchange (in Alhambra). A team in Folson was responsible for the layout of the control room—the large, circular room with the map board and the different workstations. Among other things, the team dealt with the layout of the interface that operators would use to select increment and decrement resources from the imbalance markets. The software vendor ABB had sent a team of programmers who were working with point people from the management team—economists and engineers. To manage the imbalance markets and the settlements, they had developed the BEEP software, which was running on one of the workstations in the control room. It provided the operators with the resources from the imbalance markets, determined the real-time price, and sent the results to settlement routines.

When customizing the software for the control room, the design team needed to decide what this interface should look like—how the operators would see and engage with resources on the screen. The tariff for the new markets provided only general directives. It stated that "the sources of Imbalance Energy . . . will be arranged in merit order of Energy bid prices, with respect to both incremental and decremental Energy bids."[30]

How exactly the incremental and decremental bids were to be displayed in the final "merit order" was left open. Accordingly, the team interpreted the task in terms of their general mandate to ease the work of the operators. All "applications were designed primarily to serve as tools to assist in the decision-making relating to the CAISO control area."[31] In this case, the team knew that the operators would draw on the resources with only a few minutes to spare, while considering a variety of different sources of information. To make it easy, quick, and intuitive to use BEEP, they first introduced some flexibility into the software. Without confronting obstacles, operators could easily mix and match resources from the BEEP stack. The team noted that this was the only way to ensure that the operators could take all the information around them into consideration. They later wrote that "the BEEP system is also automated; however, its execution involves manual procedures and human judgment, applied primarily by control room dispatch operators, who determine which generation units are ultimately utilized to satisfy the CAISO real time energy needs."[32] Giving operators the discretion to dispatch resources out of merit order was important to allow the "human judgment" that was necessary to meet the challenges of real-time balancing.

The same thinking applied to the layout of the software. After trying several different configurations, the designers settled on an interface that separated bids into two stacks.[33] This made it easy to see what resources were available for either task and deploy them accordingly. The discretion and layout of the BEEP software did not outright violate the directives the designers had received. The freedom to choose arbitrary resources from the stack left it up to operators to choose the optimal combination of increments and decrements.[34] But the bifurcation of the two stacks also made it convenient for operators to dispatch the two sides separately. The interface thus guided operators' attention in such a way that they ended up using the two types of resources for separate tasks rather than combining them into ideal configurations.[35]

Because they only had to work on the control room, the teams did not consider how their decisions would affect the incentives the actors faced in the Power Exchange. Even if they had wanted to, this would have been difficult. For one, the Power Exchange was halfway across the state in Alhambra, and the flow of information was severely restricted. If teams at the system operator wanted to know about decisions at the Power Exchange, they had to submit formal requests at FERC after the two entities had split into separate organizations. The teams therefore tended to treat the scheduling coordinators as black boxes—they considered them only in terms of their abstract interfaces. This is particularly visible in the way the teams dealt with the results that came from the scheduling coordinators. The design rules specified the appearance of the schedules the coordinators transmitted to CAISO's interfaces. Before the start of the market system, the system operator ran fifty extended system tests. They invited market participants into the building, taught them how to use the software, and cooperated with the Power Exchange. Throughout these tests, the team only examined whether the data had arrived in the correct format.[36] Working with random data and users who followed the rules, the team's main concern was to get the input-output relations right.

The decision to give operators the freedom to dispatch generators out of order and separate the increment and decrement stacks made sense in terms of the goals in the module. It was a prudent response (operators found it practical) to a local problem (how to organize the layout of the control room). Following the dictate of modularization, the designers ignored how these decisions affected the incentives in the financial markets, which were considered in terms of inputs and outputs.

The same logic explains why teams working on other modules did not detect the problems these decisions would create. In 1996, the team working on bidding rules for the new auctions in the PX hired the market designer Robert Wilson from Stanford. He worked with the experimentalist Charles Plott and a firm called London Analytics. Wilson wrote activity rules, and Plott tested them in laboratory experiments. As early as 1997, Wilson filed a brief with the WEPEX Steering Committee, noting that there should be avenues to allow for arbitrage between the different components of the system: "A central requirement in the overall design of the energy markets is enabling sufficient arbitrage."[37] At the time, such rules were still missing, and Wilson was thinking of ways to solve the problem.

Because he was working on the financial side of the system, his main concern was the relationship between scheduling coordinators rather than the one between them and the imbalance markets. He suggested that one might solve the problem by "enabling a market for trading Inc/Dec options among the various scheduling coordinators, including the [Power Exchange]."[38] Designers on the financial side of the system were thus well aware of the danger posed by unlicensed arbitrage opportunities. After all, the design community had objected to the separation and equality provisions as well as the rules that implemented them. But the designers could describe the problem only in terms of the interface relationships between modules. There clearly needed to be a way to enable arbitrage between modules, but it was not clear how or where exactly to create it.

For any more detailed proposals, the team would have needed to probe into the black box below the interface that linked the imbalance markets with the Power Exchange markets. This was not part of their job, so Wilson merely noted the problem as an aside and moved on. Interestingly, he complained early and publicly about the low level of cooperation and transparency between the different parts of the design process.[39] Bounded by the modularized structure of the project, the designers on the financial side did not perceive the decisions that created the problematic incentives in their own modules.

The same dynamic explains the flaws in the representation of the grid in the congestion management system. The system had two elements that were complexly linked: a market for inter- and a market for intrazonal transmission capacity. An independent design team worked on the implementation of the interzonal system. Software designers and former traders worked together to create a system that would make it easy and intuitive for traders to identify price differences between locations and adjust their portfolios accordingly. Because they focused on the experience of market participants, they were concerned about cognitive limitations. In terms of market design, they were trying to ensure that the participants could always identify the most rational trade in terms of the existing incentives.

The global pattern of power flows could affect the availability of transmission capacity anywhere in the system at any time. Strictly speaking, a market for transmission capacity would therefore need to reflect these constant fluctuations. But if the designers had built a system that reflected every line and every change in power flows, an average trader would have needed to sort through billions of possible trades to identify the most profitable one. This clearly exceeded what could be expected from an average human. The design team therefore settled on a simplified representation with only three locations. The two main zones, SP15 and NP15, captured the main source of congestion in the past—the path that linked the old service territory of Pacific Gas & Electric in the north with that of Edison. The team assumed that this would capture the most serious and predictable sources of congestion. New zones might be defined should the congestion patterns change.

A separate set of teams were working on CONG, the congestion management system for intrazonal congestion in the whole grid. It accepted the results from the interzonal market at the Power Exchange, checked them for inaccuracies, and finally adjusted the schedules to real-time flows of energy. Following the logic of modularization, the team assumed that the inputs from the other markets would be correct. Their main concern was how best to integrate CONG with the rest of the infrastructure and how to reconcile the market schedules with the residual congestion on the paths not reflected in the zones. Because the system operator had to correct the results from each scheduling coordinator separately, this was a complicated and mathematically demanding procedure.

Again, each team defined their tasks in terms of the local concerns of the module they were working on. While the interzonal teams focused on the question of how they could make a market environment that allowed rational action in terms of the model, the teams working on the intrazonal software considered how to use the information from the markets to manage the system. Neither side considered that they represented the market at a different resolution from the other. Since the two systems were presumed independent modules, fragmented attention obscured these inconsistencies. This brings us to the next problem.

PROBLEM 2: INCOMPLETE COORDINATION

Because no modularization of complex problems is perfect, organizations do not completely seal off their teams from one another. They employ executives and intermediaries who analyze the relationships between teams and update the design rules in response to new interdependencies. The WEPEX Steering Committee constantly looked for problems like Ricochet or Death Star. They hired economists and engineers who analyzed the protocols for the new markets with these concerns in mind. However, these intermediaries considered problems at a certain level of abstraction. They focused on decisions that were related to problems in the interplay between modules in the larger system. While they identified many potential gaming opportunities, they also ignored decisions that seemed to pertain only to local problems. The decisions about the layout of the BEEP stack are a good example because they affected the relationship between the imbalance markets and the financial markets and thus fell into the purview of intermediaries' work. Yet they somehow missed these decisions, nonetheless.

The relationship between the financial and the physical sides of the system was a topic of explicit concern at the steering committee. Because all experts had opposed the memorandum, it was clear that market separation would cause problems. The idea was not backed by economic theory; it represented an article of faith. Implementing the separation therefore presented a variety of technical and conceptual challenges. In a comment, a prominent market designer wrote, "The difficulty is not with power exchanges separate from the ISO per se, the difficulty is in the definition of the role of the ISO and the connection with the power exchanges."[40] It was a high-level conceptual problem, and the members of the steering committee spent much time pondering it.

In the initial FERC application to establish the new system, the steering committee had already recognized the basic problem at the heart of games like Ricochet. They note that "the Power Exchange cannot function effectively without the system operator, since the Power Exchange bidders depend on the system operator for real-time balancing of load and generation resources." Correctly, they conclude that the separation can "only work if there are no substantial price differences" between the markets.[41]

But they quickly settled on a potential solution to the problem. In 1996, they determined that the financial markets "will establish an initial merit order dispatch for each hour in the next day" and that, in the next step, "the system operator redispatches power exchange loads and resources in merit order . . . based on incremental/decremental prices."[42] Both entities were to clear the market on the basis of "merit order dispatch"—in other words, the cheapest combination of generator outputs to meet demand in a given hour, relative to system constraints.

With consistent market clearing protocols, the only differences between the two markets would be random fluctuations in the price of exceedingly small quantities of "physical capacity." This decision shaped the directive of the tariff, which was then handed to the dispatch integration team. From the global perspective, the problem was resolved. All decisions about how this directive would be implemented were relegated to local teams. As long as the teams did not violate the directive, there was no need to check on this process in any detail. Accordingly, intermediaries examined whether the rules were consistent with merit order dispatch.

As we saw, the design team's implementation did not violate the directive outright. Rather, they operated with a different definition of merit order dispatch. Giving the operators the freedom to identify the ideal combination of resources enabled them to balance the grid in light of the complex technical contingencies they might encounter. Nonetheless, the resulting inconsistencies were not visible on the level of the tariff. For example, it was the layout of the BEEP software that nudged actors to use increments and decrements separately. The design features (software layout) thus prompted one practice that created incentives for Ricochet. Importantly, these incentives only emerged in the interplay of different local factors. The control room was a case of "extended cognition"—a system where human actors and the material environment interacted to create particular cognitive abilities.[43] The reports about the design process and the tariff depict the markets at the Power Exchange and the system operator as working synchronously. But in the context of the control room, "merit order dispatch" simply gained a different, practical meaning.

This problem is even clearer for operators' practice of skipping bids. In the control room, the map and control stations allowed operators to see the power system in quite some detail. In this environment, it was sometimes reasonable to skip resources in the imbalance markets. When the resources were scattered too far across the map, could provide only small amounts of energy, or could provide valuable backup services, operators chose to skip them. From this perspective, these decisions preserved merit order dispatch by optimizing the reliability of the system as represented in the control room. But from the perspective of the financial markets, which represented locations and generators in simplified form, these decisions violated the ideal dispatch and generated price differences.

The decisions about the rules that prompted these practices were not visible from the global level. They seemed to pertain to purely local issues, such as how to set up a screen layout or where to put a map. Furthermore, from the center it looked as if the general problem had been resolved already. Mandating merit order dispatch seemed sufficient to prevent the inconsistent prices because the term did not appear ambiguous and decisions that might lead to divergent interpretations did not register on the global level. This is the deeper sense in which problematic design decisions were irreducibly local: their significance could only be comprehended relative to the full context of work in the control room. Intermediaries could not see the relevance of these decisions to the interplay between the different modules. Incomplete coordination meant that inconsistencies remained unseen if they did not raise to the same level of abstraction intermediaries operated on.

Some of the decisions that could have far-ranging implications for the market system as a whole took place in local modules where those implications were not easily visible. On the global level, designers did not perceive these decisions because they considered the problems at too high a level of abstraction.

PROBLEM 3: TEMPORAL INSTABILITY

The parallelism of modularized design work made it difficult to remove problematic incentives even when designers did discover problems. Throughout the design process, the steering committee hired market design experts who worked for Perot Systems, London Analytics, and Price Waterhouse. They actively searched for ways in which protocols might lead to gaming activities. After the markets started, monitoring units continued this work. Here we are approaching the root of a problem that provided a puzzling observation in chapter 4: market designers constantly discovered games and fixed them even before the crisis started. But the efforts to identify and resolve inconsistencies between rules in different parts of the system did not actually push the system toward perfection. Instead, new games and new versions of old games kept emerging. In the first month of market operation, CAISO filed seven amendments to its tariff. By the end of 1999, they had filed twenty-three major tariff changes. Many amendments contained references to games that had to be eradicated via rule changes.[44]

The basic problem was this: even if designers detected an issue in the interplay between different rules, adjustments necessarily occurred on the local level. Since multiple reactions occurred concomitantly, designers could never account for all interactions between components on the global level. One market designer described the work process in an interview from 1999: "There was a lot of work, a lot of fast changes, a lot of reactions—as soon as [one issue] was done, we started the next one."[45] The fast reactions required designers to rely on experimentalism. As one engineer remembers, "We tried in the design to deal with mismatches and holes the best we could, but the thought was that we were going to do the best we could. And then if something came up, we'd change it."[46] Designers would identify problems, develop a quick local fix, and then move on to the next issue. But because this happened everywhere, the global baseline of incentives kept changing. Since the behavioral foundation of the system was not stable, iterative attempts to identify problems and solve them via rule changes never came to an end. Solutions to old problems could suddenly produce new problems as fixes in other parts of the system affected the global balance of incentives.

Ricochet provides a useful illustration here because attempts to fix this game interacted with an older solution and merely shifted the problem to a different venue. One of the most persistent problems during the first year of operation occurred in the ancillary service markets—these markets traded four different kinds of backup service that could be traded in day-ahead and real-time markets. These services could come online at different speeds. For example, spinning reserves are already running and can therefore provide energy faster than nonspinning reserves. Those services that come online faster are generally considered higher quality than those that are slower be- cause they can be substituted for slower resources. The system operator had inflexible needs for each of these services and had separate auction markets for them. When there was not enough supply in one of the markets, sellers could drive up prices without fear of losing business. This created the bi- zarre situation where lower-quality resources could command much higher prices than higher-quality resources. On July 9, 1998, the market for the in- ferior replacement reserves spiked to $9,999—the maximal input value on the software interface—even though there were ample supplies of higher- quality services.[47]

To solve this problem, a special task force under leadership of Stanford economists restructured the entire ancillary service market system. Forced by the complexity of the system to take a cognitively narrow perspective, they presumed that the rest of the system remained fixed and focused on the relationship between the ancillary markets. Apart from new market mech- anisms that enabled CAISO to substitute higher-quality for lower-quality services, CAISO moved 7 percent of its demand from the day-ahead mar- ket to the day-of market. This was supposed to depress the price in the day- ahead markets. The price for the whole market was set at that of the last generator necessary to meet demand. Accordingly, the less demand there was in the market, the lower the price would be. Shifting demand therefore succeeded, and the cost of ancillary services declined by roughly 50 percent from April 1998 to March 1999.[48]

However, operators now bought a substantial amount of ancillary ser- vice capacity so close to dispatch that there was limited time to verify the resources or substitute them for alternatives. This created a latent prob- lem. Just like the imbalance markets, the ancillary service markets were supposed to be independent from the financial markets. But there was a link between the ancillary service markets and the imbalance markets. If they did not need the ancillary services, operators could select increments or decrements from generators who had previously sold their capacity as ancillary services. In that case, the generator was paid twice: for providing the backup capacity in the ancillary markets and for providing the energy in the imbalance market. The potential for double payments could amplify the price differences between the PX markets and the CAISO markets substantially. Such mechanical price differences might, once again, trigger a game like Ricochet—moving energy in and out of California to circumvent the access restrictions on the system operator's markets. Benefiting from the lax controls in the real-time ancillary markets, participants might illegally enter first the real-time ancillary markets and then the imbalance markets.

However, at first this did not happen because capacity in the ancillary service markets was cheap and operators usually skipped these resources. There was simply no good way for power marketers to move high-priced bids from the ancillary markets to the imbalance markets. Because the path was blocked, power marketers played the standard version of Ricochet and left these markets alone. However, the 7 percent rule eventually made clear the inherent risk of this setup.

Ironically, this happened when the designers addressed the original Ricochet strategy. During the energy crisis, the system operator discovered the problem. Because Ricochet relied on false imports, a local team from the market monitoring unit implemented a new rule to limit out-of-market purchases for imbalance. Again, they considered the problem in isolation— they saw that imports created problems, so they increased the barriers. But the change reverberated through the system as a whole. To compensate for the loss of imports, the system operator needed to increase its purchase of increments and decrements from ancillary services. Thus, it became more likely that energy bid into the real-time ancillary service market would be sold in the imbalance markets.

Because the system operator had moved a large amount of its demand for ancillary services into the real-time market (the 7 percent rule) and would draw on them to provide imbalance energy, power marketers now had an incentive to circumvent the access restrictions and enter imbalance markets via the real-time ancillary service markets. They would use the same old import-export scheme to enter the ancillary markets—where imports were still acceptable—and enjoy being paid twice when the operators had to use these resources. Shortly after the rule change took effect, a report diagnosed the issue: "It appears the purchase of significant amounts of Replacement Reserve . . . may have created an additional incentive for suppliers . . . to shift additional capacity into the Ancillary Services . . . and real time markets."[49]

What used to be a solution to a behavioral problem (shifting demand into real-time ancillary markets) created a new problem when a rule in another part of the system shifted (restrictions on imports for imbalance energy). The new rule changed the configuration of incentives that actors faced in the old market (large potential arbitrage profits between financial and ancillary service plus imbalance markets), leading to different behavior (gaming the imbalance market via the ancillary market) that turned the old solution into a source of new problems.

At the heart of the matter is a general problem: the management of electricity systems is technically demanding and complex. Teams working on individual parts constantly confront new, small problems requiring local adaptations that should be sustained by the inherent modularization of the system. These local adaptations are based on a targeted search for solutions given the assumption that the rest of the system can be treated as constant. The cognitive narrowing has substantial implications. Since market actors can connect each part of the system to any other, every adjustment can shift the balance of incentives and lead to new types of behavior that derail the design. This changes the baseline against which the designers need to define solutions and renders old solutions potentially ineffective. Likewise, the development of the new Ricochet variant shows that market actors shift their behavior and exploit different blind spots in the information architecture as teams resolve old ones. In that way, the organizational structure of market design work is at odds with the internal logic of designer markets. It tends to create gaming opportunities as a matter of course, and it produces only locally optimal rules when it should produce globally consistent ones. This leads to differential simplification—the paradoxical process by which the effort to make it easy and intuitive to follow designers' plans actually multiplies the ways actors can deviate from it.

PROBLEM 4: INCOMPLETE DECOMPOSITION

Modularization has yet another and more general drawback: it is not always possible to decompose design problems neatly into interrelated modules. Of course, all designers know this. The solution is simple: designers either draw the boundaries of the module around the problem or carefully control the interrelations between modules that have to play together.[50] However, these solutions require that the problem be apparent at the stage when designers draw up the design rules. If it only emerges at a later stage, repartitioning becomes difficult. Most importantly, the modularized teams might simply miss the decomposition problem because they are organized along the lines of the existing architecture. The relevant issues might simply fall between the cracks of team responsibilities.

The California system featured dozens of scheduling coordinators.

Between 1998 and 2001, forty-two entities submitted schedules to CAISO.[51] Several of these companies were energy producers who simply resubmitted commitments from long-term contracts on a daily basis.[52] They did not play an active role as intermediaries. But roughly a dozen power marketers operated their own brokerage services and alternative auction markets. As I have pointed out before, the designers intended to create markets that would find an approximate solution to the economic dispatch—the cheapest configuration of generator outputs to meet demand at all locations. Conceived as a search algorithm, the markets had to iterate over all generators in the system. Because the many different markets fragmented the search, the designers should have effected measures to reconcile the results from the different markets. We already saw that the equality provision prevented the system operator and the Power Exchange from doing so centrally. Accordingly, the designers should have found an alternative mechanism to do so.

One solution would have been an auction for schedule adjustment bids. The system operator already used these bids to adjust schedules that violated dispatch requirements. The bids indicated the price at which companies were willing to adjust the production or consumption of energy. They communicated opportunity costs and helped dispatch operators to adjust the output of generators to optimize the global dispatch structure. But market participants only communicated their bids to their scheduling coordinator, and scheduling coordinators submitted adjustment bids independently from each other. Both the imbalance and the congestion management systems therefore calculated the necessary adjustment for the submissions from each scheduling coordinator, rather than for the combined schedules from all coordinators. Clearly, this was not efficient: generators in other markets may have had lower opportunity costs to reduce their output or cheaper resources to increase it. It would therefore have made sense to collect these bids from all scheduling coordinators and then create a market where they could be traded to optimize across the different portfolios. As we have seen, Robert Wilson proposed precisely this kind of mechanism.[53]

Yet, the design rules did not contain such a market module. No one had noticed the problem beforehand because the concept of a scheduling coordinator did not emerge until halfway through 1995.[54] One engineer remembered that the idea simply popped up in response to a technical problem one day: "In one of those [WEPEX] meetings, a woman who worked for us had introduced the term *scheduling coordinator*. We were trying to figure out how the transmission operator would deal with the tens of thousands of schedules that would be coming in. It wasn't feasible. So we decided we needed these entities that aggregated the schedules and called them scheduling coordinators."[55]

At that point, the basic architecture for the system was already in place, and team responsibilities had been set. The teams working on modules that used adjustment bids treated them as simple inputs. Dutifully, they noted that there was no mechanism to arbitrage between scheduling coordinators, sent the information up the chain, and moved on with their work. No team was responsible for organizing the relationship between scheduling coordinators. To keep things as simple as possible, the tariff envisioned that scheduling coordinators would only interface with the system operator—not with one another. The steering committee noted the complaints about a missing market for adjustment bids, but things were moving too fast on too many levels to change anything about the basic architecture in 1997. In a filing to FERC, the WEPEX Steering Committee vowed to create a bulletin-board mechanism that would facilitate trades of schedule adjustment bids. But nothing happened. In the handbook for the Power Exchange from 1999, the author merely hints at a future software update that might allow such inter-scheduling-coordinator arbitrage.[56]

The missing market illustrates the key problem of modularization: once the design rules are in place and teams are working on the modules, changes become difficult. Because a market for schedule adjustment bids would have represented an additional layer between the scheduling coordinators and the system operator, it would have required changes to many different modules. The steering committee therefore postponed decisions on the matter. More importantly, the issue fell through the cracks of team responsibilities. Precisely because teams were responsible for existing modules, no team was charged with thinking through the substantial adjustments to the overall architecture. At the level of the steering committee and the California Public Utility Commission, this kind of change was no longer deemed possible when the need finally registered. Accordingly, it fell by the wayside as the designers hurtled toward the magical deadline of January 1, 1998.

The same dynamic explains why the system did not encourage companies to construct sufficient reserve capacity—the central reason for the emergence of market power. Recall the problem. The blueprints required the financial markets to produce an approximate solution to the dispatch problem in the short run. But they also needed to convince companies to invest in new generation capacity over the long term. During the political process, the stakeholders had discarded the biennial resource plan update—the existing regulatory framework for long-term investments.

Enron's comments capture the reasoning behind this move well: "The entire Biennial Resource Plan Update ('BRPU') process . . . proves that no matter how well-intentioned, centralized, governmental planning of generation investment is inefficient, and ultimately, arbitrary. . . . Going forward it would be much more productive if parties were encouraged to compete in the context of a direct access market for power."[57]

Unlike the memorandum, this argument encountered little resistance from market designers. Opposition would have been political suicide. One of the main reasons for restructuring was that the California Public Utility Commission had approved the utilities' costly and inefficient investments in the past. The whole rationale for introducing markets was to shift the risk of bad investments to producers. Accordingly, market designers would have destroyed themselves politically if they had advocated for an administrative solution to the capacity problems. This was also not necessary because Hogan and others had argued that a pure-energy market could be trusted to create incentives for investment.

Nonetheless, the market design here faced a problem of understanding—it was difficult for market actors to perceive the relevant incentives. The interfaces of the PX had to help companies anticipate future shortfalls of capacity early enough to build the plants in time. An engineer at Edison summarized the problem. Unless the market provided this information early on, "the market would have to experience three years of load growth, ever tightening demand/supply balance, degradation of reliability, and increasing prices until new generation arrived."[58] Yet the designers in California never addressed this problem. As we have seen, the interfaces of the spot markets were optimized for short-term decisions. Predicting when exactly new generation would pay off was therefore both risky and uncertain. I have given two primary reasons that the markets produced these difficulties.

First, companies did not know whether other companies were also investing. If there were alternative investments and thus a glut of supply, excess generation would not be recompensed. Second, companies had to recoup their investments through markets that priced individual hours of operation in the future. In other words, they had to bet that several years later, they would make windfall profits in a particular hour of operation. This was a risky bet indeed. Because everyone with a morsel of generation benefited from price spikes if there was a shortage, there was no strong reason to make such a risky bet. Theoretically, there were incentives to build generation: if you timed it just right, you could set an adequate market clearing price as the pivotal generator and, if the price spike was recognized as a marginal cost, make enough money to recover fixed costs. But it was practically impossible to discern when this incentive would material-ize into profits.

A case in point is the fact that the California Energy Commission re-ceived no applications for new power plants between 1994 and 1997 — the period during which the markets were first created. Since no one knew under what conditions they would be able to sell their output, no one in-vested.[59] This was a classic problem of understanding: at some point, there would be shortages and generation companies would receive high prices. The designers just had to ensure that the companies knew far enough in ad-vance that this would be the case and that they understood the incentives. There was a clear call for simplification: the designers needed to create an infrastructure to get this information to market participants quickly and re-liably.

But no particular team had been assigned the task of optimizing the sys-tem for the long run. No specific module — like a capacity market — fulfilled the function. Accordingly, multiple parts of the architecture dealt with new capacity, but none were targeted to communicate the incentives to in-vestors in time. For example, the teams working on the system operator's open-access same-time information system, called WEnet, produced infor-mation about future capacity needs. They set up protocols for making reg-ular resource adequacy assessments and getting this information to inves-tors. Several regulatory bodies also dealt with this issue. The management team ran regular adequacy checks, and the California Energy Commission did studies to forecast demand growth. But communicating increasing de-mand was not enough. Companies needed to know that they would recoup the costs of their investments. They needed clear signals of how and when these costs would be covered in the financial markets.

The steering committee tasked the Emergency Response Team with en-suring that there would always be capacity to draw on. But this team was not responsible for any of the markets.[60] Instead, they considered the prac-tical problem of what to do when the system operator ran out of supplies. They put together a set of measures for extreme situations, including pro-visions to draw on ancillary services and out-of-market transactions. The relevant document states that "the system operator has the ability to call on ANY unit within the control area, after all Market and RMR [reliability-must-run] sources have been exhausted."[61] The out-of-market transactions allowed the operators to buy energy from utilities in adjacent service terri-tories at very flexible prices if they were in a pinch.[62] The team also put to-gether protocols for rolling blackouts. But they did not work on signals to investors.

The steering committee told the team working out the activity rules for the Power Exchange that the main goal was to facilitate self-scheduling—selling energy for production on the same or the next day. When Robert Wilson and Charles Plott presented the activity rules, they committed themselves to the principle of simplicity: "As a practical matter, the activity rules must be easily understood by the traders and simple for the power exchange to implement."[63] They therefore offered tightly specified rules that "should be applied automatically by the power exchange software." The generic step function made short-term trading easier and gave traders a certain flexibility in how they recovered their costs. But it also made it almost impossible to signal to market participants which costs they would be able to recover in the long term. The designers could have introduced side payments for capacity or allowed companies to decompose their bids into production and investment costs. But this would have made the short-term more complicated and thus violated their mandate.

Again, the problem is that a crucial design challenge simply fell through the cracks. Because the signals for long-term investments were not associated with a single module, no team was responsible for them. The emergency team presupposed the existence of generation assets and clarified how the system operator would access them. The WEnet team considered how to communicate information about future demand. Because these other teams dealt with capacity issues, the Power Exchange team was supposed to focus on interfaces that would simplify and bound the decisions about short-term energy production and consumption. The issue just drifted off into the margins of the process as the WEPEX teams worked frantically to get their modules operational.

Of course, the emergence of market power could have been prevented with a capacity market or a powerful control structure. Yet the designers somehow failed to advocate for either of these provisions to check the problems that kept escalating around them. The final chapter looks more closely at the way the designers approached their work to explain why.

Conclusion

This chapter has dealt with relatively intricate, technical problems, but the core message can be summarized in one sentence: the designers were forced to adopt an organizational structure that was at odds with the requirements for successful design. Modularization prevented designers from deploying strategies of simplification and bounding effectively. Because market actors did not respect the boundaries between modules, rule changes in nominally independent parts of the system began to interact with one another. Efforts to simplify markets in one module created inconsistencies elsewhere and escalated the global complexity of the system. The inconsistencies gave rise to mechanical price differences, and actors began to explore their newfound freedoms to profit from these price differences. This derailed the logic of the system. The incomplete decomposition of some design problems, furthermore, created problems for the relationships between modules. There were no dedicated teams to fix these issues (missing market for schedule adjustment bids), while a variety of residual issues fell through the cracks of team responsibilities (interface optimization for long-term investments). The political process set a baseline that not only forced designers to adopt not only some rules that violated design logic (rules for scheduling coordinators) but also an organizational structure that was at odds with their goals.

As WEPEX proceeded, more and more inconsistencies emerged, pushing the system out of alignment with the designers' goals. Whether market actors followed the calculative logic of the designers' blueprints became increasingly arbitrary. To some extent, these problems were visible: the intermediaries kept identifying new games and changing the rules in response to little problems. It should have been clear that the requirements for active control and firm boundaries constantly increased. The more likely inconsistencies between rules, procedures, and interfaces became, the tighter the control should have been. I have already shown that the system had passed the point where a centralized oversight regime could have managed the market on the basis of formal criteria. Regardless of how powerful the control structure had been, the system would always have produced new avenues for gaming. These would have been difficult to detect because the space of possible behavior was too broad to allow a standardized assessment of transactions.

Yet the market designers might at least have pushed for a strong control structure to keep the worst excesses at bay. There should have been active enforcement against market power at the very least. The more ways actors could deviate from the requirements of the blueprints, the more emphasis there should have been on active and ongoing control. The inconsistencies between the financial and imbalance markets called for a strict enforcement of the access rules. But practically anyone could become a scheduling coordinator and circumvent them. The designers should have introduced strict controls on scheduling coordinator transactions. The signals for long-term investments were weak. Accordingly, there should have been a regulatory mandate for high reserve margins and a way to allocate the costs for these margins. If the markets could not guarantee long-term investments, the designers should have ensured that regulatory processes did. But none of this happened.

These absences are a matter of neither modularization nor politics. The designers were free to advocate for and build these architectural elements, yet they did not. Why exactly did the designers not recognize the many ways in which the market system was moving out of alignment with their plans, and why did they not try to counterbalance the escalating complexity with firm boundaries and active control? What about their vision for the system obscured these fundamental flaws? This will be the topic of the last chapter.

CHAPTER SEVEN

The Chameleonic Market

In the political negotiations, key stakeholders and politicians ignored the Cassandra cries that echoed from ivory towers far and wide. When the designers finally took control in technical working groups, they had to contend with a hybrid proposal that violated core principles of market design. The complex architecture and the tight deadlines led them to adopt a modularized approach to their design work. But the technique obscured the global impact of local decisions and debilitated routines for identifying and resolving inconsistencies between submarkets. Efforts to simplify and bound each submarket had the opposite effect: designers' decisions led to differential simplification. Different parts of the market architecture simplified the representation of the electricity system in different ways. This escalated the permutations of possible behavior in the interplay between markets and multiplied the ways in which actors could violate the design rules to extract bandit profits. Inconsistencies in decisions about boundaries made it easy to circumvent the few firm boundaries that existed; the chain was only as strong as its weakest link.

Designers' political and organizational problems explain why they were unable to create rules that guided market actors to the desired logic of action. But these problems do not tell the whole story. Neither the inability to neutralize interest politics nor the tension between modularization and the logic of designer markets can explain the strange silences and absences in the design process. As we followed the designers into the depths of technical working groups, we found a variety of instances where they could have done something to fix the problems but did not. There was no institutional structure in place to guarantee that companies would make the crucially important, long-term investments in new generation capacity. Interest politics had gotten rid of the biennial resource plan update—the regulatory process to ensure long-term investments. And the need to optimize short-term markets for long-term decisions had fallen through the cracks of modularized teamwork. Yet the designers never attempted to create an administrative or market solution to compel these investments. This, in turn, raised the very real specter of market power—and yet the designers created weak monitoring units with limited oversight. Similarly, it was crucially important for scheduling coordinators to act as neutral brokers. To encourage the creation of a market for intermediaries, WEPEX members enacted application rules that made it easy for power marketers to assume this role. They had little choice in the matter. But why did market designers not demand that these rules be accompanied by rigid reporting and transparency standards for the monitoring units? In other words, as problems with attempts to simplify and bound the markets compounded, designers did little to create vigilant, regulatory structures to keep market behavior in check.

The remaining design flaws all concern the administrative structure that implemented, managed, and adjusted the market processes to maintain a match between the desired and the real market mechanisms. The requirements for this control structure continuously grew as the design process moved forward. To ensure that the participants followed the algorithm as required, designers had to constrain the ways in which actors could frame their context of action. This required consistent incentives and information in all domains of action that participants could access. As the design process multiplied the inconsistencies between subsystems, the requirements for control became more intense. By the time the markets opened in 1998, the structure had grown so unwieldy that no centralized control structure could have kept it in check; the spectrum of possible behavior had become so large that there was no way to apply formal criteria to assess whether a given transaction fit the designers' blueprints. Fixing the problem would have required an all-knowing, centralized planner. Apart from the fact that such an all-knowing planner remains a technocratic fantasy, it would subvert the very point of introducing markets.

But designers did not even try to put a reasonably strong oversight structure into place or impose administrative burdens on market participants to pay for excess capacity. Indeed, when the political, regulatory, and technical design processes were dealing with the administrative structure that would manage the market process, the designers advocated for minimal and fragmented structures.[1]

Consider the testimony of Robert Michaels, an economics professor, during the Blue Book proceedings in 1995. Shortly after his appearance, he published an article in the *Electricity Journal* that anticipated the problematic temporal logic of the markets. He writes: "Numerous specialists are laboring to squeeze every possible inefficiency out of the short-term energy exchanges before they begin to operate, but hardly anyone is thinking about future investments in the capital that will produce and move this energy. . . .

If the sunk costs of a plant of any size (as distinguished from its fixed costs) are high enough, investments will be inefficiently timed unless there is a market for capacity commitments."[2]

In this statement, Michaels shows that he is well aware of the need for regulatory intervention to ensure the correct long-term investments. He explicitly points to the need for capacity side payments and criticizes the designers for ignoring the problem. Such side payments—or a full capacity market—would be based on administrative judgments about the need and timing of the necessary investments.

Yet in his presentation to the California Public Utility Commission, Michaels does not argue for the creation of a capable oversight structure that could play this role. Instead, he proposes the opposite. He begins with a joke: "Electricity was once an industry that was so simple, you could actually regulate it." After the laughter subsides, he explains that the development of market processes made the industry too complex to be regulated: "When you get a lot of opportunities, when you get a lot of potential buyers, a lot of potential sellers, regulation can at best follow behind. It either becomes redundant or it becomes pernicious."[3] Restructuring is the solution to this problem because it involves genuine deregulation: the creation of market mechanisms will allow regulators to reduce their oversight and step into the background.

While his article suggests that electricity markets were structurally unable to self-regulate, his statements before the California Public Utility Commission seems to suggest that they do precisely this. The statements contradict each other. Statements by Paul Joskow in 1996 constitute another example of this ambivalent stance. One of the most prominent market designers in California, he consulted for Pacific Gas & Electric and acted as an independent expert witness on both federal and state levels. Deeply worried about the possibility of market power and aware of the engineering realities behind electricity systems, he warned that market power might become an important issue in California.

But then he described the necessary monitoring system like this: "Finally, because of the many novel features because of the proposed structure and other elements of the California restructuring program as well as the inevitable uncertainties associated with diagnosing market power, the applicants have recommended a three-year monitoring program be put in place to collect data that can be used by interested parties and this Commission."[4]

Here, he describes the monitoring units as a purely precautionary measure, something that might be disassembled after three years. They collect information and evaluate whether the market process works as it should. If not, the rules can be adjusted. After the time is up, the commission can evaluate whether additional changes are necessary or everything works according to plan.[5] The monitoring units may then be disbanded. Once the market process flows as needed, oversight can recede into the background and only enter the markets in case of anomalous events.

Over and over, the archival record shows us market designers who argue for specific regulatory interventions in one moment and then turn around in the next to argue against an expansion of regulatory structures. Even William Hogan, the main proponent of an integrated pool with centralized markets, vacillated on this issue. In his presentations, he argued for a pure-energy market with caps at the value of lost load (VOLL) level. High prices in the spot markets would pay for investments. This setup would require the careful monitoring of prices to ensure that they reflected real scarcity rather than market power. The imposition of the corresponding price caps would have required substantial regulatory intervention. Yet, as if discussing a self-regulating process, he writes, "A bid based pool . . . induces economic dispatch of the entire system. It also offers the right marginal incentives to build, to maintain, to run, and to close plants."[6]

At other times, market designers were present when lawyers and utility executives made problematic decisions about the administrative structure. But, in contrast to their actions during the political proceedings, they did not weigh in and try to prevent these decisions. The rules for scheduling coordinators are a case in point. A group of stakeholders wrote these rules while following the political dictates of the memorandum. An engineer from San Diego Gas & Electric presented these rules during the Direct Access Working Group on January 2, 1997, but the archival record reflects no opposition from market designers in the "Issues Raised" section of the report.[7] Instead, the debates rotate around purely technical questions about the robustness of the interface relationships between the system operator and scheduling coordinators during various contingency events.

All of this is puzzling. Here, we have a group of experts whose primary means of enforcing the desired algorithm—creating a highly simplified, bounded, and controlled market environment—was failing. It was generally clear that the memorandum had set a flawed baseline for the markets. The WEPEX Steering Committee also frequently revised the tariffs because intermediaries and consultants had found new ways to game the rules. The designers now had the chance to constrain the escalating complexity either by shoring up subsystem boundaries or by actively controlling the system. And yet they did neither.[8] Why?

Unlike acolytes of free market ideology, the market designers were not oblivious to the problem of oversight. They try to build institutional and computational structures that generate a social process with desirable attributes. Market design therefore starts with the very premise that markets do not self-regulate but require carefully tuned institutional and material structures. It is somewhat mystifying that Richard Tabors, one of the original architects of Schweppe's spot-pricing proposal, retrospectively suggested that he and the other designers had "assumed that people would act economically rationally but hadn't thought our way through all the things that might mean or not mean."[9] Tabors did advocate on behalf of Enron at the time. But he was not alone; practically all designers—including those who represented the victims of the energy crisis or who testified on their own behalf—advocated for weak oversight structures or failed to raise their voices when the issue was on the table. They helped to write the tariffs for the new system, weighed in on the new oversight structure, and talked about the danger of market power. In each case, they were confident that limited oversight and hands-off regulation would be enough. What explains the designers' halting stance, their fondness of minimal oversight, and their unwillingness to weigh in when lawyers and utility executives implemented rules that weakened both the boundaries and the control system?

This is the final puzzle an explanation of the California energy crisis faces. When I first tried to come to terms with this question, I focused on the material about the design process itself. But even though I could reconstruct the problematic design decisions on a relatively granular level, the reasons for the designers' reticence kept eluding me. How do you explain an absence or a silence with fragmentary archival material? The questions not posed, the decisions not made, and the conversations not had remained out of reach, forever tantalizing.

This chapter focuses on the last level of the institutional field: the group level, where different teams of market designers approach specific technical problems. As I will show, the answer to the puzzle has to do with the intellectual fragmentation of market designers into two intellectual camps— economics and engineering. Economics itself was split into two slightly distinct perspectives. The ambiguities below the sleek surface of shared mathematical and conceptual tools obscured the differences between these camps. Since they worked independently of one another in different parts of the design process, they did not become aware of these differences. Missing crucial insights from the other camp, each side then arrived at the conclusion that minimal oversight would suffice. In the academic nexus of research institutes and think tanks, the designers did not notice these differences because the problem of designing the oversight architecture was ill structured at the high level of abstraction the conferences assumed. Here, the design questions admitted too many different ways to parse the problem to reveal conceptual differences in the underlying approaches. After the political and organizational crises of market design expertise, then, the third crisis was intellectual. There was no informal culture that regulated precisely how the formal blueprints should be translated into practical arrangements, and this lack created room for substantial discrepancies.

I first began to develop a sense for this problem while I was chasing down leads to understand a puzzling episode that took place in 1998–99. Because this occurred after the California markets had opened, I had ignored the relevant part of the archival material until then. In this episode, a group of market monitors displayed a strange obsession with a minor operational problem in the ancillary service markets. As I followed a group of newly hired market monitors, I soon realized that their struggles held the key to the puzzle of the designers' silence three years earlier.

A Key to the Puzzle: CAISO's Ancillary Market Crisis

Only two months after the markets first opened to the public, in May 1998, the operators in CAISO's control room encountered a strange problem in the market for replacement reserves. This ancillary market was designed to procure a small amount of standby capacity to balance the difference between scheduled demand and the system's forecast one hour in advance. It was not supposed to be either very large or particularly volatile. Yet the operators observed large price spikes during times when there was almost no demand. The numbers were suspicious: $5,000 on July 9 and $9,999 on July 13, 1998.[10] Confusingly, the markets cleared with these prices when the demand was low but with reasonable prices when it was high. Also, the relationship between the prices for different ancillary services did not make sense. Lower-quality services gained higher prices than higher-quality services. Alarmed by these developments, the governing stakeholders board imposed price caps and asked monitoring teams to find out what was happening.[11]

Initially, the problem seemed like a routine issue. The numbers looked like input mistakes, and the confusing price swings indicated a software error. There were still dozens of glitches that required minor fixes from the software vendors. On the very first day, the hour-ending one, such a glitch had almost prevented the launch of the new system. Before Jim Macias, the head of grid operations, could push the button that transferred power to the system operator, the operators suddenly realized that the control number — the algebraic sum of all the energy transactions entering or leaving the network over the twenty-six intertie points that linked California's grid with adjacent control areas — was missing. The screen was blank. Without this information, the imports and exports would not be factored into the final balance of energy flows. Hurriedly, one of the operators fetched a whiteboard from a conference room. While he was gone, the other operators started calling the balancing authorities at different interties, collecting the missing information on the incoming energy flows by hand. As they jotted down numbers on the whiteboard, one operator tallied the results on a pocket calculator. They finished just barely time.[12]

Three months in, the employees were used to such glitches and the manual fixes they required. But as the monitors investigated the ancillary markets, it became clear that neither software glitches nor manual insertions could explain the main issue. Rather, the problem seemed to originate with the bidding behavior itself. A familiar explanation quickly emerged: scarcity. At the time, not many companies had the authority to sell at market-based rates, and so a few ill-considered inputs set the prices too high. This, too, seemed like a minor problem. Because of the low volume of transactions, the financial implications were minor, and new companies would soon be able to sell at market-based rates. Or so concluded the regulators at FERC. They approved price caps and moved on with their lives.[13] But while FERC was willing to let things go, the market monitors in California stuck with the issue for over a year. As an economist in the unit remembered, "The ancillary service markets occupied most of my attention for the rest of my time in the ISO."[14]

The system operator breathed the culture of Silicon Valley. Before 1998, the head of human resources had worked with tech start-ups and wanted to hire employees who had the right values. One of the system operators' founding members explained the search like this: "We need somebody who really wants to do this because it's cool, 'cause I can make this work, this is the new stuff, this is where I want to be."[15] They were looking for highly motivated people. Employees were expected to work sixty to eighty hours a week in a high-stress environment with much demand on flexible and creative problem-solving. But more importantly, they wanted to select according to commitment to the project itself. An early hire told me that the recruiters had described the culture like this: "If your mindset is that you want to continue command-and-control, then this is probably not the right place for you."[16] The system operator therefore tended to hire people—primarily economists and engineers—who were enthralled by the prospects of market efficiency.

Since it was the 1990s and free market ideology was rampant, these hires tended to share a strong belief that the markets would converge on equilibria without much additional help. Perhaps nothing illustrates this sentiment better than the market monitors' initial confusion about their jobs. When one of the new monitors first started, she did not know what she should be doing, and no one could tell her. Trained to think about the markets as analogous to the natural gas and trucking industries, she thought they would be guided by "Adam Smith's invisible hand." To gain some orientation, she even "tried to visit a couple of other industries that had market monitoring and tried to figure out, well, what it is that they call the exercise of market power" and other problems.[17]

To people like her—trained economists with a rudimentary understanding of electricity systems and no clear sense of market design—the flaws of the ancillary markets were almost offensive. It was highly counterintuitive that lower-quality services could obtain higher prices than higher-quality services or that prices would increase during times of lower demand. It looked as if the market participants behaved irrationally. But that was simply unacceptable to the monitors who identified deeply with the system operators' mission to achieve "reliability through markets." The mystery therefore justified a deeper investigation.

But as soon as they began to dig, the mystery only deepened. The databases were not providing data that was ready for analysis. Instead, they collected a variety of market and system information, much of it amended by manual insertions and edits from different departments that struggled to get their jobs done with software that kept throwing up glitches. "One of our biggest challenges at the start-up," one monitor remembered, "was understanding how the market systems themselves produced the data, because there was so much of it. . . . A tremendous amount of effort goes into just setting up the database and the analytic tools to drill into that database."[18] When they finally extracted the required data and tried to assemble it into supply and demand curves for standard econometric analyses, the results made no sense. Neither did the quantitative relations between the categories—the behavior continued to appear irrational and did not fit into the expected logic of supply and demand. Much of the data also did not fit into their models, suggesting that the analytical frameworks were missing important parts of the market process. In other words, the economists had a hard time fitting the process the designers had wrought into the standard categories of econometric analysis.

At that point, the monitoring units realized that their approach to the data must be wrong, that their analytical framework was inappropriate, and that their very understanding of the problem was insufficient.[19] To get to the bottom of the mystery, they created an independent working group that brought together two economists, two electrical engineers, a lawyer, and three administrators with expertise in data management.[20] The group had the freedom to draw on expertise from other departments. It worked in concert with the market surveillance committee, monitoring staff at the Power Exchange, the operations department, and input from other stakeholders.

In the past, cooperation between economists in the monitoring group and engineers in the operations department had been difficult. They tended to blame each other for problems and avoided engaging too deeply with each other's perspective. The problem was exacerbated by the difference in age and expertise: the economists were young and tended to come from outside the utility industry, while most engineers were older and had largely spent their careers in regulated monopolies. Instead of cooperating, they preferred to divide tasks and stick to their area of expertise.

However, to solve the ancillary market mystery and overcome the confusing complexity of the data, they had no other choice but to talk to each other. Both groups perceived the problem and wanted to solve it. While the economists had strong expectations about flawless market performance because they did not fully understand the constraints of the electricity systems, the engineers had similar expectations because they did not fully understand how these constraints would affect market performance. After a relatively brief period, they realized that the two perspectives had to be "married to each other," as one manager put it.[21] An engineer described the unfolding interactions like this:

> I used to go to the market monitoring folks and would basically have long debates with them about what causes the problem and what we are going to do about it. And it's very challenging because you have a group of people . . . who are very smart, but . . . they have never really run an electric grid before. . . . So here I am pulling my hairs, and I say, "That is not how it works." And they say, "Well, that is how it *should* work." And I say, "I don't know what it should. It just doesn't work that way." And they say, "Well, explain why it doesn't work that way." So I would explain it to them.[22]

Economists told similar stories from their perspective, suggesting that engineers had no idea how incentives worked and that it was hard to convince them to sort through all the different ways in which players might thwart the system. The interactions between the two groups would often involve little numeric examples and toy models, hashed out with pen and paper, to illustrate basic elements of system functionality (to the economists) and games of strategic interaction (to the engineers). In this way, the two sides slowly began to integrate their respective viewpoints into a unified perspective.

When the working group began to compile its internal report on what was going on, terrifying insights emerged. The group realized that companies could exercise vast amounts of market power in the course of just a few hours and that this had little to do with their market share. From this realization, a new metric for market power emerged—the pivotal supplier test, which captured the relational and flexible aspect of market power. The group also recognized that the market protocols set a variety of highly problematic incentives for strategic games. Indeed, the strange bids in the ancillary service markets had not been input mistakes, glitches, or even attempts to exercise market power. Instead, they were experiments in gaming the system. When the team pressured the power marketers for an explanation, they found out that the company had played around with the markets to identify profitable trades. They simply limited the bid to $9.999 for a MW/h because "the rumor went around the market that the ISO computers ... could only handle four digits, so 9.999 dollars. ... But, after the fact, it turned out that looking at the code, they could have gotten up to 99.999 dollars, bankrupting the utilities on the spot."[23] Naturally, the team quickly and silently fixed these input limits that could have brought down the entire financial structure of the industry with a single key stroke.

From the end of 1998 on, the market monitoring units at CAISO were alert. The ancillary service markets had been the canary in the coal mine, and the monitoring team had listened. They revised their perspective on the markets and filed multiple reports with FERC, informing them of flaws in the market architecture and warning of the potential for vast market power abuses. But since their oversight and enforcement capabilities were extremely limited, there was little they could do without FERC.[24] The market designers' efforts to identify and solve the flaws that created gaming opportunities suffered from the problem of temporal instability discussed in the previous chapter—solutions tended to interact and create new loopholes, starting an endless merry-go-round between the market designers and the participants. As I have outlined, the efforts to redesign the ancillary service markets succeeded but created avenues for new variants of the Ricochet game. Nonetheless, the experience helped the monitoring regimes to evolve.

The more I read about the development of market monitoring, the more I became convinced that the story held the key to the designers' silences during the period of market construction. It was not *just* free market ideology. Of course, the episode in 1998–99 had much to do with that. The monitors believed in the myth of the self-regulating market, and that rendered the problems in the ancillary markets perplexing enough to encourage critical reflection. However, the market designers who put the system together between 1995 and 1998 carried specialized PhDs in economics, engineering, and system operations research. For them, markets were the product of explicit institutional design. They did not perceive a general tension between regulatory oversight and the markets. They did not believe in the "stark utopia" of the self-regulating market, to use a nice phrase by Karl Polanyi.[25]

To me, how difficult it had been to overcome the epistemic disconnect between engineers and economists seemed more significant. This disconnect lingered for institutional, cultural, and even demographic reasons. The monitors only began to understand and address this barrier to understanding when very concrete problems with their data and analytical models forced them to communicate with each other directly and in depth. I started to suspect that, perhaps, there had been a similar disconnect among the market designers and that the market design work had simply not given them a good enough reason to confront and resolve these differences. Once I approached the archival material with this hypothesis, the evidence soon fell into place.

I begin by tracing the origin of the ambiguities in the intellectual project of electricity market design. Then, I show how these ambiguities sustained distinct perspectives on the nature of and requirements for oversight. Finally, I trace how these differences affected design decisions and how the organization of the design process sustained them.

The Chameleonic Market

Designers view the market as an information processor and the market mechanisms as algorithms that solve optimization problems.[26] These algorithms are composed of software and strategic interactions between individuals. The logic of these algorithms needs to be enforced via institutional infrastructures. While market design's emphasis on explicit institutional design is relatively new, we have seen that the idea of the market as an information processor traces to socialist undercurrents that characterize the beginning of modern economics.[27] With the utilities' adoption of state-space representations in the 1960s, equivalences opened up between the tools used to manage the grid and the economic vision of markets as algorithms. Carried by these equivalences, the homeostatic control framework that Schweppe and his colleagues developed at MIT and Harvard could travel easily between economics and engineering departments.[28]

However, the conceptual frameworks contained multiple ambiguities, in terms of both the conceptual language and the math they used for communication. On the drawing board, electricity markets thus had a chameleonic quality. Chameleons can change the order and form of colored skin cells to alter their appearance. This allows them to blend more easily into different environments. Interestingly, this does not just provide camouflage but also helps to signal the chameleon's physiological condition to others. Similarly, the ambiguities in the designers' conceptual apparatus made it easy for this apparatus to travel between engineering and economic contexts. But these ambiguities also made communication across distinct work cultures deceptively easy.

This is most visible in the mathematical models themselves. In the blueprints for the new markets, the precise nature of the human actors and the relationship between markets and grid management remains open to interpretation. This enables communication across distinct camps because it sustains subtle changes in the meaning of ideas like information, competition, and the actor. Consider only the blueprint for California's congestion management system. Researchers at the Electric Power Research Institute in Palo Alto developed the theoretical basis for this system in a series of papers that were later published in academic venues.[29] The authors, Hong-po Chao and Stephen Peck, started with Schweppe's basic approach but developed a plan for a decentralized system of bilateral trades to find the complete economic dispatch. They worked in conversation with colleagues Shmuel Oren, Felix Wu, and William Hogan at Harvard and Robert Wilson at Stanford.[30]

The goal was to create a market that would find an economic dispatch of available generation relative to the available transmission capacity. The designers began by formally defining the problem. The task of finding the economic dispatch can be written as an optimization problem:

$$\max_{0,q^s q^d} \sum_{i=1}^{n} [B_i(q_i^d, w^d) - C_i(q_i^s, w^s)]$$

where $B_i(q_i^d, w^d)$ is a benefit function for demand at node i and $C_i(q_i^s, w^s)$ is a supply function at node i. These functions are defined by two variables: the quantity of demand q_i^d and the quantity of supply q_i^s at node i as well as the random variables w^d and w^s, which represent locational idiosyncrasies. Stated in ordinary language, the problem is to find for a particular node the quantities of supply and demand that maximize benefit and minimize the cost of generation—in other words, to find the cheapest generators to meet aggregate demand at all locations. This problem then becomes subject to two constraints that capture the presence of limited transmission capacity and condition the space of possible solutions. Note that the benefit and supply functions are exogenously given. They are simple curves that note supply and demand at different price levels. You could imagine these as preferences ranked by a human actor or as information about the characteristics of generators. Similarly, you can think about the information as price preferences or as signals of cost. In one case, you could think about the supply curve as the result of competition that pushes the generator to submit their true, marginal cost. In the other, you could simply think about it as a submission of technical information in the interest of running the system efficiently.

By using this formalization of combinatorial optimization problem, the blueprint required the market to work as a search algorithm, and more specifically as a dynamic program. This program had to find the best combination of generator outputs that meets the demand requirements while obeying the transmission limits. To conceptualize this program, the designers define institutional rules for the new market mechanism. For each directed link in the network, they create capacity rights that represent the maximum power flow on that line. This leads to a system of property rights, where each link (i, j) has a fixed set of transmission capacity rights (P): $P = \{P_{ij} \mid 1 \leq ij \leq n\}$.

A trading rule then makes energy transactions between two locations contingent on the possession of transmission capacity rights. Each energy transaction requires rights that represent the increase in real power flow on all links that are affected by the injection of power at the origin node. These bundles can be described as sets of coefficients $B = \{\beta_{ij}^k \mid 1 \leq i, j, k \leq n\}$ that represent quantities of transmission capacity rights on the links (i, j) that a trader needs to transfer a unit of power from node k to node n.[31]

When the energy market is linked to the transmission capacity market, the two constraints of the optimization problem are represented in the energy market: no energy transaction is possible that does not conform to the existing power flows, because they require transmission rights that reflect the changes in these flows. And no transaction can exceed the existing transmission capacity because the rights correspond to the real capacity of the lines.

The transmission rights, β_{ij}^k, can be calculated as an expression of the quantity of energy inserted at node k and the current transmission capacity, P_{ij}. Because this calculation requires knowledge of all power flows, the authors imagine a centralized bulletin board that always states how many rights are needed or would be received for a particular transaction (B). The market operator constantly updates this bulletin board by calculating the power flows at the current transaction structure and the marginal changes that new transactions would create. In other words, a centralized computation system generates prices that reflect the optimality of the energy flows and transmission capacity rights. Traders can then react to this state by trading energy and transmission rights.

This trading process solves the optimization problem in much the same way as a search algorithm would. In the market for transmission capacity, traders or consumers of energy who will benefit the most from capacity can pay the most for the transmission rights. In a perfectly competitive market with perfect information, the price of capacity rights would tend to the largest possible profit that could be realized in the underlying energy transaction. This would optimize the usage of scarce capacity relative to the optimization of energy transactions. Iteratively, the system thus converges on the global optimum.

Formally, the economists show that there exists a vector of prices and quantities at each node, as well as a vector of transmission rights for transactions between each set of nodes that fulfill the optimization problem. They also run simulations that mimic the market process thus defined and show that it converges on the equilibrium from arbitrary starting positions and in short periods of time ("Lyapunov stability"). This establishes that the market mechanism is a valid and computable solution.

Nothing about the formalization requires that the trading be done by human beings or even considers the possibility. The program describes an interplay between central and decentral computation, but it does not make any provisions for human cognitive limitations. The model implicitly presumes that all local traders uniformly follow the same basic calculation with different inputs from their local positions, identify the best trade, execute it, submit the information to the center, and then recalculate. The bilateral trading process can therefore be imagined as a distributed set of computations by humans who follow a fixed calculation in a closed system. Or it can be imagined as a set of information exchanges between machines. Mathematically, the two realizations of the algorithm are identical. The blueprint is thus agnostic about the specific implementation of the trading process, the precise role of control, and the relationship between center and periphery. The two markets simply solve the problem and do so from arbitrary starting points.

For the implementation, it matters tremendously how exactly human traders are supposed to behave and how computations are split between software and humans. Indeed, figuring out these questions constitutes the bread and butter of market designers during implementation processes. And, as we have seen, the WEPEX teams spent substantial energy to identify how they could simplify the representation of the grid to enable real humans to find the most profitable trades. Wrestling with the problem of ensuring the correct incentives and understanding produced the zonal congestion management model in 1995.

But on the level of the blueprints that designers assess in research settings, these issues remain ambiguous. Any mathematical statement needs to be embedded in a referential universe of practical context, which means that such statements sustain substantial levels of ambiguity—they are chameleonic and adjust their meaning relative to the context of use. Unless an informal culture stabilizes this referential universe, alternative interpretations can coexist.[32] Depending on who is reading the paper, the practical meaning of the model may thus appear to be quite different.

To see how this ambiguity led to subtle differences in perspective, consider two quotes that look very similar on the surface. In *Spot Pricing of Electricity*, Schweppe and his coauthors write, "Electric energy must be treated as a commodity which can be bought, sold and traded, taking into account its time- and space-varying values and costs. This book presents a complete framework for the establishment of such an energy marketplace."[33] Responding to Schweppe's proposal, the economist Vernon Smith wrote, "This procedure [Schweppe's spot-pricing mechanism] incorporates large amounts of information into simple price signals, just as a market might do, and it provides the basis for an economic dispatch center, or regional energy exchange."[34]

Both authors talk about the same proposal, and both agree that the spot-pricing approach turns electricity into a commodity. But while Schweppe equates his approach with the creation of a marketplace, Smith asserts that the system only works *as if it is* a market ("just as a market might do"). For Schweppe, the important thing about a marketplace is that a commodity is sold according to information about the price. It does not matter that both prices and outputs are set by an integrated monopoly and merely react to demand information from sensors (FAPER devices).

For Smith, however, this is crucial. Since the system involves neither decentralized decisions by individuals nor competition between individuals, it is a simulacrum, a system that mimics certain features of a market but does not qualify as one. While market designers with an economics background thus tended to view markets as distinct and genuinely human domains of action, engineers viewed them as a way to coordinate machines in the system as a whole.

This difference in the imagination of markets might seem rather inconsequential at first. Both engineers and economists wanted to make room for trading processes between humans. The difference seems to be merely an issue of emphasis: if you think about machines as the basic unit, you tend to view the market as an exchangeable component or module of a larger sociotechnical system. The market is a way to coordinate the operation of machines—and humans have to play some role in this process. If you think about the basic unit as human actors, you tend to describe markets as distinct domains of human action that play some role for a larger system.

Both sides agree that markets have to work within the structure of the electricity system. Both agree that prices have a coordinative function and that the market works as an algorithm. But while engineers saw continuity between the logic of the market and the logic of the electricity system, economists viewed them as distinct parts that needed to be integrated.[35] Engineers extended the mathematical tools used to describe grid management to the description of markets. Economists separated the discussion of the market logic from the logic of grid management after deciding how much of the grid should be represented in the market.

This somewhat subtle difference was not apparent in the 1990s. Market designers divided along a variety of architectural issues, but these seemed to hinge on specific technical questions and trade-offs among different design objectives.[36] The most important debates concerned whether markets should be centralized auctions or bilateral contract markets, whether markets should be pure exchanges or pools, and how congestion management should be organized.[37] The choices seem to come down to technical issues rather than philosophical differences about the nature of human actors and the role of markets in the larger structure of the electricity system.[38] As Shmuel Oren put it in a review article, "The dispute centers on the 'how much' questions, on what is essential and what is optional, on the relationship between short-term and long-term efficiency and on the tradeoffs involved in the short-term policy choices."[39]

Nonetheless, the debates always come back to the philosophical difference just discussed. If you view markets as an informational infrastructure that organizes how machines talk to each other in the larger electricity system, there is no reason to oppose centralized power pools. The centralization simply makes the coordination of decentralized signals easier. However, such centralization seems problematic if you view markets as decentralized systems of interaction between individuals. Centralization would constrain competition and decentralized decision-making. This would reduce markets' ability to find the superior solution to the efficiency problem. The importance and distinct character of human agency in markets, in other words, was directly related to the questions of how far markets should be trusted and what they should look like. There was simply a distinct flavor to a market that looked like individuals competing for monetary profit and a market where individuals operated generators and tried to make a living. As decisive as the philosophical differences were, they did not become readily apparent. Electricity market design could thus present a largely united front to the world, with experts disagreeing only on technical details. However, below this level of unity, the ambiguities produced quite distinct ideas about what the implementation of markets actually required. Yet these groups did not detect and resolve the underlying differences.

Intellectual Fragmentation at WEPEX and FERC

Different groups of market designers worked on different modules for California's new architecture. They were responsible for different parts of the administrative structure that implemented the new markets.[40] Auction designers primarily developed the activity rules for the public exchange markets. Robert Wilson and his team from the University of Stanford developed the rules. Charles Plott and his colleagues from Caltech (as well as a firm called London Analytics) then used computer-assisted laboratory experiments to test them. These experts worked as outside consultants for the WEPEX process and helped to create the software interfaces for the different markets.

Other economists had a stronger background in industrial organizations. People like Paul Joskow were not working on the details of auction design but addressing questions of industry structure in regulatory proceedings at FERC and the California Public Utility Commission. These experts talked about market power as well as architectural issues, such as the correct procedure for settlements. They came from California's public universities, from think tanks and research institutes, and from private universities in the East, particularly MIT and Harvard.

A third group of market designers were engineers. They worked primarily for the three utilities. Like SCE's lead engineer, Vikram Budhraja, or Pacific Gas & Electric's Ziad Alaywan, they typically held engineering PhDs with MAs in economics or system operations but had no direct affiliation with a university. For some tasks, they hired economists and engineers from the Electric Power Research Institute in Palo Alto or Berkeley's Energy Institute. They had expertise that related primarily to the period of regulated monopolies. Accordingly, they worked on the creation of the system operator and on problems that concerned congestion management, the integration of grid management, and markets for reliability services.

Each group interpreted the basic vision of electricity market design differently. Mechanism designers like Robert Wilson viewed the market process as akin to a deterministic algorithm. In one of his filings, he outlines the activity rules that describe how bidding can take place in the hourly auction at the Power Exchange. He writes, "The purpose of the activity rules is to encourage convergence to an efficient outcome while suppressing gaming."[41] In other words, market design is fundamentally about designing the rules for the market process, which is viewed as distinct from its wider environment. If the rules are right, they will set the correct incentives and the market will converge on the desired outcome. The initial conditions of the market determine the trajectory of its process through different states. This is encapsulated in an early paper on design principles where Wilson writes that the most basic principle is "to treat the market design as establishing a mode of competition among the traders. The key is to select a mode of competition that is most effective in realizing the potential gains from trade."[42] Set the incentives right, and you create mode of competition that converges on the desired results.

Since opportunities for gaming often emerge if the rules do not reflect the technical details that shape opportunities for profits, these designers were attuned to the threat that the technical complexity of the electricity industry posed to successful market design. Plott and his team repeatedly recommended intensive testing and iterative improvements to the rule structures. However, while they were worried about loopholes that would derive from mismatches between the rules and technical conditions, they thought that market rules were the place to address these problems.

Control was provided by the institutions that configured the market mechanisms by organizing the incentives for the players. Though institutions are centralized regulatory structures, they create processes that self-regulate if the incentives are set correctly. The institutions must thus merely protect the structure of incentives that generates the pure market mechanism. This leads to a distinct style of analysis where designers reason backward from the desired equilibrium result: they identify a market mechanism that leads to a particular equilibrium and then show how a given set of institutions configures a logic of interaction that gets you there. In that sense, the economic perspective was not unlike Leibniz's idea of a preestablished harmony: once all the cogs and wheels are in the right place and the market is wound up in the right way, it will steadily march toward equilibrium. Or as Ziad Alaywan, the chief engineer for Pacific Gas & Electric, put it, when economists discover a problem with the markets, they "say, 'Well, the problem will solve itself if you basically put all the incentives in the right place.' But they don't understand the nature of the grid."[43]

These market designers did not think of ongoing oversight and intervention as an explicit matter of market design. Rather, they viewed the institutional setup as their task and simply deferred on all other issues. This explains the silence about the rules for scheduling coordinators. As outlined previously, these followed political and legal considerations. More sensible rules would have included reporting standards and the right to screen scheduling coordinators' transactions. But since this would have been related to ongoing oversight, the auction designers ignored the issue. These rules surrounding the enforcement of compliance seemed separate from the rules that structured the different steps of the auction and the incentives that they set. Here, the silence of the market designers thus opened the path toward purely political decisions about rules.

Economists with a background in the subfield of industrial organizations had a slightly different reason to be unconcerned about extensive control structures. Unlike the mechanism designers, they were attuned to the problem of changing industry conditions and their dynamic effect on the incentives of market participants. That is, while the economists also thought about the market in algorithmic terms, they did not buy into the idea that rules predetermine the trajectory of a system completely. In their statements, they frequently talk about the market as an evolutionary process in which constant innovation occurs against the backdrop of competition. As Professor Michaels points out: "Nobody would have even a year ago envisioned half of the new types of financial and related instruments that were discussed by the various commentators late yesterday afternoon."[44] Yet, because these designers focused on the structural features of the industry, they did not consider incentives in terms of local rules in individual subsystems or hour-to-hour variations in supply-and-demand balances.

Accordingly, they underestimated the speed with which market conditions can subvert the algorithmic logic of the design. In line with the existing literature on electricity systems, they viewed market power largely in static terms. They thought that market power problems could be addressed by either forcing companies to divest generation assets or switching to regulated rates for certain generators (must-run contracts). Since these mitigation measures would play out over longer stretches of time, the economists reasoned that a monitoring function would suffice. Should problems emerge, the monitoring institutions could inform FERC, which could then decide if any kind of mitigation was necessary. In other words, these economists thought about the administrative structure that would administer the market as a more traditional regulator that might observe developments from a distance. This explains why Joskow thought about the monitoring units as mere information-gathering services that might be taken down after a few years. He seems to have assumed that problems of implementation might lead to unexpected behavior but that all real problems would develop slowly enough to fit into the standard regulatory approach. This explains, in other words, why the new markets started with monitoring units whose function was ill specified and whose members were mainly focused on the short-term issues of implementation.

Engineers and system operations researchers tended to interpret the market design project differently. In contrast to the mechanism designers, they were closely attuned to the fact that any complex system can take on a variety of different states and that only some of these lead to the desired equilibrium. In contrast to the industrial organization researchers, they also recognized that this could happen from moment to moment. They were familiar with the properties of complex systems—phase shifts, nonlinearity, and tipping points. Accordingly, they always wanted to create feedback mechanisms that could monitor the ongoing operation of the system and then adjust inputs to keep the system in check.

However, the engineers reasoned about this control structure in terms of grid management—not in terms of market oversight. Vikram Budhraja stated the central importance of CAISO: "This issue of requiring somebody who can perform the integration, coordination, and synchronization between production and consumption is a fact that cannot be controverted."[45] Once CAISO had the power to coordinate supply and demand in real time, he said, "everything around that is free market, and again, unimpeded by any central control and so forth."[46] As far as they were concerned, grid management was the center of the system. This was the place where the actual balancing of generators took place, where power flows had to be adjusted and managed. The market appears to be a separate sphere that produces inputs for grid management. This center would be carefully protected, but the markets themselves would be "unimpeded by any central control."

But why did they not think that the markets would require particularly strong oversight? As outlined before, the engineers and system operations researchers thought of the market as one of multiple different ways to coordinate machines in the interest of grid management. Since they were a natural extension of the larger system, engineers tended to transpose their view of feedback-control mechanisms from the grid to the market. Just like components in a larger sociotechnical system, markets here appear as conduits of information that generators and consumers transmit neutrally. The main question is therefore how a system of information exchanges can converge on a desired solution that takes all aspects of the technical dispatch into consideration. Ongoing control and oversight are necessary because of the complex permutations of possible states in the transformation of a dynamic system of energy flows.

But detecting and constraining manipulative behavior is not the first priority. Steven Stoft, who wrote an introduction to energy economics for engineers, explained this mindset to me in an interview: "In engineering, you have all these transformers and wires and transistors and whatnot that you arrange, and they do what you want them to do. And [the engineers] keep thinking they can arrange people and tell them what they're supposed to do and they'll do it."[47] The engineers therefore equated the supply function of a generator with the expected behavior of market participants. As the notorious Dr. Backus explained during the Perot hearings, "the tools that were used for that analysis [of the potential problems] continued to assume an optimization approach only appropriate to a regulated market."[48] Under this approach, market participants would continue to act as generators had in the regulated system. They would submit the marginal costs for the generators because they wanted to cover their costs. In other words, they understood that a company needed a good incentive to make the correct bids. But by interpreting the market as a signaling device to coordinate between generators and consumers, the engineers missed that market participants would try to make money in any way possible. They understood the principle of self-interest but not the capacity of self-interest and guile to pitch the market against the grid.

While the engineers were aware of the dynamic complexity of the electricity system and the need to control its balance carefully, they did not think that the markets would do anything but provide information to complete this task. Now and then, the markets might be off from the technically correct solution. But they would not actively contradict the reliable operation of grid management. It would be business as usual. In the proceedings, engineers were therefore happy to assure the audience that technical monitoring would suffice. The monitoring units would receive all technical information about grid operations and the schedules of market participants. If problems emerged, they could always just call the generators and ask them to change their behavior. The possibility of deception, opportunism, and strategic manipulation did not enter their arguments. Regulators would therefore not have much to do, ultimately. As one of the designers put it, "And if all goes well, basically the report [by the local monitors to FERC] would say that the system is working well. So, in that case, I do not see it being potentially reams of data [for FERC to handle]."[49]

Revealing their lack of suspicion about sellers' intentions, engineers repeatedly suggested that the monitoring program would not need strong powers of mitigation because it would primarily work as a vehicle for stakeholder deliberations about the market rules.[50] At other times, they

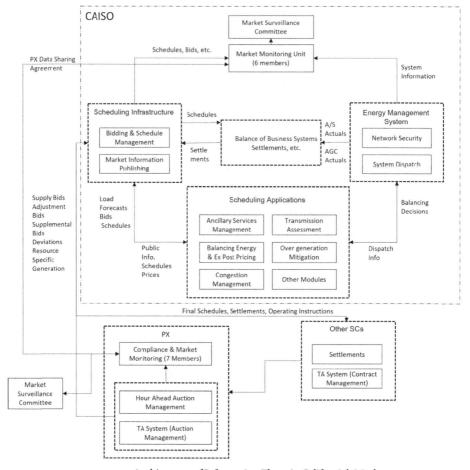

FIGURE 7.1. Architecture of Information Flows in California's Markets

suggested that sellers of electricity should just file quarterly reports about their generation costs to the system operator or FERC. This would enable the system operator to determine fixed costs and compile benchmarks of competitive prices. This suggestion only makes sense under the assumption that generators would freely submit adequate data about generation costs without further scrutiny.

We can see the different points of view at work in the informational architecture of California's administrative structure. Figure 7.1 displays the flows of information in the markets. The center of the figure describes CAISO's information system. All bids enter the scheduling infrastructure on the left side of the diagram. From there, they are passed on to the energy management system and the scheduling applications. As the figure indicates, there is no independent step where CAISO evaluates the genesis of the schedules on the level of the scheduling coordinators or the Power Exchange. Yet the system contains extensive checks and balances. The architecture is set up to determine whether market results, in the form of schedules, can be used to balance the system. Each step of the software environment checks the formal accuracy of the bids with the requirements of grid management. The monitoring units appear as classic regulators in a feedback-control system, but their capacities are strictly limited to the organization—they observe all inputs and their place in the internal systems, but they do not have access to behavior outside the system.

The structure of information flows shows that the designers did not worry about the interplay between incentives and that they focused on ensuring correct inputs for reliable grid management. It describes a complex feedback system that is entirely dedicated to identifying and fixing operational flaws in the system operators' internal systems. Here, we see the engineers' view at work: they thought about the markets as mechanical systems that were part of the larger electricity system. They conceptualized market failure in terms of human error and problems immanent to the rules of a given market. Accordingly, they thought control could be modularized and focused on ensuring the output's compatibility with reliable grid management.[51] Conversely, every single step of the auctions at the Power Exchange and the system operator were carefully laid out in rules and hardwired into the software interface of the scheduling applications. In these isolated but complex modules, we see the work of auction designers who focused on the optimization of short-term bidding behavior alone. Finally, the cumbersome information pipelines between the monitoring units, the market surveillance committee, and FERC demonstrate the influence of the industrial organization experts, who thought of market power mitigation as a slow and bureaucratic process.

In sum, then, the two types of economists and the engineers had subtly different ways of thinking about electricity markets and the requirements for their implementation. The heterogeneous information architecture shows how each group shaped different parts of the administrative structure. Extremely stringent and closely monitored auction mechanisms stood opposed to monitoring units that had limited oversight of the market and rudimentary enforcement tools. A meticulously designed information architecture ensured that all inputs to the system operators' internal systems met technical requirements, and yet there were practically no measures to ensure that these inputs did not reflect manipulative intent.

Unfortunately, each group arrived at the conclusion that a limited and transient form of market oversight would suffice. While mechanism designers ignored the fact that shifting operational conditions can affect a dynamic market process that is based on static rules, engineers appreciated the need for continuous oversight and adjustments to the balance of supply and demand. However, they underestimated the market players' antagonism and therefore thought that market oversight should be focused on technical issues. Economists with a background in industrial organizations recognized the potentially shifting incentives in electricity markets but underestimated the speed with which such changes might occur. Accordingly, they thought the existing regulatory authorities would suffice. The way they framed their understanding of the new markets led to different interpretations of the models and the problems they might encounter. Each group ignored crucial pieces of the puzzle that the other groups knew to be important.

The intellectual fragmentation does not lack a certain irony. If they had put their different perspectives together, they would have quickly realized that the escalating complexity of the market system required extensive and forceful control structures. After all, the engineers' sensitivity to the need for ongoing control would have revealed both the speed and the ease with which misalignments in the incentive structure could emerge.

Why did this convergence not happen? When we looked at the monitors' work from 1998, we saw that problems with the ancillary markets eventually forced them to confront each other, make these ambiguities visible, and evolve their understanding of electricity markets. So why did something like this not happen during the design process?

Certainly, the work at WEPEX was highly modularized. The different groups of designers worked on different modules and different aspects of the overarching administrative structure. The industrial relations experts worked on different modules than the auction designers and engineers. The general organizational structure therefore sustained the intellectual fragmentation. But many designers cooperated outside WEPEX in the nexus of research institutes, academic departments, and conferences that integrated the community of electricity market designers. Why did the practical problems of implementation not trigger the kind of self-reflexive and recursive learning processes that would take place in 1998 and clarify the ambiguities?

The problem of designing an oversight structure for California was ill structured at the level from which abstraction designers pondered it during conferences and workshops. Ill-structured problems are those whose limits are hard to specify, that cannot easily be mathematized, and that admit to near-endless possible solutions. Note that such problems *do* have solutions that are in principle available to the experts. The problems are just not specified clearly enough to point to a single answer. When approaching these problems, groups can bring slightly different information to bear and come up with different definitions.[52] These solutions may be incompatible, but unless they cause immediate problems, this is not readily apparent. In that case, "accidents happen because information is incomplete but the gaps are smoothed over in ways that sustain the illusion of safety."[53]

How to design the correct administrative system for the new market was precisely such an ill-structured problem. It was complex because it referred to the market infrastructure as a whole as well as to the individual submarkets. It touched on multiple, seemingly discrete issues: the capabilities of monitoring units, the rules for scheduling coordinators, the oversight protocols for different parts of the market, the administrative solutions to plan for capacity and transmission upgrades, and so on. Because behavior could deviate from the blueprints in both the short and the long term, the problem could also not easily be turned into a discrete mathematical model. The interactions among the different parts of the system were too complex to be simulated on a computer, as designers do today, or even represented in a game theoretical model. During the 1990s, the computational and mathematical tools of market design did not allow such comprehensive models. But since the problem was ill structured, it did not easily facilitate a self-reflexive discourse. In abstract discussions about the global architecture of the market, different groups could therefore maintain different positions without the conceptual tensions and problems becoming obvious; this was just another version of the same problem that derailed efforts to establish jurisdiction in political debates. And in the local contexts of the WEPEX process, each group could sustain its perspective on market design without confronting challenges from the other sides. The problems of modularization thus combined with the problems derived from the chameleonic nature of the intellectual vision the designers pursued.

And with this final insight, all the puzzle pieces have snapped into place. Political, intellectual, and organizational challenges undercut a straightforward approach to the creation of California's markets. First, they blocked strategies of simplification and bounding; then they obscured the escalating control requirements that grew in the shadow of the ever more complex market system. On all three fronts, designers were overwhelmed: they failed to control crucial policy decisions because they could not assert their standing as experts. They failed to work around the resulting design flaws because they were forced to adopt an organizational structure that made it impossible to meet the consistency standards of market design. Finally, without a stable culture of artisanship that could have guided the translation of formal blueprints into institutions, the markets assumed a chameleonic character, and crucial requirements remained hidden. Market designers thus faced a deep crisis of expertise in California. With these observations, it is time to step back and ask, What can we learn for market design more generally?

Conclusion

As we step back from the intricate details of California's design process, a clear picture emerges. Three practical problems explain why the designers ended up with a flawed system. First, designers did not have the *political standing* to control central design decisions. Second, designers' *organizational tools* were insufficient to meet the consistency requirements of their market mechanisms and contain the behavioral complexity of the system. Modularization tended to produce only locally optimal sets of rules and practices, while the markets required globally consistent rules and practices. Third, different groups of designers did not agree about the requirements to implement their blueprints. Their *practical meaning* was not sufficiently stable across the different parts of the design process. Together, these three problems overwhelmed even sophisticated designers. They prompted decisions that were locally prudent but that gradually escalated the market complexity, created porous boundaries, and deceived the designers about the growing control requirements. In this way, the California energy crisis was truly a failure by design.

By now, the traumatic events of 2000–2001 have safely faded into the past. Some litigation may still be playing out in FERC's courts, and the legal shell of the Power Exchange is still reimbursing former clients. But enough time has gone by for some of Enron's executives to have entered and left prison again.[1] Likewise, designers have long drawn their lessons from the California disaster. Modern electricity markets no longer look like the vastly complex experiment that California's architects created between 1993 and 1998.[2] But if today's electricity markets have evolved to a point where they work relatively well, what can the case teach us about market design as it is practiced today? Can we draw general lessons from the difficulties the designers once faced in California, almost twenty-five years ago?

Before we dive into the mechanics of the argument, it is worth pointing out that the analytical framework offers a different way to think about market creation. Existing theories are not well suited to explain the limits of market design because they view the market as an evolutionary process and order as the emergent product of decentral decisions that are embedded in the society surrounding the market.[3] This makes it difficult to understand market order as something that could be planned. For a world in which economic transactions are increasingly mediated via designed platforms, this is a serious lacuna. To improve our understanding of such markets, I have developed a framework that analyzes market design on its own terms and views market creation as a form of social engineering.[4] This framework begins with the plans of the designers, conceptualizes how they go about realizing them, derives scope conditions for success, and explains the difficulties of meeting them.

This theory not only adds a new perspective to the sociological work on market creation but also reopens the books on an old and all but forgotten topic: social engineering. In sociology, social engineering is largely seen as hubris or political ideology. And, of course, there are good reasons to be wary of technocratic ambitions. As the literature on centralized planning has shown time and again, ill-fated attempts to "improve the human condition" have surfaced throughout modern history.[5] In the 1960s, sociology earned recognition by pointing to the many ways in which the fundamental uncertainty of the future lays waste to human dreams of technocratic rule.[6] Sociology is, after all, the science of unintended consequences.[7]

In line with this general sentiment, most work on market design assumes that it is destined to fail. Even the social studies of finance, which look closely at the aspirations of market designers, assume that every successful framing produces its own overflows—any victory of market design will be transient, partial, and nongeneralizable.[8] Similarly, most work on digital capitalism and platforms has ignored the supply side of the industry.[9] Instead of figuring out what the designers are trying to do with the platforms and how the results relate to these plans, the literature has mainly tried to understand how technologies of control shape the conditions for labor and how labor, in turn, reacts to these new technologies.[10]

But market design works well in many cases. It seems that digitalization has breathed new life into projects of social engineering. Inside the computer, the world turns into a sandbox where engineers have endless powers of control and vision. They can quickly and flexibly mold the basic structure of interactions and understand the resulting processes in real time. Computer simulations can model even very complex forms of strategic behavior, and databases can collect and process even granular information about actual behavior. It is therefore possible to register problems and apply experimental fixes quickly and flexibly. In other words, under digital capitalism, social engineering has become more widespread, less visible, and more powerful than it has ever been. Rather than assume that market design is destined to fail, the book therefore asks, Under what conditions does it fail?

The basic outlines of the resulting framework can be summarized in a few sentences. Designers view markets as information processors and market mechanisms as search algorithms that solve constrained optimization problems. To realize these algorithms, market actors, often in conjunction with software, need to enact subroutines of the larger algorithm. To get actors to follow this calculative logic, the designers need to shape the interpretive lens that actors bring to contexts of decision-making. Using strategies of simplification, bounding, and control, they try to create an environment where it is intuitive and beneficial for actors to do so. Generally, designers have to find a balance between the three types of strategies. Because it is never possible to exclude every form of undesirable behavior in advance, all designer markets work as feedback-control mechanisms. The designers constrain the space of possible behavior as much as possible with strategies to simplify and bound the market. They seek to limit the set of possible behaviors as much as they can to the behaviors in line with the algorithm. Then, they impose a control structure to identify and constrain hazardous behaviors that can still occur within the space defined by the rules and procedures of the market.

Finding the right balance between the three strategies is easiest when a given allocation problem can be solved within an integrated software environment and very narrow behavioral options. It gets harder with complex allocation problems because they require that the designers give more discretion to market actors. The more freely participants can act, the less tightly the designers can regulate the space of possible behaviors, and the oversight requirements expand. Market design fails when the space of behaviors becomes so vast that the oversight structure can no longer apply standardized metrics to evaluate whether behavior matches the blueprint. Accordingly, it becomes more and more difficult to strike the right balance between the three strategies as the complexity of the allocation problem increases.

This basic framework is an analytical tool. It translates questions of market evolution and undesirable market dynamics into questions of human techniques of control and their limits. It also offers a general scope condition—a point where market design comes to its limits as a form of social engineering. Thus, this framework can be used to explore cases of market creation by design. However, which specific strategies are available and where exactly the limits of control are located will vary on a case-by-case basis. They will depend on the specific organizational setup of the control regime, the available monitoring technologies, and the hazards of destructive behavior.[11] The empirical analysis in chapters 3–4 has demonstrated how this framework can be put to use. It explains the California energy crisis by looking at the structural features that introduce the avenues for undesirable behavior and make it impossible to detect and constrain them. It understands these problems in terms of efforts to meet the high consistency requirements behind designer markets. The decisive question is now whether we can say something more general about these dynamics. What can the California case teach us about the practical limits of market design more generally? I will consider each domain in turn.

The Political Limits of Market Design

Market design is not a purely neutral or even just a technical activity.[12] Allocation questions invariably touch on issues of justice, fairness, and equity. It is always about the highly loaded question of "Who gets what—and why?" to cite the title of a book that introduced market design to a lay audience.[13] The creation of designer markets is therefore often embedded in politics. Designers rarely start with a clean slate; usually, their structures displace some previous arrangement. Design projects therefore often raise legal questions and affect vested interests. Just like any other engineering project, market design has a fundamental political component.

Because it is impossible to have market design without politics, and because market design both succeeds and fails under conditions of political contestation, there is no inherent contradiction between the two sides. Designers' conceptual and practical tools are quite flexible. They can alter blueprints, recode software, and work around problematic political decisions. Where one algorithm has become infeasible, another may fit. Where a market no longer works, an administrative rule might. Had California set a rule to enforce long-term investments in excess capacity, the market logic would not have derailed quite so spectacularly. Market design is a flexible suite of tools that can work around political decisions.

That being said, there are two points of tension. On the one hand, designers need to ward off decisions that affect the basic applicability of their methodology. This is what made the Memorandum of Understanding so problematic in California. The decision to separate the market from grid management severed the definition of the design problem (finding the optimal dispatch) from the algorithmic tools to solve it (the market). It was no longer possible to combine computational and human calculations to identify the solution to the optimization problem. Instead, the market produced approximate results that the system operator had to process further. Even if the designers had created a perfectly balanced system of rules and procedures for the market, the system would still have been flawed because each side missed the tools of the other. This is somewhat obvious: market design cannot work if its methodological tools are not applicable to the problem at hand.

On the other hand, designers need to ensure consistency between the rules and procedures of the market at some point. This follows directly from the previous discussion of how market design works. To keep the control requirements manageable, rules and procedures must be largely consistent with each other. They must make it beneficial and easy for actors to follow the calculative logic the blueprint requires. While it is impossible to rule out all inconsistencies, these need to be minimized as much as possible. In that way, political decisions can orient and configure the baseline of the market, but they cannot establish substantial inconsistencies in the system of rules and procedures that define actors' context of decision-making.

Market designers therefore need to be able to wrest control over some decisions from the political process, and they need to dominate the implementation process at some point. For both, they need to assert jurisdiction. In a personal conversation, Peter Cramton pointed out to me that market design works well in modern electricity markets because the technical character of most decisions is now widely recognized and academic market designers are frequently appointed to powerful positions in the governance apparatus. Today, designers hold substantial jurisdiction in electricity and other financial markets—but this does not translate naturally into other market contexts. The analysis in chapter 6 has shown why it can be difficult for designers to break in. Experts draw their political credibility from their standing as neutral arbiters of truth. To assert jurisdiction, they have to convince audiences that the relevant questions are, in fact, technical and not political questions. Rhetorically, they do this by pulling the debate onto their terrain and demonstrating superior skill in wielding the tools of their craft. Ideally, this prompts audiences to recognize their own ignorance and defer jurisdiction to the experts. For this mechanism to work, the terms of the debate must be reasonably stable, and the experts need to hold the monopoly over the interpretation of the relevant concepts. Otherwise, audiences will not recognize the performance of the experts as a superior display of skill.

This can be quite tricky, particularly for allocation problems where markets have not been established yet. Take the Blue Book proceedings. Electricity markets did not exist yet. Accordingly, the questions that stakeholders, politicians, and designers negotiated dealt with a highly abstract and fictional entity. Fundamental concepts like market, efficiency, and competition could assume a variety of meanings for different professions as well as in common sense. When stakeholders freely projected a variety of inchoate ideas onto this entity, the inconsistencies were not readily apparent. Ambiguity both facilitated conversation and made it harder to identify points of divergence. Without a stable baseline that would have defined narrow standards of argument, the market designers could do very little to establish their superior understanding of the subject matter. Instead, they appeared to be just another group with strange opinions. Once the questions were viewed as political, the experts were seen as interested parties, and the uncertainty of the scientific statements is attributed to partisan leanings.[14] This is a fairly general problem and shows up whenever scientists are drawn into broad political debates with fuzzy concepts and general questions. But what does this mean for market design more generally? Here, we can only venture some hypotheses for future research.

First, market design will presumably be most successful in settings that already have a largely functioning market. When the design interventions are narrow and target specific solutions, the terms of the debate will be more technical and settled. Designers can then more easily demonstrate the competence that is necessary to establish jurisdiction and assume political control. Once a largely functioning market is in place, it is already solving some problem relevant to the design process. Accordingly, political compromises will less likely concern questions that affect the basic applicability of market design. Likewise, with fewer decisions at stake, there is also less of a risk that politics will introduce fundamental inconsistencies into the architecture of the market. Examples of such forms of market design are proposals to reform the clearing rules in stock exchanges or measures to reform the auctions for US Treasuries.[15] In each case, designers can avoid the points of tension with politics by defining their interventions as narrowly technical.

Conversely, politics will be at odds with the imperatives of market design when the project requires far-ranging and fundamental reforms—as in cases where designers try to solve complex allocation problems that deal with collective goods like water, electricity, or clean air. To create the required markets, the relevant goods and services first need to be commodified. They need to be translated into tradable rights, and the designers need to create the corresponding trading regimes. These new regimes need to replace existing legal structures and must be compatible with the complex, technical infrastructures involved in the provision of these goods and services. Such a foundational design project will generate the kinds of general questions that designers cannot control politically.

Even if the political compromises do not sever the connection between problem and method, it is likely that politics will make market design substantially harder. The more political decisions a design requires to get the fundamental changes on track, the more inconsistencies the designers have to deal with during implementation. As we have seen in the case of the equality provision, early political compromises can imply cascades of further decisions that exacerbate the problem during implementation—the lax standards for scheduling coordinators were implied by the equality provision of the memorandum.

Other compromises will make it harder to apply strategies of simplification. Here, we can find another reason the political dynamics of design work are particularly problematic for complex allocation problems. As I argued in the second chapter, complex allocation problems complicate the balance among simplification, bounding, and control because designers need to give more discretion to market players. The more complex the allocation problem, the more perfectly and carefully designers need to control the space of possible behavior around that inevitable discretion. Any system with complex interdependencies and underdetermined contexts of decision-making will therefore teeter on the brink of being too complex for an integrated control structure to handle. Accordingly, such a system is considerably more vulnerable to the complexities added by the political process than systems that can define acceptable behavior more narrowly.

This consideration draws out a basic truth: when designer markets work, they usually work better than alternative arrangements. But these systems are fragile. To work, the rule system has to be highly internally consistent and must leave the market actors little room for anything but the actions the algorithm requires. Otherwise, the profit motive becomes separated from the productive uses of the commodities, and substantial misallocations occur.[16] The earlier mismatches between blueprint and reality enter the system, the harder they will be to fix later. The more complex the allocation problem and the greater the hazard of deviant behavior, the more precarious the global balance of simplicity and control and the more devastating the ripple effects of early political decisions. In that sense, the risk-and-reward structure of market design for complex allocation problems is highly disadvantageous as soon as politics is involved.

But as long as the basic applicability of designers' methodology is not affected, politics does not overdetermine the success or failure of design projects. For the most part, market design is technical work to build and maintain market infrastructures. Politics configures this work, but it is not the end of the story. Perhaps worse than the Memorandum of Understanding were the tight deadlines for the implementation. Together, these two factors forced WEPEX into a highly modularized design structure that could not handle the complex architectural baseline. But the organizational problems were themselves distinct from the political ones. Any theory of market design failure therefore has to account for the practical conditions of this technical work and its effects on designers' ability to strike the balance among simplification, bounding, and control.

The Organizational Limits of Market Design

The modularized structure of the WEPEX process motivated many of the decisions that led to arbitrage and congestion games as well as market power. Market designers worked in local teams that could not identify the consequences their decisions had in other parts of the market architecture. Structurally, they were required to consider the rest of the system only in terms of the simplified interface relationships defined by the design rules. But market actors looked for opportunities below the level of these interface relationships and potentially derailed the intended architecture. Intermediaries who should have discovered problematic interdependencies considered the problem at a level of abstraction that obscured many of these interdependencies. The continual changes in rules in different modules also made it impossible to iteratively perfect the system in response to problems. Modularized design work produced only locally optimal sets of rules. But market design called for a globally consistent set of rules and procedures.

Of course, the situation in California was extreme. Modularization maximally fragmented the work among teams and weakened lines of authority.[17] It complicated the review of decisions and recalcified the architecture envisioned by the design rules. At the same time, the complex dependencies between the different forward markets meant an unusual level of interdependency between modules. A highly fragmented division of labor has never been a great match for situations with high task interdependence.[18] Had the political process not forced the designers to use a modularized approach and had they dealt with a less complex architecture, they would doubtlessly have been able to deploy their strategies of simplification and bounding more successfully.

But the organizational dynamics in California still point to a general problem. Market design has deep roots in behavioral economics and the theory of bounded rationality.[19] Designers strive to build market interfaces that compensate for the limited cognitive capacities of actors and ensure the optimal rationality their algorithms demand. But the cognitive limitations of the market actors also affect the designers themselves.[20]

One of the most basic insights about organizations is that they both compensate for and inherit some of the cognitive weaknesses of their human members. Organizations focus limited cognitive capacities on different parts of the environment. This allows them to compensate for certain human biases and process more complex sets of information reliably.[21] But local attention within the division of labor is still limited and can become myopic with respect to the organization's larger goals or changing aspects of the environment. In *any* organization, there will therefore be inconsistent decisions between divisions, technical failures, normalized deviance, and dynamics that can incubate disasters below the routines of administrative attention.[22] For example, Diane Vaughan's masterful account of the *Challenger* disaster shows how cultural differences between departments structured attention in ways that normalized risks and misdirected the flow of signals that could have revealed the problem.[23] Similarly, Scott Snook's analysis of the friendly-fire incident in Iraq shows how local divisional cultures can begin to drift from standard operating procedures and then normalize this deviance.[24] Graham Allison's famous analysis of the Cuban Missile Crisis also reveals the problematic role of dysfunctional politicking between intragovernmental units. As members of different branches of the government were trying to increase their spheres of influence, they pushed an agenda that ignored important signals and escalated the crisis.[25]

Organizations create hierarchies and various processes of oversight to deal with these problems.[26] Higher levels manage interdependencies between subunits by imposing tasks, allocating funds, setting incentives, and organizing both formal and informal relationships. In particular, managers can resolve tensions between local frames by redirecting members' attention to crucial information they are not aware of or by reorganizing their task structures. Simon called this the "exception management" function of administration.[27]

But the different levels of the hierarchy always operate at some remove from the details of local decisions. Managers have limited cognitive resources and review local decisions in terms of the larger context that their role defines. To become visible as problematic, local decisions must therefore pass a cognitive threshold.[28] Signals can get lost as they traverse the different parts of the organization. Diane Vaughan has called this general class of phenomena "structural secrecy"; the ways different divisions filter, pass on, and interpret information can engender systematic blind spots.[29]

Regardless of how tightly hierarchical structures regulate the division of labor and regardless of how thorough the review processes, there will be mismatches between the global goals of the organization and the decisions made within the different departments. Recall the example from chapter 7: ABB's computer programmers built the interfaces for the imbalance markets in CAISO's control room. They followed instructions the WEPEX Steering Committee had carefully adjusted to the creation of the financial markets. Despite modularization, there was a highly concentrated effort to coordinate the design efforts across modules. But decisions like the one to separate the two bid stacks were in keeping with the instructions and therefore did not become subject to any further scrutiny. Yet such decisions engendered dispatch practices that produced incentives for arbitrage games. Because these design decisions did not cross the cognitive threshold of managers, they disappeared from the purview of hierarchy.

In most complex organizations, these basic features of organizational life do not pose general obstacles. Even the theory of normal accidents suggests as much.[30] It focuses on the most complex technical organizations, such as nuclear power plants, where failures in seemingly independent parts of the system can quickly interact to produce new problems. Yet, even if accidents are unavoidable, they will be exceedingly rare in organizations in which the members share a baseline allegiance to the group's goals. A whole literature on high-reliability organizations has explored these local, interactional, and informal practices that compensate for the many stopgaps in formal structures.[31] In other words, informal norms of cooperation, interactional strategies to solve local problems, and routines for collaborative learning bind formal organizations together. They explain why inconsistent decisions, dysfunctional politicking, and cognitive errors do not usually lead to accidents and disasters.[32]

This is lacking in designer markets. Their creators cannot rely on cooperation but depend on sanctions and incentives to coordinate their markets. At the same time, the market actors always have a meta-incentive to look for ways to play the system to evade the pressure of competition and realize bandit profits. While designers are trying to carefully align incentives and sanctions, market actors are forever searching for ways to leverage and exploit, rather than compensate for, the blind spots that exist in every complex organization.[33] For example, once the market players identified the mechanical price differences between the financial and imbalance markets in California, they did not alert the designers to the problem. Instead, they kept quiet and worked to exploit them.

In sum, modularization poses extreme versions of a very general problem. Because no complex organization can completely avoid decisions that are inconsistent with the organizational goals, market design will generally lead to rules and procedures that engender gaming opportunities. The more complex the organizational structure, the higher the chance that many such inconsistencies will emerge. Just as economists generally accept that regulators will forever chase creative market actors in a dialectical struggle of rule evasion and redefinition, so do market designers forever struggle to identify a consistent rule set from within complex divisions of labor.[34]

This general insight has a relatively clear practical implication. Market design will work best when the organizational structure of the design process can be kept small, ensuring that the interactions among all rules and procedures can be assessed by a handful of people. The most successful forms of market design usually involve relatively small teams who make decisions in a narrow and tightly coordinated division of labor. This makes it easy to control the kinds of blind spots that emerge when different teams set rules in response to local problems. A highly centralized design process vouchsafes for the required consistency between rules and procedures that define the market context—where sanctions and incentives are enough to coordinate the behavior of antagonistic players.[35]

However, unless a working market is already in place, a simple organizational structure will often not be feasible for complex allocation problems. The organizational context of design work will therefore move into tension with the behavior of market actors, and the system will begin to experience episodes of gaming and manipulation. The severity of this problem depends on two factors. First, what are the hazards associated with deviant behavior? If the algorithms are robust to minor deviations, designers only need to create a system where most people follow the logic of the algorithm most of the time. Inconsistent design decisions will therefore be more tolerable.

This is not the case for the allocation of collective goods like water, electricity, and health care. Apart from the ethical concerns that emerge when these goods become subject to dysfunctional speculations, even minor deviations from the intended allocation of these goods can affect people's survival. Markets for these allocation problems would therefore be vulnerable to even moderate levels of deviant behavior. For cases where such behavior can be tolerated, the decisive policy question is how the resulting losses in efficiency relate to the costs of alternative administrative solutions.

The second factor to consider is the cost of control. Whenever the designers create rules and procedures that generate opportunities and incentives for hazardous behavior, a control structure needs to take over. This has an important policy implication. When weighing whether to solve a complex allocation problem via a market or an alternative administrative structure, the discussion should involve the costs and feasibility of a capable control structure. As this book has suggested, electricity markets are substantially harder to regulate than utilities with monopoly rights. Market power can emerge very quickly and requires real-time oversight, rather than the old system of periodic company reviews.

After the California energy crisis, FERC gave up on its original plan to shrink agency size and started to build a new department of market over-sight.[36] This turned out to be a more sophisticated and extensive regulatory apparatus than the oversight structures of the bygone era. Electricity systems are another case that proves the old adage that "freer markets [mean] more rules."[37] It is still an open question whether these additional monitoring and enforcement costs are offset by the efficiency gains that markets introduce. This seems to be the case for many US electricity markets. For example, a recent paper estimates yearly savings that are "worth roughly 5 percent of the total variable cost of generating electricity in market areas."[38] This amounts to a reduction of between $3 billion and $5 billion per year. These savings offset the cost of regulation by far. But it is difficult to tell whether they may not themselves be offset by the loss of system resilience over the long term—disasters like those in Texas or California in 2020 and 2021 carry substantial costs. Because it is difficult to stabilize the relevant counterfactuals, it quickly becomes impossible to compare these costs and gains.

A second, even more important consideration is the limits of the control structure. The organizational problems that apply to the design process *also* apply to oversight. As soon as the control structure needs to employ a complex division of labor, the different departments will begin to develop blind spots and gaps in the responsibilities between experts. This echoes a basic insight from Perrow's work on normal accidents. Adding redundancies is not always a good way to improve safety because it increases the dynamic complexity of the system and thus makes room for unexpected interactions between component failures.[39] Similarly, the capacity of oversight regimes does not necessarily become better when it expands. Naturally, market actors will begin to innovate in the perceptual gaps between departments. Somewhat ironically, market design will therefore be most successful when either the design process or the control structure can exist as a highly centralized authority; even though market designers like to position their craft as the opposite of centralized planning, the fingers of their invisible hand should not be divided. If possible, the designers should oversee the market as all-knowing watchmakers. Once the organizational apparatus adopts a complex division of labor, undesirable behaviors begin to proliferate in the perceptual gaps of the oversight regimes.

Here, we thus come back to a distinction I introduced at the end of the second chapter. For the most part, this book has identified contingent empirical reasons that market designers broach the scope conditions for successful market design. While these problems are basic enough to suggest that they will show up in many other contexts, only future research can truly tell. But the preceding argument points to a way in which market design can fail on principle. When the allocation problem becomes complex enough that designers have to adopt a complex division of labor for the construction *and* oversight of the market, not only will gaming incentives and opportunities emerge as a matter of course but it will also be impossible to correct them iteratively. The markets will necessarily fail if the designers' objectives are vulnerable to this behavior. Arguably, this is the core reason we should be careful to use markets for the most pressing problems of our time: they tend to be both complex and, once embedded in a market, vulnerable to deviant behavior. This combination is all but sure to overwhelm the organizational capabilities of designers' control regimes.

The Cognitive Limits of Market Design

Market design is an effort to impose a formal system of rules on a domain of social action. We have seen that this requires a relatively high level of consistency in the rules, interfaces, and procedures that structure market actors' interpretative approach to situations of exchange. So far, I have focused on political and organizational reasons that market designers might arrive at rules and procedures that violate these consistency requirements. But, as we have seen, problematic decisions in California also involved designers' conceptual work. Divergent interpretations of the mathematical models prompted inconsistent design decisions.

To understand how general this problem is, it helps to return to an example Stinchcombe uses to explain why formal systems of rules may work effectively: building a house on the basis of a blueprint. The basic problem is that any blueprint or set of formal rules is ambiguous because it is abstract. With inimitable style, he writes, "Plain meaning is the extreme value (namely, zero) of a variable that describes the variance of meanings in a linguistic community, given a text."[40] When construction workers implement a blueprint, they can follow it correctly in a number of ways—just as the ABB programmers did in CAISO's control room. To reduce the variance of meanings, communities come up with institutions and understandings that establish a common interpretation. In particular, they develop informal standards of good artisanship that can fill in missing details—where exactly to put pipes or how to perform certain elements of the assembly.

Now, market designers do have informal systems of artisanship that explain the meaning of a given assumption. The formal system of mathematical abstractions only works as a practical guide because there are conventions for inferring the requirements of their realization. But we saw a substantial drift among different camps of market designers. For example, those with engineering backgrounds had a much different sense of the assumptions about "rational action" than those with an economic background in game theory. This created problems because practical inferences diverged in different settings.

The market was chameleonic: working in different contexts, designers had different ideas about they required to build it. Methods to establish agreement among the informal systems of artisanship would have been crucial. Such methods make it possible to build houses. For example, there are special classes on how to write and read technical drawings. These classes are closely coordinated with others that establish the norms of artisanship among those who work with them. Construction workers learn to interpret the different formal signs in terms of the craft, architects learn how construction workers interpret the different elements of technical drawings, and so on. Divergent, informal practices of interpretation are themselves the result of formal practices of practical education, which are related to each other. Precisely such an alignment among different informal cultures of interpretation was missing in California.

Indeed, it is still missing in the world of market design, and this marks one of the major differences between civic and social engineering. To this day, market design is fragmented into a variety of communities in computer science, engineering, economics, and operations research who use the same formal languages in slightly different ways. Experimental, computational, formal, and empirical analysis rely on similar formal languages and are often meant to complement one another in market design experiments. But these different uses are not undergirded by efforts to align these different ways of reading and writing blueprints. Not only should there be an effort to create a standardized practice for writing blueprints, but there should also be classes on translating blueprints into working sociomaterial systems. As long as disparate cultures of artisanship continue to coexist, the practical meaning of designers' formalizations will remain ambiguous, regardless of how carefully the mathematical definitions are laid out in the beginning.[41] As soon as these ambiguities are obscured and become impossible to resolve collaboratively in face-to-face interactions, the design process will produce problematic decisions. Precisely this happens when the design work takes place in a complex division of labor, as is the case with complex allocation problems. Furthermore, the more complex the allocation problem, the more variegated the different forms of expertise brought to the table. Without informal systems of artisanship to negotiate their interrelations, the experts will come up with divergent instructions or begin to compete with one another, engendering a dysfunctional politicking for influence over technical questions.[42] For the third time, then, we encounter a fairly general reason that market design should stay away from complex allocation problems: the informal practices of artisanship have not become stable enough to sufficiently reduce the variance in the possible interpretations of formal design blueprints. However, this may already be changing as market design moves more firmly into the purview of computer scientists. Their highly applied work has always lent itself to the development of such informal standards of good practice.

Last Thoughts

We now have the outlines for a theory of market design failure. We began with a conceptual framework that provided the intellectual ambitions of the designers and the practical requirements to realize those ambitions. The empirical analysis then provided a variety of reasons the designers found it difficult to meet these requirements. Abstracting from the California case, the conclusion has suggested that many of these reasons describe fairly general obstacles in the political, organizational, and conceptual contexts of market design. Indeed, the organizational problems mark a point where this form of social engineering fails on its own terms. Designer markets are always at risk of separating actors' drive to profit from the logic of production. The more complex the allocation problem, the more acute this danger becomes. Once designers give discretion to market actors, the link between possible and desirable behavior implied by the rules becomes more tenuous—the rich interpretative practices of actors can give rules new meanings or connect them in surprising ways across contexts.

To prevent the control requirements from escalating beyond the limits of bureaucracy, designers must use strategies of simplification and bounding with brutal efficiency. Yet this becomes difficult when they have to contend with the messy world of real implementation processes. For complex allocation problems, they may find themselves surrounded by political players who have their own interests; submerged in complex organizational structures that are internally opaque; and segregated into diverse cultures of expertise that are not conversant with one another. The recent blackouts in California and Texas are painful remainders of this fact.[43] Even with twenty years of experience and the most extensive oversight regimes of any market in existence, these structures remain precariously controlled spaces of antagonistic behavior. It remains to be seen whether markets can truly offset these problems by unleashing the innovative forces that enable the green transition or whether the innovative solutions will emerge from the administrative structures of state-funded research projects. At the very least, this book suggests that market design for essential goods and services is a fickle and tenuous matter because designers need to use imperfect tools to contain and organize the antagonistic, roaming self-interest of reflexive parties.

But if market design does not provide a silver bullet, what else are we to do? How do we escape the complacency and inefficiency of governmental bureaucracies? My core argument is that when market design fails, it does so because coordination without cooperation does not scale well beyond self-contained and simple platform architectures. But if coordination without cooperation is difficult, perhaps social engineering works better if we give coordination *with* cooperation another shot.[44] Indeed, corporate giants like Google, Amazon, and Walmart already manage to solve vastly complex allocation problems within their administrative structures. Amazon, for example, is replacing entire markets with its logistic systems. For certain commodities, it coordinates every step from production to consumption.[45] To do so, it uses optimization tools similar to the ones that undergird designer markets. In a sense, Amazon's tools are just different implementations of the same ideas that drive market design.

Where it is successful, market design rests on the immense coordinative powers of digitalization and digital platforms. They make it possible to streamline incentives and follow through with sanctions. It seems to me that we should ask whether the same tools might be used to reform governmental organizations. This would be not market design but government design. After all, it is certainly possible to build markets that do not presuppose antagonistic players. This is how we already understand certain market design experiments. I mentioned the Feeding America auctions in passing before, but it is worthwhile to discuss them at a bit more length here. Not only are these auctions an example of market design at its best but they also represent a market without profit incentives.

Feeding America is a national nonprofit organization that distributes three hundred million pounds of food donations to forty-six million Americans each year. Before 2005, the organization used a centralized queuing system to allocate donations. Before a branch received any donations, it had to progress through a queue, which was organized by a relatively rough algorithm. This algorithm defined a branch's need for donations by the number of patrons and the donations the bank had already received. When it was the bank's turn, the center would offer a truckload of donations. If the bank refused the offer, the center would offer the same load to the next food bank on the list. Regardless of whether a branch accepted or refused the offer, it moved down in the queue.

This system was inefficient for several reasons. Because branches also received their own local donations, demand for particular products constantly changed in ways that were not visible to the center. Food banks might therefore value donations differently at different points in time. Refusing a truckload at one point did not mean that the branch would also refuse the same load at a later point. Food banks also had a reason to accept donations even if they did not need them: they had to do so to avoid getting fewer offers in the future.[46] Furthermore, the queuing system was extremely slow because it only made one offer at a time, progressing slowly down a list of potential takers while the food was in danger of spoiling. All this led to waste — a suboptimal allocation of food to food banks, given a distributed set of preferences.

A team from the University of Chicago headed by Canice Prendergast developed a new allocation mechanism for, and with, Feeding America.[47] The team of sixteen employees and academics created the Choice System, a centralized spot market that used a first-price, sealed-bid auction. In this type of auction, every participant submits a sealed bid for an object. The one with the highest bid gets the object and pays the offered price. The designers implemented this auction in a web-based software interface. The website listed the available food items, quantities, weights, and locations. Participants could submit a sealed bid for each item. After the auction closed, bidders received an email with the outcomes. The auction took place twice a day from Monday to Sunday.

The system improved the efficiency of the allocations in both the short and the long run. Banks could now discriminate between more or less desirable products because the bidding system allowed them to express the marginal rates of substitution for different items. Food-poor banks could increase their consumption of donations with lower prices (for which there was less overall demand), and food-rich banks could leave the cheaper food in favor of more expensive items (i.e., they could concentrate their spending). The overall allocation of food was improved because winning bids corresponded more accurately to the availability of food at the different local branches.[48]

The food allocation mechanism is an example of a successful market design. It worked exactly as intended because all participants understood the choice situation in the same way and followed the calculative steps that the blueprints required — they only had incentives to express their relative preferences for different food items and could easily understand how to act on these incentives. The underlying allocation problem had several properties that enabled market designers to use the strategies of simplifying, bounding, and controlling almost without limit, thus creating a perfectly self-contained and internally consistent market system.

First, the problem was well defined. A discrete set of donations needed to be allocated in a way that gave equal weight to the preferences at different food banks. This allowed the designers to solve the problem within a single-market environment with highly standardized interfaces. Second, the problem was static. Twice a day every day, the actors confronted exactly the same problem. The substantive preferences and the items themselves changed, but the structure of the problem itself remained the same. Accordingly, the designers had to leave little room for a trajectory of improvement and could therefore constrain the behavior of market actors almost completely. Together these two features meant that designers could simplify the market structure to an almost deterministic set of choices. Third, the allocation problem was separable from other domains of action. No other context of action mattered for the activities in the auction markets. This made it easy to bound the market. With almost no limits to simplification and bounding, the designers could implement a simple control structure. A small team of experts could build and oversee the market, sidestepping most of the problems that plagued California or any complex market.

This example illustrates how market design can improve on alternative administrative allocation mechanisms. But the most remarkable feature of the Feeding America mechanism is its ability to eradicate profit motives. The design team was concerned that the use of money would quickly introduce inequality into the system. Indeed, the Feeding America staff was deeply suspicious about the whole project. One employee told the design team, "I am a socialist. That's why I run a food bank. I don't believe in markets. I'm not saying I won't listen, but I am against this."[49] To introduce market mechanisms into this altruistic environment, the designers needed to take the risk of inequality off the table. They invented a scrip currency called shares and distributed this currency to the food banks on the basis of perceived need. The balances of shares did not depreciate, and the designers replenished budgets by redistributing spent shares each evening. With these rules, the scrip currency retained only the signaling function of money. The currency could not be taken out of the system, accumulated, or arbitrarily enlarged. Accordingly, food banks of varying sizes could always express their preferences equally well, and the system could not produce inequality among the food banks. Here, we see an example of market design that is used to coordinate cooperative players. This relaxes the fundamental challenge substantially. Not only do market actors usually try to use the auctions as intended but they also have a reason to report problems to designers. The Feeding America mechanism thus indicates some of the benefits that might accrue to market design as government design.

Of course, the strongest argument for markets is always the power of profit incentives. Bureaucrats simply do not face the same pressure as entrepreneurs to work efficiently and innovatively. Who is to say that the food banks will truly bid in the interest of their patrons if they have no profit incentive to do so? But maybe incentive design does not have to be tethered to market competition. Perhaps one could build incentive systems that rely not on monetary profit but on recognition and status—like Wikipedia or Yelp.

Regardless of where these ideas may lead, market design for cooperative players could tap into the very tools that complex organizations use to integrate their formal structures: the informal mechanisms for problem-solving, learning, and interpersonal coordination. Without a doubt, these mechanisms are the key to the many high-reliability organizations that manage other hazardous and risky technologies.[50] Once we look at the issues from this perspective, it seems less laughable that government reform may be our best shot at addressing the most difficult allocation problems of our time.

If coordination with cooperation seems like an obvious solution to problems that emerge with antagonistic market players, why is this idea so undesirable politically? To me, it seems that the main reason is the politicians' incentives to abdicate responsibility for hard questions.[51] No politician wants to be caught deciding whose access to water should be rationed, who should move out of an area affected by global warming, or who should pay for the transition to green energy. Those who want to be elected by a majority find it easier to defer hard questions to the market than to involve research staff in a ministry under their responsibility. The market thus becomes a space of deferred political responsibility, and the politicians can focus on pandering to the majority on symbolic issues.

However, as the intense political polarization shows, we are entering a period where the hard questions have to be posed and answered one way or another. As we run out of water, land, food, and clean air, our democracies have to decide how to ration and preserve these goods. There can be no doubt that administrative structures must address these problems. This book has shown that designer markets are no silver bullet here. For administrative structures built in an imperfect world, the danger of noncooperative market participants is substantial. It is therefore high time that we consider alternative administrative solutions.[52] This requires a different political perspective on the issues at hand. We have to find a way to face these problems politically, take responsibility for the answers, and then use the newfound powers of planning and coordination to search for the best way to implement them. A sociology of social engineering might make a small contribution to this larger project.

Acknowledgments

Six years ago, I became interested in the California energy crisis. I thought that Enron had caused the near collapse of the electricity system, and I wanted to understand how a single company could have done it. But as soon as I began to push below the surface level, I realized that Enron was a side story. Nearly every seller in the market had engaged in the same destructive behavior—and worse. How was that possible? How could a market unravel so completely? As I dug into the question, I realized that the California markets were unlike most others. They had been *designed* in the full sense of the term. Leading world experts had carefully planned the transaction platforms and market institutions, trying to create a social process that would work as their theories predicted. Yet, despite much attention to the problems of gaming and market power, they ended up with a system that was vulnerable to dozens of different manipulations. How could that be? The more I tried to understand what they had been working on, the more I realized that market design is all around us. As commerce moves online, markets increasingly morph into transaction platforms. These platforms are built by design experts in proprietary organizations, who can shape and control the market process on a granular level. And they try to organize the market process in line with higher-order objectives. The mystery of California's crisis, which involved an early form of market design, suddenly seemed to hold the key to a pair of tantalizing questions: What does it mean to plan a market, and under what conditions do such projects of social engineering fail or succeed?

This book is an attempt to answer these questions. On the long and winding path to its completion, I would have given up at least a dozen times without the support of mentors, friends, and family. Nonetheless, my first words of thanks have to go to the interviewees who took the time to talk to me, often multiple times. Without the insights they provided, the archival material would have been hard to decipher, and the book could not have been written.

But even with the best data, a book is nothing without analysis. Here, I owe my greatest debts of gratitude to my mentor and friend Andrew Abbott. More than anyone else, he helped me to develop this project and overcome the challenges I confronted. He was never too busy to chat with me or read drafts on short notice. Whenever I got stuck, he provided guidance by walking through the argument with me, pointing out angles I had not explored, or giving me new things to read. His influence and his ideas are visible on every page of this book and have shaped my thinking since I first entered sociology. Another major influence was Gary Herrigel. His multidisciplinary orientation and his deep appreciation of social theory helped me to bring empirical questions back to theoretical debates. Whenever the topic seemed parochial and esoteric, he reminded me what was at stake and why the questions were interesting. He read drafts upon drafts and has shaped the way I think about regulation and the political economy.

During my time at the University of Chicago, there were many others whose critical questions and sympathetic feedback shaped the arguments of this book. In particular, I want to thank Kyla Bourne, Tim Elder, Kimberly Hoang, Karin Knorr-Cetina, Austin Kozlowski, Jane McCamant, John Padgett, Benjamin Rohr, Jonathan Schoots, and Andrew Swift. Their unfailing support carried me through the hardest part of the project.

When I finished my PhD, in 2020, the COVID pandemic had a fierce grip on the world, and I was extremely fortunate that Jens Beckert offered me a postdoctoral position at the Max Planck Institute in Cologne. This safe harbor not only allowed me to wait out the worst of the pandemic but also offered an intellectual hub for anyone interested in economic sociology and provided enough time to write the first draft of *Failure by Design*. Among the many people I met in Cologne, I owe particular gratitude to Daria Tisch, Leon Wansleben, Kathleen Griesbach, Arjen van der Heide, Sebastian Kohl, and Timur Ergen, who read and discussed parts of the book with me, often on long walks along the Rhine. During my first year at MIT Sloan, I found the time and inspiration to finish the manuscript thanks to a light teaching load, an invigorating intellectual community, and the unfailing support of my mentors Cat Turco, Susan Silbey, and Ezra Zuckerman, who help to deepen my understanding of economic sociology every day. A big thanks also to Michael Cusumano, who took the time to provide feedback on the first part of the book and introduced me to the strategic management literature on transaction platforms. At the University of Chicago Press, I would like to thank my editor Elizabeth Branch Dyson and her team for their tireless efforts to improve the manuscript. In particular, I would like to thank my copy editor, Angelique Dunn, who did a tremendous job with the language in this book and corrected my various Germanisms. Finally, I want to thank my family for supporting me throughout the years it took to write this book. To my wife, Katrin Rilinger, and our son, Arthur, finally, I want to say thanks for everything and every moment together.

[APPENDIX A]

Data and Methods

This book is a historical case study. Because archival material is inevitably fragmentary and all archives are subject to selection bias, the book triangulates material from different sources. It relies on two types of primary data: archival material from various sources and in-depth interviews with market designers, stakeholders, and regulators. Most of the archival materials stem from three archives: those of the California Public Utility Commission in San Francisco, the California State Archives in Sacramento, and the online filing system of the Federal Energy Regulatory Commission. These three archives contain materials that document the work of the organizations that were tasked with designing, implementing, and monitoring the electricity markets in California. They also contain the voluminous records of litigation on the California energy crisis.

The archives in San Francisco house sixty-three boxes of filings, transcripts, and submittals in a docket that chronicles the entire period of deregulation. Early files contain transcripts and filings from the negotiations between regulators and stakeholders after the California Public Utility Commission published the decision to deregulate in 1994. Boxes from later dates contain various filings that document the technical process of implementation during the WEPEX (later Trust Advisory Committee) process between 1994 and 1998. The last folders chronicle state actions dealing with the unfolding crisis between 2000 and 2001. I visited the archive in the summer of 2018 and digitized over ten thousand pages of transcripts and filings, primarily documenting the period of market design between 1994 and 1997.

The California State Archive contains documents that chronicle the political processes leading to the creation of AB 1890 and business documents that were preserved from the California energy crisis. Of particular importance were the business documents of the Power Exchange and the California System Operator, which chronicle the initial design, operation, adjustment, and monitoring of these markets in great detail (1997–2002). The archives also contain material that pertains to the Senate Select

Committee's investigation of fraudulent behavior during the energy crisis, a highly political investigation of power marketers' behavior. I visited the state archives twice, once in the winter of 2017 and once in the summer of 2018. Here, I digitized about seven thousand pages.

Finally, the online archives at FERC contain an abundance of materials on all aspects of restructuring in California. Since FERC had to sanction all design decisions as well as decisions about changes to the tariffs governing the operation of the markets, the archival record gives a close overview of the initial design process and the adjustments to California's markets between 1998 and 2001. Because FERC was also the main regulatory entity of the California wholesale markets, most of the litigation took place there, and the dockets contain a vast paper trail of filings, evidence, hearing transcripts, technical statements, expert analyses, and affidavits that allow us to dive into any aspect of the crisis. Throughout the period of data collection between January 2017 and the summer of 2018, I scraped all substantial filings from the dockets.[1] Transcripts of hearings and dockets associated with the standards of legal oversight were relevant to my reconstruction of how the monitoring regimes were developed.

I supplement the sources from the three archives with a variety of other archival material. I retrieved transcripts from fifteen congressional hearings on the Western energy crisis, the Enron collapse, and FERC's oversight of the energy markets. I added four reports from the United States Accounting Office on different aspects of the regulatory structure. Further, for descriptive purposes I used a quantitative dataset from the California Energy Institute that captures key metrics of the California energy markets for the period from 1998 to 2002. To reconstruct the intellectual history of market design, I relied on a variety of working papers and publications from the Energy Institute in Palo Alto, the Working Paper Series of the California Center for the Study of Energy, William Hogan's working paper archive, and the working paper series of the MIT-Harvard workshop on homeostatic systems. I supplemented these sources with the dominant trade publications: the *Electricity Journal*, the *Energy Law Journal*, and the *Public Utility Fortnightly* for the years between 1993 and 2000. To reconstruct the crisis, I also drew on general newspapers like the *Los Angeles Times* and the *San Francisco Chronicle*. Finally, I made use of the WEPEX coordination website, which was stored in the Internet Archive (1996–98). Tables A.1–4 summarize the main sources by archive, leaving out newspapers, working papers, trade publications, and materials from the Internet Archive. These were used more selectively and will be cited in full in the analysis.

Most, though not all, of the archival material reflects formal procedures and not the informal practices surrounding them (excluding certain

TABLE A.1. Archival Material, Congressional Investigations

Congressional Investigations	Description & Date
Electric Utility Industry Restructuring: The California Market	Subcommittee on Energy and Power, Committee on Commerce, House of Representatives, 107th Congress, First Session, September 11, 2000
California's Electricity Crisis	Committee on Energy and Natural Resources, House of Representatives, 107th Congress, First Session, January 31, 2001
Electricity Markets: Lessons Learned from California	Subcommittee on Energy and Air Quality, Committee on Energy and Commerce, House of Representatives, 107th Congress, First Session, February 15, 2001
Congressional Perspectives on Electricity Markets in California and the West and National Energy Policy	Subcommittee on Energy and Air Quality, Committee on Energy and Commerce, House of Representatives, 107th Congress, First Session, March 6, 2001
Electricity Markets: California	Subcommittee on Energy and Air Quality, Committee on Energy and Commerce, House of Representatives, 107th Congress, First Session, March 20 and 22, 2001
Assessing the California Energy Crisis: How Did We Get to This Point, and Where Do We Go from Here?	Joint Hearings, Subcommittee on Energy Policy, Natural Resources, and Regulatory Affairs and the Committee on Government Reform, House of Representatives, 107th Congress, First Session, April 10–12, 2001
Wholesale Electricity Prices in California and the Western United States	Committee on Energy and Natural Resources, Senate, 107th Congress, First Session, May 3, 2001
The California Energy Crisis: Impacts, Causes and Remedies	Committee on Financial Services, House of Representatives, 107th Congress, First Session, June 20, 2001
FERC: Regulators in Deregulated Electricity Markets	Committee on Government Reform, House of Representatives, 107th Congress, First Session, August 2, 2001
The Effect of the Bankruptcy of Enron on the Functioning of Energy Markets	Subcommittee on Energy and Air Quality, Committee on Energy and Commerce, House of Representatives, 107th Congress, Second Session, February 13, 2002
California Independent System Operator: Governance and Design of California's Electricity Market	Subcommittee on Energy Policy, Natural Resources, and Regulatory Affairs, Committee on Government Reform, House of Representatives, 107th Congress, Second Session, February 22, 2002

(*continued*)

Congressional Investigations	Description & Date
Examining Enron: Electricity Market Manipulation and the Effect on the Western states	Subcommittee on Consumer Affairs, Foreign Commerce, and Tourism, Committee on Commerce, Science, and Transportation, House of Representatives, 107th Congress, Second Session, April 11, 2002
Examining Enron: Developments regarding Electricity Price Manipulation in California; Energy Market Manipulation	Subcommittee on Consumer Affairs, Foreign Commerce, and Tourism, Committee on Commerce, Science, and Transportation, House of Representatives, 107th Congress, Second Session, May 15, 2002
The Role Enron Energy Service Inc (EESI) Played in the Manipulation of Western Energy Markets	Committee on Commerce, Science and Transportation, House of Representatives, 107th Congress, Second Session, July 18, 2002
California's Electricity Market: The Case of Perot Systems	Committee on Government Reform, House of Representatives, 107th Congress, Second Session, July 22, 2002
Asleep at the Switch: FERC's Oversight of Enron Corporation, vols. 1–4	Committee on Governmental Affairs, Senate, 107th Congress, Second Session, November 12, 2002

TABLE A.2. Archival Material, California Public Utility Commission

California Public Utility Commission (CPUC)	Archival Material	Description
CPUC, *Order Instituting Rulemaking and Order Instituting Investigation*	CPUC Archives San Francisco, R.94-04-031 / I.94-04-132, boxes 10–50	All filings responding to the Blue Book that formally started the process of restructuring in 1994. Contains information on the political processes before the CPUC and reports about or filings from technical WEPEX processes of implementation.
Ibid.	CPUC Archives San Francisco, R.94-04-031 / I.94-04-132, boxes 50–53	CPUC's attempts to cope with the energy crisis (consolidated docket)
Ibid.	CPUC Archives San Francisco, R.94-04-031 / I.94-04-132, boxes 69–71	Transcripts from hearings during the design process (1994–97)

TABLE A.3. Archival Material, California State Archives

California Independent System Operator (CAISO)	Archival Material	Description
Market Surveillance Committee, Reports (1998–2001)	California State Archive, R400.007, boxes 12–14	Material (academic papers, analyses, data charts, etc.) related to the problems in the ancillary markets
Electricity Oversight Board, Subject Files (related to market power analysis at CAISO, 1997–2001)	California State Archive, R400.005, boxes 4–5 R400.010, boxes 18–19	Background material pertaining to specific issues (including market power in ancillary markets)
CAISO Market Surveillance Committee and Board of Governor Meeting Files (1998–2000)	California State Archive, R400.006, box 6, folder 1–box 9, folder 6	All material used during board meetings, including all material presented to the subcommittees (contains memos, memoranda, and status reports on problems with ancillary markets)

Other		
Sheila J. Kuehl Papers: Sen. Select Committee to Investigate Price Manipulation of the Wholesale Energy Markets	California State Archive, LP402:338–53, boxes 17–18	Personal files documenting work for the Senate Select Committee to Investigate Price Manipulation in Wholesale Markets

Power Exchange	Archival Material	
Teaching Material (Market Primer, etc.) for Board of Governors	2 reports (available online)	Background information on how the interface of the market works
Electricity Oversight Board, Subject Files	California State Archive, R400.005, box 5, folders 10–25 R400.010, box 18, folder 1–box 19, folder 14	Background material related to market power analysis at PX, 1997–2001
Board of Governor's Meeting Files (1998–2000)	California State Archive, R400.008, box 13, folder 15–box 14, folder 9	Agenda, minutes and background material presented during meetings of the Stakeholders Board, including material of committee meetings
PX Compliance Filings	George Sladoje, PX CEO, Personal Archive	DVD containing detailed documents chronicling the PX's investigation of Enron's early gaming activities

TABLE A.4. Archival Material, FERC

Federal Energy Regulatory Commission	Docket Number (Accessible via eLibrary)	Notes
Contract Path Methodology	ER93-706-000	Docket that first develops the legal standards for market oversight in a case against Indiana MI Power Co. Subsequently used until after the Western energy crisis.
Merger Applications and Technical Conferences regarding Market Power Methodology	PL98-6 RM98-4 RM98-6	FERC's early, fruitless attempts to revise their market power standard in the context of mergers (1998).
California Parties' Application for Establishment of CAISO/PX	ER96-1663 EC96-19	All material related to the design of the markets. In particular, WEPEX hearings that debate the correct approach to measuring market power and overseeing the California markets (1996–99). Contains all formal filings pertaining to the design and implementation of the California markets.
Development of Orders concerning Deregulation and Market Power Analysis (592, 888, 2000)	RM96-6 RM95-8 RM99-2	Landmark decisions to open the transmission system to prepare the ground for deregulation (Order 888 in 1996) and the subsequent development of Regional Transmission Organizations (Order 2000 in 1999). Contains transcripts that debate market power and methodology in energy markets.
Ancillary Market Crisis	ER98-2843	Crisis in ancillary markets at CAISO, consolidated docket. Contains all filings relevant to the crisis and redesign of the markets.
Gaming Case	EL03-180	Case that investigates the various manipulative games first discovered through the Enron memos.
Enron Investigation	PA02-2	Contains all material relevant to the investigation of manipulation of Western energy markets through Enron and others. In particular, evidence of transactions from all sellers in the Western energy markets.
Refund Case	EL00-95 EL00-98	Investigation of market power abuses in the California energy markets in 2000–2001. Contains all settlements regarding market power abuses as well as the evolution of the oversight standards during the crises. Cross-references to all individual cases involving the Western energy crisis.

transcripts and internal reports). The archival sources therefore offer only a fragmented view of the social processes that generated it. Besides relying on more than one archive, the best strategy to deal with this problem is to triangulate archival data with semistructured, in-depth interviews. I therefore added a series of such qualitative interviews to the material for this book.

Interviewing elites like politicians and business leaders harbors particular challenges related to their professional skills, like the ability to dodge questions and generate convincing yet misleading accounts. But the biggest challenge was access.[2] To deal with this problem, I relied on a mixture of quota and snowball sampling. Engaging with the archival material, I drew up lists of relevant actors from several different parts of the design process. In particular, I tried to interview regulators (state and federal), stakeholders, engineers, and economists who participated in the political, regulatory, or technical processes of market design and oversight. After identifying key players in each group and convincing a few to participate, I used their contacts to find new interviewees.

The interviews followed a semistructured format that was based on an interview guide with modifications for each group. The guide was approved by the Institutional Review Board in November 2017. It asks several questions about the person's role in the restructuring effort and the internal processes at the organizations they worked at. The questions were meant to elicit narratives about their experiences during the crisis. Apart from asking simple, factual questions not well supported by the archival data (e.g., how many people worked in the departments), I used the interviews to get information on the culture of market design, the narratives of the crisis, and the texture of everyday life in the organizations that ran the markets. I stopped conducting further interviews when the answers to my questions started to become redundant. Upon completion of the interviews, I took notes about my observations. Over the course of about one and a half years, I conducted seventy-six interviews with sixty-three individuals.

To facilitate shadow comparisons, I did not speak only to designers of the California system; I also talked to some who contributed to a more successful experiment with electricity market design at the time: the electricity markets for the PJM Interconnection. While several of the market designers I talked to contributed to the creation of both the PJM and the California markets, eight of the interviewees worked on PJM exclusively. See tables A.5 and A.6 for a detailed overview of the coverage of the different aspects of the design process. Since many interviewees participated in different parts of the design process, the numbers in A.5 do not reflect discrete interviews but rather indicate how many interviews contributed to an understanding of the processes in question. A.6 lists the actual number of

TABLE A.5. Expert Interviews by Organizational Affiliation and Profession

	Economists / Designers	Engineers / Designers	Stakeholders	Lawyers / Politicians / Other
Technical Process / Implementation (WEPEX/ TAC)	9	8	9	6
Political Design Process: Public Utility Commission / California Assembly	8	6	10	5
Regulatory Design Process: FERC	11	7	8	6
Affiliation after Market Started				
System Operator / Power Exchange	10	6	7	9
FERC	12	5	3	5
CA Government	3	2	4	5
Market Actors	2	1	4	1
PJM	2	7	3	4

TABLE A.6. Number of Interviews and Interviewees by Profession

	Interviews	Interviewees	Market Designers
Economists	23	19	12
Engineers	17	16	13
Stakeholders	10	6	—
Lawyers/Politicians	26	22	—
Total	76	63	25

interviews and participants by profession. The third column identifies the number of market designers in each category.

For transcription, I either paid for the services of REV.com with money from a Henderson Grant or transcribed the interviews by hand. The seventy-five interviews amount to approximately nine hundred to one thousand pages of transcripts. Relying on grounded theory guidelines, I analyzed these transcripts by building primary and secondary codes and refining them in a process of constant comparison.[3]

Because the transcripts were used in combination with archival material, I never used the entire corpus but selected interviews with participants whose experiences were relevant to the analytical question at hand. This approach yielded themes and patterns that helped to elaborate the archival analysis. Because the interviews were retrospective and dealt with events that lie twenty years in the past, I only used them to corroborate or elaborate on evidence that I found in the archival materials. However, in some cases, I do report interview statements that are not covered by archival material. These usually refer to evaluative judgments about the crisis. In these cases, at least three interviews contain statements that make similar claims. Some of my interviewees preferred to be quoted anonymously. To these quotes, I have assigned an alias. Aliases can be distinguished from real names because the fictional last names are single letters only.

Key to Archival Sources

LAT—*Los Angeles Times*
NYT—*New York Times*
SFC—*San Francisco Chronicle*
WP—*Washington Post*

CPUC—docket R.94-04-031/I.94-04-032, California Public Utility Commission Archive, San Francisco, California
CSA—California State Archives, Sacramento, CA
FERC—Federal Energy Regulatory Commission

For FERC statements (opinions, orders, questions): "Commission Statement Name," statement number FERC paragraph number, (date).
For Cases: *Party Name*, decision number FERC paragraph number, (date).
For Evidence and Other Submissions: Author (if identified), "Document Title," FERC docket number.

Notes

INTRODUCTION

1. Geertz 1978; Hayek 1945.

2. Callon 2008; Fligstein and Mara-Drita 1996; Granovetter 1985.

3. Padgett and Powell 2012.

4. Beckert 2009.

5. Coase 1988; Williamson 1985. Hybridity between markets and organizations then creates coordination problems that require explanation (Eccles and White 1988; Foss 2003; Magelssen, Rich, and Mayer 2022).

6. Hayek 1940, 1945. Of course, the intellectual history is far more complex than this simple opposition suggests (Bockman 2011).

7. As will become clear later, even market designers are somewhat inconsistent in their use of models and metaphors. While realizing a model means creating a deterministic machine, the dominant metaphors to justify market design are evolutionary. The tension between the mechanistic and evolutionary imaginary has been part of economics for a long time. It goes back to the writings of the physiocrats in the nineteenth century (Samuels 1962).

8. The growing literature that revives the debate for the twenty-first century has rarely appreciated this twist (Morozov 2019; Phillips and Rozworski 2019; Shapiro 2009).

9. Viljoen, Goldenfein, and McGuigan 2021.

10. Kominers, Teytelboym, and Crawford 2017; Prendergast 2017; Roth 2008; Waldinger 2021.

11. Kominers, Teytelboym, and Crawford 2017.

12. McAfee and Wilkie 2020.

13. Filippas, Horton, and Zeckhauser 2020; Horton 2017.

14. Pathak 2017. For a fascinating discussion of market design for equality, see also Dworczak, Kominers, and Akbarpour 2021.

15. For the papers in the different working groups of Mechanism Design for Social Good, see https://www.md4sg.com/, accessed May 16, 2023.

16. Lehdonvirta 2022; Rahman and Thelen 2019; Viljoen, Goldenfein, and McGuigan 2021.

17. Krippner 2011.

18. Frankel, Ossandón, and Pallesen 2019.

19. Liang and Parkinson 2020.

20. CAISO 2021.

21. Chiu et al. 2015.

22. Cramton 2021; Rilinger 2021.

23. Commission 2021; Cramton 2021; Rilinger 2021; Schechter 2020; Wheeler and Garrick 2020.

24. For this reason, very little research has explored the design processes in platform organizations (Schüssler et al. 2021; Bailey and Barley 2020).

25. P. Joskow 2001.

26. Sweeney 2002a.

27. G. Taylor et al. 2015.

28. McLean and Elkind (2003) 2013.

29. For the first narrative, see Hogan 2002; Sweeney 2002b. For the second, see Beder 2003; G. Taylor et al. 2015.

30. The economist Esther Duflo (2017) has made the same point.

31. McCabe, Rassenti, and Smith 1991. On online transaction platforms, A/B tests and other experiments can be applied directly, eradicating the difference between lab and field. Nonetheless, scaling experimental interventions to the market as a whole remains a problem (Luca and Bazerman 2021).

32. G. Carroll 2019; Velupillai and Zambelli 2013.

33. Roth 2008.

34. Klemperer 2002, 2003; Roth and Wilson 2019; Vulkan, Roth, and Neeman 2013.

35. Duflo 2017.

36. Granovetter 1985; White 1981.

37. For example, Baker 1984.

38. Aspers, Bengtsson, and Dobeson 2020, 422.

39. Indeed, the embeddedness perspective is so focused on antecedents that the market itself has remained a somewhat elusive category in this research program (Krippner 2002; Krippner and Alvarez 2007).

40. Lusher, Koskinen, and Robins 2012.

41. DiMaggio and Powell 1983; Nee 2005.

42. Bourdieu 2005; Martin 2003.

43. Bourdieu 2005; Fligstein 2002; Fligstein and McAdam 2011; Martin 2003.

44. Dobbin 1994; Nee 2005; Vogel 2018.

45. Mirowski and Nik-Khah 2007.

46. Reverdy and Breslau 2019.

47. Breslau 2013.

48. Ahrne, Aspers, and Brunsson 2015.

49. Callon 1998.

50. Brisset 2018; Guala 2001, 2005; Pallesen and Jenle 2018; Roscoe and Willman 2021; Wansleben 2018.

51. Guala 2001.

52. Blok 2011; Breslau 2013; Frankel, Ossandón, and Pallesen 2019; Garcia-Parpet 2007.

53. Scholars recognize this irony (MacKenzie 2009), but it nonetheless undermines the critical verve behind the performativity argument (Hirschman 2015).

54. It goes back to early research in the social studies of science (Latour 1999).

55. Though it would not have to be (Rilinger 2022a). The basic criticism is well established by now (Brisset 2018; Zuckerman 2010, 2012).

56. MacKenzie 2022.

57. Callon 2009; Guala and Mittone 2005.

58. MacKenzie 2008.

59. Preda 2009.

60. The literature is not committed to explaining market design success or failure from the perspective of designers, in terms of their plans and capabilities. The prototype of performative effects is a self-fulfilling prophecy. Such Barnesian performativity occurs when the use of a theory makes the world more like that theory. Importantly, such effects can occur without the actors' intention. While actors perceive themselves to be describing the world, they are, in fact, making it (MacKenzie 2007).

61. This requires immanent critique rather than description (Rilinger 2015).

62. I here follow a recent line of research in economic sociology and management that has made this point forcefully but has not begun to develop its implications (Ahrne, Aspers, and Brunsson 2015; Frankel, Ossandón, and Pallesen 2019; McIntyre et al. 2021; Pallesen and Jenle 2018; Stark and Pais 2020). I also draw on insights about the way platform infrastructures utilize techniques of evaluation and protocol to exercise control over users (Kornberger, Pflueger, and Mouritsen 2017).

63. Bichler 2017.

64. Ockenfels 2009, 31 (my translation).

65. Auction theory helps here because it gives information about which situations can be ignored (Vickrey 1962).

66. The most famous and sustained discussion of this problem can be found in *Seeing like a State* (J. Scott 1998), but the arguments go back to a long line of anarchist and libertarian thinkers. Indeed, even though market designers usually invoke Friedrich Hayek as their figurehead, he argued that it is impossible to plan and control the market because information cannot easily be aggregated and evaluated by a center (Hayek 1945).

67. This observer-dependent definition of complexity is inspired by Luhmann's (2012) abstract, cybernetic definition.

68. C. Y. Baldwin and Clark 2000.

CHAPTER ONE

1. O'Donnell 2003, 165–68.

2. Roe and Schulman 2008, 25–29.

3. David Lazarus, "Lights Out—Juice Cut Again: S.F. Sues Power Firms," *SFC*, January 18, 2001, A1.

4. O'Donnell 2003, 167.

5. O'Donnell 2003, 167.

6. Chuck Squatriglia, Justino Aguila, Patrick Hoge, and Matthew Stannard, "Rolling Blackouts Hit/Power Cut to Parts of Bay Area at Midday—PG&E Defaults on Debt," *SFC*, January 18, 2001, A1.

7. O'Donnell 2003, 168.

8. US Energy Information Administration, "Subsequent Events—California's Energy Crisis," accessed April 10, 2023, https://www.eia.gov/electricity/policies/legislation/california/subsequentevents.html.

9. This is the reason CAISO has been studied as an instance of high-reliability management (Roe and Schulman 2008).

10. Contrary to common belief, the electricity crisis did not have a lasting effect on the state budget. The state had to pay for electricity through 2001 and used its general fund to do so. But it repaid the general fund by selling $6.2 billion in electricity bonds. These were financed by ratepayers, not taxpayers. The crisis was therefore largely paid for by the customers of the utilities—it was socialized by state intervention but not with tax revenues (S. Sheffrin 2004, 215–16).

11. The California Energy Commission was mainly in charge of forecasting energy needs and siting new power plants for the utilities.

12. In the electricity industry, day- and hour-ahead markets are often referred to as spot markets. This is not technically correct, because they also refer to future points of delivery. I will nonetheless stick with the conventions and refer to the energy imbalance markets in CAISO as spot markets because their results were not open to revision (Biggar and Hesamzadeh 2014, 73).

13. The data for the PX ends in February 2001 because the organization declared bankruptcy and stopped operating auction markets.

14. P. L. Joskow 2001, 1. The quantity of energy that generators deliver is measured in MW/h, while the capacity is measured in MW. The capacity, the *rate* at which power flows over a line, indicates the maximum output rate of the generator under ideal operating conditions. Since *rate* is a relative term, energy is sold and priced in MW/h. To get a certain job done, you need a specific amount of energy. Any specific power level gets a job done relative to how long the power continues to flow. A megawatt flowing for one hour is a MW/h. For example, to boil some water, you need about thirty watt-hours, i.e., a generator needs to supply energy at a rate of 0.00003 MW for one hour (Biggar and Hesamzadeh 2014, 34).

15. Sweeney 2002a, 145.

16. The stranded costs were calculated as the asset's market value in a competitive setting minus the book value that ratepayers would still have to pay under the regulated

structure. Current net book values of utility assets are the allowable costs that have not yet been recovered (Blumstein, Friedman, and Green 2002, 8).

17. They also imposed a 10 percent reduction on retail rates, paid for with bonds that reflected deferred increases in rates.

18. This problem was exacerbated by a regulatory imbalance in the new retail markets. The utilities had to serve all customers and even had to take them back after they had switched to a different supplier. Alternative retail suppliers, however, did not have such an obligation and had no regulatory limitations on their retail prices. When the crisis hit, retail customers thus came back to utilities, who had to charge low prices and could not turn them away (Cicchetti, Dubin, and Long 2004; Duane 2002).

19. This issue is more complicated than presented here and is discussed later in greater detail. There were other ways for the utilities to hedge their risk and the literature has different views about why they did not do this (Cicchetti, Dubin, and Long 2004, 67–68; Wolak 2003, 17). Later, I argue that the restriction on forward contracts was less relevant to the occurrence of the crisis than has usually been claimed.

20. Thomas K., interview, March 15, 2018.

21. Andrew F., interview, January 25, 2018.

22. To prepare for deregulation, the California Public Utility Commission started a $90 million publicity campaign to alert end users of their ability to choose their own provider. Even though "retail choice" had been one of the leading issues during the debates about restructuring, these efforts largely evaporated without effect. Less than 3% of small commercial and residential customers decided to switch their provider; cf. CEC data cited by Weare (2003, 41).

23. George Sladoje, interview, March 30, 2018.

24. McNamara 2002, 40–43.

25. This opinion can be found in a joint report by the president of the Electricity Oversight Board and the California Public Utility Commission to Gray Davis. Michael Kahn and Loretta Lynch, "EOB-CPUC Report," submitted in Joint Informational Hearing, Senate Committee on Energy, Utilities and Communications and Assembly Committee on Utilities and Commerce, August 10, 2000, CSA. The core claim that the markets may be manipulated appeared prior to the release of the report.

26. Nancy Vogel, "Davis Seeks Price Ceiling on Soaring Electricity Rates," *LAT*, July 28, 2000.

27. This part of the crisis played out in response to San Diego's complaint from August 2000. They were asking for restrictions to sellers' behavior and price caps of $250. The other utilities and the Public Utility Commission joined the complaint in support (G. Taylor et al. 2015, 72).

28. R. O'Neill and Helman 2007, 144; "Order Accepting for Filing in Part and Rejecting in Part Proposed Tariff Amendment and Directing Reevaluation of Approach to Addressing Intrazonal Congestion," 90 FERC 61,0006 (January 7, 2000).

29. Quoted in Peter Behr, "Calif.'s Davis Lacked Legal Ability to Solve Energy Crisis," *WP*, August 24, 2003.

30. Nancy Vogel, "Crisis Darkens State Christmas Tree.," *LAT*, December 6, 2000.

31. Weare 2003, 44–46.

32. In January and March 2001, the California Public Utility Commission finally granted utilities rate increases, but these measures were too little, too late and could not resolve the utilities' financial troubles.

33. De Vries 2007, 96.

34. Pacific Gas and Electric Company, "Pacific Gas and Electric Company Files for Chapter 11 Reorganization," press release, April 6, 2001, https://www.pgecorp.com /news/press_releases/Release_Archive2001/040601press_release.shtml.

35. Southern California Edison, "SCE Proposes Plan to Stabilize Rates, Protect Customers from San Diego–Type Rate Shock," press release, November 17, 2000, https://newsroom.edison.com/releases/sce-proposes-plan-to-stabilize-rates-protect -customers-from-san-diego-type-rate-shock.

36. Weare 2003, 4.

37. Sweeney 2002a, 29.

38. See the appendix for a list of sources.

39. McNamara, 2002, xv.

40. More recent, cursory treatments of the crisis sometimes bring the sides together and claim that both are true. Isser's (2015) recent recounting in his monumental history of electricity restructuring in the United States takes this route. Other examples are short overviews in collected editions, like Considine and Kleit 2007; Nix, Decker, and Wolf 2021; J. Taylor and VanDoren 2002. These treatments simply report the facts that are not in dispute. Accordingly, they do not contribute to a resolution of the debate: neither side denies the existence of the factors the other side focuses on (supply, market power, manipulation, demand, political errors). What is in dispute is the relative weight of these factors for the train of events outlined in the first section.

41. An important part of the story is that the California Energy Commission's biennial resource plan update reflected the belief that demand management can be counted as a gain in supply (i.e., by reducing demand, they reduced the requirements for new capacity). These reductions, or "negawatts," were then counted positively in the report. This may have contributed to an overly optimistic view of the existing supply in the 1990s (Marcus and Hamrin 2001, 2–3).

42. In 1996, the California Energy Commission had projected an 11.7 percent total growth in demand between 1995 and 2000. The real growth rate was 14.5 percent, only 3 percent higher than had been generally anticipated by the regulators (CEC 1996; Sweeney 2002a, 94).

43. Between 1977 and 1988, the eleven states added capacity at an annual growth rate of 4.5 percent. In the decade between 1988 and 1998, this rate reduced to 0.5 percent. This did not correspond to the growth in demand. Between 1977 and 1998, consumption grew by 2.4 percent per year, with an increase of just below 10 percent in the decade between 1988 and 1998 (Fisher and Duane 2001, 4).

44. Reserve margin is calculated by subtracting peak demand from installed capacity and then dividing by demand. It is a measure for how much capacity exists in excess of demand. About 15 percent is necessary for reliable operation.

45. The analysis includes coal plants outside California because they are owned or controlled by the three utilities in the state. If we exclude those plants, the situation

looks somewhat different. The claim that the output of the natural gas plants increased massively in 2000 is not borne out by the data. Nonetheless, the output did increase during the time of interest, so the evidence from before 2000 supports Sweeney's (2002a, 97) argument.

46. Annual applications for certification averaged about 250 MW per year between 1990 and 1996, while annual retirements averaged about 450 per year. Over the seven years, installed capacity declined by about 1,400 MW. From 1997 through 2000, applications averaged 3,300 MW per year; however, in 2000 none of this new supply was yet operational (Sweeney 2002a, 101).

47. McNamara 2002, 32–37.

48. Borenstein 2002; Borenstein, Bushnell, and Knittel 1999; Borenstein et al. 2008; Borenstein, Bushnell, and Wolak 2002; Bushnell 2004; Bushnell and Wolak 2000; Wolak 2003, 2005.

49. P. L. Joskow and Kahn 2002, 10.

50. Borenstein, Bushnell, and Wolak 2002, 2.

51. See, for example, the objections voiced by Harvey and Hogan (2001b, 9).

52. With very few exceptions, related to accusations of physical withholding.

53. G. Taylor et al. 2015, 83.

54. McLean and Elkind (2003) 2013.

55. G. Taylor et al. 2015, 83–97.

56. Michael Liedke, "Trading Floors Represent Ground Zero in Energy Crisis," *Las Vegas Sun*, March 26, 2001, https://lasvegassun.com/news/2001/mar/26/trading -floors-represent-ground-zero-in-energy-cri/. Of course, not all this profit accrued from operations in California; sorting out what did or did not constituted a major problem during litigation.

57. Carol J. Loomis, ". . . And the Revenue Games People (like Enron) Play: Got Energy Trading Contracts?," *Fortune Magazine*, April 15, 2002; McNamara 2002, 52–58.

58. Carl Ingram, "Freeman 'Surprised' at Alleged Gouging by DWP," *LAT*, August 2, 2002, https://www.latimes.com/archives/la-xpm-2002-aug-02-me-freeman2-story .html.

59. Richard A. Oppel Jr. and Laura M. Holson, "While a Utility May Be Failing, Its Owner Is Not," *NYT*, April 30, 2001, https://www.nytimes.com/2001/04/30/business /while-a-utility-may-be-failing-its-owner-is-not.html.

60. "Order Affirming Factual Findings, Directing Compliance Filing and Ordering Refunds re San Diego Gas & Electric Company v. Sellers of Energy and Ancillary Services et al under EL00-95," 149 FERC 61, 116 (November 10, 2014).

61. George Sladoje, interview, March 30, 2018.

62. The operations of the West Desk are outlined in, for example, Robert Mc-Cullough, "Enron Discovery, June 9, 2004," FERC EL03-137/180. Strategically disaggregating deals into strips that traders entered into the general accounting software (Enpower) made it difficult even for insiders to see how the profits were generated. But the West Desk also used private accounting ledgers (Inc Sheet and others), in which the trades were clearly listed. These ledgers were eventually found in a warehouse and ana-

lyzed by a team of investigators. They reveal the extent to which the West Desk used the schemes outlined in the famous Enron memos.

63. In 2005, an administrative law judge of the Federal Energy Regulatory Commission released this tape and others to the public. They can be found in docket EL03-180-000.

64. Julian Borger, "Tapes Reveal Enron's Secret Role in California's Power Blackouts," *Guardian*, February 4, 2005, https://www.theguardian.com/business/2005/feb/05/enron.usnews.

65. Beder 2003, 109.

66. Greg Palast, "Why the Lights Went Out All over California," *Observer*, July 1, 2001.

67. Stoft 2002.

68. The various explanations for a legitimate reduction of generator output are discussed in Harvey and Hogan, 2001a, 2001b.

69. G. Taylor et al. 2015, 178–82.

70. The economic theory of regulatory capture is, in its original formulation, little more than a theory of corruption. It suggests that regulators sell the desired policy to the highest bidder (Stigler 1971). The book does not evaluate this question head-on, but I have done so in a separate article (Rilinger 2023).

71. Ernest Hollings, "Time for a Special Counsel," *NYT*, February 9, 2002.

72. McLean and Elkind (2003) 2013.

73. Duane 2002, 474.

74. Beder 2003; Bushnell 2004; Cicchetti, Dubin, and Long 2004; Marcus and Hamrin 2001; McCullough 2001; McNamara 2002; Navarro and Shames 2003; Rights 2002; Walsh 2004; Woo 2001; Woo, Lloyd, and Tishler 2003. But see Smith, Rassenti, and Wilson 2002.

75. In particular, Beder 2003; Blumstein, Friedman, and Green 2002; de Vries 2007; Sueyoshi 2010.

76. Didion 2006, 131.

77. Jan Smutny-Jones, interview, February 21, 2017.

78. Hirsh 1999, vii; O'Donnell 2003, 50–51.

79. P. L. Joskow and Schmalensee 1988, 9.

80. Jan Smutny-Jones, interview, February 21, 2017.

81. Of course, there were other efforts to describe market designs for electricity in Europe and the US, but the MIT-Harvard connection proved decisive for the foundational work by Schweppe (in engineering) and Joskow and Kahn (in economics), which, in turn, became influential in California.

82. Richard Tabors, interview, April 18, 2018.

83. Tabors 2018.

84. Breslau 2020, 231.

85. It is therefore a natural tool for market design. Control theory provides a mathematical framework to conceptualize issues of ongoing feedback control in non-

linear systems. It is mainly a tool to formalize problems. Linear and nonlinear programming—as well as other numerical techniques for finding solutions to systems of differential equations by approximation—can often be used to solve optimal control problems (Weber 2011, 253–54).

86. The research had a distinct connection to cybernetics, which emerged in the same nexus and gave rise to systems engineering (Ashby 1957; Wiener 1965).

87. Schweppe, Tabors, et al. 1980.

88. Schweppe, Tabors, et al. 1980, 1151.

89. Schweppe, Tabors, et al. 1980, 1154.

90. At several points the book quotes William Vickrey (1978), who discussed congestion management and explicitly considered the homeostatic control theory as well.

91. For example, Paul Joskow and Jean Tirole (2000) acknowledge Robert Wilson and William Hogan. In the articles that sketch the design for the California congestion management system, the authors explicitly acknowledge Hogan for "many incisive comments and constructive suggestions" (Chao and Peck 1996, 25). In 1997, Hong-po Chao and Hillard G. Huntington organized a conference about the design of competitive electricity markets, where many of the issues in California were discussed. Again, the most important members of the MIT-Harvard nexus joined the representatives from the Energy Institute (Chao and Huntington 1998, 1–2).

92. Paul Joskow at MIT, for example, wrote recommendations for Pacific Gas & Electric. Harvard's William Hogan worked for San Diego Gas & Electric and for Enron. His work stood behind most of the proposals that San Diego submitted to the Public Utility Commission and FERC. In 1988, Richard Tabors and Michael Caramanis, members of the original workshops, founded Tabors, Caramanis & Associates, a consulting firm for market design. They were hired first by stakeholders and later by CAISO when the organization got off the ground.

93. As early as 1982, the California Energy Commission and the California Department of Public Utilities oversaw projects to test the feasibility of engineering proposals conceived in the context of the homeostatic system workshops. Southern California Edison and Pacific Gas & Electric funded experiments to develop differentiated metering technologies that would allow end users to react to time-sensitive rate changes in their service territories. Their employees took leading roles in the implementation of these experiments and created ties to the MIT-Harvard nexus that solidified during the next decade (Schweppe, Caramanis, Tabors, and Bohn 1988, xiv; Schweppe, Caramanis, Tabors, and Flory 1982). John Flory helped design the Power Exchange and was involved in the research that led to *Spot Pricing of Electricity*.

94. Roth and Wilson 2019, 135.

95. Minutes of the WEPEX/TAC Steering Committee, January 8, 1996, https://web
.archive.org/web/20000817212105/http://www.energyonline.com/wepex/.

CHAPTER TWO

1. Lambert 2006; Walsh 2004.

2. Market designers have proposed this distinction themselves (Smith 2008).

3. For a careful history of different traditions of market design, cf. Mirowski and Nik-Khah 2017.

4. Beckert 2016.

5. The debate has been recast multiple times, with different victors emerging in each retelling (Cottrell and Cockshott 1993; Lavoie 1981; J. O'Neill 2006).

6. Historically speaking, the debate is a retrospective construction by Hayek, who published Mises's essay together with a recounting of the debate in a collected edition in 1935. Hayek's reading influenced subsequent narratives of the debate even though it was extremely selective and misrepresented Mises's centrality to the debate. Arguably, the exchange did not start with Mises's essay but with Otto Neurath's writings on planned economies, or even earlier with Enrico Baronne's 1908 model of a socialist economy (Bockman 2011, 24–29). Here, these exegetical points do not matter because I am only interested in the broad outlines of the argument.

7. Mises 1935.

8. Nove 1991.

9. Mises 1935.

10. The evolution of the Lange-Lerner-Taylor solution is subject to a broad literature on the calculation debate. The main formulation appeared in 1936–37 (Lange 1936, 1937).

11. Lavoie (1981) has argued that the socialist economists narrowed the debate to mathematical models and thereby misunderstood the foundational challenge of the Austrians.

12. Hayek 1945.

13. Lange 1967, 158.

14. Akerlof and Shiller 2010.

15. Right now, the debate over luxury socialism is playing out once more. Authors ponder the possibility of nationalizing the logistic systems of companies like Walmart and Amazon that have proved that entire markets can be replaced by centrally planned, algorithmic logistic systems (Morozov 2019; Phillips and Rozworski 2019).

16. Vickrey 1962.

17. Börgers 2015, 2.

18. Nik-Khah and Mirowski 2019.

19. Rassenti, Smith, and Bulfin 1982.

20. Mirowski and Nik-Kah (2017) have traced the development of experimentalist market design as one of three overarching traditions.

21. In fact, these techniques have rarely been used in electricity systems because their operation is less comprehensible to an external observer. ISOs have relied on more traditional linear and quadratic linear programming techniques. They generate only approximate solutions, but errors can be easily detected and resolved in secondary analyses (Yang et al. 2017).

22. Here, I hearken back to the origins of the social studies of finance — the literature on sociotechnical systems (Hughes 1987).

23. I am adapting these from Stinchcombe's (2001, 10) original terms "cognitive adequacy," "communicability," and "trajectory of improvement."

24. Herman K. Trabish, "California Regulators See Signs of a New Energy Crisis—Can They Prevent It?," Utility Dive, May 18, 2018, https://www.utilitydive.com/news/california-regulators-see-signs-of-a-new-energy-crisis-can-they-prevent-i/523414/.

25. Akerlof (1970) 1995.

26. Bolton, Greiner, and Ockenfels 2018.

27. W. Scott 2013.

28. Interestingly, white-collar crime usually happens in the interest of furthering the organizations' objectives, not to undermine them (Soltes 2016).

29. Freeland and Zuckerman Sivan 2018; Z. Lei, Naveh, and Novikov 2016; Lyles 2014.

30. Stinchcombe 2001, 56–58.

31. This is an old insight from the literature on organizational learning (Orr [1996] 2016).

32. Roberts 1990; Roe and Schulman 2008; Weick, 1988, 2005; Weick and Roberts 1993.

33. Abdulkadiroğlu and Sönmez (2003) provide a general account of matching problems and the foundational work of David Gale and Lloyd Shapley. The Boston mechanism had to be changed several times because sophisticated parents found ways to game the system to the disadvantage of less-informed parents.

34. Roth and Peranson 1999.

35. Abdulkadiroğlu et al. 2006, 6.

36. Schutz and Luckmann 1973.

37. Roth and Wilson 2019, 126.

38. Budish and Kessler 2016.

39. This idea goes back to pragmatist philosophy, which stresses the creative and fundamentally open character of the future (Dewey [1922] 2002, 190).

40. Emirbayer and Mische 1998, 966.

41. The problem of determining the rules of inference outside practice is immortalized in Lewis Carroll's famous story about Archimedes and the Tortoise (L. Carroll 1895), where Archimedes is forever unable to convince the Tortoise about the rules of inference because each set of rules needs to be justified with yet another inference, leading to an infinite regress.

42. Perrow (1984) 1999.

43. Downer 2011.

44. The concept of safety underlying Perrow's argument ignores crucial differences between hazards (Leveson et al. 2009). However, in the present context, it is only the epistemic argument that matters.

45. Perrow (2010) himself highlighted that the application of normal accident theory to markets is problematic because financial crises are the product of intentional action.

46. Merton 1936.

47. Many of these failures hinge on the organizational limits of processing vast quantities of information between different departments in response to real-time developments. Others hinge on incentive problems with reporting the correct information to and within the bureaucracies (Ellman 2014).

48. Kellogg, Valentine, and Christin 2020; F. Taylor (1947) 2004.

49. Cramton and Schwartz 2002.

50. Gode and Sunder 1993.

51. Leveson 2011, 66.

52. Cameron and Rahman 2022.

53. In the 1990s, most generators used turbines that induced electricity by spinning copper wire inside a magnet. Power plants usually contain several generators that are dispatched separately. For accounting, managerial, and regulatory purposes, these plants are treated as units (P. L. Joskow and Schmalensee 1988, 46).

54. Biggar and Hesamzadeh 2014, 46–49.

55. Rilinger 2021.

CHAPTER THREE

1. Cited in Joel Roberts "Enron Traders Caught on Tape," CBS, June 1, 2004, https://www.cbsnews.com/news/enron-traders-caught-on-tape/.

2. Van Vactor 2000.

3. Greg Palast, "Why the Lights Went Out All over California," *Observer*, July 1, 2001.

4. Milton 2005, 17.

5. The details can be found in the last version of the 1998 Tariff for CAISO, filed with FERC: "California ISO, ISO Tariff, Version 7," 82 FERC 61,327 (1998), sections 2.1–2.5.

6. Borenstein 2002, 199.

7. Initially, this market was referred to as an "hour-ahead" market. Until January 1999, it operated on a rolling basis, with each market closing three hours before the hour of operation. After that, it was only open three times a day, each time dealing with a different block between five and twelve hours in the future.

8. James G. Kritikson, "California Electricity Market Primer," prepared for the CalPX Board of Governors (February 2000), R400.010, box 18, folder 12, Electricity Oversight Board subject files, CSA, 8.

9. Economists do not assume that the future is completely unpredictable. Rather, they use *uncertainty* to indicate that actors only know a probability distribution of future states. As new information becomes available, the probabilities shift and require new trades (Varian 1992).

10. Many of them also simply acted on their own behalf, selling energy from affiliated producers.

11. They played several other functions apart from improving the search for the ideal unit commitment: they could act as financial intermediaries hedging price risks for

consumers, manage energy purchases for disaggregated buyers, help with congestion management, and provide ancillary services (Stoft 1997, 36).

12. The following discussion is reconstructed from the detailed descriptions in the submissions of the CAISO Market Surveillance Committee in FERC ER98-2843, chapter 2 of the annual report of the system operator from 1999, and the detailed descriptions of the reports of the Market Surveillance Committee, R400.006-R400.007, folder 1–12, box 12, CSA.

13. CAISO, *Annual Report on Market Issues and Performance* (Folsom, CA: CAISO 1999), chap. 2.3, http://www.caiso.com/Documents/1999-2000AnnualReporton MarketIssuesandPerformance.pdf.

14. If the imbalance markets did not produce sufficient resources to adjust the system, the system operator also had recourse to so-called "reliability must run" contracts and out-of-market purchases. The contracts were used when parts of the market were blocked off from one another (load pockets) and companies did not face competition. The contracts substituted standard rates for market prices because the lack of competition would not produce prices at marginal cost. The out-of-market purchases were a tool of last resort in case California did not have enough generation capacity and operators needed to import energy from other states.

15. CAISO report on Management Assertion Relating to Ancillary Services Management, Balancing Energy and Ex-post Pricing, and Congestion Management Systems, May 27, 1998, R401.005, box 6, folder 4, CSA, 3–5 (hereafter cited as CAISO report 1998).

16. CAISO report 1998, 24–33.

17. Breslau 2020.

18. Shared with me by the former CEO of the Power Exchange.

19. *California's Electricity Market: The Case of Perot Systems, Hearing before the Subcomm. on Energy Policy, Natural Resources and Regulatory Affairs, of the House Comm. on Government Reform*, 107th Cong., 2nd Sess. (2002) (statement of Charles J. Cicchetti, PhD), 91.

20. The system operator used the definition provided by the FTC: "Market power to a seller is the ability profitably to maintain prices above competitive levels for a significant period of time." In economics, the qualification "significant period of time" is not used because it introduces qualitative considerations into the calculation. CAISO Market Surveillance Committee, "The Competitiveness of the California Energy and Ancillary Service Markets, March 9, 2000," FERC ER98-2843, 1.

21. Borenstein 2000; Borenstein, Bushnell, and Knittel 1999.

22. Market participants are "pivotal" if they are necessary to meet aggregate demand at a given moment. California's independent system operator developed a pivotal supplier test (PSI) in 1998 to detect market power. If the supply margin is greater than the capacity offered by a supplier being evaluated, the PSI is less than one, and buyers have supply alternatives. If the PSI is greater than one, the supplier is pivotal. Cf. Rahimi and Sheffrin 2003; A. Sheffrin 2002.

23. Borenstein 2002.

24. Lennie W., interview, February 2, 2018.

25. Carmella G., interview, November 28, 2017.

26. Anelise S., interview, December 13, 2017.

27. San Diego Gas & Electric, "California Parties' Supplemental Evidence of Market Manipulation by Sellers, Proposed Findings of Fact, and Request for Refunds and Other Relief," FERC Dockets EL00-95-000 / EL00-98-000, 34–35.

28. Brian S., interview, March 13, 2018.

29. Early insights about the interaction between congestion and market power in California can be found in a research report commissioned by the system operator in 1999. See London Economics, "Assessing Market Power in Newly Deregulated Electricity Markets, July 1999," R400.010, box 19, folder 18, Electricity Oversight Board subject files (I–T), CSA.

30. CAISO Market Surveillance Committee, *Annual Report on Market Issues and Performance*, June 1999, chap. 2, http://www.caiso.com/Documents/Chapter2_1998 AnnualReport_MarketIssuesandPerformance.pdf.

31. During the litigation of the crisis, the power marketers argued that the utilities had defrauded the Power Exchange by understating their demand and that they were to blame for the shift of business into the imbalance markets. For example, see *Hearing before the House Comm. on Energy and Commerce, Exhibit No. CA-228*, 106th Cong., 2nd Sess. (2000) (statement of John Stout), FERC EL00-98-000, 2. California's Parties contested this heavily in *Hearing, Exhibit No. CA-3* (prepared Testimony of Dr. Gary A. Stern), FERC EL00-98-000, 31–45.

32. They could make use of prearranged contracts to curtail the load in emergency situations, and they could reduce reserve margins and use replacement reserves to supplement imbalance energy. They could also try to use out-of-market purchases (i.e., buy from other balancing authorities). See CAISO report 1998, 2–14. But because of the games outlined in sections 1-B and C, this recourse was not likely to lower the prices.

33. CAISO Market Surveillance Committee, "Competitiveness of the California Energy," 4.

34. There were other problems with the system operator's markets. Most important were incentives to withhold power to activate reliability-must-run contracts, software problems that prevented those outside California from offering their supplies, and clearing rules for the auctions that created perverse incentives in the beginning. These problems are discussed in the Market Surveillance Committee meetings between 1998 and 2000. See "Presentation: Top Three Issues, Discussed at August 12th 1998 Meeting," R400.006-R400.007, box 12, folder 1, CAISO Market Surveillance Committee meeting files, CSA.

35. The next two sections draw from the detailed descriptions in Lambert 2006; G. Taylor et al. 2015.

36. In theoretical economics, arbitrage is considered "riskless"—it is an instantaneous realization of profits from price differences between locations. In reality, arbitrage also includes speculative trades, where traders bet that they can profit at a later time without insurance that they will be able to do so (Ito and Reguant 2014).

37. FERC, *Final Report on Price Manipulation in Energy Markets*, FERC PA02-2-000, VI.11–26 (hereafter cited as *FERC Final Report*).

38. Cited in *Prepared Direct Testimony of Gerald A. Taylor on Behalf of the California Parties, Part 2, Exhibit No. CAL-324*, May 15, 2015, FERC EL02-60-007, 91.

39. *Prepared Testimony of Gerald A. Taylor on Behalf of California Parties, Exhibit No. CAL-055*, September 21, 2012, FERC EL01-10-085, 1.

40. *FERC Final Report*, VI.12–14.

41. The utilities used the same strategy to understate their load in the Power Exchange. Once CAISO imposed price caps on its markets, they could protect themselves from the escalating prices in the Power Exchange because they lowered the intersection between supply and demand in the day- and hour-ahead markets and would never pay more than the price caps.

42. The regulators' price caps on both the Power Exchange's and CAISO's markets exacerbated the price differences and thus the arbitrage opportunities. Since CAISO eventually capped prices at $250, they effectively encouraged the utilities to move most of their demand into the real-time market. But even before these escalating factors were in place, the power marketers faced strong incentives to avoid the system operator's tariff restrictions and devised strategies to this effect (Borenstein et al. 2008).

43. For an extensive discussion, see G. Taylor et al. 2015.

44. Outlined in Alaywan, Wu, and Papalexopoulos 2004, 2–3.

45. *FERC Final Report*, VI.26.

46. McCullough Research, memorandum to research clients, "Congestion Manipulation in ISO California," June 5, 2002, 4–5. He elaborated further on this analysis in *Examining Enron: Electricity Market Manipulation and the Effects on the Western States, Hearing before the Subcomm. on Consumer Affairs, Foreign Commerce and Tourism, of the Senate Comm. on Commerce, Science, and Transportation*, 107th Cong., 2nd Sess. (2002), 69–83.

47. Enron, trading memorandum, December 8, 2000, 5, https://www.ferc.gov/industries/electric/indus-act/wec/enron/12-08-00.pdf (hereafter cited as second Enron memo).

48. See, for example, the famous description of "Forney's Perpetual Loop" in G. Taylor et al. 2015 (166).

49. Second Enron memo, 2–3.

CHAPTER FOUR

1. Twenty-eight separate events are mentioned in section 2.2. of the PX's annual report to FERC from 1999: *Electricity Markets of the California Power Exchange: Annual Report to the Federal Regulatory Commission, Market Compliance*, July 30, 1999, FERC ER-96-1663. Confidential material from the compliance unit details the conversations between Enron and the market monitoring team. The CEO confirmed Enron's cooperative stance to me in an interview. George Sladoje interview, March 30, 2018.

2. *Energy Market Manipulation, Hearing before the Senate Comm. on Energy and Natural Resources,* 107th Cong., 2nd Sess. (2002) (statement by Terry Winter, president and CEO, California Independent System Operator, Folsom, CA), 19.

3. A lawyer representing Enron at the time put much weight on this cooperative attitude in an interview with me. Michael Day, interview, January 18, 2018.

4. The argument in this chapter partly draws on articles and expert testimony by the market designers William Hogan and Vernon Smith. See Hogan 2002; Smith, Rassenti, and Wilson 2002. See also *FERC: Regulators in Deregulated Electricity Markets, Hearing before the House Comm. on Government Reform,* 107th Cong. (2001), 93–98. However, my explanation combines their partial arguments and introduces a new theory to explain the crisis.

5. For the argument about the importance of forward contracts, cf. Borenstein 2002. For the importance of the retail price freeze, cf. Smith, Rassenti, and Wilson 2002. For all three arguments, cf. P. L. Joskow 2001.

6. Sweeney 2002b, 31.

7. The PX also set single market clearing prices, which exacerbated the effects of market power. Every buyer would be charged more if a company with market power set the market price.

8. Smith, Rassenti, and Wilson 2002.

9. Duane 2002.

10. A single contract is equal to 1 MW for sixteen hours per day for one month, excluding Sundays. Companies could buy blocks of contracts to reflect the capacity they required. For example, 1,600 contracts equal 1,600 MW for sixteen hours each day for one month, excluding Sundays.

11. These numbers stem from table 17 of Power Exchange, Market Monitoring Committee, *Second Annual Report to the Federal Energy Regulatory Commission,* July 31, 2000, FERC ER98-2843, 48 (hereafter cited as *Second Surveillance Report 1999*).

12. Zarnikau and Hallett 2008.

13. The restructuring was premised on excess supply in California. In 1995, the CEC had issued a biennial planning document that projected the growth of demand and available supply until 2001. It estimated a vast excess of supply, with reserve margins of 21–23 percent (16 percent was the North American Electric Reliability Corporation's standard). But the two utilities had vastly inflated their descriptions of available supply. For example, they treated interruptible contracts as surplus energy and made projections about purchases that they never intended to make (Marcus and Hamrin 2001). So the planning horizon for the new generation was flawed before the restructuring. The utilities wanted to increase the stranded costs they could recover while restructuring. Contrary to their statements, they were trying to minimize their generation assets to avoid market risk. This problematic baseline was exacerbated by the dynamic described here.

14. Between 1997 and 2000, applications averaged about 3,300 MW (Sweeney 2002a, 103).

15. Duane 2002.

16. Particularly for assets whose costs had been recovered before deregulation—these generators did not have to factor their investment costs into the bid and therefore operated at an advantage to new entrants. This is a classic accounting problem within economics: the theory does not account for the uneven history of recouped costs among the participants in the market.

17. Forward markets do not solve this problem because they do not compensate generators that merely keep the fringe of the system competitive.

18. P. L Joskow 2022.

19. This is the reason some markets, such as the wholesale markets in Australia, explicitly allow prices at around $10,000 per MW/h.

20. Incidentally, this is also why a moderately elastic demand in the short run would not solve the problem of market power. In the long run, demand would grow, and the supply would dwindle until demand became inelastic again.

21. Beckert 2013.

22. Polanyi (1944) 2001.

23. Other electricity markets, most notably the PJM Interconnection in the eastern states, ultimately avoided this problem by introducing separate capacity markets that would deal with the addition of new generation assets over longer periods of time. However, these capacity markets have no real demand—the demand curve is constructed on the basis of political negotiations between stakeholders. There is no solution to this problem that would find the adequate balance on the basis of purely decentralized decisions. Hence, these structures are also referred to as "market-like" entities (Breslau 2013).

24. After the day- and hour-ahead auctions and after trades had been accepted, the sellers needed to specify the technical details for the generators that would execute these trades. The SCE would then submit this information to the system operator. See "California Electricity Market Primer," prepared for the CalPX Board of Governors, February 2000, R400.010, box 18, folder 12, Electricity Oversight Board subject files, CSA.

25. "ISO System Functionality Staged for Implementation after January 1, 1998," R.400.010, box 18, folder 8, Electricity Oversight Board subject files, CSA, 5–6.

26. Stoft 2002, 243–54.

27. Borenstein et al. 2008.

28. Borenstein et al. 2008, 9. "Report on Redesign of California Real-Time Energy and Ancillary Services Markets, October 18, 1999," CAISO Market Surveillance Committee meeting files, box 13, folder 4, CSA.

29. These and other differences are explored in the CAISO Market Surveillance Committee, "Preliminary Report on the Operation of the Ancillary Services Markets of the California Independent System Operator," August 19, 1998, FERC ER-98-2843, 34.

30. There were a few other sources of price difference that are too negligible to be considered extensively here. Using CAISO rather than the Power Exchange was associated with lower transaction costs because CAISO had a fixed charge for all energy produced or consumed in California, while the Power Exchange transaction charge only applied to energy sold or bought in the Power Exchange market. Before August 1999,

those who promised to sell or buy a certain quantity of energy also needed to procure ancillary services. In the Power Exchange markets, these ancillary services were originally sold relative to the scheduled energy rather than consumed energy. If you did not schedule any demand or supply in the forward markets, you therefore did not have to pay for the ancillary services that responded to whatever you produced or used in the real-time markets.

31. For example, see Enron West Power Trading Presentation, FERC EL03-180, Ex. S-98, 42, where the regional network of interacting trading desks is depicted without marked boundaries for the two market settings.

32. San Diego Gas & Electric, "CAISO Scheduling Coordinator Application Protocol, FERC Electric Tariff First Replacement," vol. 2, exhibit no. MID 18, October 13, 2000, FERC EL00-95.

33. This is what Pacific Gas & Electric did when it moved profits from stranded cost recovery into an unregulated affiliate that gamed the markets (Beder 2003, 115).

34. Beder 2003.

35. The California Public Utility Commission and the California Energy Commission oversaw the retail markets in California and the operations of the utilities.

36. Federal Power Act, 16 U.S.C. §§ 824d, 824e ¶¶ 205, 206 (1940).

37. US General Accounting Office, "Concerted Actions Needed by FERC to Confront Challenges That Impede Effective Oversight," June 2002, 33, https://www.gao.gov/assets/a157237.html (hereafter cited as "Concerted Action Needed").

38. G. Taylor et al. 2015, 183.

39. *Second Surveillance Report 1999*, 62–66.

40. D. Jermain, memorandum, "Completion of Report on Enron's Actions for May 25, 1999," George Sladoje private archive.

41. CAISO, "Market Monitoring and Information Protocol," section 4.4.2, February 1998, https://www.caiso.com/Documents/AttachmentI-14_MMIP_pdf.

42. Between 1997 and 2001, FERC was restructured according to the FERC First initiative, which tried to optimize the agency for the new market conditions. Offices changed names and responsibilities shifted, but according to one of my interviewees, the initiative was mostly window dressing. Not much of the actual workflow changed. This was confirmed by a report of the General Accounting Office from 2002. "Concerted Action Needed," 37. The report stated that the changes had not produced improvements in the oversight activities. The Office of Markets, Tariffs and Rates was the product of FERC First.

43. Donald J. Gelinas, associate director, FERC Office of Markets, Tariffs and Rates, to jurisdictional sellers and nonjurisdictional sellers in the West, March 5, 2001, FERC PA02-2-000, 1.

PART TWO

1. Kleit 2018, 81; Miller 2002, 266.

2. Cramton 2003, 1.

3. Isser 2015, 233.

4. Gary Ackerman, interview, November 17, 2017.

5. Özden-Shilling (2021) makes this point forcefully. She shows that the creation of electricity markets should be understood in terms of work by highly local expert cultures.

6. For example, Beder 2003, 153.

7. Many of the Snohomish tapes are part of FERC's public record in docket EL03-180. Testimony from analysts who listened to these tapes contains passages that make the experimental approach clear. For example, "Prepared Initial Tape Testimony of Barry E. Sullivan, Witness for the Staff of the Federal Energy Regulatory Commission, Exhibit S-129," March 1, 2005, FERC EL03-180.

8. Nix, Decker, and Wolf 2021.

9. See, for example, criticisms of Enron's position by SCE in "Reply Comments of SCE (U-338-E) on Commission Proposed Policy Decisions," box 18, folder 42a, CPUC, 3–4. In an interview with SCE's Vikram Brudhraja, (February 2, 2018), he confirmed that Enron's point of view had "not been consistent" with the utilities' perspective.

10. The chapters will rely on core categories of institutional analysis in this way (DiMaggio and Powell 1983).

CHAPTER FIVE

1. Here, we are talking about the political action field where multiple stakeholders were vying for control over the legal foundations of the restructuring project (Fligstein and McAdam 2012).

2. Hirsh 1999, 249–50.

3. In 1998, Enron paid about $500,000 to lobbyists and experts who worked for the California Public Utility Commission and the legislature. The other power marketers did not get into the electricity game until 1997. Despite later revelations, there can be no doubt that the power marketers' influence was eclipsed by that of the other industry groups on the state level (Isser 2015, 237).

4. Marcus and Hamrin 2001, 1–2.

5. Duane 2002, 488–89.

6. Brian S., interview, March 13, 2018.

7. The initial decision was made in December 1995 but amended in January 1996.

8. This has generally been acknowledged in the literature. Because most studies consider the retail price freeze one of the decisive flaws, they still ascribe substantial importance to the bill. I do not share this view and will therefore focus on the structural features of the California Public Utility Commission proposal (Isser 2015, 241–42).

9. Bill Bradley, "Master of Disaster: How Pete Wilson's Energy Chief Short-Circuited the California Grid," *LA Weekly*, February 14, 2001, https://www.laweekly.com/master-of-disaster/.

10. Blumstein and Bushnell 1994.

11. Initially, the Blue Book did not clearly differentiate between the two proposals. The commissioners entered majority and minority proposals at the beginning of 1995, but the basic outline of the two alternatives are already visible in the Blue Book. Kevin

Porter, *A Summary of the California Public Utility Commission's Two Competing Electric Utility Restructuring Proposals*, NREL/TP-461-8330 (Golden, CO: National Renewable Energy Laboratory, 1995).

12. Isser 2015, 238; interview with Jan Smutny-Jones, October 24, 2017.

13. Ron Russell, "Dim Bulbs: Greedy Out-of-State Profiteers Make Easy Targets, but the Real Villains of California's Energy Debacle Are the Ones under the State Capitol Dome," *San Francisco Weekly*, March 7, 2001, 3, https://www.ronrussell.org/dim-bulbs.

14. Jan Smutny-Jones, interview, October 24, 2017.

15. Bill Booth and Barbara Barkovich represented CLECA; Keith McCrea and Glenn Sheerin spoke for CMA; Jan Smutny-Jones and Doug Kerner represented IPP; and Vikram Budhraja, Alex Miller, and Ann Cohn came from SCE.

16. O'Donnell 2003, 17.

17. Barbara Barkovich, interview, August 21, 2018.

18. Barkovich 2018.

19. One of the negotiators of the MOU explains this in *Hearing before the Public Utility Commission of the State of California*, Pasadena, August 21, 1995, reporter's transcript, 32:4299–489, box 71, CPUC, p. 4312–13; Jan Smutny-Jones, interview October 24, 2017.

20. O'Donnell 2003, 18.

21. Barbara Barkovich, interview, August 21, 2018.

22. Stoft 1997, 36.

23. Hogan 1995; Stoft 1996; Eric Woychik, "California's Schedule Coordinator: Market Maker with Advantage, November 26, 1997," in Conference Proceedings, "Opportunities in the New Electricity Marketplace: The Race for the Customer," CONF-980380, Banff, 22–24; Larry Ruff, "The California PX Auction: Whatever Happened to the System Operator and Why Should Anybody Care" (UC Power Conference, March 10, 1997); Charles R. Imbrecht, statement before the FERC (Technical Conference on the WEPEX Applications, August 1, 1996), FERC ER96-1663.

24. Nix 2021, 785.

25. William Hogan, interview, December 11, 2017.

26. "California Energy Commission Comments on the Memorandum of Understanding," October 2, 1995, box 19, folder 1, CPUC, 5.

27. How the categories of market design configure political negotiations while being subject to political contestation is the subject of Daniel Breslau's (2013) research on the topic.

28. The concept of jurisdiction is used in the sociology of professions (Abbott 1988). Professions try to establish control over work by making a variety of different claims to jurisdiction by defining the problem and the appropriate solution.

29. Aune 2002; Porter 1995.

30. Haas 2004; Weingart 1999.

31. Eyal 2019.

32. Goodwin 1988.

33. *Hearing before the California Public Utility Commission*, San Francisco, June 15, 1994, reporter's transcript, 2:299–596, box 69, CPUC, 301.

34. *Hearing*, 304.

35. *Hearing*, 304.

36. *Hearing*, 304.

37. *Hearing*, 304.

38. *Hearing*, 304.

39. For other examples at the California Public Utility Commission, cf. *Hearing before the California Public Utility Commission*, Los Angeles, June 14, 1994, reporter's transcript, 1:1–298, box 69, CPUC. For FERC, cf. *Official Hearings in the Matter of Pacific Gas & Electric Company, San Diego Gas & Electric Company, and Southern California Edison Company*, Washington, DC, August 1, 1996, 1:1–279, FERC ER96-1663.

40. *Hearing before the California Public Utility Commission*, San Francisco, June 15, 1994, reporter's transcript, 2:299–596, box 69, CPUC, 373.

41. William Hogan, interview, December 11, 2017; *Official Hearings*, FERC ER96-1663.

42. Colander 2007; Fourcade 2009; Berman 2022.

43. Fourcade and Khurana 2013.

44. Derthick and Quirk 1985.

45. I have already pointed out that market design feeds from many different disciplines and is somewhat eclectic. The point holds for economics in general as well. Like any social science, economics is fragmented into subfields that differ in their use of central concepts and in their methods. The discipline appears to be unified because it ties the different subfields back to a minimal set of common conventions, practices, and tools (Reay 2012).

46. The concept of multivocality was initially developed to explain the characteristics of "robust action" (Leifer 1991; Padgett and Ansell 1993). Such actions can be interpreted coherently from multiple perspectives, which is usually advantageous. Multivocality gives political actors the flexibility to react freely to changed situations. In the literature on expert authority, the concept sometimes describes experts' ability to present their knowledge compellingly to a variety of audiences (Menchik 2020). But multivocality can also refer to symbols and artifacts and thus the discursive situation itself (Ferraro, Etzion, and Gehman 2015). That is the sense in which I use it here.

47. Suryanarayanan and Kleinman 2012.

48. Enron Power Marketing, initial comments in response to the California Public Utility Commission's *Order Instituting Rulemaking and Order Instituting Investigation*, June 8, 1994, box 10, folder 5a, CPUC, 19–20.

49. Southern California Edison Company (U 338-E), comments in response to *Order Instituting Rulemaking and Order Instituting Investigation*, April 1994, box 11, CPUC, 12.

50. "Comments of Industrial Users on Blue Book Policy Issues," June 8, 1994, box 10, folder Formal 4a, CPUC, 8.

51. Rilinger 2022b.

CHAPTER SIX

1. Ferdinand M., interview, February 19, 2018.

2. How these systems initially developed is the topic of Thomas Hughes's book (1993).

3. O'Donnell 2003, 16.

4. Deb Le Vine, interview, November 29, 2017.

5. Gary Ackerman, interview, November 17, 2017.

6. Electricity Oversight Board, hearing, March 14, 1997, box 4, folder 11, Electricity Oversight Board hearing files, CSA, 13.

7. Beder 2003; Isser 2015; Stoft 1997.

8. Hogan 1998.

9. Stoft 1997.

10. It is true that power marketers attended the meetings and exercised some influence as market experts. "Joint Application of Pacific Gas & Electric Company, San Diego Gas & Electric Company, and Southern California Edison Company for Authority to Sell Electric Energy at Market-Based Rates Using a Power Exchange," FERC ER96-1663, A-5. But they did not hold seats on the steering committee, and independent power producers were outvoted. In 1996, utilities and their allies chose most members of the steering committee.

11. For example, in a letter to the Public Utility Commission, the utilities had to justify themselves against the accusation of dominance and did so by asserting that they had to make the system work in the end. WEPEX Steering Committee to Dan Fessler, president of the CPUC, February 20, 1996, WEPEX Forum, captured November 9, 1999, https://web.archive.org/web/20000817212105/http://www.energyonline.com /wepex/.

12. Cramton 2017.

13. Edwards 2010; Hughes 1987, 1998.

14. Galloway 2004; Simon 1962.

15. C. Y. Baldwin and Clark 2000, 64.

16. Direct Access Working Group, Workshop on Communication and Data Systems, January 9, 1997, box 30, folder 17, CPUC.

17. Minutes of the WEPEX Steering Committee, January 8, 1996–April 2, 1997, https://web.archive.org/web/20000817212105/ http://www.energyonline.com /wepex/.

18. "Phase II Work Item Status, CAISO Management, 1997," CAISO Board of Governors and committee meeting files, box 6, folder 5, CSA.

19. S. David Freeman, testimony before the California Senate Energy Committee, February 25, 1997, FERC ER96-1663, 3.

20. C. Y. Baldwin and Clark 2000.

21. Just as in the case of normal accidents, problems emerge because parts of the system begin to interact in unexpected ways (Perrow [1984] 1999). However, in the case of

market design, participants systematically search for overlooked interactions below the level of the interfaces. The resulting problems are therefore neither particularly rare nor dependent on cascades of interacting failures.

22. Hughes 1998.

23. Leveson et al. 2009.

24. Vaughan (1996) 2016.

25. Hayek 1945.

26. J. Scott 1998.

27. Interestingly, this is a problem that transaction cost economics has pointed out as well (Williamson and Winter 1993).

28. Cf. Paul Gribik, "Consequences of the Imbalance Energy Market Protocols," submitted to *California's Electricity Market: The Case of Perot Systems, Hearing before the Subcomm. on Energy Policy, Natural Resources and Regulatory Affairs, of the House Comm. on Government Reform*, 107th Cong., 2nd Sess. (2002), 207.

29. It is a general problem of modularization that it depends on a static architecture of design rules (Chesbrough 2003; Tee, Davies, and Whyte 2019).

30. CAISO Management, "ISO Scheduling Protocol, CAISO Tariff," April 1998, FERC EC96-19-017, section 11.2.

31. CAISO report 1998, 12.

32. Price Waterhouse, report of independent accountants to board of governors, May 27, 1998, CAISO Board of Governors and committee meeting files, Box 6, Folder 4, CSA.

33. Cf. Gribik, "Consequences," 207.

34. CAISO, *Annual Report on Market Issues and Performance* (Folsom, CA: CAISO, 1999), section 4.1–2, http://www.caiso.com/Documents/1999-2000Annual ReportonMarketIssuesandPerformance.pdf.

35. PX Compliance Unit, "Price Movement in California's PX Markets, May– September 2000," November 7, 2000, FERC ER96-1663, 82.

36. The tests revealed problems that led to amendments to the CAISO tariff. The testing process is described in the applications for these amendments. For example, see Amendment No. 4 to the ISO Operating Agreement and Tariff, Including the ISO Protocols, CAISO Management, March 3, 1998, FERC EC96-19017, 6–8.

37. Robert Wilson, *Activity Rules for the Power Exchange and Priority Pricing of Ancillary Services, Reports to the California PX and ISO Trusts for Power Industry Restructuring*, WEPEX Reports, March–May 1997, captured September 8, 2008, https://web .archive.org/web/20000817212118/http://www.energyonline.com/wepex/reports /reports2.html (hereafter cited as *Activity Rules for Power Exchange*).

38. *Activity Rules for Power Exchange*.

39. Stoft 1996.

40. San Diego Gas & Electric Company, comments to Coordinating Commissioner Ruling," 1995, docket I.94-04-032, box 19, folder 49a, CPUC.

41. "Joint Application of PG&E, SDG&E, and SCE for Authority to Sell Electric Energy at Market-Based Rates Using a Power Exchange, Pacific Gas & Electric et. al.," April 29, 1996, FERC ER96-1663, 5.

42. Minutes of the WEPEX Steering Committee, February 20–21, 1996, https://web.archive.org/web/20000817212105/http://www.energyonline.com/wepex/.

43. Hutchinson 1995.

44. FERC ultimately stopped allowing further amendments and insisted on a fundamental redesign of the system. "Order Accepting for Filing in Part and Rejecting in Part Proposed Tariff Amendment and Directing Reevaluation of Approach to Addressing Intrazonal Congestion," January 7, 2000, 90 FERC 61,0006.

45. O'Donnell 2003.

46. CAISO engineer, interview, November 22, 2017.

47. "Enron Silver Peak Investigation—Investigation Timeline, January 2000," George Sladoje private archive.

48. CAISO Market Surveillance Committee, *Report on Redesign of California Real-Time Energy and Ancillary Services Markets*, October 18, 1999, CAISO Market Surveillance Committee meeting files, box 13, folder 4, CSA.

49. CAISO Department of Market Analysis, *Report on California Energy Market Issues and Performance: May–June 2000*, August 10, 2000, FERC PA02-2-000.

50. C. Y. Baldwin and Clark 2000.

51. This is the number of CAISO trading partners in a network that I derived from submissions to FERC PA-02-02, where all active sellers of energy in California submitted trading records to document their activities during the energy crisis.

52. Borenstein et al. 2008.

53. *Activity Rules for Power Exchange*.

54. "Joint Application of Pacific Gas and Electric Company, San Diego Gas & Electric Company, and Southern California Edison Company for Authority to Sell Electric Energy at Market-Based Rates Using a Power Exchange, PG&E, SDG&E, SCE," May 29, 1996, FERC ER96-1663.

55. Carla B., interview, November 22, 2017.

56. Kirshner 1997. For the handbook, see "California Electricity Market Primer," prepared for the CalPX Board of Governors, February 2000, box 18, folder 12, Electricity Oversight Board subject files, CSA.

57. Enron Power Marketing, initial comments in response to the California Public Utility Commission's *Order Instituting Rulemaking and Order Instituting Investigation*, June 8, 1994, box 10, folder Formal 5a, CSA, 12.

58. Gary Stern, "Resource Adequacy in Competitive Electricity Markets," presentation, Rutgers University Center for Research in Regulated Industries Advanced Workshop in Regulation and Competition, 16th Annual Western Conference, New Brunswick, June 27, 2003, 4.

59. Sweeney 2002a.

60. CAISO, "Emergency Response Team: Events Requiring Immediate Executive in Charge Notification," June 15, 1998, Board of Governors meeting files, box 6, folder 4, CSA.

61. CAISO, "Summer Operations Plan," 1998, box 6, folder 4, Board of Governors meeting files, CSA, 3.

62. California Council of Science and Technology, retrospective report on California's Electricity Crisis prepared for the California Energy Commission, June 2002, 26. Characteristically, the out-of-market transactions became the target for some of Enron's games during the energy crisis. Conceived in the context of emergency response, the existence of such transactions affected the incentives in the imbalance markets.

63. *Activity Rules for Power Exchange*, 3.

CHAPTER SEVEN

1. The debates about the oversight structure and regulatory standards for California's markets took place in several venues. Most relevant are the debates in a series of technical conferences at FERC in 1996 and their precursor at the Public Utility Commission in 1994–95. Because FERC held final jurisdiction over the new markets, it also had to sanction the feedback-control structure for the new system. The debates can be found in FERC ER96-1663.

2. Michaels 1997, 62.

3. *Hearing before the California Public Utility Commission*, Los Angeles, June 15, 1994, reporter's transcript, 2:299–596, box 69, CPUC, 343–44.

4. *Hearing*, 154.

5. In testimony to FERC after the crisis, Joskow and other market designers argued for much more extensive market oversight. In this respect, the creation of California's markets was a learning experience. Today, the oversight of electricity markets is comprehensive and takes place in real time. For the learning process in California during the crisis, see Rahimi and Sheffrin 2003; Wolak 2005. For the development of monitoring generally, see García and Reitzes 2007.

6. Garber, Hogan, and Ruff 1994, 48.

7. Report on January 9, 1997, Direct Access Working Group Workshop on Communications and Data Systems, January 17, 1997, box 30, folder 108A, CPUC, 27–45.

8. I am focusing on the monitoring units at the Power Exchange and the system operator because these were built from scratch when the designers created the two organizations. The larger control structure included FERC, the Public Utility Commission, and the Energy Commission. As we have seen, these agencies suffered from weaknesses and contributed to the crisis. But these problems are not directly related to the market design process in California. To explain the broader regulatory problems, the literature has pointed to political rivalries between Washington and California, an outdated and weak legal mandate, regulatory capture, adherence to pro-market ideology, and insufficient resources in terms of personnel, data, and money (Beder 2003; Bushnell 2005; Rilinger 2023; Wolak 2003).

9. Özden-Schilling 2021, 54.

10. There were corresponding investigations of anomalous behavior at the Power Exchange. Cf "Enron Silver Peak Investigation—Investigation Timeline, January 2000," George Sladoje private archive.

11. Cf. "Emergency Motion to Stay, Notice of Action Taken, Request for Rehearing, and Motion for Clarification of the California Independent System Operator Corporation," July 13, 1998, FERC ER98-2843.

12. O'Donnell 2003, 86–87.

13. "Order Denying Motions for Stay, Authorizing the ISO to Take Interim Action, Requiring Market Monitoring Reports, and Providing Opportunity to Comment," July 17, 1998, FERC ER98-2843.

14. Jan S., interview, January 23, 2018.

15. O'Donnell 2003, 30.

16. Deb LeVine, interview, November 29, 2017.

17. Anelise S., interview, December 13, 2017.

18. Theo C., interview, November 27, 2017.

19. This argument flows from an analysis of internal debates at the market monitoring units. The minutes from these meetings can be found in CAISO Market Surveillance Committee meeting files, 1998–2000, boxes 12–13, CSA. I supplemented the sources with material from the interviews with members of the Market Surveillance Committee and the market monitoring unit.

20. Jan S., interview, January 23, 2018.

21. Ziad Alaywan, interview, August 31, 2018.

22. Alaywan 2018.

23. Jason Christian, interview, January 23, 2018.

24. Why exactly FERC did not react to the warnings that came from California has been a topic of considerable controversy. I discuss this question in Rilinger 2023.

25. Polanyi (1944) 2001.

26. For the differences in the mathematical treatment of design problems, cf. Mirowski and Nik-Khah 2017.

27. Bockman 2011, 17–50.

28. These connections are fairly visible in the context where the spot-pricing idea developed. For example, one of Schweppe's collaborators at MIT, Roger Bohn, wrote his PhD thesis about spot pricing for electricity. Located in the Sloan School of Management, he was closely associated with economists interested in the prospect for electricity markets. Bohn's supervisor at Sloan was Richard Schmalensee, and his adviser in the economics department was Paul Joskow, a student of Edward Kahn, who took part in early experiments with market design.

29. Chao and Huntington 1998; Chao and Peck 1996.

30. The available approaches to the problem of congestion management were limited. Academics, industry insiders, and consultants negotiated these solutions in the nexus among universities, think tanks, and the implementation process. The acknowl-

edgment sections of the relevant articles in the trade press and academic journals document this nexus and the influence of the blueprints on the WEPEX process (Chao and Huntington 1998; Chao and Peck 1996).

31. The introduction of separate capacity rights for links requires that the nodes be renamed.

32. Stinchcombe 2001, 55–75.

33. Schweppe, Caramanis, Tabors, and Bohn 1988, xvii.

34. Smith 1987, 26.

35. See, for example, the conclusion of the efficiency analysis in P. L. Joskow and Schmalensee 1988 (176–78).

36. Cramton 1998.

37. Pools are characterized by side payments to cover the varying costs of generators. Systems of side payments make bids more transparent, but they also remove generators' control over how they represent their fixed costs in their prices. It is a strategy to simplify and bound the interface.

38. For a quick overview, see Stoft 2002, 204–6.

39. Oren 1998, 80.

40. The discussions are predominantly located in FERC ER96-1663 and ER96-29. For my analysis, I used commission orders and inquiries as well as the transcript of different technical conferences.

41. Robert Wilson, "Activity Rules for a Power Exchange" (report to the California Trust for Power Industry Restructuring, Stanford Business School, Stanford, CA, February 21, 1997).

42. Wilson 1998, 161.

43. Ziad Alaywan, interview, August 31, 2018.

44. *Hearing before the California Public Utility Commission*, Los Angeles, June 15, 1994, reporter's transcript, 2:299–596, box 69, CPUC, 343–44.

45. *Hearing before the California Public Utility Commission*, Los Angeles, October 24, 1994, reporter's transcript, 15:2351–615, box 70, CPUC, 2360.

46. *Hearing*, October 24, 1994, 2362.

47. Steven Stoft, interview, December 11, 2018.

48. *California's Electricity Market: The Case of Perot Systems, Hearing before the Subcomm. on Energy Policy, Natural Resources and Regulatory Affairs, of the House Comm. on Government Reform*, 107th Cong., 2nd Sess. (2002), 171.

49. *Hearing before the California Public Utility Commission*, Los Angeles, June 15, 1994, reporter's transcript, 1:1–299, box 69, CPUC, 100.

50. Pacific Gas & Electric Company, San Diego Gas & Electric Company, and Southern California Edison Company, *Official Transcript of Proceedings*, Washington, DC, August 1, 1996, vol. 1, FERC ER96-1663, 79 (hereafter cited as WEPEX Transcript).

51. This is tangible in an exchange between Pacific Gas & Electric's Joe Pace and Richard O'Neill. They discuss what should be monitored and what should not. When O'Neill points to the many different bidding protocols and their obscuring of the composition of market prices, Pace is surprised at the suggestion that this information might not easily be available from generators. WEPEX Transcript 1:34–35.

52. Turner 1976, 382.

53. Weick 1998, 74.

CONCLUSION

1. Andy Fastow is touring the academic circuits to speak of the accounting magic that enabled Enron to appear uniquely profitable while it was teetering on the brink of bankruptcy. "Post-Prison, Former Enron CFO Hits Speaking Circuit," Bloomberg Law, February 20, 2016, https://news.bloomberglaw.com/business-and-practice/post -prison-former-enron-cfo-hits-speaking-circuit.

2. Cramton 2017, 2021.

3. Abolafia 2001; Ahrne, Aspers, and Brunsson 2015; Arora-Jonsson, Brunsson, and Hasse 2020; Beckert 2009, 2016; Fligstein 1996.

4. Beginnings of such a perspective are visible in efforts to understand the relationship between markets and digitalization (Burrell and Fourcade 2021; Fourcade and Healy 2016).

5. J. Scott 1998.

6. Putnam 1977.

7. The view of sociology as the science of unintended consequences goes back to the influential article by Robert Merton (1936).

8. Çalışkan and Callon 2010; Muniesa 2014.

9. Rahman and Thelen 2019; Stark and Pais 2020; Vallas and Schor 2020. But see Viljoen, Goldenfein, and McGuigan 2021.

10. Griesbach et al. 2019; Y.-W. Lei 2021.

11. For a useful framework for analyzing safety in feedback-control systems, see Leveson 2011.

12. Hitzig 2020.

13. Roth 2015.

14. Weingart 1999.

15. Budish, Cramton, and Shim 2015; Liang and Parkinson 2020.

16. This, of course, is one of the oldest insights about the relationship between financial and productive capital (Veblen [1904] 2016).

17. Albert 2018; Chesbrough 2003.

18. Thompson (1967) 2017.

19. Smith 2008.

20. Duflo 2017.

21. Beniger 2009; Cyert and March (1963) 2013; March and Simon 1958; Simon 1962.

22. Jacobides 2007.

23. Vaughan (1996) 2016.

24. Snook 2002.

25. Allison and Zelikov 1971.

26. Joseph and Ocasio 2012; Thompson (1967) 2017; Weick and Roberts 1993.

27. Simon (1969) 1996.

28. Dutt and Joseph 2019; Sullivan 2010.

29. Vaughan (1996) 2016.

30. Perrow (1984) 1999.

31. La Porte 1996; Roe and Schulman 2008; Weick and Roberts 1993; Weick and Sutcliffe 2015.

32. Vaughan 2021.

33. As happens more generally in financial markets between regulators and the regulated (Funk and Hirschman 2014; MacKenzie 2011; Thiemann and Lepoutre 2017).

34. Rose 2014.

35. Incidentally, this explains why online transaction platforms have increasingly moved to private corporate structures with centralized decision-making (C. Baldwin 2023).

36. Cf. William Massey's discussion of agency changes in *Asleep at the Switch: FERC's Oversight of Enron Corporation, Hearing before the Senate Comm. on Governmental Affairs*, 107th Cong., 2nd Sess. (2002), 37–60.

37. Vogel 1996.

38. Cicala 2022, 438.

39. Perrow 1994.

40. Stinchcombe 2001, 55.

41. Mirowski and Nik-Khah 2017; Nik-Khah and Mirowski 2019.

42. Mirowski and Nik-Khah 2007.

43. Cramton 2021; Rilinger 2021.

44. A similar argument for democratic socialism can be found in Adler 2019.

45. Phillips and Rozworski 2019.

46. Kominers, Teytelboym, and Crawford 2017, 547.

47. Prendergast 2017.

48. For a detailed explanation, see Prendergast 2017.

49. Prendergast 2017, 146.

50. Vaughan 2021.

51. Krippner 2011.

52. For a book that thinks into a very similar direction, cf. Adler, 2019.

APPENDIX A

1. For larger dockets, I wrote a Python script to scrape all submissions. It circum-vented the cumbersome interface of the FERC eLibrary and eased the analysis by stan-dardizing file names.

2. Hertz and Imber 1995.

3. Saldaña 2015; Strauss and Corbin 1990.

References

Abbott, A. 1988. *The System of Professions: An Essay on the Division of Expert Labor.* Chicago: University of Chicago Press.

Abdulkadiroğlu, A., P. Pathak, A. E. Roth, and T. Sönmez. 2006. *Changing the Boston School Choice Mechanism. NBER Working Papers* (11965), Cambridge, MA. https://doi.10.3386/w11965.

Abdulkadiroğlu, A., and T. Sönmez. 2003. "School Choice: A Mechanism Design Approach." *American Economic Review* 93 (3): 729–47.

Abolafia, M. Y. 2001. *Making Markets: Opportunism and Restraint on Wall Street.* Cambridge, MA: Harvard University Press.

Adler, P. S. 2019. *The 99 Percent Economy: How Democratic Socialism Can Overcome the Crises of Capitalism.* New York: Oxford University Press.

Ahrne, G., P. Aspers, and N. Brunsson. 2015. "The Organization of Markets." *Organization Studies* 36 (1): 7–27.

Akerlof, G. A. (1970) 1995. "The Market for 'Lemons': Quality Uncertainty and the Market Mechanism." In *Essential Readings in Economics*, edited by S. Estrin and A. Marin, 175–188. London: Macmillan Education UK.

Akerlof, G. A., and R. J. Shiller. 2010. *Animal Spirits: How Human Psychology Drives the Economy, and Why It Matters for Global Capitalism.* Princeton, NJ: Princeton University Press.

Alaywan, Z., T. Wu, and A. D. Papalexopoulos. 2004. "Transitioning the California Market from a Zonal to a Nodal Framework: An Operational Perspective." Paper presented at the Power Systems Conference and Exposition, IEEE Power and Energy Society, New York, October 10–13, 2004.

Albert, D. 2018. "Organizational Module Design and Architectural Inertia: Evidence from Structural Recombination of Business Divisions." *Organization Science* 29 (5): 890–911.

Allison, G. T., and P. Zelikov. 1971. *Essence of Decision: Explaining the Cuban Missile Crisis.* Boston: Little Brown.

Arora-Jonsson, S., N. Brunsson, and R. Hasse. 2020. "Where Does Competition Come From? The Role of Organization." *Organization Theory* 1 (1). https://doi.org/10.1177/2631787719889977.

Ashby, R. W. 1957. *An Introduction to Cybernetics.* London: Chapman and Hall.

Aspers, P., P. Bengtsson, and A. Dobeson. 2020. "Market Fashioning." *Theory and Society* 49 (3): 417–438.

Aune, J. A. 2002. *Selling the Free Market: The Rhetoric of Economic Correctness*. New York: Guilford.

Australian Competition and Consumer Commission. 2021. *Murray-Darling Basin Water Markets Inquiry*. Canberra, Australia: Commonwealth of Australia.

Bailey, D. E., and Barley, S. R. 2020. "Beyond Design and Use: How Scholars Should Study Intelligent Technologies." *Information and Organization* 30 (2). https://doi.org/10.1016/j.infoandorg.2019.100286.

Baker, W. E. 1984. "The Social Structure of a National Securities Market." *American Journal of Sociology* 89 (4): 775–811.

Baldwin, C. 2023. *Capturing Value in Digital Exchange Platforms*. Cambridge, MA: Harvard Business School.

Baldwin, C. Y., and K. B. Clark. 2000. *Design Rules: The Power of Modularity*. Vol. 1. Cambridge, MA: MIT Press.

Beckert, J. 2009. "The Social Order of Markets." *Theory and Society* 38 (3): 245–69. https://doi.org/10.1007/s11186-008-9082-0.

———. 2013. "Imagined Futures: Fictional Expectations in the Economy." *Theory and Society* 42 (3): 219–40. http://www.jstor.org/stable/43694686.

———. 2016. *Imagined Futures*. Cambridge, MA: Harvard University Press.

Beder, S. 2003. *Power Play: The Fight for Control of the World's Electricity*. New York: Scribe.

Beniger, J. 2009. *The Control Revolution: Technological and Economic Origins of the Information Society*. Cambridge, MA: Harvard University Press.

Berman, E. P. 2022. *Thinking like an Economist: How Efficiency Replaced Equality in US Public Policy*. Princeton, NJ: Princeton University Press.

Bichler, M. 2017. *Market Design: A Linear Programming Approach to Auctions and Matching*. Cambridge: Cambridge University Press.

Biggar, D. R., and M. R. Hesamzadeh. 2014. *The Economics of Electricity Markets*. Chichester, UK: John Wiley and Sons.

Blok, A. 2011. "Clash of the Eco-Sciences: Carbon Marketization, Environmental NGOs and Performativity as Politics." *Economy and Society* 40 (3): 451–76.

Blumstein, C., and J. Bushnell. 1994. "A Guide to the Blue Book: Issues in California's Electric Industry Restructuring and Reform." *Electricity Journal* 7 (7): 18–29.

Blumstein, C., L. S. Friedman, and R. Green. 2002. "The History of Electricity Restructuring in California." *Journal of Industry, Competition and Trade* 2 (1–2): 9–38.

Bockman, J. 2011. *Markets in the Name of Socialism*. Palo Alto, CA: Stanford University Press.

Bolton, G., B. Greiner, and A. Ockenfels. 2018. "Dispute Resolution or Escalation? The Strategic Gaming of Feedback Withdrawal Options in Online Markets." *Management Science* 64 (9): 4009–31.

Borenstein, S. 2000. "Understanding Competitive Pricing and Market Power in Wholesale Electricity Markets." *Electricity Journal* 13 (6): 49–57.

———. 2002. "The Trouble with Electricity Markets: Understanding California's Restructuring Disaster." *Journal of Economic Perspectives* 16 (1): 191–211.

Borenstein, S., J. Bushnell, and C. R. Knittel. 1999. "Market Power in Electricity Markets: Beyond Concentration Measures." *Energy Journal* 20 (4): 65–88.

Borenstein, S., J. Bushnell, C. R. Knittel, and C. Wolfram. 2008. "Inefficiencies and Market Power in Financial Arbitrage: A Study of California's Electricity Markets." *Journal of Industrial Economics* 56 (2): 347–78.

Borenstein, S., J. Bushnell, and F. A. Wolak. 2002. "Measuring Market Inefficiencies in California's Restructured Wholesale Electricity Market." *American Economic Review* 92 (5): 1376–405.

Börgers, T. 2015. *An Introduction to the Theory of Mechanism Design*. New York: Oxford University Press.

Bourdieu, P. 2005. *The Social Structures of the Economy*. Cambridge: Polity.

Breslau, D. 2013. "Designing a Market-like Entity: Economics in the Politics of Market Formation." *Social Studies of Science* 43 (6): 829–51.

———. 2020. "Redistributing Agency: The Control Roots of *Spot Pricing of Electricity*." *History of Political Economy* 52 (S1): 221–44. https://doi.org/10.1215/00182702 -8718023.

Brisset, N. 2018. *Economics and Performativity: Exploring Limits, Theories and Cases*. London: Routledge.

Budish, E., P. Cramton, and J. Shim. 2015. "The High-Frequency Trading Arms Race: Frequent Batch Auctions as a Market Design Response." *Quarterly Journal of Economics* 130 (4): 1547–621.

Budish, E., and J. B. Kessler. 2016. "Can Agents "Report Their Types"? An Experiment That Changed the Course Allocation Mechanism at Wharton." Chicago Booth Research Paper, No. 15-08.

Burrell, J., and M. Fourcade. 2021. "The Society of Algorithms." *Annual Review of Sociology* 47: 213–37.

Bushnell, J. 2004. "California's Electricity Crisis: A Market Apart?" *Energy Policy* 32 (9): 1045–52.

———. 2005. "Looking for Trouble: Competition Policy in the U.S. Electricity Industry." In *Electricity Deregulation: Choices and Challenges*, edited by J. M. Griffin and S. L. Puller, 256–96. Chicago: University of Chicago Press.

Bushnell, J., and F. Wolak. 2000. "Regulation and the Leverage of Local Market Power in the California Electricity Market." Competition Policy Center, working paper no. CPC00-13, University of California, Berkeley.

CAISO. 2021. *Final Root Cause Analysis, Mid-August 2020 Extreme Heat Wave*. Folsom, CA: CAISO. http://www.caiso.com/Documents/Final-Root-Cause-Analysis-Mid -August-2020-Extreme-Heat-Wave.pdf.

Çalışkan, K., and M. Callon. 2010. "Economization, Part 2: A Research Programme for the Study of Markets." *Economy and Society* 39 (1): 1–32.

Callon, M. 1998. "An Essay on Framing and Overflowing: Economic Externalities Revisited by Sociology." *Sociological Review* 46 (S1): 244–69.

———. 2008. "Economic Markets and the Rise of Interactive Agencements: From Prosthetic Agencies to Habilitated Agencies." In *Living in a Material World: Economic Sociology Meets Science and Technology Studies*, edited by T. Pinch and R. Swedberg, 1:29–56. Cambridge, MA: MIT Press.

———. 2009. "Civilizing Markets: Carbon Trading between In Vitro and In Vivo Experiments." *Accounting, Organizations and Society* 34 (3–4): 535–48.

Cameron, L. D., and H. Rahman. 2022. "Expanding the Locus of Resistance: Understanding the Co-constitution of Control and Resistance in the Gig Economy." *Organization Science* 33 (1): 38–58.

Carroll, G. 2019. "Robustness in Mechanism Design and Contracting." *Annual Review of Economics* 11 (1): 139–66. https://doi.org/10.1146/annurev-economics-080218 -025616.

Carroll, L. 1895. "What the Tortoise Said to Achilles." *Mind* 104 (416): 691–93.

CEC. 1996. *Gas Prices: Gouging or Supply and Demand.* Sacramento, CA: California Energy Commission.

Chao, H.-P., and H. G. Huntington, eds. 1998. *Designing Competitive Electricity Markets.* Boston: Kluwer Academic.

Chao, H.-P., and S. Peck. 1996. "A Market Mechanism for Electric Power Transmission." *Journal of Regulatory Economics* 10 (1): 25–59.

Chesbrough, H. 2003. "Toward a Dynamics of Modularity." In *The Business of System Integration*, edited by A. Prencipe, A. Davies, and M. Hobday. Oxford: Oxford University Press: 174–81

Chiu, Y. H., J. C. Lin, W. N. Su, and J. K. Liu. 2015. "An Efficiency Evaluation of the E.U.'s Allocation of Carbon Emission Allowances." *Energy Sources, Part B: Economics, Planning, and Policy* 10 (2): 192–200. https://doi.org/10.1080/15567249.2010.527900.

Cicala, S. 2022. "Imperfect Markets versus Imperfect Regulation in US Electricity Generation." *American Economic Review* 112 (2): 409–41.

Cicchetti, C. J., J. A. Dubin, and C. M. Long. 2004. *The California Electricity Crisis: What, Why, and What's Next.* Norwell, MA: Kluwer Academic.

Coase, R. H. 1988. *The Firm, the Market, and the Law.* Chicago: University of Chicago Press.

Colander, D. C. 2007. *The Making of an Economist, Redux.* Princeton, NJ: Princeton University Press.

Considine, T. J., and A. N. Kleit. 2007. "Can Electricity Restructuring Survive? Lessons from California and Pennsylvania." In *Electric Choices*, edited by A. N. Kleit, 9–38. Oakland, CA: Rowman and Littlefield.

Cottrell, A., and W. P. Cockshott. 1993. "Calculation, Complexity and Planning: The Socialist Calculation Debate Once Again." *Review of Political Economy* 5 (1): 73–112.

Cramton, P. 1998. *Efficiency Considerations in Designing Electricity Markets.* Ontario: Competition Bureau of Industry Canada.

———. 2003. "Electricity Market Design: The Good, the Bad, and the Ugly." Paper presented at the System Sciences, 2003, Proceedings of the Thirty-Sixth Annual Hawaii International Conference (HICSS'03), Big Island, HI. https://dl.acm.org/doi/proceedings/10.5555/820754.

———. 2017. "Electricity Market Design." *Oxford Review of Economic Policy* 33 (4): 589–612. https://doi.org/10.1093/oxrep/grx041.

———. 2021. "Lessons from the 2021 Texas Electricity Crisis." *Utility Dive*, March 23. https://www.utilitydive.com/news/lessons-from-the-2021-texas-electricity-crisis/596998/.

Cramton, P., and J. A. Schwartz. 2002. "Collusive Bidding in the FCC Spectrum Auctions." *Contributions in Economic Analysis & Policy* 1 (1): 1538-0645.107.

Cyert, R. M., and J. G. March. (1963) 2013. *A Behavioral Theory of the Firm.* Illustrated ed. Eastford, CT: Martino Fine Books.

Derthick, M., and P. J. Quirk. 1985. *The Politics of Deregulation.* Washington, DC: Brookings Institution.

de Vries, L. J. 2007. "The California Electricity Crisis: A Unique Combination of Circumstances or a Symptom of a Structural Flaw." In *Institutional Reform, Regulation and Privatization: Process and Outcomes in Infrastructure Industries*, edited by R. W.

Kuenneke, A. F. Correlje, and J. P. M. Groenewegen, 153–76. Cheltenham, UK: Edward Elgar.

Dewey, J. 2002. *Human Nature and Conduct*. Mineola, NY: Dover.

Didion, J. 2006. "Notes from a Native Daughter." In *We Tell Ourselves Stories in Order to Live: Collected Nonfiction*, edited by J. Didion, 131–42. New York: Everyman's Library.

DiMaggio, P. J., and W. W. Powell. 1983. "The Iron Cage Revisited: Institutional Isomorphism and Collective Rationality in Organizational Fields." *American Sociological Review* 48 (2): 147–60.

Dobbin, F. 1994. *Forging Industrial Policy: The United States, Britain, and France in the Railway Age*. Cambridge: Cambridge University Press.

Downer, J. 2011. "'737-Cabriolet': The Limits of Knowledge and the Sociology of Inevitable Failure." *American Journal of Sociology* 117 (3): 725–62. https://doi.org/10.1086/662383.

Duane, T. P. 2002. "Regulation's Rationale: Learning from the California Energy Crisis." *Yale Journal on Regulation* 19 (471): 471–540.

Duflo, E. 2017. "The Economist as Plumber." *American Economic Review* 107 (5): 1–26.

Dutt, N., and J. Joseph. 2019. "Regulatory Uncertainty, Corporate Structure, and Strategic Agendas: Evidence from the US Renewable Electricity Industry." *Academy of Management Journal* 62 (3): 800–27.

Dworczak, P., S. D. Kominers, and M. Akbarpour. 2021. "Redistribution through Markets." *Econometrica*, 89 (4): 1665–98

Eccles, R. G., and H. C. White. 1988. "Price and Authority in Inter-profit Center Transactions." *American Journal of Sociology* 94:S17–S51.

Edwards, P. N. 2010. *A Vast Machine: Computer Models, Climate Data, and the Politics of Global Warming*. Cambridge, MA: MIT Press.

Ellman, M. 2014. *Socialist Planning*. Cambridge: Cambridge University Press.

Emirbayer, M., and A. Mische. 1998. "What Is Agency?" *American Journal of Sociology* 103 (4): 962–1023.

Eyal, G. 2019. *The Crisis of Expertise*. New York: John Wiley and Sons.

Ferraro, F., D. Etzion, and J. Gehman. 2015. "Tackling Grand Challenges Pragmatically: Robust Action Revisited." *Organization Studies* 36 (3): 363–90.

Filippas, A., J. J. Horton, and R. J. Zeckhauser. 2020. "Owning, Using, and Renting: Some Simple Economics of the 'Sharing Economy.'" *Management Science* 66 (9): 4152–72.

Fisher, J. V., and T. P. Duane. 2001. "Trends in Electricity Consumption, Peak Demand, and Generating Capacity in California and the Western Grid." Program on Workable Energy Regulation, Berkeley, CA.

Fligstein, N. 1996. "Markets as Politics: A Political-Cultural Approach to Market Institutions." *American Sociological Review* 61 (4): 656. https://doi.org/10.2307/2096398.

———. 2002. *The Architecture of Markets: An Economic Sociology of Twenty-First-Century Capitalist Societies*. Princeton, NJ: Princeton University Press.

Fligstein, N., and I. Mara-Drita. 1996. "How to Make a Market: Reflections on the Attempt to Create a Single Market in the European Union." *American Journal of Sociology* 102 (1): 1–33. https://doi.org/10.1086/230907.

Fligstein, N., and D. McAdam. 2011. "Toward a General Theory of Strategic Action Fields." *Sociological Theory* 29 (1): 1–26.

———. 2012. *A Theory of Fields*. Oxford: Oxford University Press.

Foss, N. J. 2003. "Selective Intervention and Internal Hybrids: Interpreting and Learning from the Rise and Decline of the Oticon Spaghetti Organization." *Organization Science* 14 (3): 331–49.

Foundation for Taxpayer and Consumer Rights. 2002. *Hoax: How Deregulation Let the Power Industry Steal $71 Billion from California*. Santa Monica, CA: Foundation for Taxpayer and Consumer Rights.

Fourcade, M. 2009. *Economists and Societies: Discipline and Profession in the United States, Britain, and France, 1890s to 1990s*. Princeton, NJ: Princeton University Press.

Fourcade, M., and K. Healy. 2016. "Seeing like a Market." *Socio-economic Review* 15 (1): 9–29. https://doi.org/10.1093/ser/mww033.

Fourcade, M., and R. Khurana. 2013. "From Social Control to Financial Economics: The Linked Ecologies of Economics and Business in Twentieth Century America." *Theory and Society* 42 (2): 121–59.

Frankel, C., J. Ossandón, and T. Pallesen. 2019. "The Organization of Markets for Collective Concerns and Their Failures." *Economy and Society* 48 (2): 153–74. https://doi.org/10.1080/03085147.2019.1627791.

Freeland, R. F., and E. W. Zuckerman Sivan. 2018. "The Problems and Promise of Hierarchy: Voice Rights and the Firm." *Sociological Science* 5:143–81.

Funk, R. J., and D. Hirschman. 2014. "Derivatives and Deregulation: Financial Innovation and the Demise of Glass–Steagall." *Administrative Science Quarterly* 59 (4): 669–704.

Galloway, A. R. 2004. *Protocol: How Control Exists after Decentralization*. Cambridge, MA: MIT Press.

Garber, D., W. W. Hogan, and L. Ruff. 1994. "An Efficient Electricity Market: Using a Pool to Support Real Competition." *Electricity Journal* 7 (7): 48–60.

García, J. A., and J. D. Reitzes. 2007. "International Perspectives on Electricity Market Monitoring and Market Power Mitigation." *Review of Network Economics* 6 (3): 397–424.

Garcia-Parpet, M.-F. 2007. "The Social Construction of a Perfect Market: The Strawberry Auction at Fontaines-en-Sologne." In *Do Economists Make Markets? On the Performativity of Economics*, edited by D. MacKenzie, F. Muniesa, and L. Siu, 20–54. Princeton, NJ: Princeton University Press.

Geertz, C. 1978. "The Bazaar Economy: Information and Search in Peasant Marketing." *American Economic Review* 68 (2): 28–32.

Gode, D. K., and S. Sunder. 1993. "Allocative Efficiency of Markets with Zero-Intelligence Traders: Market as a Partial Substitute for Individual Rationality." *Journal of Political Economy* 101 (1): 119–37.

Goodwin, C. D. 1988. "The Heterogeneity of the Economists' Discourse: Philosopher, Priest, and Hired Gun." In *The Consequences of Economic Rhetoric*, edited by A. Klamer, D. N. McCloskey, and R. M. Solow, 207–20. New York: Cambridge University Press.

Granovetter, M. 1985. "Economic Action and Social Structure: The Problem of Embeddedness." *American Journal of Sociology* 91 (3): 481–510.

Griesbach, K., A. Reich, L. Elliott-Negri, and R. Milkman. 2019. "Algorithmic Control in Platform Food Delivery Work." *Socius* 5. https://doi.org/10.1177/2378023119 870041.

Guala, F. 2001. "Building Economic Machines: The F.C.C. Auctions." *Studies in History and Philosophy of Science* 32 (3): 453–77.

———. 2005. *The Methodology of Experimental Economics*. New York: Cambridge University Press.

Guala, F., and L. Mittone. 2005. "Experiments in Economics: External Validity and the Robustness of Phenomena." *Journal of Economic Methodology* 12 (4): 495–515.

Haas, P. 2004. "When Does Power Listen to Truth? A Constructivist Approach to the Policy Process." *Journal of European Public Policy* 11 (4): 569–92. https://doi.org/10 .1080/1350176042000248034.

Harvey, S. M., and W. W. Hogan. 2001a. "Identifying the Exercise of Market Power in California." LECG research paper, Cambridge, MA.

———. 2001b. "On the Exercise of Market Power through Strategic Withholding in California." LECG research paper, Cambridge, MA.

Hayek, F. A. 1940. "Socialist Calculation: The Competitive 'Solution.'" *Economica* 7 (26): 125–49. https://doi.org/10.2307/2548692.

———. 1945. "The Use of Knowledge in Society." *American Economic Review* 35 (4): 519–30.

Hertz, R., and J. B. Imber. 1995. *Studying Elites Using Qualitative Methods*. Vol. 175. New York: Sage.

Hirschman, D. 2015. "Has Performativity Lost its Punch?—Fabian Muniesa, *The Provoked Economy: Economic Reality and the Performative Turn* (New York, Routledge, 2014)." *European Journal of Sociology* 56 (3): 531–34. https://doi.org/10.1017 /S0003975615000417.

Hirsh, R. F. 1999. *Power Loss: The Origins of Deregulation and Restructuring in the American Electric Utility System*. Cambridge, MA: MIT Press.

Hitzig, Z. 2020. "The Normative Gap: Mechanism Design and Ideal Theories of Justice." *Economics & Philosophy* 36 (3): 407–34.

Hogan, W. W. 1995. "A Wholesale Pool Spot Market Must Be Administered by the Independent System Operator: Avoiding the Separation Fallacy." *Electricity Journal* 8 (10): 26–37.

———. 1998. "Rethinking W.E.P.E.X.: What's Wrong with Least Cost?" *Public Utilities Fortnightly* 136:46–49.

———. 2002. "Electricity Market Restructuring: Reforms of Reforms." *Journal of Regulatory Economics* 21 (1): 103–32.

Horton, J. J. 2017. "The Effects of Algorithmic Labor Market Recommendations: Evidence from a Field Experiment." *Journal of Labor Economics* 35 (2): 345–85.

Hughes, T. P. 1987. "The Evolution of Large Technological Systems." In *The Social Construction of Technological Systems: New Directions in the Sociology and History of Technology*, edited by W. E. Bijker, T. Hughes, and T. Pinch, 51–82. Cambridge, MA: MIT Press.

———. 1993. *Networks of Power: Electrification in Western Society, 1880–1930*. Baltimore: Johns Hopkins University Press.

———. 1998. *Rescuing Prometheus*. New York: Random House.

Hutchinson, E. 1995. *Cognition in the Wild*. Cambridge, MA: MIT Press.

Isser, S. 2015. *Electricity Restructuring in the United States: Markets and Policy from the 1978 Energy Act to the Present*. Cambridge: Cambridge University Press.

Ito, K., and M. Reguant. 2014. "Blowin' in the Wind: Sequential Markets, Market Power and Arbitrage." *American Economic Review* 106 (7): 1921–57.

Jacobides, M. 2007. "The Inherent Limits of Organizational Structure and the Unfulfilled Role of Hierarchy: Lessons from a Near-War." *Organization Science* 18 (3): 455–77. https://doi.org/10.2139/ssrn.871738.

Joseph, J., and W. Ocasio. 2012. "Architecture, Attention, and Adaptation in the Multibusiness Firm: General Electric from 1951 to 2001." *Strategic Management Journal* 33 (6): 633–60.

Joskow, P. 2001. "California Can Tame Its Crisis." *New York Times*, January 13, 2001.

Joskow, P. L. 2001. "California's Electricity Crisis." *Oxford Review of Economic Policy* 17 (3): 365–88.

———. 2022. "From Hierarchies to Markets and Partially Back Again in Electricity: Responding to Decarbonization and Security of Supply Goals." *Journal of Institutional Economics* 18 (2): 313–29.

Joskow, P. L., and E. Kahn. 2002. "A Quantitative Analysis of Pricing Behavior in California's Wholesale Electricity Market during Summer 2000." *Energy Journal* 23 (4): 1–35.

Joskow, P. L., and R. Schmalensee. 1988. *Markets for Power: An Analysis of Electrical Utility Deregulation*. Cambridge, MA: MIT Press

Joskow, P. L., and J. Tirole. 2000. "Transmission Rights and Market Power on Electric Power Networks." *RAND Journal of Economics* 31 (3): 450–87. https://doi.org/10.2307/2600996.

Kellogg, K. C., M. A. Valentine, and A. Christin. 2020. "Algorithms at Work: The New Contested Terrain of Control." *Academy of Management Annals* 14 (1): 366–410.

Kirshner, D. 1997. "Did Power Marketers Cripple the California Power Exchange? A Response to Steven Stoft." *Electricity Journal* 10 (7): 56–60.

Kleit, A. N. 2018. "Were California's Electricity Markets Manipulated, and by Whom?" In *Modern Energy Market Manipulation*, 81–103. Bingley, UK: Emerald Group.

Klemperer, P. 2002. "What Really Matters in Auction Design." *Journal of Economic Perspectives* 16 (1): 169–89. https://doi.org/10.1257/0895330027166.

———. 2003. "Using and Abusing Economic Theory." *Journal of the European Economic Association* 1 (2–3): 272–300. https://doi.org/10.1162/154247603322390937.

Kominers, S. D., A. Teytelboym, and V. P. Crawford. 2017. "An Invitation to Market Design." *Oxford Review of Economic Policy* 33 (4): 541–71.

Kornberger, M., D. Pflueger, and J. Mouritsen. 2017. "Evaluative Infrastructures: Accounting for Platform Organization." *Accounting, Organizations and Society* 60:79–95. https://doi.org/10.1016/j.aos.2017.05.002.

Krippner, G. R. 2002. "The Elusive Market: Embeddedness and the Paradigm of Economic Sociology." *Theory and Society* 30 (6): 775–810.

———. 2011. *Capitalizing on Crisis*. Cambridge, MA: Harvard University Press.

Krippner, G. R., and A. S. Alvarez. 2007. "Embeddedness and the Intellectual Projects of Economic Sociology." *Annual Review of Sociology* 33:219–40.

Lambert, J. D. 2006. *Energy Companies and Market Reform: How Deregulation Went Wrong*. Tulsa, OK: PennWell.

Lange, O. 1936. "On the Economic Theory of Socialism: Part One." *Review of Economic Studies* 4 (1): 53–71.

———. 1937. "On the Economic Theory of Socialism: Part Two." *Review of Economic Studies* 4 (2): 123–42.

———. 1967. "The Computer and the Market." In *Socialism and Economic Growth*, edited by C. Feinstein, 158–61. Cambridge: Cambridge University Press.

La Porte, T. R. 1996. "High Reliability Organizations: Unlikely, Demanding and at Risk." *Journal of Contingencies and Crisis Management* 4 (2): 60–71.

Latour, B. 1999. "Circulating Reference: Sampling the Soil in the Amazon Forest." In *Pandora's Hope: Essays on the Reality of Science Studies*, edited by B. Latour, 24–79. Cambridge, MA: Harvard University Press.

Lavoie, D. 1981. "A Critique of the Standard Account of the Socialist Calculation Debate." *Journal of Libertarian Studies* 5 (1): 41–87.

Lehdonvirta, V. 2022. *Cloud Empires: How Digital Platforms Are Overtaking the State and How We Can Regain Control*. Cambridge, MA: MIT Press.

Lei, Y.-W. 2021. "Delivering Solidarity: Platform Architecture and Collective Contention in China's Platform Economy." *American Sociological Review* 86 (2): 279–309.

Lei, Z., E. Naveh, and Z. Novikov. 2016. "Errors in Organizations: An Integrative Review via Level of Analysis, Temporal Dynamism, and Priority Lenses." *Journal of Management* 42 (5): 1315–43.

Leifer, E. M. 1991. *Actors as Observers: A Theory of Skill in Social Relationships*. Routledge: New York.

Leveson, N. 2011. *Engineering a Safer World: Systems Thinking Applied to Safety*. Cambridge, MA: MIT Press.

Leveson, N., N. Dulac, K. Marais, and J. Carroll. 2009. "Moving Beyond Normal Accidents and High Reliability Organizations: A Systems Approach to Safety in Complex Systems." *Organization Studies* 30 (2–3): 227–49.

Liang, N., and P. Parkinson. 2020. "Enhancing Liquidity of the US Treasury Market under Stress." Hutchins Center on Fiscal and Monetary Policy at Brookings Working Papers, Washington, DC.

Luca, M., and M. H. Bazerman. 2021. *The Power of Experiments: Decision Making in a Data-Driven World*. Cambridge, MA: MIT Press.

Luhmann, N. 2012. *Theory of Society*. Vol. 1. Palo Alto, CA: Stanford University Press.

Lusher, D., J. Koskinen, and G. Robins, G. 2012. *Exponential Random Graph Models for Social Networks: Theory, Methods, and Applications*. Cambridge: Cambridge University Press.

Lyles, M. A. 2014. "Organizational Learning, Knowledge Creation, Problem Formulation and Innovation in Messy Problems." *European Management Journal* 32 (1): 132–36.

MacKenzie, D. 2007. "Is Economics Performative? Option Theory and the Construction of Derivatives Markets." In *Do Economists Make Markets? On the Performativity of Economics*, edited by D. MacKenzie, F. Muniesa, and L. Siu, 54–86. Cambridge, MA: Princeton University Press.

———. 2008. *An Engine, Not a Camera: How Financial Models Shape Markets*. Cambridge, MA: MIT Press.

———. 2009. *Material Markets: How Economic Agents Are Constructed*. New York: Oxford University Press.

———. 2011. "The Credit Crisis as a Problem in the Sociology of Knowledge." *American Journal of Sociology* 116 (6): 1778–841. https://doi.org/10.1086/659639.

———. 2022. *Trading at the Speed of Light: How Ultrafast Algorithms Are Transforming Financial Markets*. Princeton, NJ: Princeton University Press.

Magelssen, C., B. Rich, and K. Mayer. 2022. "The Contractual Governance of Transactions within Firms." *Organization Science* 33 (6): 2226–49. https://doi.org/10.1287/orsc.2021.1536.

March, J. G., and H. A. Simon. 1958. *Organizations*. New York: Wiley.

Marcus, W., and J. Hamrin. 2001. *How We Got Into the California Energy Crisis*. Sacramento, CA: JBS Energy.

Martin, J. L. 2003. "What Is Field Theory?" *American Journal of Sociology* 109 (1): 1–49.

McAfee, P., and S. Wilkie. 2020. "Teaching Old Markets New Tricks." Project Syndicate, January 23, 2020. https://www.project-syndicate.org/onpoint/market-design-strategies-improve-outcomes-by-preston-mcafee-and-simon-wilkie-2020-01.

McCabe, K. A., S. J. Rassenti, and V. L. Smith. 1991. "Smart Computer-Assisted Markets." *Science* 254 (5031): 534–38. http://www.jstor.org/stable/2879381.

McCullough, R. 2001. "Price Spike Tsunami: How Market Power Soaked California." *Public Utilities Fortnightly* 139 (1): 22–33.

McIntyre, D., A. Srinivasan, A. Afuah, A. Gawer, and T. Kretschmer. 2021. "Multisided Platforms as New Organizational Forms." *Academy of Management Perspectives* 35 (4): 566–83.

McLean, B., and P. Elkind. (2003) 2013. *The Smartest Guys in the Room*. New York: Portfolio Penguin.

McNamara, W. 2002. *The California Electricity Crisis*. Tulsa, OK: PennWell.

Menchik, D. A. 2020. "Authority beyond Institutions: The Expert's Multivocal Process of Gaining and Sustaining Authoritativeness." *American Journal of Cultural Sociology*, 9:450–517.

Merton, R. K. 1936. "The Unanticipated Consequences of Purposive Social Action." *American Sociological Review* 1 (6): 894–904.

Michaels, R. J. 1997. "MW Gamble: The Missing Market for Capacity." *Electricity Journal* 10 (10): 56–64. https://doi.org/10.1016/S1040-6190(97)80320-X.

Miller, R. M. 2002. *Paving Wall Street: Experimental Economics and the Quest for the Perfect Market*. New York: John Wiley and Sons.

Milton, J. 2005. *Paradise Lost*. Indianapolis: Hackett.

Mirowski, P., and E. Nik-Khah. 2007. "Markets Made Flesh: Performativity, and a Problem in Science Studies, Augmented with Consideration of the F.C.C. Auctions." In *Do Economists Make Markets? On the Performativity of Economics*, edited by D. MacKenzie, F. Muniesa, and L. Siu, 190–255. Cambridge: Princeton University Press.

———. 2017. *The Knowledge We Have Lost in Information: The History of Information in Modern Economics*. Oxford: Oxford University Press.

Mises, L. von. 1935. "Economic Calculation in the Socialist Commonwealth." In *Collectivist Economic Planning*, edited by F. A. von Hayek, N. G. Pierson, L. von Mises, G. Halm, and E. Barone, 87–130. London: Routledge.

Morozov, E. 2019. "Digital Socialism? The Calculation Debate in the Age of Big Data." *New Left Review*, no. 116, 33–67. https://newleftreview.org/issues/ii116/articles/evgeny-morozov-digital-socialism.

Muniesa, F. 2014. *The Provoked Economy: Economic Reality and the Performative Turn*. New York: Routledge.

Navarro, P., and M. Shames. 2003. "Electricity Deregulation: Lessons Learned from California." *Energy Law Journal* 24 (1): 33–64.

Nee, V. 2005. "The New Institutionalisms in Economic Sociology." In *The Handbook of Economic Sociology*, 2nd ed., edited by N. J. Smelser and R. Swedberg, 49–74. Princeton, NJ: Russel Sage Foundation.

Nik-Khah, E., and P. Mirowski. 2019. "On Going the Market One Better: Economic Market Design and the Contradictions of Building Markets for Public Purposes." *Economy and Society* 48 (2): 268–94. https://doi.org/10.1080/03085147.2019 .1576431.

Nix, A., S. Decker, and C. Wolf. 2021. "Enron and the California Energy Crisis: The Role of Networks in Enabling Organizational Corruption." *Business History Review* 95 (4): 765–802. https://doi.org/10.1017/s0007680521001008.

Nove, A. 1991. *The Economics of Feasible Socialism Revisited*. 2nd ed. London: Harper-Collins Academic

Ockenfels, A. 2009. "Marktdesign und Experimentelle Wirtschaftsforschung." *Perspektiven der Wirtschaftspolitik* 10:31–53.

O'Donnell, A. 2003. *Soul of the Grid: A Cultural Biography of the California Independent System Operator*. Lincoln, NE: iUniverse.

O'Neill, J. 2006. "Knowledge, Planning, and Markets: A Missing Chapter in the Socialist Calculation Debates." *Economics and Philosophy* 22 (1): 55–78. https://doi.org/10 .1017/S0266267105000702.

O'Neill, R., and U. Helman. 2007. "Regulatory Reform of the U.S. Wholesale Electricity Markets." In *Creating Competitive Markets: The Politics of Regulatory Reform*, edited by M. K. Landy, M. A. Levin, and M. M. Shapiro, 128–57. Washington, DC: Brookings Institution.

Oren, S. S. 1998. "Authority and Responsibility of the ISO: Objectives, Options, and Tradeoffs." In *Designing Competitive Electricity Markets*, edited by H. G. Huntington and H.P. Chao, 79–96. Boston: Kluwer Academic.

Orr, J. E. (1996) 2016. *Talking about Machines: An Ethnography of a Modern Job*. Ithaca, NY: Cornell University Press.

Özden-Schilling, C. 2021. *The Current Economy: Electricity Markets and Techno-economics*. Palo Alto, CA: Stanford University Press.

Padgett, J. F., and C. K. Ansell. 1993. "Robust Action and the Rise of the Medici, 1400–1434." *American Journal of Sociology* 98 (6): 1259–319.

Padgett, J. F., and W. W. Powell. 2012. "The Problem of Emergence." In *The Emergence of Organizations and Markets*, edited by J. F. Padgett and W. W. Powell, 1–29. Princeton, NJ: Princeton University Press.

Pallesen, T., and R. P. Jenle. 2018. "Organizing Consumers for a Decarbonized Electricity System: Calculative Agencies and User Scripts in a Danish Demonstration Project." *Energy Research & Social Science* 38:102–9.

Pathak, P. A. 2017. "What Really Matters in Designing School Choice Mechanisms." *Advances in Economics and Econometrics*, edited by B. Honoré, A. Pakes, M. Piazzesi, and L. Samuelson, 176–214. Cambridge, MA: Cambridge University Press.

Perrow, C. (1984) 1999. *Normal Accidents: Living with High Risk Technologies*. Princeton, NJ: Princeton University Press.

———. 1994. "The Limits of Safety: The Enhancement of a Theory of Accidents." *Journal of Contingencies and Crisis Management* 2 (4): 212–20.

———. 2010. "The Meltdown Was Not an Accident." In *Markets on Trial: The Economic Sociology of the U.S. Financial Crisis: Part A*, edited by M. Lounsbury and P. M. Hirsch, 309–30. Bingley, UK: Emerald Group.

Phillips, L., and M. Rozworski. 2019. *The People's Republic of Wal-Mart: How the World's Biggest Corporations Are Laying the Foundation for Socialism.* Brooklyn: Verso.

Polanyi, K. (1944) 2001. *The Great Transformation: The Political and Economic Origins of Our Time.* 2nd ed. Boston: Beacon Paperback.

Porter, T. M. 1995. *Trust in Numbers: The Pursuit of Objectivity in Science and Public Life.* Princeton, NJ: Princeton University Press.

Preda, A. 2009. *Framing Finance: The Boundaries of Markets and Modern Capitalism.* Chicago: University of Chicago Press.

Prendergast, C. 2017. "How Food Banks Use Markets to Feed the Poor." *Journal of Economic Perspectives* 31 (4): 145–62.

Putnam, R. D. 1977. "Elite Transformation in Advanced Industrial Societies: An Empirical Assessment of the Theory of Technocracy." *Comparative Political Studies* 10 (3): 383–412.

Rahimi, A. F., and A. Y. Sheffrin. 2003. "Effective Market Monitoring in Deregulated Electricity Markets." *IEEE Transactions on Power Systems* 18 (2): 486–93.

Rahman, K. S., and K. Thelen. 2019. "The Rise of the Platform Business Model and the Transformation of Twenty-First-Century Capitalism." *Politics & Society* 47 (2): 177–204. https://doi.org/10.1177/0032329219838932.

Rassenti, S. J., V. L. Smith, and R. L. Bulfin. 1982. "A Combinatorial Auction Mechanism for Airport Time Slot Allocation." *Bell Journal of Economics*, 13 (2): 402–17.

Reay, M. J. 2012. "The Flexible Unity of Economics." *American Journal of Sociology* 118 (1): 45–87.

Reverdy, T., and D. Breslau. 2019. "Making an Exception: Market Design and the Politics of Re-regulation in the French Electricity Sector." *Economy and Society* 48 (2): 197–220. https://doi.org/10.1080/03085147.2019.1576434.

Rilinger, G. 2015. "Methodenprobleme immanenter Kritik: Das Beispiel der Entfremdung." *Leviathan* 43 (1): 88–112.

———. 2021. "The Texas Blackouts and the Problems of Electricity Market Design." *Promarket*, March 24.

———. 2022a. "Conceptual Limits of Performativity: Assessing the Feasibility of Market Design Blueprints." *Socio-Economic Review* 21 (2): 885–908.

———. 2022b. "Discursive Multivocality: How the Proliferation of Economic Language Can Undermine the Political Influence of Economists." *Socio-Economic Review* 20 (4): 1991–2015.

———. 2023. "Who Captures Whom? Regulatory Misperceptions and the Timing of Cognitive Capture." *Regulation & Governance* 17 (1): 43–60. https://doi.org/10.1111/rego.12438.

Roberts, K. H. 1990. "Some Characteristics of One Type of High Reliability Organization." *Organization Science* 1 (2): 160–76.

Roe, E., and P. R. Schulman. 2008. *High Reliability Management: Operating on the Edge.* Stanford, CA: Stanford Business Books.

Roscoe, P. J., and P. Willman. 2021. "Flaunt the Imperfections: Affective Governance and London's Alternative Investment Market." *Economy and Society* 50 (4): 565–89.

Rose, N. L., ed. 2014. *Economic Regulation and Its Reform: What Have We Learned?* Chicago: University of Chicago Press.

Roth, A. E. 2008. "What Have We Learned from Market Design?" *Innovations: Technology, Governance, Globalization* 3 (1): 119–47.

———. 2015. *Who Gets What — and Why*. New York: Houghton Mifflin Harcourt.

Roth, A. E., and E. Peranson. 1999. "The Redesign of the Matching Market for American Physicians: Some Engineering Aspects of Economic Design." *American Economic Review* 89 (4): 748–80.

Roth, A. E., and R. B. Wilson. 2019. "How Market Design Emerged from Game Theory: A Mutual Interview." *Journal of Economic Perspectives* 33 (3): 118–43.

Saldaña, J. 2015. *The Coding Manual for Qualitative Researchers*. New York: Sage.

Samuels, W. J. 1962. "The Physiocratic Theory of Economic Policy." *Quarterly Journal of Economics* 76 (1): 145–62.

Schechter, A. 2020. "Was the 2017 FCC Spectrum Auction a Success — or a Disappointing Failure?" *Promarket*, June 17.

Schüssler, E., W. Attwood-Charles, S. Kirchner, and J. B. Schor. 2021. "Between Mutuality, Autonomy and Domination: Rethinking Digital Platforms as Contested Relational Structures." *Socio-Economic Review* 19 (4): 1217–43.

Schutz, A., and T. Luckmann. 1973. *The Structures of the Life-World*. Vol. 1. Evanston, IL: Northwestern University Press.

Schweppe, F. C., M. C. Caramanis, R. D. Tabors, and R. E. Bohn. 1988. *Spot Pricing of Electricity*. Boston: Kluwer.

Schweppe, F. C., M. C. Caramanis, R. D. Tabors, and J. Flory. 1982. *Utility Spot Pricing: California, Prepared for Pacific Gas and Electric and Southern California Edison*. Cambridge, MA: Cambridge University Press.

Schweppe, F. C., R. D. Tabors, J. L. Kirtley, H. R. Outhred, F. H. Pickel, and A. J. Cox. 1980. "Homeostatic Utility Control." *IEEE Transactions on Power Apparatus and Systems*, PAS-99 (3): 1151–63.

Scott, J. C. 1998. *Seeing like a State: How Certain Schemes to Improve the Human Condition Have Failed*. New Haven, CT: Yale University Press.

Scott, W. R. 2013. *Institutions and Organizations: Ideas, Interests, and Identities*. New York: Sage.

Shapiro, D. 2009. "Reviving the Socialist Calculation Debate: A Defense of Hayek against Lange." *Social Philosophy and Policy* 6 (2): 139–59. https://doi.org/10.1017/S0265052500000674.

Sheffrin, A. 2002. "Empirical Evidence of Strategic Bidding in the California ISO Real-Time Market." In *Electricity Pricing in Transition*, edited by A. B. Faruqui and K. Eakin, 267–81. New York: Springer.

Sheffrin, S. M. 2004. "State Budget Deficit Dynamics and the California Debacle." *Journal of Economic Perspectives* 2 (18): 205–26.

Simon, H. A. 1962. "The Architecture of Complexity." *Proceedings of the American Philosophical Society* 106 (6): 467–82.

———. (1969) 1996. *The Sciences of the Artificial*. 3rd ed. Cambridge, MA: MIT Press.

Smith, V. L. 1987. "Currents of Competition in Electricity Markets." *Regulation* 11 (2): 23–29. https://heinonline.org/HOL/P?h=hein.journals/rcatorbgll&i=89.

———. 2008. *Rationality in Economics: Constructivist and Ecological Forms*. Cambridge: Cambridge University Press.

Smith, V. L., S. J. Rassenti, and B. Wilson, B. 2002. "California: Energy Crisis or Market Design Crisis?" Paper presented at the Hoover Institute Conference on the California Electricity Problem, Stanford, CA.

Snook, S. A. 2002. *Friendly Fire: The Accidental Shootdown of US Black Hawks over Northern Iraq*. Princeton, NJ: Princeton University Press.

Soltes, E. 2016. *Why They Do It: Inside the Mind of the White-Collar Criminal*. New York: PublicAffairs.

Stark, D., and I. Pais. 2020. "Algorithmic Management in the Platform Economy." *Sociologica* 14 (3): 47–72.

Stigler, G. J. 1971. "The Theory of Economic Regulation." *Bell Journal of Economics and Management Science* 2 (1): 3–21.

Stinchcombe, A. L. 2001. *When Formality Works: Authority and Abstraction in Law and Organizations*. Chicago: University of Chicago Press.

Stoft, S. 1996. "California's I.S.O.: Why Not Clear the Market?" *Electricity Journal* 9 (10): 38–43.

———. 1997. "What Should a Power Marketer Want?" *Electricity Journal* 10 (5): 34–45.

———. 2002. *Power System Economics*. New York: IEEE Press.

Strauss, A., and J. M. Corbin. 1990. *Basics of Qualitative Research: Grounded Theory Procedures and Techniques*. New York: Sage

Sueyoshi, T. 2010. "Beyond Economics for Guiding Large Public Policy Issues: Lessons from the Bell System Divestiture and the California Electricity Crisis." *Decision Support Systems* 48 (3): 457–69.

Sullivan, B. N. 2010. "Competition and Beyond: Problems and Attention Allocation in the Organizational Rulemaking Process." *Organization Science* 21 (2): 432–50.

Suryanarayanan, S., and D. L. Kleinman. 2012. "Be(e)coming Experts: The Controversy over Insecticides in the Honey Bee Colony Collapse Disorder." *Social Studies of Science* 43 (2): 215–40. https://doi.org/10.1177/0306312712466186.

Sweeney, J. L. 2002a. *The California Electricity Crisis*. Stanford, CA: Hoover Institution.

———. 2002b. "The California Electricity Crisis: Lessons for the Future." *Bridge* 32 (2): 23–32.

Taylor, F. W. (1947) 2004. *Scientific Management*. New York: Routledge.

Taylor, G., S. Ledgerwood, R. Broehm, and P. Fox-Penner. 2015. *Market Power and Market Manipulation in Energy Markets: From the California Crisis to the Present*. Arlington, VA: Utilities Report.

Taylor, J., and P. VanDoren. 2002. "California's Electricity Crisis." In *Electricity Pricing in Transition*, edited by A. B. Faruqui and K. Eakin, 245–65. New York: Springer.

Tee, R., A. Davies, and J. Whyte. 2019. "Modular Designs and Integrating Practices: Managing Collaboration through Coordination and Cooperation." *Research Policy* 48 (1): 51–61.

Thiemann, M., and J. Lepoutre. 2017. "Stitched on the Edge: Rule Evasion, Embedded Regulators, and the Evolution of Markets." *American Journal of Sociology* 122 (6): 1775–821.

Thompson, J. D. (1967) 2017. *Organizations in Action: Social Science Bases of Administrative Theory*. New York: Routledge.

Turner, B. A. 1976. "The Organizational and Interorganizational Development of Disasters." *Administrative Science Quarterly* 21 (3): 378–97.

Vallas, S., and J. B. Schor. 2020. "What Do Platforms Do? Understanding the Gig Economy." *Annual Review of Sociology* 46:273–94.

Van Vactor, S. 2000. "East vs. West: Comparing Electric Markets in California and PJM." *Public Utilities Fortnightly* 138 (14): 24–35.

Varian, H. R. 1992. *Microeconomic Analysis*. 3rd ed. New York: Norton.

Vaughan, D. (1996) 2016. *The* Challenger *Launch Decision: Risky Technology, Culture, and Deviance at N.A.S.A.* Enlarged ed. Chicago: University of Chicago Press.

———. 2021. *Dead Reckoning: Air Traffic Control, System Effects, and Risk.* Chicago: University of Chicago Press.

Veblen, T. (1904) 2016. *The Theory of Business Enterprise.* Chicago: Charles Scribner and Sons.

Velupillai, K. V., and S. Zambelli. 2013. "Computability and Algorithmic Complexity in Economics." In *A Computable Universe: Understanding and Exploring Nature as Computation*, 303–31. Singapore: World Scientific.

Vickrey, W. 1962. "Auction and Bidding Games." In *Recent Advances in Game Theory*, edited by M. Maschler, 15–27. Princeton, NJ: Princeton University Press.

———. 1978. "Efficient Pricing under Regulation: The Case of Responsive Pricing as a Substitute for Interruptible Power Contracts" *Resources and Energy* 14:157–174.

Viljoen, S., J. Goldenfein, and L. McGuigan. 2021. "Design Choices: Mechanism Design and Platform Capitalism." *Big Data & Society* 8 (2). https://doi.org/10.1177/20539517211034312.

Vogel, S. K. 1996. *Freer Markets, More Rules: Regulatory Reform in Advanced Industrial Countries.* Ithaca, NY: Cornell University Press.

———. 2018. *Marketcraft: How Governments Make Markets Work.* New York: Oxford University Press.

Vulkan, N., A. E. Roth, and Z. Neeman, eds. 2013. *The Handbook of Market Design.* Oxford: Oxford University Press.

Waldinger, D. 2021. "Targeting In-Kind Transfers through Market Design: A Revealed Preference Analysis of Public Housing Allocation." *American Economic Review* 111 (8): 2660–96.

Walsh, J. 2004. *The $10 Billion Jolt: California's Energy Crisis: Cowardice, Greed, Stupidity and the Death of Deregulation.* Los Angeles: Silver Lake.

Wansleben, L. 2018. "How Expectations Became Governable: Institutional Change and the Performative Power of Central Banks." *Theory and Society* 47 (6):773–803.

Weare, C. 2003. *The California Electricity Crisis: Causes and Policy Options.* San Francisco: Public Policy Institute of California.

Weber, T. A. 2011. *Optimal Control Theory with Applications in Economics.* Cambridge, MA: MIT Press.

Weick, K. E. 1988. "Enacted Sensemaking in Crisis Situations." *Journal of Management Studies* 25 (4): 305–17.

———. 1998. "Foresights of Failure: An Appreciation of Barry Turner." *Journal of Contingencies and Crisis Management* 6 (2): 72–75.

———. 2005. "Making Sense of Blurred Images: Mindful Organizing in Mission STS-107." In *Organization at the Limit: Lessons from the Columbia Disaster*, edited by W. Starbuck and M. Farjoun, 159–77. Malden, MA: Blackwell.

Weick, K. E., and K. H. Roberts. 1993. "Collective Mind in Organizations: Heedful Interrelating on Flight Decks." *Administrative Science Quarterly* 38 (3): 357–81.

Weick, K. E., and K. M. Sutcliffe. 2015. *Managing the Unexpected: Sustained Performance in a Complex World.* New York: John Wiley and Sons.

Weingart, P. 1999. "Scientific Expertise and Political Accountability: Paradoxes of Science in Politics." *Science and Public Policy* 26 (3): 151–61.

Wheeler, S. A., and D. E. Garrick. 2020. "A Tale of Two Water Markets in Australia:

Lessons for Understanding Participation in Formal Water Markets." *Oxford Review of Economic Policy* 36 (1): 132–53.

White, H. C. 1981. "Where Do Markets Come From?" *American Journal of Sociology* 87 (3): 517–47.

Wiener, N. 1965. *Cybernetics, or Control and Communication in the Animal and the Machine.* Vol. 25. Cambridge, MA: MIT Press.

Williamson, O. E. 1985. *The Economic Institutions of Capitalism: Firms, Markets, Relational Contracting.* New York: Simon and Schuster.

Williamson, O. E., and S. G. Winter, eds. 1993. *The Nature of the Firm: Origins, Evolution, and Development.* New York: Oxford University Press.

Wilson, R. 1998. "Design Principles." In *Designing Competitive Electricity Markets*, edited by H. P. Chao and H. G. Huntington, 159–83. Boston: Kluwer Academic.

Wolak, F. A. 2003. "Diagnosing the California Electricity Crisis." *Electricity Journal* 16 (7): 11–37.

———. 2005. "Lessons from International Experience with Electricity Market Monitoring." Policy, Research Working Paper WPS3692, World Bank Group, Washington, DC. http://documents.worldbank.org/curated/en/639831468140966929/Lessons-from-international-experience-with-electricity-market-monitoring.

Woo, C.-K. 2001. "What Went Wrong in California's Electricity Market?" *Energy* 26 (8): 747–58.

Woo, C.-K., D. Lloyd, and A. Tishler. 2003. "Electricity Market Reform Failures: U.K., Norway, Alberta and California." *Energy Policy* 31 (11): 1103–15.

Yang, Z., Q. Xia, H. Zhong, and C. Kang. 2017. "Fundamental Review of the O.P.F. Problem: Challenges, Solutions, and State-of-the-Art Algorithms." *Journal of Energy Engineering* 144 (1). https://doi.org/10.1061/(ASCE)EY.1943-7897.0000510.

Zarnikau, J., and I. Hallett. 2008. "Aggregate Industrial Energy Consumer Response to Wholesale Prices in the Restructured Texas Electricity Market." *Energy Economics* 30 (4): 1798–808.

Zuckerman, E. W. 2010. "What If We Had Been in Charge? The Sociologist as Builder of Rational Institutions." In *Markets on Trial: The Economic Sociology of the US Financial Crisis; Part B*, 359–78. Bingley, UK: Emerald Group.

———. 2012. "Market Efficiency: A Sociological Perspective." In *The Oxford Handbook of the Sociology of Finance*, edited by K. Knorr-Cetina and A. Preda, 223–49. Oxford: Oxford University Press.

Index

Note: Page numbers in italics refer to figures and tables.

AB 1890, 26, 48, 138, 146–47, 151, 157, 167, 243

ABB (software vendor), 176, 228, 231

Ackerman, Gary, 138

AES (energy company), 84

Alaywan, Ziad, 209, 210

algorithms: and allocation problems, 77, 229; derailed by games, 82, 108; inefficient, 234–36; interpretation of rules, 68–71, 74, 89, 161, 194, 203, 205, 225, 229; markets as, 11, 17, 55–62, 88, 108, 134, 161, 186, 196, 203, 208, 209–11, 222; as metaphor, 168

Allison, Graham, 227

allocation problems: with design strategies, 18–19, 56, 77–82, 84, 174, 221, 225, 231–33, 235–36; and market failure, 230–31; success at preventing, 235–36

altruism, market mechanisms and, 65, 236

Amazon, 3, 65, 234, 264n15

ancillary service markets, *86*, 91, 183, 198; crisis in CAISO's, 198–203, 216, *248*; and imbalance markets, 183–84; and market power, 100, 102; within market structure, *86*, 91–92; restructured, 183; types of, 91

arbitrage: as desirable, 121; function among power marketers, 87, 93, 100–101; illegal, to manipulate market, 100–104, *103*, 135, 175, 228, 269n42; legitimate, 83, 84, 93, 101, 121, 125, 168; as necessary within system,

178, 187; as "riskless," 268n36; and simplification, 120–26; unlicensed, 178. *See also* game playing; loopholes in market structure

arbitrage games, 100–104, *103*, 226, 228; Fat Boy, 102–4; import-export, 101–2, *103*; Ricochet, 101–2, 110, 127–28, 179, 180, 181, 183, 184–85, 202; Ricochet variant, 185

auctions, 60, *86*; centralized, in restructured system, 88, 150; circumventing rules of, 135; day-ahead, 89, 91, 93, 183; designers of, 209, 211, 215; Feeding America's, 235; operations of, 116; at PX, 89, 91, 112, 124, 177; replaced, 35; for schedule adjustment bids, 186; simplification of interfaces, 120. *See also* ancillary service markets; congestion; day-of market (PX); imbalance (real-time) markets; Power Exchange (PX)

Backus, George, 152, 213

bankruptcy: Enron, 41; PG&E, 35

Barkovich, Barbara, 149–50

Barone, Enrico, 59

battle of two narratives, 5, 36–47, 84, 110–11, 260n40. *See also under* California; electric energy crisis

BEEP (balancing energy and ex post energy) software, 124–25, *170*, 176–77, 180, 181

Belden, Tim, 95–96

biennial resource plan update, 187–88

blackouts, rolling, 25, 79. *See also* electric energy crisis

Blue Book proceedings: blocked by conflicts, 150; controversies within, 146–51, 162–63, 273n11; corrupted by interest politics, 166–67; CPUC archives on, *246*; WEPEX and, 166. *See also* Memorandum of Understanding (1995); Western Power Exchange (WEPEX)

Bohn, Roger E., 50, 52–53, 280n28

Bonneville Power Administration, 84

bounding: and allocation problem, 81; contradicted, 112; as design strategy, 12–14, 76, 82, 185, 194, 221; exemplified, 122; failure of, 15, 193, 196; failure to use, 127, 217; mandatory, 233; successful, 19, 235; unconstrained, 236; weakened, 197. *See also* controlling; control structures; market design, strategies of; simplification

Bourdieu, Pierre, 8

Brulte, Jim, 146

Budhraja, Vikram, 149, 150, 157, 209, 212

Bush, George W., 46

CAISO. *See* California Independent System Operator (CAISO)

California, electricity markets in, 4–6; "cathedral" architecture of, *27, 86*, 86–93, *88*, 108, 111; control structure of, 111, 129–34; porous boundaries among, 127–29, 133, 135, 164, 166, 192, 219; previous history of, 26, *27*, 49–54, 143–45; restructured, 26–28, *27, 28*, 48–49, 113–14, 145–51, 270n13

California, energy crisis in, 14–18, 24–26, 233; CAISO's initial actions to combat, 23–25; as failure by design, 47–49 (*see also* market design); losses from, 35–36, 230; and manipulations, 42, 43 (*see also* Enron; game playing); practical problems of, 18–20, 219, 226–33; state budget socializing, 26, 35–36, 258n10; transcripts of congressional hearings

on, 244; two narratives of, 5, 36–42, 110–11, 260n40

California Center for the Study of Energy, 244

California Department of Public Utilities, 263n93

California Energy Commission, 37, 53, 90, 116, 152, 258n12, 263n93

California Energy Institute, 244

California Large Energy Customer Association (CLECA), 149

California Manufacturers Association (CMA), 149

California Public Utility Commission (CPUC), 16, 156; archives from, 243, *246*; and Backus, 152; coup against, 147–51; and energy crisis, 26–32, 35; and forward contracting, 114; and long-term contracts, 29; and Michaels, 195; and origins of system redesign, 144; payments to from Enron, 273n3; politics and, 167; rate increase, 35; restructuring program, 36; and utilities' bad investments, 188; as toothless, 167

California Independent System Operator (CAISO), 26, 84, 110, 128; ancillary market crisis at, 198–203, 216; on arbitrage, 269n41; boundary with Western Interconnection, 129; business documents of, 243; and congestion issues, 92–93, 105–6, *107*; congressional hearing on, *245*; control structure of (*see* market monitoring units [CAISO]; market surveillance committee [CAISO]); distance from PX as hindrance, 177; within electric energy architecture, *86*, 87, 90–93, 94, 106, 177; FERC oversight of, 130–31, 167; function of, 23–24, 86–87, *86*, 90–93; gamed by sellers, 98, 184; information architecture of, 214–15, *214*; investment in nuclear plants, 148; isolated from PX, 122; and January 2001 energy crisis, 23–25, *27*, 33, 42, 44, 45; limited jurisdiction of, 127–29; and redesign, 97. *See also* control structures; Western Power Exchange (WEPEX)

California State Archives, 243–44, *247*

Callon, Michael, 9

Calpine (energy company), 41

capitalism: digital, and social engineering, 220–21; and socialism, 1–2

Caramanis, Mike, 50, 52–53

Carroll, Lewis, 263n41

Carter, Jimmy, 166

centralization: as counterproductive, 13–14, 19, 57, 59, 74, 173, 208; as desirable in design process, 2, 52–53, 159, 160–61, 169, 229, 230; Enron's opposition to, 159–60, 187–88; sociology on, 220; as solution to California's energy crisis, 35. *See also* control structures; decentralization

Challenger disaster, 227

Chao, Hong-po, 53, 204

Cicchetti, Charles, 96

climate change, 237

computers: compared with markets, 11, 57–60, 70, 203, 221; market moved into, 61; and markets, 220–21

computer scientists, 6, 233

CONG (congestion management system), 179

congestion, 104, 132; blueprint for management of, 42, 93, 126, 204–7; CAISO and, 92–93; controlling, 126–27, 179; detecting, 133; emergence of, 135; Enron and artificial, 95–96, 106; fictional, 92, 95, 104, 132; flaws in grid representation, 178; games, and differential simplification, 126–27; market power and, 98, 104–8, *107*; as predictable, 92; worst sources of, 179. *See also* game playing

congestion games, 104–8, *107*, 132–34, 135, 226; Death Star, 106, 127–28, 179; DEC, 105; and differential simplification, 126–27; Forney's Perpetual Loop, 106; load shift, 107–8

congressional investigations, *245–46*

Conlon, Greg, 147

contracts, long-term, 186; avoided in past, 113–14, 116; utilities and, 29, 30–31, 37, 38, 112, 113–14, 164

controlling: as design strategy, 12–14, 76–77, 185, 221; difficulties of, 225; as easy, 19; failure of, 18–19, 196; limits of, 221–22; requirements, 217; successful, 235; theoretical, 210. *See also* bounding; control structures; market design, strategies of; simplification

control structures: as always necessary, 13, 18, 56, 212, 216; California's weak, 111, 129–31, 133–34, 137, 175–82, 191, 194; designers' ambivalence on weakness of, 197; designers' disagreement on, 210–15, *214*; designing, as ill-structured problem, 216–17; in design process, 85–86, 138, 171, 221; and gaming, 229; holes in, 15, 17, 131–34, 193, 228–29; limits of, 13–14, 15, 73–74, 81, 131–34, 191, 194, 215–16, 230; and modularization, 18, 169–90; need for strong, 190, 191–92, 194, 211–12, 219; and PX, 168; rules on energy supply depletion, 189; and separation of market from operator, 150–51, 153, 154, 159–62, 212; successful, 236; today's simplified, 219; weakened, 18, 169–90, 197. *See also* California Independent System Operator (CAISO); Federal Energy Regulatory Commission (FERC)

control theory, 50–51, 262n85

counterflows, 106–7, *107*

Cowles Commission, 58–59

Cramton, Peter, 137–38, 223

Cuban Missile Crisis, 227

Davis, Gray, 32, 34, 36

day-ahead market (PX), 87–88, *88*, 91, 93; fake congestion in, 107; price fluctuations in, 28, *28*, *88*, 89, *123*, 183; as spot market, 99–100, *123*, 258n12

day-of market (PX), *88*, 89, 91, 93, 107, *170*, 183

Death Star (game), 106, 127–28, 179. *See also* game playing decentralization: within control structures, 76–77; in market design, 71, 161; and modularization, 16–17; of utilities, 165

deregulation, 4–5, 32, 48, 49, 55, 259n22; archives on, 243, *245*, *248*; Backus on, 152; Davis on, 32; and Enron, 41, 46, 145, 150–51; Michaels on, 195; supported by Enron and politicians, 45–46, 145. *See also* restructuring, of California's electricity market

designer markets, 2–3, 11, 56, 63, 74; as algorithms, 11, 17, 55–62, 205, 209, 210, 211, 221; as chameleonic, 17, 204–9, 232; as computer-human hybrids, 61, 206; as computers, 11, 57–60, 70, 203, 221; core of, 62; and economic fluctuations during California's crisis, 4–6, *27*, 28–35, *28*, 36–37, 41–42, 93, 113–14, 183, 198; examples of, 2; failure of (*see* market design, failure of); flaws in, 166 (*see also* market design, flaws of; market designers, limitations of); forward (*see* forward markets); history of, 4–6, 49–54, 59–61, 143–44; illiquid, 121; imperfections in, 39; literature on, 137–41; manipulation of (*see* designer markets, manipulation of); as "no silver bullet," 234, 237; as organizational forms, 11–14, 55–82, *63*, 138–39; origin of concepts in, 143; perfect, 52, 88; perspectives on, 158–62; self-interest and optimizing, 65–66, 172; self-regulating, myth of, 201–2; separation from grid management, 150–51, 153, 154, 159–62, 212; short-term, 120; temporal structure of, 87–88, *88*, 118–20; and traditional markets, differences between, 64–75; and traditional organizations, 11–12, 64, 66–67, 172, 173, 227–29, 237. *See also* ancillary service markets; congestion; imbalance (real-time) markets; market design; market designers; markets, generally

designer markets, manipulation of, 5, 38, 40–47, 83–84; via arbitrage games, 100–104, 226; via congestion games, 104–8; via market power, 97–100. *See also* game playing

Diablo Canyon Nuclear Power Plant, 148, 164

Didion, Joan, 48

Duke (energy company), 41, 45, 84

Dunn, George, 149

Dynegy (energy company), 45, 145

eBay, 65

economics, 1, 255n7, 275n45; expertise in, 158–62; and market design, 2, 9, 57; socialist undercurrents of modern, 203; within sociology, 7

economists, 6; on causes of electric energy crisis, 39–40, 46, 194; compared to market designers, 228–29; defense of market manipulation, 46; on disadvantages of markets, 59–60; as interviewees for book, *250*; market designers as, 197–98, 209; philosophical differences with engineers, 203, 207–17, *214*, 219; socialist vs. Mises, 59; work with engineers, 17, 53, 199–202, 231–32. *See also specific individuals*

electric energy crisis: beginnings of, 25–26; Enron as cause of, 40–42; manipulation in, sources of, 42 (*see also* Enron; game playing); price spikes in California, 4–6, 28–35, *28*, 41–42, 93, 113–14, 183, 198; two narratives of, 5, 36–42, 260n40. *See also* California, energy crisis in

Electricity Journal, 244

electricity markets: original, 143–45; restructured into designer markets, 26–28, *27*, *28*, 48–49, 113–14, 145–51, 270n13; today's, 53, 168, 219, 223. *See also* designer markets

Electricity Oversight Board, 32

electricity systems: allocation problem within, 18–19, 79–80, 232; and balance of strategies, 109; functionality of generic, 77–82. *See also* designer markets; generators; utilities, electric (CA)

Electric Power Research Institute (Palo Alto), 53, 157, 204, 209 electric utilities in California. *See* utilities, electric (CA)

Electric Utility Restructuring Forum, 166

Energy Institute (Berkeley), 244

engineers: and designers, 134, 157; and economists, 17, 53, 199–202, 209; and economists, philosophical differences between, 203, 207–17, *214*, 219, 231–32; interviewed for book, *250*; as source of idea for electricity market design, 49–54; within system, 79, 87

English Pool, 147–48, 160

Enron, 128, 219; Backus revealing loopholes to, 152; collapse of, 5, 40–42; collusion with federal government, 46; congressional hearings on, 244, *245–46*; as conspirator in energy crisis, 40, 139–40, 149, 150–51; cooperation with monitors, 44, 83–84, 110, 269n1, 270n3; FERC archives on, *248*; limited powers of, 139–40; opposition to market centralization, 159–60, 187–88; payments to lobbyists and others, 46, 273n3; preference for deregulation and restructuring, 46, 145, 150–51; recommendation of competition in power market, 188; Silver Peak incident, 95–96, 133; as source of California's energy crisis, 5, 40–42, 83; support of Memorandum of Understanding, 150–51; violations by, 17, 41–42, 101–2, 106, 110, 120, 128, 139; West Desk, 44, 110, 261n62. *See also* game playing; loopholes in market structure; power marketers

environmentalists, opposition to restructuring, 145, 146

experts, technical, 11, 138, 153–54; failure of rhetoric of, 158–62; ignored by politicians, 139, 144, 152, 153, 156, 157; rhetorical techniques of, 16, 154–57. *See also* economists; engineers; market designers

Federal Communications Commission (FCC), 75

Federal Energy Regulatory Commission (FERC), 27, 28, 156, 177, 180; analysis of price spike, 39; archives from, 243, 244, *248*; congressional hearing on oversight of Enron, *246*; during energy crisis, 31–34, 40; on Enron violations, 45, 110; intellectual fragmentation at, 209–18; interviewees from, *250*; opposition to California's government solutions, 32–33; oversight of California's market structures, 32–33, 129–31, 167, 199; release of tapes on corruption, 44; restructured, 229–30, 272n42; SDG&E's appeal to, 32. *See also* control structures

Federal Power Act (1935), 129

Feeding America auctions, as successful market design, 234–36

Fessler, Dan, 147, 157

Fielder, John, 149–50

field theory, 8–9, 140

financial markets, 10, 88, 94, 180, 187, 191; and congestion, 127; market clearing protocols in, 175–79; principles of, 181; and recouping investment costs, 189; simplified by designers, 122, 126. *See also* bounding; controlling; market design

Fligstein, Neil, 8

forward contracts, 122, 123; during crisis, 30–31; lack of long-term, 112–14; restrictions on, 34, 38, 112, 114; utilities avoiding, 114, 115, 128–29

forward markets, 87–88, *88*; and arbitrage, 101, 103, 104, 119–20; and DEC game, 105; lack of, 112; long-term, 90; and market power, 99–100, 103, 113, 118, 123, 135; and modularization, 226; role in California's market architecture, 14, *88*, 90, 91, 92, 94, 99, 105, 116, 120–21, 122, 271n17, 272n30. *See also* day-ahead market (PX); day-of market (PX); spot markets

fragmented attention, in California's market design, 175–79

fraud, committed by Enron, 5, 41, 101–2. *See also* Enron; game playing; loopholes in market structure

Freeman, S. David, 41; WEPEX under, 166

free markets, 163, 212, 230; ideology of, 55, 158, 196, 199

Frequency Adaptive Power Energy Rescheduler (FAPER), 51–52, 207

game playing: and arbitrage (*see* arbitrage games); benefits of to market design, 96; and congestion (*see* congestion games); and corporate restructuring, 128–29; defense of, 96, 173; engineers' misconception of, 213–14, 215; by Enron, as profiteering, 95–96, 110, 111, 139–40; fictional power-flow creation, 127–28; identifying and solving problems, as unending process, 111, 179, 182–85, 191, 202, 221; with imbalance and ancillary markets, 185; incentives for, 126, 173, 174, 176, 181, 185, 202, 228, 231; and market power, 108; and modularization, 174, 175–92, 226; preventing, 196; roles, multiple, 128; threat of, to market design, 202, 210. *See also* Enron; market actors; market power; power marketers

game theory, 12, 59–60, 61–62, 68, 96, 232

generators, 27, 92, 93, 177, 258n14, 266n53; accused of market manipulation, 34; calculations of, short-term, 116–17, 119, 193–94; dispatch of, 88, *88*; excess capacity, need for, 115–20, 187–88, 222; finding cheapest to meet aggregate demand, 180, 204–7; function of, 23–24, 77–79, 85–86, 92, 258n14; in imbalance markets, 91–92; and market power, 27, 97–98, 118, 119; products, simplification of, 121; shut down, 24, 44–45, 98–99. *See also* electricity systems; utilities, electric (CA)

global warming, 3

Google, 234

government: bureaucracies obstructing designers, 234; conflicts during crisis, 28–36; reforming, 234, 237. *See also* California Public Utility Commission (CPUC); Federal Energy Regulatory

Commission (FERC); politics; *and specific organizations*

Granovetter, Mark, 7

green transition, 233

Harvard Electricity Policy Group, 53, 155

Hayek, Friedrich, 52, 59, 257n66; on Mises debate, 264n6

health care, 3

Hogan, William, 149, 204; on investment incentives, 188; opposition to Memorandum of Understanding, 152, 157; on regulation, ambivalence of, 196; rhetoric in Blue Book controversy, 155–57; working paper archive, 244

Hollings, Ernest, 46

homeostasis, 51–52, 263n93; dream of, 78; between economics and engineering, 203

homeostatic control, 49–53, 203

hour-ahead market, 107; as spot market, 258n12, 266n7

house building, as analogy for market design, 231, 232

humans: and computers, in markets, 61, 62, 206–9, 222; design decisions by, 14; limitations and biases of, 70, 134, 168, 206, 215, 226–27; vs. machines, in design process, 60, 179, 227; outrage during energy crisis, 31–32. *See also* market actors

imbalance (real-time) markets, 25; and ancillary markets, 183–84; within California's electricity market structure, *86*, 92, 93, 120–26, *123*, *170*, 228, 267n14; during energy crisis, 35; functions of, 91; inconsistencies with financial market, 191; market-clearing protocols in, 175–79; and market power, 100, 102–3, 104; price fluctuations within, 28, *28*, 122–25, *123*

Imbrecht, Charles, opposition to Memorandum of Understanding, 152–53

implicit markets, 92. *See also* forward markets

incomplete coordination, in California's market design, 179–82
incomplete decomposition, 174, 185–90
independent power producers (IPPs), 37, 87, 139–40, 144–46, 149, 153, 167
Industrial Information Resources, 45
Institutional Review Board, 249
intermittency, 78
interviews for book, 249–51; by profession, 249, *250*
investments, long-term, 118, 188–90, 191–92, 193–95, 222
Iraq, friendly-fire incident in, 227
Isser, Steve, 138

Joskow, Paul, 34, 49, 152–53, 209; and monitoring program, 195–96, 211–12

Kirchhoff's laws, 23–24, 78–79
Knight, Jesse, 148
Kuehl, Sheila J., *247*

lawyers, 196, 197; as interviewees for book, *250*; and market design, 163–64, 196, 197; among market designers, 6, 49, 165; working with designers, 63, 165, 200
Lay, Ken, 46
Leibniz, Gottfried Wilhelm, 210
Littlechild, Stephen, 147
load following, 51–52, 78
load pockets, 98, 108, 267n14
load shift (game), 107–8
London Analytics, 177, 182, 209
loopholes in market structure: Backus revealing to Enron, 152; market actors exploiting, 12, 17, 96, 110, 131, 132, 172; market designs creating, 174; market rules addressing, 210. *See also* game playing; market power
Los Angeles Department of Water and Power, 41, 84
Los Angeles Times, 244
Lumpenproletariat (Marx), as analogy for reduced bargaining power, 115–16

MacArthur, Douglas, 96
Macias, Jim, 198

market actors, 8, 11, 26–28, 87–90; antagonism of, 12, 14, 19–20, 56, 64–75, 81, 144, 172, 174, 185, 193–94, 210, 221, 226, 233, 237; defense of, 43; exploiting CAISO's limited jurisdiction, 127–29; exploiting holes in control structure, 15, 17, 131–34, 185, 193, 228–29; exploiting porous structural boundaries, 15, 17, 127–29, 135; exploiting price differences, 191, 228; freedom from, 234–36; incentivizing to cooperate, 67–71, 221, 223, 225, 236; as interviewees for book, *250*; limitations of, 226–27; and organization employees, difference between, 66–67; profits from energy price differences, 191; requirements of, 135; rewarded for violations, 108. *See also* economists; engineers; Enron; game playing; lawyers; loopholes in market structure; power marketers; retail buyers of energy (end users); utilities, electric (CA)
market creation, 1–2, 4–5; as form of social engineering, 47–48, 220; initial, in California, 143–44; and market design literature, 6–10; after restructuring, 27–29, *27*; role of politics in, 7, 8, 140–41, 143–64, 224–25; theories of, 1. *See also* designer markets; market design; politics
market design, 2, 12, 57, 62, 210, 225, 231; allocation problem of, 18–19, 77–82, 174, 229, 232–33; alternatives to, 234, 237; as "camel," 138, 139; control structure in California's, 131–34, 175–82; core challenge of, 11–12, 56, 64–75, 236 (*see also* market actors); core idea of, 71; embeddedness perspective on, 7–8, 10; failure of (*see* market design, failure of); flawed outcome of, practical reasons for, 18, 219, 222–33; flaws of (*see* market design, flaws of); as form of organizational planning, 55–82, 138–39; games undermining, 85 (*see also* Enron; game playing; market actors); house building as analogy for, 231, 232; invention of, 60–61;

market design (*continued*)
limitations of, 3–4, 20, 70–74, 112, 219–33, 266n47; literature on, 6–10; neo-institutional framework on, 8–9, 10, 140; paradigmatic examples of, 61–62, 68–69, 70; principles of, 16, 71, 74, 135, 140, 143–44, 151–53, 169–93, 217–18; requirements of actors, 135; rules for, 210; socialist tendencies behind, 57–62; and "social studies of finance," 9–10; and sociologists, 7–10, 60; successful, 10, 84, 85, 93, 112, 162, 174, 190, 220–22, 223, 224, 229, 230, 234–36, 249; temporal structure of, 87–88, *88*, 117, 118–19. *See also* modularization

market design, failure of, 4–6, 10, 14–20, 47–49, 81–82, 110–11, 137–41, 217, 221; avoiding in future, 224–25, 230–31; due to Enron, 83, 110–11

market design, flaws of, 47–49, 111, 166–67; corporate restructuring, 128–29; differential simplification, 120–27, 164, 166–67, 168; forward contracts, lack of, 112–14, 118, 187–90; history of, 49–54, 143–44; manipulation, 43–44, 97–108 (*see also* designer markets, manipulation of); and market power, 115, 190; and modularization, 169–92 (*see also* modularization); persisting today, 232; porous boundaries, 18, 111, 127–29, 133, 135, 164, 166–67, 168, 219; procedural, 137–41, 178, 232; retail-price freezing, 29, 113, 114–15, 118, 147; weak control structure, 111, 129–31, 133–34, 137, 175–82, 194, 197

market design, strategies of, 12–14, 18–19, 56–57, 75–77, 84, 85, 112, 135, 221, 226; allocation problems with, 18–19, 56, 77–82, 84, 174, 221, 225, 231, 233, 235–36; other problems with, 84, 120–26, 140–41, 143–44, 168–69, 174, 175–92, 194, 197. *See also* bounding; controlling; simplification

market designers: ambivalence of, on oversight and self-regulation, 194–97; backgrounds of, 6, 11, 49–50, 53, 182, 196–97, 200–201, 275n45; building flawed system, 15–18; and engineers, 134, 157, 207; engineers and economists as, 197–98, 200–201, 203, 207–8; and expert rhetoric, in debate with politicians, 154–57; and fragmentation between engineering and economics, 197–98, 203, 207–17, *214*, 219, 231–32; functions of, 2, 6–7, 11, 63–64, 67–74, 126, 131, 134, 172, 223; and games, 182–83; as interviewees for book, 249, *250*; and language of economics, 158–62, 275n46; limitations of, 131–34; against market actors, 12, 17, 19–20, 56, 64–75, 127–34; as market actors, 144; against market power, 98–99; "marrying" engineering and economics, 201–2; and modularization, 172–74 (*see also* modularization); motivations of, 138–41; at onset of energy crisis, 94–95; opposition to Memorandum of Understanding, 151–64; against politicians, 151–57, 162–63; and requirements for interactions among market actors, 64–66, 172; silence on optimizing short-term markets, 164, 193–94; silence on scheduling issues, 211; violating own principles, 15, 135, 140–41, 168–93, 217–18. *See also* bounding; controlling; designer markets; game playing; simplification

market mechanisms: applied to school selection, 68–69, 70, 71, 77; encouraging actors' self-interest, 65–67; as hybrid, 61; implementation of, 232; and market design, 2, 7; and market power, 100, 119; needing excess energy capacity, 115–20, 222; as search algorithms, 11, 55–62, 77, 88, 89, 161, 168, 186, 194, 203, 205, 208, 209, 221, 222, 229; violated in California, 71, 74, 97–109; zero-intelligence, 76. *See also* designer markets

market monitoring units (CAISO), 96–96, 98, 110–12, 130–31, 182, 213, 279n8; in ancillary markets crisis, 200–203; Joskow on, 211–12; limitations of, 215;

against Ricochet, 184; as temporary, 195–96; as weak, 194

market power, 97–100; blamed for crisis, 40, 123; defined, 32, 97, 267n20; detecting, 132, 202, 267n22; and differential simplification, 15, 115–20, 126–27, 135; emergence of, 135; excess capacity, kept at bay by, 117–18, 120; FERC archive on abuses, *248*; FERC definition of, 128–30; and pivotal supplier test, 202; and price spikes, 119, 123; redefined, 45; and reserve capacity, 187, 194; strategies to wield, 97–98, 108; utilities as vulnerable to, 113, 123; warding off, 113, 190, 191, 195, 196, 197, 211. *See also* game playing

markets, generally, 1; literature on, 6–10. *See also specific markets*

market surveillance committee (CAISO), 130–31, 200, *247*; in information structure, 214–15, *214*; against market power, 100, 101; pivotal supplier test, 267n22; price and protocol differences with PX, 101, 122–26, *123*, 271n30; and scheduling coordinators, 125 (*see also* game playing)

mathematics, 216, 217; in economics, 59; economists' and engineers' use of, 197, 204; formulae as chameleonic, 204–7, 232; on generation, 88; models, interpretations of, 231; as useless against mystery of market, 59

McIntosh, Jim, 25

mechanism design, 60

Memorandum of Understanding (1995), 150–51; battle over acceptance of, 153–57; disadvantaging market designers, 151, 153, 167, 168, 196, 225; Enron foreseeing inefficiencies in, 150–51; experts' opposition to, 152–53; and political negotiations, 144–51; separation and equality provisions of, 151, 155, 159–62, 166–67, 178, 186, 225

Michaels, Robert, 211; on need for investments, 194–95

microeconomic theory, 52, 88

Miller, Jeff, 95

Mirant (energy company), 41

Mises, Ludwig von: argument against socialism, 57–59; Hayek on, 264n6

MIT-Harvard workshop on homeostatic systems, 244

modularization, 16–18; advantages of, 170–71; and differential simplification, 175–82; entailing local, not global concerns, 169, 173–74, 177, 179, 181–82, 185, 193, 219, 226; incomplete decomposition in, 185–90; as inevitable, 170–71; problems of, 169–90, *170*, 217, 226, 228–29; temporal instability within, 182–85, 202

monopolies: in California's electricity system, 26–27; electricity industry as, 50; utilities as, 26, 229

multivocality: derailing designers' rhetoric, 158–59, 161–63, 201, 275n46; among market designers today, 232. *See also* rhetoric

National Energy Group, profits from energy crisis, 41–42

natural gas industry, 145, 146; and electricity systems, false analogy between, 161–62, 200

NCPA Cong Catcher (game), 106

Neumann, John von, 59

New York Times, 46

normal accident theory (Perrow), 72–73, 81, 230, 265nn44–45

Oren, Shmuel, 204, 208

Pacific Gas & Electric (PG&E), 24, 26, 41–42, 114, 179, 195, 209, 210, 263n93; bankruptcy, 35; nuclear plant construction fiasco, 148; profits from energy crisis, 41–42. *See also* utilities, electric (CA)

Peace, Steve, 32, 48; supporting AB 1890, 146–47

Peck, Stephen, 53, 204

Perot Systems, 152, 182; congressional hearing on, *246*

Perrow, Charles, theory of normal accidents, 72–73, 81, 230, 265nn44–45

PJM Interconnection, 81, 84, 163, 249

planning, long-term, 120, 163–64. *See also* forward markets

Plott, Charles, 53, 60, 177–78, 190, 209, 210

Polanyi, Karl, 119, 203

politics: and battle of two narratives, 46–47; constraining designers, 140, 191; corrupting WEPEX, 166–67; deferring hard questions to markets, 237; and design flaws, 16–17, 18, 19, 138–41, 163, 226; Enron's connections to, 46, 140; in market creation, 7, 8, 140–41, 143–64, 224–25; in market design and implementation, 4, 48, 138–39, 144–51, 222–26; and market failure, 9, 32–35; in market manipulation, 38–39, 46; operatives ignoring expert designers, 139, 144, 152, 153, 156, 157; paralyzed during California energy crisis, 4, 26, 34; and passage of AB 1890, 146–47; of restructuring, 48. *See also specific individuals and organizations*

PoolCo model: in Blue Book controversy, 147–51, 156; Edison's favor for, 160–61; Enron's opposition to centralization of, 159–61. *See also* Blue Book proceedings; Memorandum of Understanding (1995)

Power Exchange (PX), 32, 43, 45, *86*, 122, 138, 165, 171, 219, 269nn41–42; archival material from, *247*; bankruptcy, 35, 258n13; business documents from, 243; and CAISO, 93, 124, 130–31, 168, 180, 181, 183–84, 186; and CAISO, in information structure, 214–15, *214*; against congestion, 104; coordinating contract scheduling, 27, *27*, *28*; creation of, 166–67, 176–84, 188, 190; distance from CAISO, 177, 180; on Enron exploiting loopholes, 95, 110; FERC oversight of, 130; functions of, 27, 124, 130; gamed by sellers, 98 (*see also* game playing); isolated from CAISO, 122, 179; and long-run generation, 116–18, 190; market monitoring units, 130, 131, 182,

279n8; against market power, 123; order of energy provision by, 124–25; percentage of California's market, 116; price and protocol differences with CAISO, 122–26, *123*, 183, 271n30; spot markets of, 112 ; utilities buying from, 89, 114. *See also* California Independent System Operator (CAISO); scheduling coordinators

power marketers: arbitrage by, 27, 87, 89, 93, 100–104, 168; attempt to game ancillary markets, 184, 202; in energy crisis, 140; function of, 27, 87, 266n11; role within market system, 27, 89–90, 165, 186; as schedulers, 128, 194; support of Memorandum of Understanding, 150–51. *See also* Enron

power plants. *See* generators

Preferred Policy Decision (1996), 146, 151, 165–67. *See also* Memorandum of Understanding (1995); Western Power Exchange (WEPEX)

Prendergast, Canice, 235

price spikes: before electric energy crisis, 183, 198; during electric energy crisis, 4–5, 28–35, *28*, 41–42, 93, 113–14; long-term bets on, 119, 188–90; within older electricity system, 145

Price Waterhouse, 182

Public Utility Fortnightly, 244

Rassenti, Stephen, 53, 60

Red Congo (game), 84, 106

regulation: blamed for crisis, 38; in California's original system, 26, *27*, 193–94, 195; designers' ambivalence toward, 195–96; to ensure investments, 193–94; traditional, 211; in US electricity markets, 230; of utilities by California's government, 35; warding off, 119. *See also* centralization; deregulation

regulators. *See* California Public Utility Commission (CPUC); Federal Energy Regulatory Commission (FERC); Southern California Edison (SCE)

Reliant (energy company), 145

Research and Development Planning
  Forum, 166
restructuring, of California's electricity
  market, 26–28, *27*, *28*, 48–49, 113–
  14, 145–51, 270n13; compromise
  on, 150–51; controversy over, 143–
  64; industry structure after, *27*, *86*;
  industry structure before, 26, *27*,
  144–45; initial, 26–28, 53, 113, 145–
  51; modularization as impediment to,
  169–92; as preferable to regulation,
  195; purpose of, 164; supporters
  of, 145; utilities divided over, 145–
  51. *See also* Blue Book proceedings;
  Memorandum of Understanding
  (1995); Western Power Exchange
  (WEPEX)
retail buyers of energy (end users), 26–
  27, *27*, 31, *86*, 90, 259n18; inelastic
  demand, 113, 114–15
retail market, 26–27, *27*, 31, *86*, 90,
  259n18; price freezes in, 29–31, 38,
  113–15, 118, 147; and wholesale prices
  during crisis, 28, 30. *See also* utilities,
  electric (CA)
rhetoric: Enron's, 159–60; experts', 154–
  58, 223–24; SCE's, 160–61. *See also*
  Memorandum of Understanding
  (1995)
Ricochet (game), 101–2, 110, 120, 127–28,
  179, 180; variant of, 182, 202. *See also*
  game playing
Riley, Ed, 25
rolling blackouts, 25, 79. *See also* electric
  energy crisis
Romero, Philip, 149

San Diego Gas & Electric (SDG&E), 26,
  152, 196; in Blue Book controversy,
  146, 148; crisis over rate spike, 31–32,
  84. *See also* utilities, electric (CA)
San Francisco Chronicle, 244
San Onofre nuclear power plant, 148
savings and loan debacle of 1980s, 35
SCE. *See* Southern California Edison
  (SCE)
schedules, market, *27*, 90–91; and

adjustment bids, 187; aggregation
  of, 186–87; and congestion, 179; in
  information structure, 214–15, *214*
scheduling coordinators, 86, *86*, 90–
  91, 92–93, 178; anyone as, 191; and
  CAISO, 125; designers' silence on,
  196, 210–11; and modularization, 187,
  191; power marketers as, 127, 128; in
  restructured system, *27*, *27*, *86*, 88,
  90–91, 167, 186–87, 214–15, *214*; rules
  for, 196, 210–11; treated as black boxes,
  177. *See also* Power Exchange (PX)
Scheduling Coordinator User Group, 166
Schmalensee, Richard, 49
Schutz, Alfred, 69
Schwarzenegger, Arnold, 36
Schweppe, Fred, 50–53, 156, 203, 204;
  and Vernon Smith, 207–8
scientists, 154, 224
Senate Select Committee, fraud
  investigations of, 243–44
Shumway, Norm, 148
Silicon Valley culture, 199
simplification: blocked, 112, 217, 190, 196;
  and congestion games, 126–27; and
  control, difficulties of balancing, 225,
  229; as design strategy, 12–14, 75–76,
  82, 168–69, 194, 221; differential, 15,
  17, 18, 125–26, 164, 166, 168–69, 185,
  193; failure of, 15, 120–26; generating
  systemic complexity, 15, 111, 120,
  125–26, 134–35, 175, 185, 191; and
  illegal arbitrage, 120–26; incomplete,
  112, 126, 133, 175; and long-term
  strategies, 116, 168, 190; mandatory,
  233; and market power, 115–20; and
  modularization, 175–92; successful, 19,
  236. *See also* bounding; controlling;
  control structures; market design,
  strategies of
Simpsons, The (TV show), 40
Skilling, Jeff, 48
Sladoje, George, 43, *247*
Smith, Vernon, 53, 60; and Fred
  Schweppe, 207–8
Smutny-Jones, Jan, 149
Snohomish tapes, 273n7

Snook, Scott, 227

social engineering: to address allocation problems, 234; to address modern crises, 237; and digitalization, 220–21; limits of, 3–4, 10, 14, 54, 73–75, 111–12, 219, 221–22, 226–34, 237; market creation as, 47–48, 220; market design as, 2, 60–61, 220–21, 233; sociology on, 220, 237

socialism: calculation debate of, 2, 57–59; within California's old electricity structure, 145; and capitalism, 1–2; and market design, 57–62; Mises against, 57–59; and neoliberalism of 1990s, 40–41; as solution to California's 2001 energy crisis, 26, 35–36

socialists, 236; on market process, 59

sociologists: on accidents, 72–73, 81, 265nn44–45; on organizations, 7–9, 64–66, 227, 230, 237, 265n28, 279n8; on safety, 73, 230, 265n44

sociology, 1, 220, 237; of market design, 7–10

software interfaces, 75

solar energy, 65, 80

Southern California Edison (SCE), 26, 114, 179, 209, 263n93; in Blue Book controversy, 146, 157, 160–61; nuclear plant construction fiasco, 148; suit against FERC, 34. *See also* utilities, electric (CA)

spot contracts, 122

spot markets, 29, 31, *88*, 113, 121, 122, 150, 160, 168, 196, 235, 258n12; British, 147–48; Choice System, 235; imbalance markets as, 91; market power in, 115; optimized for short-term decisions, 112, 168, 175, 188–90, 211; price swings in, 112; of PX, 112; software for, and short-term decisions, 175. *See also* forward markets; Power Exchange (PX)

spot prices, 31, 52–53, 156; philosophical differences over, 207–9

Spot Pricing of Electricity (Schweppe et al.), 52–53, 207

stakeholders: environmentalists, 145–46; scientists, 154, 224. *See also* market actors

Steve Peace Death March, 48, 147

Stewart, Jon, 40

Stinchcombe, Arthur, 64, 231

Stoft, Steven, 152–53, 213

submarkets, 63, 124; and designers, 168; in new system, 14, 93, 94, 125–26, 135, 217; simplification in, 15, 125, 135, 193. *See also* game playing; market design

supply and demand: in ancillary service market system, 183; balancing, 51, 52, 216; Barone on, 59; and CAISO imbalance markets, 124; and competition, 115; control structure as coordinating, 212; economy as mathematical functions of, 59; during energy crisis, 24; and excess generation, 117, 188–89; of generation capacity, 37, 93, 97–98, 117–19, 188; and generation cost, 186, 204–5; imbalances, as cause of crisis, 33; and market power, 97–100, 115, 128; in microeconomics market, 52; in optimization problems, 204–5; and prices, illogical, 198, 200; and prices at PX, 89, 124, 175; utilities lowering intersection between, 269n41; variations in, 211

Tabors, Richard, 50–53

tariffs, 197, 244; CAISO changes to, 182; lacking manipulation oversight, 130; and market operations, 96, 105, 108, 139–40, 176, 180–81, 187; revised to prevent gaming, 182, 196; and scheduling coordinators, 187; violated, 42, 45, 127

Taylor, F. W., 75

telecommunications industry, 145

temporal instability, within modularization, 174, 182–85, 202

Texas: blackouts in, 3, 81, 230, 233; manipulation of market in by giant companies, 41. *See also* Enron

Turing, Alan, 59

Uber, 3, 61

United Kingdom, restructuring model in, 147–48, 160

United States Accounting Office, 244

Upwork, 61

utilities, electric (CA): affiliates as wholesale sellers, 90, 128–29; buying from PX, 89; buying from wholesalers, 87, 90; CPUC limiting purchases of power, 114; dominating state market, 26, 87; environmentalists threatening, 145; and forward contracts, 38, 112, 113–14; importance in market process, 140; integrating into single system, 165, 171; investments in nuclear power, 148, 164, 188; and long-term contracts, 29, 37, 112, 113–14, 164; losing cash reserves to high wholesale prices, 28–30, 32, 114, 259n18; as monopoly, 26; and network congestion, 92; position as always hedged, 128–29; on restructuring alternatives, 145–51; retaining retail market, 26–27, 27, 90, 113, 115, 259n18; role within restructured system, 147–48; "stranded costs" of, 29–30, 31, 41–42, 148, 153, 258n16, 272n33; as threat to politicians' power, 148; as victims of market power, 113, 115; and WEPEX, 166–67, 276nn10–11. See also generators; and specific companies

Vaughan, Diane, 227

Vickrey, William, 60

Walmart, 234, 264n15

Walras, Leon, 59

water resources, 37, 38

WEnet, 90, 189, 190. See also California Independent System Operator (CAISO)

WEPEX. See Western Power Exchange (WEPEX)

Western Electricity Coordinating Council, 152

Western energy crisis, 4, 5, 6, 45, 93; causes of, 14–15. See also California, energy crisis in; electric energy crisis

Western Interconnection, 24, 27, 28, 37, 87, 88, 89, 106; boundary with CAISO, 129; and fictional power flows, 127–28, 129

Western Power Exchange (WEPEX), 53, 166; coordination website, 244; corrupted by interest politics, 166–67; CPUC archives on, 243; design flaws, 166–69, 190, 191, 217, 225–26; FERC archives on, 248; intellectual fragmentation at, 209–18; and modularization, 216; origins of, 165; and power marketers, 194; revising tariffs to prevent gaming, 196; simplifying search for optimal trades, 206–7; steering committee, and global vs. local concerns, 179–80, 228. See also Blue Book proceedings; California Independent System Operator (CAISO); Memorandum of Understanding (1995)

White, Harrison, 7–8

wholesale markets, 86, 87–88, 90, 93; FERC in charge of, 129–31; pool-based, 156; price fluctuations in, 28–30, 28, 113–14, 122–23, 123; and profits from crisis, 41; and retail prices during crisis, 28–30, 31, 90, 93. See also California Independent System Operator (CAISO); Power Exchange (PX)

Wikipedia, 237

Williams (energy company), 45, 145

Williams, Bill, 44

Wilson, Pete, on Blue Book controversy, 149–51, 157

Wilson, Robert, 53, 209; on market design, 69, 71, 177–78, 190, 204, 209–10

Winter, Terry, 24–25; testimony before Congress, 110. See also California Independent System Operator (CAISO)

Wu, Felix, 204

Yellow Book, 144, 145, 163

Yelp, 237